Mastering Wartime

Margaret
Humphreys

PENNSYLVANIA PAPERBACKS

Mastering Wartime

A Social History of Philadelphia During the Civil War

J. MATTHEW GALLMAN

PENN

University of Pennsylvania Press

Philadelphia

Originally published 1990 by Cambridge University Press
Copyright © 1990 Cambridge University Press

Pennsylvania Paperbacks edition first published 2000
All rights reserved
Printed in the United States of America on acid-free paper

10 9 8 7 6 5 4 3 2 1

Published by
University of Pennsylvania Press
Philadelphia, Pennsylvania 19104-4011

Library of Congress Cataloging-in-Publication Data
Gallman, J. Matthew (James Matthew)
    Mastering wartime : a social history of Philadelphia during the Civil War /
J. Matthew Gallman.
        p. cm.
    "Originally published 1990 by Cambridge University Press"—T.p. verso.
    Includes bibliographical references (p.   ) and index.
    ISBN 0-8122-1744-6 (alk. paper)
    1. Philadelphia (Pa.)—History—Civil War, 1861–1865—Social aspects.   2. Philadelphia
(Pa.)—Social conditions—19th century.   3. Philadelphia (Pa.)—Economic conditions—
19th century.   4. United States—History—Civil War, 1861–1865—Social aspects.   I. Title.

F158.44.G35   2000
974.8′1103—dc21   00-025222

Contents

List of tables   *page* vii

Preface and acknowledgments   ix

1 Introduction   1
2 Filling the ranks   11
3 Kinfolk at war: Philadelphians' responses to death and
      separation   54
4 Old rituals for new causes: Civic celebration at war   85
5 Help from the home front: Wartime voluntarism in
      Philadelphia   117
6 The Great Sanitary Fair of 1864: Exercise in civic
      voluntarism   146
7 Preserving the peace: Order and disorder   170
8 Soldiers in the city: The military challenge to public
      order   194
9 Philadelphia's workers in wartime   217
10 The fortunes of war: The Civil War and Philadelphia's
      manufacturing development   251
11 The economic life of wartime Philadelphia   266
12 Winners and losers: The R. G. Dun credit reports   299
13 Conclusion: Toward the Centennial City   329
Appendix: The R. G. Dun data   341
Bibliographic essay   344
Index   350

Tables

			page
Table	2.1.	The 1863 draft in Philadelphia, Fifth District: distribution of paid exemptions by occupation	42
Table	2.2.	Occupational distribution of men sampled from the 1861 and 1866 city directories compared with the occupational distribution of exemption-purchasing draftees in the Fifth District	44
Table	2.3.	Experiences of drafted Quakers from Philadelphia's yearly meeting	51
Table	8.1.	Monthly arrests in Philadelphia, 1857–67	196
Table	8.2.	Philadelphia arrests for selected crimes, 1857–67	199
Table	8.3.	Share of all arrests for selected crimes, 1857–67	200
Table	8.4.	Arrests by race and age of offender	202
Table	8.5.	Violent incidents reported in the Public Ledger	205
Table	8.6.	Military involvement in reported violence	206
Table	9.1.	United States prices and real wages, 1860–70	225
Table	9.2.	Selected wage schedules for three Philadelphia factories	226
Table	9.3.	Employment shifts between 1860 and 1870	228
Table	9.4.	Wages for sewing women, 1861 vs. 1866	244
Table	10.1.	Manufacturing output in major U.S. cities, 1860	254
Table	10.2.	Type of manufacturing in Philadelphia: change in total output, 1860–66	258
Table	10.3.	Type of manufacturing in Philadelphia: change in total output, 1860–70	260
Table	10.4.	Type of manufacturing: share of total output in 1860 and 1866	262
Table	10.5.	Type of manufacturing: share of total output in 1860 and 1870	263

Table 11.1.   Philadelphia's monthly almshouse population, 1858–67   272

Table 11.2.   Hoover's wholesale price index, 1855–70   273

Table 11.3.   Buildings erected in Philadelphia, 1855–68   275

Table 11.4.   Philadelphia's foreign trade   277

Table 11.5.   Purchases at the U.S. military depots   284

Table 11.6.   Prices paid by the quartermaster's department for clothing and equipage   285

Table 12.1.   The R. G. Dun sample: all firms, final year in business   301

Table 12.2.   The R. G. Dun sample: evidence of annual fluctuations, 1855–69   302

Table 12.3.   The R. G. Dun sample: final year in business × year established   303

Table 12.4.   The R. G. Dun sample: final year in business × estimated worth   305

Table 12.5.   The R. G. Dun sample: final year in business × year established × estimated worth   306

Table 12.6.   The R. G. Dun sample: final year in business × type of enterprise   308

Table 12.7.   The R. G. Dun sample: firms with southern ties   313

Table 12.8.   The R. G. Dun sample: firms with southern ties, year of origin × final year in business   314

Table 12.9.   The R. G. Dun sample: war contractors   317

Table 12.10.   The R. G. Dun sample: war contractors, final year in business   318

Table 12.11.   The R. G. Dun sample: war contractors, annual fluctuations, 1855–69   320

Table 12.12.   The R. G. Dun sample: war contractors, year of origin × final year in business   321

Table 12.13.   The R. G. Dun sample: war contractors, final year in business × extimated worth   322

Table 12.14.   The R. G. Dun sample: men with incomes over $100,000 in 1864   325

Preface and acknowledgments

This book is the product of several overlapping interests. First, the Civil War has long seemed to me to be the most compelling event in American history. I remember when I first encountered a textbook's graph showing that America's casualties during the War Between the States dwarfed those of later conflicts. Thus I assumed that the Civil War must have left an enormous mark on everything in its wake. Later, after choosing history as a profession, my interest turned to the work of the "new" social, economic and urban historians. Ordinary events seemed more important than wars and elections; the lives of workers, immigrants, women, and blacks more vital than those of business leaders and elected officials. I found this literature particularly useful in understanding the broad movements that marked the century of growth after 1790. Whatever research topic I settled on would somehow consider the changing landscape of nineteenth century America.

Although I did not want to examine those incidents that dot history's timeline, I had long felt that major events are a useful means of illuminating everyday life. Sometimes the best way to understand a community is to examine it under crisis. And the surest way to evaluate individual attitudes toward various issues is to wait until events "ask" men and women what they think. Thus diarists will deal with the future on New Year's Day, the state of the nation on Independence Day, and their political beliefs on Election Day. Even for the historian exploring the broad sweep of ordinary life, the atypical episode sometimes provides the best backdrop.[1]

Given the seemingly endless list of volumes about the Civil War, it is really rather surprising that the Northern home front has not attracted more attention. Certain groups – intellectuals, writers, blacks, women – have been the subject of book-length studies, and numerous scholars have considered the war's impact on the economy and on the Constitution; but everyday life at home is largely an untold story.[2] And although the recent generation of new social historians has produced dozens of important monographs on various

---

1 David Hackett Fischer, a master of creative research, once suggested that one way to study family limitation practices in colonial America was to read descriptions of fires in hopes of finding whether married couples were running out of the same bedrooms.

aspects of nineteenth-century America, their work pays scant attention to the Civil War. Thus I found that the intersection of my first two interests – the Civil War and nineteenth-century social history – presented a fertile area of inquiry.

I first came to know wartime Philadelphians through their diaries, letters, and newspapers. These early explorations were guided less by a concrete set of questions than by a desire to identify the breadth of the war's impact on those who stayed behind. How did daily routines change for people living beyond the rebels' grasp? How did the conflict's ebbs and flows mold activity on the home front? How did patriotic-minded citizens contribute to the war effort? These questions yielded a series of chapter-length topics that together describe most of the ways in which the war touched individual Philadelphians.

Each chapter in this book combines a portrayal of individual experiences with an examination of broader institutional patterns. The result is, at one level, a discussion of how the Civil War touched the city and its inhabitants. But the home-front story is also a useful way of illuminating nineteenth-century American life. Historians of long-term movements in social history and urban development tend to neglect the war years – perhaps because the wartime events are deemed anomalous. However, the sectional conflict can be an ideal occasion to examine Philadelphia's institutions under stress.

One way to gauge the war's "impact" is to compare the war years with antebellum life.[3] A second, complementary, approach is to consider the evidence in a comparative perspective: How did Civil War Philadelphia compare with other home fronts? Arthur Marwick's *War and Social Change in the Twentieth Century* examined the social impact of the two world wars in four "tiers": destructive aspects, test aspects, participation aspects, and psychological aspects.[4] This model, which is particularly useful in comparing the home-front experiences of nations involved in total warfare, can also – with adjustments – aid in our understanding of Civil War Philadelphia.

2 Philip Shaw Paludan's "*A People's Contest": The Union and Civil War, 1861–1865* (New York, 1988), which surveys the impact of the war on Northern society, appeared too late to be included in this book. For bibliographies of Civil War history see Eugene C. Murdock, *The Civil War in the North: A Selective Annotated Bibliography* (New York, 1987); James M. McPherson, *Ordeal By Fire: The Civil War and Reconstruction* (New York, 1982), 656–94; and Paludan, "*A People's Contest*", 441–70.
3 My greatest concern has been to examine the war years in the context of the antebellum experience. Although the war's lasting impact is of frequent concern, a comprehensive treatment of that topic (which would consider shifts emerging long after the war) is beyond the scope of this study.
4 Arthur Marwick, *War and Social Change in the Twentieth Century* (New York, 1974), 11–14 and *passim*.

As Marwick notes, wartime destruction can force a country into entirely new patterns of social, economic, and political development. But as we shall see, although the price of the Civil War was great, Northern society never experienced the sort of physical destruction that racked much of Europe during World War I and World War II. The Union war effort in this sense is generally more comparable to that of the United States in both world wars. In all three American cases, Marwick's first two "tiers" are best considered together in a slightly more broadly construed sense of war as a "test" of a society and its institutions.

In both world wars the challenges of mobilization expanded the power of U.S. government. Wartime economic demands led to federal financing measures and government controls over private industry; manpower requirements resulted in selective service legislation; and the desire to promote patriotism in the face of dissent led to suppression of civil liberties.[5] Of course the degree of wartime centralization varied, reflecting the material demands, the political climate, and the existing structure of government. But generally speaking, in the absence of dramatic destruction, modern warfare tends to place more power in government hands: In Randolph Bourne's vivid formulation, "war is the health of the state."[6] We shall therefore consider the extent to which the enormous challenge posed by the Civil War pushed power from local to central and from private to public hands. But we will also ask how the war's tests molded actions within Philadelphia's vast network of private institutions. How did existing bodies meet the new demands? What new organizations emerged? How did "the private city" answer this public demand?[7]

Marwick's third tier, "participation," encompasses the benefits accrued by social groups who contribute to their nation's war effort. Again, the results vary but the broad patterns are consistent. In both world wars American workers acted from strength, and organized labor reaped some rewards. And in each case the wartime demands led to expanded roles for America's women and blacks. The Civil War presented Philadelphia's workers, women, and blacks with similar

5 For accounts of the American home front during the two world wars see David M. Kennedy, *Over Here: The First World War and American Society* (New York, 1980); Richard Polenberg, *War and Society: The United States, 1941–1945* (Philadelphia, 1972); James L. Abrahamson, *The American Home Front* (Washington, D. C., 1983).

6 Carl Resek, ed., *War and the Intellectuals: Essays by Randolph S. Bourne, 1915–1919* (New York, 1964), 69.

7 See Sam Bass Warner, Jr., *The Private City: Philadelphia in Three Periods of Its Growth* (Philadelphia, 1968).

opportunities for participation in the war effort. The results of their efforts will provide a second comparative focus.[8]

The "psychological aspects" of the wartime experience, Marwick's final tier, encompasses many issues that are beyond the scope of this study. But two topics will suggest some of Philadelphians' personal and collective responses to the war's emotional strains. First, we will consider how families responded to the separation and losses that the conflict brought. And later, we will ask how the war's many dramatic moments fit into the city's established array of rituals.[9]

This book began as a dissertation at Brandeis University. My greatest debt is to the community of friends and scholars that made my years there so pleasurable. My early drafts were improved by comments and suggestions from Daniel Cohen, Ruth Friedman, Wendy Gamber, C. Dallett Hemphill, John Hill, Alex Keyssar, James Kloppenberg, Tammy Miller, David Palmer, Tom Pegram, David Sicilia, Howard Wach, and Susan Tananbaum. While writing the dissertation I received support and travel grants from an Irving and Rose Crown Fellowship.

The Hemphill family took me into their homes whenever I visited Philadelphia. Without their kindness my research trips would have included far less revelry and more drudgery. And in addition to their warmth and hospitality, they provided me with one of my principal sources: the magnificent James Tyndale Mitchell diary in a cardboard box under my bed.

I was fortunate that many of the manuscript sources for this book are in the Historical Society of Pennsylvania's excellent collection. I would like to thank the HSP's archivists for both their expertise and their unflagging good cheer. I would also like to thank the librarians and archivists at the American Antiquarian Society, Brandeis University, Columbia University, Eleutherian Mills, the Germantown Historical Society, Harvard University's Baker Library, Haverford College, the Library Company of Philadelphia, the Library of Congress Manuscript Room, Loyola College, the National Archives (Washington and Philadelphia branches), the Philadelphia City Archives, and Swarthmore College. I would also like to thank Kenneth Finkel, of the Library Company, for helping me track down the illustrations.

8 The experience of Philadelphia's workers will be considered in a distinct chapter, but women and blacks will appear in several topical chapters.

9 Marwick tends to include the intellectual and cultural aspects of war in the fourth tier of his model. Neither topic seems particularly well suited to a community study. However, my sense from the diaries and newspapers is that traditional entertainment persisted in Philadelphia throughout the war with an occasional patriotic song or play added to the familiar mix.

Since beginning this project I have become quite adept at seeking advice. The list of scholars who have taken time to answer a letter, read a chapter, or comment on a paper has become quite long. I would like to thank Amy Bridges, Michael Frisch, Lori Ginzburg, Claudia Goldin, Arnold Hirsch, J. Morgan Kousser, Roger Lane, Eric Monkkonen, Allen Steinberg, Stephan Thernstrom, and Henry Williams for their words of advice.

My colleagues at Loyola College have offered a supportive atmosphere and sound suggestions as I hammered out my seemingly endless revisions. I am particularly indebted to Steve Hughes, Carole Fink, Chuck Cheape, and Bill Donovan for their careful critiques and enthusiastic support.

Frank Smith, at Cambridge University Press, has guided this manuscript to publication with patient professionalism. My anonymous reader offered a lengthy critique with many useful comments, large and small. While I lack a frame of reference, I suspect that this book has been peculiarly fortunate to have been in such hands.

I would like to make special mention of three eminent scholars who both helped make this a better book and, in very different ways, provided me with the sort of models that every aspiring professional hopes to find. When I was an undergraduate at Princeton, James McPherson's courses kindled my interest in American history and the Civil War. Nearly a decade later, his comments on the penultimate draft of this book caught several errors of fact and interpretation. I worked with John Demos when I thought that I would make a career studying colonial America. When I shifted my attention to the Civil War, he revealed a long-neglected fascination with the topic. Together we spent an afternoon puzzling over the importance of wartime separations. I learned long ago to pass my work over Stanley Engerman's desk before bringing it to the public eye. I am proud to add my name to the roll of authors who have profited from his generous comments.

My intellectual debt to my father, Robert Gallman, goes far beyond these pages. He has lent his editorial hand to much of what follows. Anyone who knows his meticulous scholarship and wide-ranging interests will not be surprised to learn that his comments have improved nearly every chapter. But equally important, he has managed to offer long hours of help and guidance without ever stepping in uninvited or threatening my autonomy.

When I first began mulling over dissertation topics, my father sent me a long letter describing the ideal adviser. In Morton Keller I found such a scholar. The first chapter I turned in came back within a week with penciled comments throughout. In the years to come

Professor Keller battled his way through thousands of pages with the same painstaking care. And as I have reshaped the manuscript for publication, he has continued to offer wise counsel. I only wish that the final product was worthy of his enormous efforts.

Toni Rosen Gallman's contributions to this book have been both great and small. When I first knocked on Toni Rosen's office door I came in search of computer wizardry. She lent her enormous talents to navigating my manuscript through a maze of antagonistic software and uncooperative hardware. Any scholar who has ventured onto such perilous terrain without a guide will recognize how great her assistance has been. But as I contemplate our world today, those labors seem a very small part.

Finally, I would like to thank my sisters, Eve and Anita, and my parents, to whom this book is dedicated.

1   *Introduction*

In 1860 Philadelphia's population of 565,529 put it behind only London, Paris, and New York among the world's large cities.[1] Two-thirds of the citizenry was native born, with most immigrants from Ireland (16.7 percent of the population) and Germany (7.5 percent). Blacks made up less than 4 percent of the population.[2] Through the first half of the century, the city's official jurisdiction included only the area between the Delaware River and the Schuylkill River from Vine Street to South Street. The rest of Philadelphia County extended south of South Street, into the farmland far north of the city, and across the Schuylkill into Haddington. The Consolidation Act of 1854, prompted by demands for improved utilities and better organized police and fire protection, brought the county's dozens of political units into the City of Philadelphia.[3] In the second quarter of the nineteenth century Philadelphia, which had long been one of the nation's leading commercial and banking centers, was at the forefront of northeastern industrial developm nt. By the outset of the Civil War the city's economy boasted a wide array of manufacturing concerns, with textiles and machinery among its leading sectors. Much of this early production still took place in small shops, but these were steadily giving way to larger establishments.[4]

Despite the economic, demographic and political developments of the previous decades, Sam Bass Warner has found that Philadelphians on the eve of the Civil War "clung to their tradition of privatism." Where dramatic growth had upset familiar associational

1   Russell F. Weigley, "The Border City in Civil War, 1854–1865," in R. Weigley, ed., *Philadelphia: A 300-year History* (New York, 1982), 363.
2   Scott Campbell Brown, "Migrants and Workers in Philadephia: 1850 to 1880" (Ph.D. diss., University of Pennsylvania, 1981), 27.
3   Elizabeth Geffen, "Industrial Development and Social Crisis, 1841–1854," in *Philadelphia*, ed. Weigley, 359–62; Howard Gillette, Jr., "The Emergence of the Modern Metropolis: Philadelphia in the Age of its Consolidation" in *The Divided Metropolis: Social and Spatial Dimensions of Philadelphia, 1800–1975*, eds. William W. Cutler, III and Howard Gillette, Jr. (Westport, Conn., 1980), 3–21.
4   See Chapter 10. For discussions of mid-nineteenth-century Philadelphia see Sam Bass Warner, Jr., *The Private City: Philadelphia in Three Periods of Its Growth*, 2nd ed. (Philadelphia, 1987), 49–157; Allen F. Davis, "Introduction," in *The Peoples of Philadelphia: A History of Ethnic Groups and Lower-Class Life, 1790–1940*, eds. Allen F. Davis and Mark H. Haller (Philadelphia, 1973), 7–11.

1

networks, citizens of all classes turned to a wide array of clubs and organizations ranging from church groups, fraternal societies, and political clubs to fire companies and street gangs. In 1861 the city had 400 churches, and Warner estimates that it had "twice that number of organized lodges, clubs, and benefit associations."[5]

Although it had a sizable Quaker population with a long abolitionist tradition, defenders of racial equality were in a distinct minority in the City of Brotherly Love.[6] In the 1856 Presidential election, Pennsylvania Democrat James Buchanan received 53 percent of Philadelphia's votes, the American Party candidate 36 percent, and antislavery Republican James C. Fremont a mere 11 percent. In 1858 the local Republicans and Americans joined together in the "People's Party," which although allied with the National Republicans, sidestepped the slavery issue in favor of a more politically viable protariff platform. In the critical state elections of 1860, Philadelphia reelected Mayor Alexander Henry as the Constitutional Union candidate, but gave the unsuccessful Democratic gubernatorial candidate 51 percent of the local vote. The following month Republican Abraham Lincoln won 57 percent of the Pennsylvania vote, but only 52 percent in Philadelphia. Even this was no triumph for abolitionism. Lincoln ran locally at the top of the People's Party ticket, which stressed tariff protection and profited from a divided Democratic opposition.[7] In the hotly contested 1864 elections, Philadelphia voters reelected Mayor Henry, favored the Unionist Curtin in his successful bid for reelection, and supported Lincoln over Peace Democrat George McClellan.[8] But the victorious parties consistently evoked the call of patriotism over abolitionism.

Several factors combine to make Philadelphia a particularly attractive focus for this study. The city's size assures access to a greater range of personal papers, newspapers, and printed materials than would have been available from a smaller community. Moreover, as a leading metropolis, Philadelphia was less likely than a smaller town to swing wildly in response to specific events or shifts in

5 Warner, *The Private City*, 49, 61; Timothy L. Smith, *Revivalism and Social Reform: American Protestants on the Eve of the Civil War* (New York, 1957), 20.
6 See William Dusinberre, *Civil War Issues in Philadelphia, 1856–1865*, (Philadelphia, 1965), *passim*; Wayne Smith, "Pennsylvania and the Civil War: Recent Trends and Interpretations," *Pennsylvania History* 3 (July 1984): 206–31; Philip S. Foner, "The Battle to End Discrimination Against Negroes on Philadelphia's Streetcars," *Pennsylvania History* 40 (July 1973): 261–90; (October 1973): 355–79.
7 Dusinberre, *Civil War Issues*, 78–79, 98–103; Weigley, "The Border City in Civil Way," 385, 391–2; Erwin Stanley Bradley, *The Triumph of Militant Republicanism: A Study of Pennsylvania and Presidential Politics, 1860–1872* (Philadelphia, 1964), Chapter 2.
8 Weigley, "The Border City in Civil War," 413; Bradley, *Triumph of Militant Republicanism*, Chapter 5.

a particular sector. Thus, although many facets of Philadelphia's wartime experience were certainly unique, the possibility of finding extremely atypical patterns is not great.[9]

As the Union's second largest city, Philadelphia played a vital role in providing the army with men and matériel. Its central location made the City of Brotherly Love a major depot for recruits bound for the front as well as for wounded soldiers on their way home. And though Philadelphians never faced enemy troops in their streets, Rebel forces entered Pennsylvania on three occasions, presenting local citizens with particularly compelling tests of their patriotism and their institutions. It is by examining Philadelphia's responses to these various challenges, as filtered through the city's vast economic and social diversity, that we will be able to achieve a broad sense of the war's impact on various aspects of life.

The Civil War's events produced simultaneous responses in many aspects of Philadelphia life. In the days after the Battle of Gettysburg, for instance, many mourned lost loved ones, others commemorated Independence Day, thousands prepared to care for trainloads of wounded, and the bulk of the citizenry quickly returned to familiar routines. By addressing a series of distinct issues, I have sacrificed narrative for topical analysis (while maintaining a chronological structure within each chapter). This, I think, is a necessary evil. It is unfortunate because the tides of enthusiasm, which were often molded by events on the battlefield, are critical to an understanding of local movements. With that in mind, let us begin with a brief version of wartime Philadelphia as experienced by a handful of the citizens who will reappear periodically throughout later chapters.

Lincoln's November 1860 election and South Carolina's secession the following month raised fears in Philadelphia's households. On New Year's Day 1861, young Quaker Anna Yarnall wrote: "We are peaceful now tho' I am afraid for not long. Buchanan will give place to Lincoln and then – Oh anything but sucession or Civil War – but yet compromise would be as bad." A few days later contractor William Eyre added: "Our wisest statesmen are at their wits end to know what course to recommend. . . . The public mind is greatly inflamed."[10]

Many defended the Southern point of view, most denounced forceful coercion of the disloyal states, and nearly all passionately

9 For an example of the impact of the demand for arms on a small New England city see Michael Frisch, *Town Into City: Springfield, Massachusetts and the Meaning of Community, 1840–1880* (Cambridge, 1972).
10 Anna Yarnall diary, 1 January 1861, Haverford College Library, Haverford, Pa.; William Eyre diary, 6 January 1861, microfilm, Swarthmore College Library, Philadelphia.

hoped to avoid war.[11] The first months of 1861 saw numerous peace rallies. In February the president-elect visited Philadelphia on his journey to Washington and citizens cheered as Lincoln promised that "there is no need of bloodshed and war." But this momentary euphoria did not ease the city's doubts.[12]

Two months after the inauguration, crowds filled the streets at news of the fall of Fort Sumter in South Carolina. When she heard of the Federal fort's danger, Katherine Brinley Wharton, the young wife of a Philadelphia lawyer, admitted: "I had no idea I wd care so much – I felt a shock & thrill of terror, surprise & dread of all that may be coming, & then indignant defiance & a feeling that *we must* come well out of it." A few days later, when the fort fell, Wharton added: "It is useless to speak of my feeble, or rather powerless, indignation at the idea of our flag being lowered to these crazy traitors."[13] All over the city, diarists described private fears and public hysteria.[14]

Sarah Butler Wister, the daughter of Southern sympathizer Pierce Butler, kept a careful account of the days immediately following Sumter's fall. On April 15 she recorded that "[a]ll the world [is] awake & alive with the news that Ft. Sumter has surrendered." Later that evening "[t]here was the most tremendous excitement. Thousands assembled furious at the news of the surrender, & swearing revenge on all disunionists or disaffected." On the seventeenth Wister went into town:

> Chestnut Street is a sight; flags large & small flaunt from every building, the dry-goods shops have red[,] white & blue materials draped together in their windows, in the ribbon stores the national colors hang in long streamers, and even the book sellers place the red, white, and blue bindings together; the streets are filled with a crowd of idle, eager, hurrying, lounging, talking, listening people, men & women, old & young, rich & poor, wherever there is a telegraph office, there is a regular jam at the corner to read the last message which has just been posted up on a board.[15]

11 On January 28 seventy-two-year-old diarist Jacob Elfreth, Sr., surveyed recent events and recorded: "If in the ordering of divine Providence we may be favored to escape the desolating effects of Civil War I think I shall rejoice if all the Slave States go out of the Union & stay out." See Jacob Elfreth, Sr., diary, 28 January 1861, Haverford.
12 Weigley, "The Border City in Civil War," 392–3; See Chapter 6.
13 Katherine Brinley Wharton diary, 6, 14 April 1861, Historical Society of Pennsylvania, Philadelphia (hereafter HSP).
14 See for instance Anna Ferris diary 15 April 1861, Swarthmore; Nicholas B. Wainwright, ed., *A Philadelphia Perspective: The Diary of Sidney George Fisher* (Philadelphia, 1967), 385, entry of 15 April 1861; Lewis Walker diary, 15 April 1861, HSP.
15 Fanny Kemble Wister, "Sara Butler Wister's Civil War Diary," *Pennsylvania Magazine of History and Biography* 102 (July 1978): 273–7, entries of 15, 17 April 1861.

Suddenly calls for peace gave way to enthusiasm for war. Sidney George Fisher wrote that "The town is in a wild state of excitement. Everybody is drilling."[16] For the next several months Philadelphians turned their attention to the task ahead. Recruiting tents dotted the landscape, volunteers drilled wherever they could find open space, and hundreds of women flocked to the Girard Hotel to sew uniforms. On Sundays patriotic citizens began church services by singing the "Star Spangled Banner."[17] With her husband drilling with the Home Guard, the suddenly politicized Katherine Wharton exclaimed: "I never knew before how much I had to be proud of in my country."[18]

This enthusiasm lasted until the opposing forces clashed in July 1861 near Manassas Junction, Virginia. In the days following the first Battle of Bull Run, Northern optimism dimmed at word that McDowell's Union troops had broken and run from the field. The news left Philadelphia "in a perfect frenzy."[19] On July 22 twenty-seven-year-old lawyer James Tyndale Mitchell went into town and found "every body very much depressed at the news of the great defeat." But the next day Mitchell wrote that "[n]ews from Manassas not so bad as was at first reported" and that the "general feeling [was] more cheerful and much more determined than ever."[20] When he heard the news, Henry Wharton's "hand clenched till it must have been positive pain." But after a long silence he declared: "Well we must pick up our flint & try again."[21] Shortly after Bull Run the ninety-day regiments that had formed in April returned to Philadelphia, and many volunteers reenlisted for three years. At home, citizens prepared for a long conflict. Public and private efforts merged to spur enlistment, outfit the troops, bring comfort to men at the front, and provide support for the families of volunteers.

A year after Sumter fell, Jacob Elfreth, Jr., wrote: "victory seems with us and the Rebellion is fast waning."[22] A few months later Sidney George Fisher judged that "I think the war virtually over, tho how soon we may have peace is doubtful."[23] But General George McClellan's failures in Virginia that June disturbed many in Philadelphia.[24] On July 2, 1862, Lincoln called for 300,000 new three-

16 Wainwright, ed., *A Philadelphia Perspective*, 386, entry of 22 April 1861.
17 Henry Benners diary, 28 April 1861, HSP.
18 Wharton diary, 30 April 1861.
19 Philadelphia *Evening Bulletin*, 22 July 1861 (hereafter *EB*).
20 James Tyndale Mitchell diary, 22,23 July 1861, privately owned.
21 Wharton diary, 22 July 1861.
22 Jacob Elfreth, Jr., diary, 16 April 1862, Haverford.
23 Wainwright, ed., *A Philadelphia Perspective*, 428, entry of 12 June 1862.
24 See Wainwright, ed., *A Philadelphia Perspective*, 429, entries of 30 June, 3 July 1862; Yarnall diary, 3 July 1862; Mitchell diary, 3 July 1862; Lewis Ashhurst diary, 3 July 1862, HSP.

year volunteers, with provisions for conscription if local quotas were not met. In Philadelphia citizens set to work filling the local 5,000-man quota.

Two months later Philadelphians turned to even more energetic recruiting as rebel troops moved north and threatened the City of Brotherly Love.[25] News of General Lee's successes left Anna Yarnall "more worried now than ever before" and Lewis Ashhurst reported a "Great Fear in Philad[elphia] of an invasion of the state."[26] On September 12 George W. Fahnestock observed that "there is in fact a regular panic here, although the idea is absurd."[27] As the panic heightened, Sidney George Fisher found that "[t]he aspect of the city is greatly changed. Fewer people in the streets, recruiting stations with flag flying & drum beating in all directions, wounded soldiers walking about, tents pitched in Independence Square - these," he added, "are novel sights in America." On the eighteenth Fisher wrote of "news . . . that a terrible battle raged all of yesterday with great loss on both sides" and the once complacent Fahnestock reported that "[t]he whole country hangs breathless."[28]

The Union stopped Lee's 1862 advance at Antietam, and Philadelphia's emergency volunteers returned. At home, the threatened militia draft dominated popular attention. Although Philadelphia successfully filled its enlistment quota, Pennsylvania conscripts soon began arriving at "Camp Philadelphia" on the outskirts of town.[29]

In late 1862, as Copperhead sentiment mounted, a group of Philadelphians founded the Union Club, a patriotic organization that soon expanded into the Union League of Philadelphia.[30] In January 1863 Lincoln issued his Emancipation Proclamation. The city's Peace Democrats responded to these developments by forming the Democratic Club and by launching the *Age*, an antiwar newspaper. As political differences increasingly moved into the open, tensions within the city grew.[31]

That June Philadelphians faced another crisis as Rebel troops once again invaded Pennsylvania. On June 15 Lewis Ashhurst noted

25   Frank H. Taylor, *Philadelphia in the Civil War, 1861–1865* (Philadelphia, 1913), 215–20; See Chapter 2.
26   Yarnall diary, 2 September 1862; Lewis Ashhurst diary, 4, 12 September 1862.
27   George W. Fahnestock diary, 12 September 1862, HSP.
28   Wainwright, ed., *A Philadelphia Perspective*, 438, entries of 9, 16, 18 September 1862; Fahnestock diary 18 September 1862.
29   Taylor, *Philadelphia in the Civil War*, 270.
30   Maxwell Whiteman, *Gentlemen in Crisis: The First Century of the Union League of Philadelphia, 1862–1962* (Philadelphia, 1975), 18–26.
31   Winnifred K. Mackay, "Philadelphia During the Civil War," *Pennsylvania Magazine of History and Biography* 70 (January 1946); Weigley, "The Border City in Civil War," 405–7; Chapters 6 and 7.

a "[g]reat excitement about the Rebel raid into Penna."[32] In the next few days the fears escalated: "The city is alive with excitement"; "altogether the excitement is without parallel"; "City full of rumors and absurdly exaggerated reports of invasion"; and "[t]hings near a gloomy aspect."[33] As Lee neared, Governor Curtin and Mayor Henry called for emergency recruits, but their pleas fell largely on deaf ears. Fortunately, Meade's troops stopped Lee and Philadelphia's feeble defenses remained untested. Jacob Elfreth, Sr., described "great rejoicing . . . in our city at the result of this great victory."[34] And on July 7, on learning of the Union's victory at Vicksburg, James Mitchell wrote: "Good news seems to rain on us. . . . The state house bell was rung and everybody quit work for the day and turned out in the streets to have a good time."[35] Soon after Gettysburg, Philadelphians' celebrations were interrupted by the July 1863 draft. And that summer black recruits appeared in the city for the first time. These two developments helped the Union to fill its ranks, but not without creating controversy on the home front.

After the 1863 victories, Philadelphians began to anticipate a speedy end to the conflict. On December 31, Anna Ferris wrote: "The retrospective of the past year is very different from its predecessor & leaves us full of hope for the future & we feel as if it might indeed prove the 'year of jubilee' to the country."[36] But once again the casualties mounted as Grant launched his bloody campaign north of Richmond. When she learned of the Battle of the Wilderness, Katherine Wharton felt "sick at heart" and her husband "was too anxious to sleep."[37] At home the city's attention turned to June 1864's Great Central Fair to raise money for the United States Sanitary Commission.

In July 1864 Pennsylvania faced its third Rebel invasion when the Confederate troops marched through the state and burned Chambersburg. The response in Philadelphia was not as pronounced as a year before. Mary Ashhurst noted that "[w]e certainly [have] become accustomed to horrors. *This* outbreak did not terrify us as the one of last year."[38] But the city did send emergency troops into the field and opened its arms to refugees from Chambersburg.[39]

32 Lewis Ashhurst diary. 16 June 1863.
33 *EB,* 16 June 1863; Fahnestock diary, 16 June 1863; Mitchell diary, 16 June 1863; Sarah Richardson diary, 16 June 1863, Swarthmore.
34 Elfreth, Sr., diary, 6 July 1863.
35 Mitchell diary, 7 July 1863.
36 Ferris diary, 31 December 1863. Ferris was actually from nearby Wilmington, Delaware, but she spent much of her time in Philadelphia.
37 Wharton diary, 11 May 1864.
38 Mary Ashhurst diary, 22 July 1864, HSP.
39 Mackay, "Philadelphia During the Civil War," 33–4; Chapters 2 and 4.

As 1864 came to a close, public attention turned to Democrat George McClellan's challenge to Lincoln in the national election. Both the October state election and the presidential vote the following month produced vigorous campaigning on both sides. On November 4, Jacob Elfreth, Jr., reported that "[t]he election draws near and the excitement grows intense."[40] Many Philadelphians favored McClellan, but Katherine Wharton felt torn: "God knows I dont want a dishonorable peace – if for no other reason for the sake of my brother who gave up his life for the cause. . . . But I think that the Administration has mismanaged everything."[41]

In the months following Lincoln's reelection, Philadelphians reveled in a series of victories that signaled the death of the Confederacy. When Lincoln met Rebel leaders in early February, Jacob Elfreth, Jr., wrote: "everybody seems crazy about the Peace rumors." However, a few days later he reported that "the Peace affair has entirely fallen through."[42] But this disappointment was soon offset by General Sherman's successes in South Carolina. On February 22 Henry Benners observed "[m]uch excitement over the war news the opinion being rebellion in collapse." Lewis Ashhurst agreed that there was "apparent good reason to hope for peace before long."[43]

That April Philadelphians joined the rest of the North in ecstatic celebration. On the third Federal troops occupied Richmond. Six days later General Robert E. Lee surrendered at Appomattox Court House in Virginia. These victories sparked spontaneous displays all over the city. But Northerners did not celebrate long. On April 14, 1865, John Wilkes Booth shot Abraham Lincoln at Ford's Theater, and on the following day Philadelphians learned that the president had died from his wounds. This news brought citizens into the streets in quite a different mass display of emotions. A week later the funeral train that took Lincoln's remains home to Springfield, Illinois, stopped in Philadelphia where the body rested in state. Thousands of mourners stood in line for hours to pass through Independence Hall to pay their final respects.

Contemporary accounts reveal repeated moments when Philadelphians responded passionately to the Civil War. The greatest public attention turned to the battlefield when Confederate troops threatened the City of Brotherly Love. On other occasions citizens debated Lincoln's policies ranging from conscription, emancipation, and political arrests, to his manipulation of the Union's generals. But

40 Elfreth, Jr., diary, 4 November 1864.
41 Wharton diary, 11 October 1864.
42 Elfreth, Jr., diary, 3, 5 February 1865.
43 Benners diary, 22 February 1864; Lewis Ashhurst diary, 23 February 1865.

the diaries and newspapers also show that after the war's first months, Philadelphians on the home front returned to their routine lives.

Although they quickly adjusted to reports of bloody battles, Philadelphians felt the war's daily impact in dozens of more personal ways. Thousands of young men enlisted in the army, leaving thousands more at home fearing for absent loved ones. Citizens on the home front contributed to the war effort by raising bounty funds and by forming and supporting a vast array of voluntary societies aiding soldiers in Philadelphia and in the field. In addition to the conflict's military component, the Civil War touched life in Philadelphia by challenging existing benevolent societies, spawning new civic rituals, creating numerous disruptive tensions, providing new opportunities for local entrepreneurs, and raising prices.

The following chapters will consider various ways in which Philadelphia and its citizens felt the impact of the Civil War.[44] In the topics under investigation – enlistment and conscription, responses to separation and death, civic ritual, benevolence, the Great Sanitary Fair, public disorder, the military presence, labor, long-term economic change, annual economic fluctuations, and the entrepreneurial experience – several common themes will emerge. First, the diverse forces unleashed by the war created an equally varied range of experiences. The institutions that emerged to meet the crisis left individual citizens with innumerable options and yielded wide-ranging responses. And repeatedly this investigation has found strong continuities with the past: Philadelphia's wartime world evolved out of established peacetime practices. This is not to suggest that the war had no impact, but rather that by the eve of the war Philadelphia had developed a complex system of private and public institutions – institutions that were sufficiently flexible to answer the new demands without requiring substantial revision. The Civil War strained life in Philadelphia, but for the four wartime years the city and its inhabitants were able to maintain their peacetime routines while meeting the requirements of a major conflict.

How do these findings fit into our understanding of war and modern society? Like later conflicts, the Civil War certainly posed a

44 I have tried to address the war's principal social and economic effects; however, I am not proposing to offer a complete political history of the war years. Political issues will certainly arise–particularly as they concern potentially disruptive tensions and the centralization of power–but party politics will remain on the periphery. For greater political detail see Bradley, *The Triumph of Militant Republicanism;* Dusinberre, *Civil War Issues;* Weigley, ed., *Philadelphia;* and J. Thompson Scharf and Thomas Westcott, *History of Philadelphia, 1609–1884* 3 vols. (Philadelphia, 1884).

major "test" for Northern institutions. As we shall see, numerous familiar forces, including the demands for men, matériel, and civic order, pushed power toward the center. But Philadelphia's experience shows the other side of that coin: the persistence of localism and voluntarism in the face of new challenges. And during the Civil War, as during the two world wars, traditionally weak or powerless groups sought to parlay "participation" into social and political gains. The ledger sheet for these groups reveals mixed results. Workers won short-term gains but enjoyed few long-term improvements; women won the nation's gratitude but their energies did not typically yield increased powers; and whereas black military participation helped earn them postwar access to Philadelphia's streetcars, the victory was not won with a concomitant shift in local attitudes.

2 Filling the Ranks

The United States was unprepared in 1861 to engage in a major conflict. The regular army had less than 16,000 men; seven of the eight army bureau commanders had served in the War of 1812; and General in Chief Winfield Scott was seventy-four years old. When the Civil War started, a third of the army's officers resigned to serve the Confederacy.[1] The Pennsylvania state militia numbered 56,500 ill-trained and mostly unarmed men.[2] Philadelphia's branch of the militia comprised three Brigades and a special Reserve Brigade. The city was also the home of several independent military organizations.[3]

By the war's close, between 80,000 and 100,000 Philadelphians had served in the Union army. The city's 1870 population included 138,000 males between eighteen and forty-five years of age.[4] This chapter will examine the process by which so large a share of Philadelphia's military-aged men were brought into uniform. It will concentrate on two themes: (1) How was recruiting in Philadelphia organized? (2) Who served? (Was the conflict really a "rich man's war and a poor man's fight?")

Citizen soldiers and the call to arms

On April 15, 1861, Lincoln called for 75,000 three-month troops to put down the rebellion.[5] Recruiting tents sprang up all over Philadelphia as men hurried to enlist, anxious to share in the glory before the infant Confederacy fell. One Fourth Ward merchant offered $100 for a place in a newly formed company but could find no recruit willing to relinquish his spot. For a few frenzied weeks volunteers drilled in

---

1 James M. McPherson, *Ordeal By Fire: The Civil War and Reconstruction* (New York, 1982), 163; Allan Nevins, *The War for the Union*, 4 vols. (New York, 1959), 1:163–4.
2 Frank H. Taylor, *Philadelphia in the Civil War, 1861–1865* (Philadelphia, 1917), 15–17.
3 These included the First Troop Philadelphia City Cavalry, the Washington Grays, and the Scott Legion. Taylor, *Phildelphia in the Civil War*, 18–23. For a discussion of these nineteenth-century private military organizations see Marcus Cunliffe, *Soldiers and Civilians: Martial Spirit in America, 1775–1865* (New York, 1968), 215–35.
4 Bureau of the Census, *Ninth Census of the United States, Population* (Washington, 1970). This figure includes blacks.
5 McPherson, *Ordeal By Fire*, 149.

squares, armories, and empty buildings.[6] By April 29, Philadelphia had filled its quota of ninety-day volunteers, and hundreds of locals left town to enlist in neighboring states.[7]

The war fever of April 1861 spurred much of Philadelphia into action. One diarist reported that "most every other man in the street is in some kind of uniform."[8] On the twentieth, young lawyer James Tyndale Mitchell wrote that he had "[c]ommenced to drill with a squad."[9] Godfrey Brinley lost patience when his company was not immediately called into service and joined the Washington Grays.[10] Even gout-ridden, fifty-two-year-old Sidney George Fisher spoke of joining the Germantown Home Guard.[11]

Philadelphia sent eight infantry regiments, one cavalry troop, one artillery company, and one independent company in response to Lincoln's April 1861 call. On April 17 a Captain Archambault issued the following notice: "To the French residents of Philadelphia":

> Comrades – Our country of adoption is attacked in its Constitution and its laws – our duty is to aid the Government constitutionally elected, to maintain the Union. We appeal to our countrymen and others to come and increase the ranks of the Gardes Lafayette, so as to be ready at the first call for any contingency.[12]

Philadelphia's German, Irish, and British immigrants answered similar calls. In the next few days, the University of Pennsylvania Classics Department, the Harrison Literary Institute, the Tivoli Hose Company, the Maennercher Vocal Society, young men from the Fifteenth Ward, and workers from numerous manufacturing establishments all offered their services.[13]

The composition of these ninety-day forces suggests the associational network that supported Philadelphia's activities for the next

6 For good descriptions of April 1861 in Philadelphia see Winnifred K. MacKay, "Philadelphia During the Civil War, 1861–1865," *The Pennsylvania Magazine of History and Biography* (January 1946): 7–11; Ellis Paxson Oberholtzer, *Philadelphia: A History of the City and its People* (Philadelphia, 1912), 2:361; J. Thomas Scharf and Thompson Westcott, *History of Philadelphia*, 3 vols. (Phildelphia, 1884), 1:753–63; and Russell F. Weigley, "The Border City in Civil War, 1854–1865," in *Philadelphia: A 300-Year History*, ed. Weigley (New York, 1982), 394–6.

7 Edward G. Everett, "Pennsylvania Raises an Army, 1861," *Western Pennsylvania Magazine* 39 (Summer 1956): 100.

8 Nicholas B. Wainwright, "Education of an Artist: The Diary of Joseph Boggs Beale," *Pennsylvania Magazine of History and Biography* (October 1973): 500, entry of 30 April 1861.

9 James Tyndale Mitchell diary, 20 April 1861, privately owned.

10 Katherine Brinley Wharton diary, 18, 20 April 1861, Historical Society of Pennsylvania, Philadelphia (hereafter HSP).

11 Nicholas B. Wainwright, ed., *A Philadelphia Perspective: The Diary of Sidney George Fisher, 1834–1871* (Philadelphia, 1961), 386, entry of 22 April 1861.

12 *Philadelphia Public Ledger*, 17 April 1861 (hereafter *PL*).

13 *PL*, 18, 19, 20, 22 April 1861; Scharf and Westcott, *History of Philadelphia*, 1:764; Taylor, *Philadelphia in the Civil War*, 33–9.

INDEPENDENT RANGERS' SONG.

Dedicated to CAPTAIN WM. McMULLIN,

BY FRANK WHITAKER, Esq.

Our Country is now in great danger,
  And calls aloud for freemen all,
To rally around our noble standard,
  And answer bravely to the call.

    So buckle on in freedom's cause,
    The majesty of all our laws,
    That majesty to us was given,
    In '76, bestowed by heaven.

The President, though not *our* choice,
  Now holds his seat in hallowed land,
And we'll protect him, though we perish,
  By a brother, hand to hand.
    Chorus.

Disunion in our midst is raging,
  In social circles, and midst Firemen all,
And McMULLIN's Band's the first responded,
  To our President's appeal to all.
    Chorus.

A MANN has answered to his summons,
  A DEGAN nobly takes his stand,
But a bold McMULLIN bravely steps forth,
  With his true and gallant band.
    Chorus.

One of the many song sheets for sale in Philadelphia praising the
exploits of local companies or regiments. The Independent Rangers –
organized on May 20, 1861 – was composed of men from the
Moyamensing Hose Company. Library Company of Philadelphia.

four years. Each numbered regiment was composed of colorfully named companies reflecting Philadelphia's complex social mosaic. The Eighteenth included two companies from the State Fencibles, a local infantry corps dating back to the War of 1812, the Garde Lafayette and Zouaves, the Washington Blues, the National Grays, and the Minute Men of '76. The Twenty-first was mostly German, the Twenty-fourth primarily Irish. The Twentieth was manned by the "Scott Legion," an organization of Mexican War veterans. The firemen of the Moyamensing Hose Company formed the core of McMullin's Rangers, an independent company.[14]

Allan Nevins has called the 75,000 ninety-day militia volunteers "the merest stopgap."[15] But by the time they were mustered out, much of the Union's military structure was already in place. Under the direction of Treasury Secretary Salmon P. Chase, the North settled on a system that recognized state sovereignty while attending to national needs. When Lincoln called for 42,000 three-year volunteers on May 3, the War Department assigned each state a quota to be distributed evenly across congressional districts. Volunteers enlisted into local companies of a hundred men, and were then mustered into ten companies per regiment, these bearing state – not national – numerals. The enlistees elected their own company officers, whereas the state governors commissioned regimental officers, often merely ratifying the volunteers' choices. These original three-year regiments eventually dwindled in size. But rather than channel new recruits into old regiments, the states usually created new regiments. Such a system pleased the locals, but it left the generals with the task of maneuvering regiments of dramatically different strengths.[16]

In the spring of 1861 the Union army answered to many masters. The nation's executive called for troops, Congress approved the request, and Cabinet officers orchestrated the details. But at the local level, hundreds of town dignitaries put up tents, hired bands, and filled enlistment books. Between the officials in Washington and the recruiters on the village greens stood the Northern governors who were both implementers of federal policies and defenders of states' rights.

In the Keystone State Governor Andrew Curtin frequently found himself at odds with fellow Pennsylvanian and party adversary, Secretary of War Simon Cameron. Early in the war Cameron repeatedly commissioned political cronies and sent them into Pennsyl-

14   Taylor, *Philadelphia in the Civil War*, 33–9.
15   Nevins, *The War for the Union*, 1:167
16   Nevins, *The War for the Union*, 1:167–9; McPherson, *Ordeal By Fire*, 165–9.

COL. E. D. BAKER'S
CALIFORNIA
REGIMENT.

A RENDEZVOUS

For the enrollment of a

COMPANY OF PICKED MEN

WILL BE OPENED ON

Monday, August 12, 1861,

AT THE HOUSE OF HENRY MEHRING,

PASSYUNK ROAD

OPPOSITE QUEEN STREET.

This Company will leave for the Seat of War in two weeks, or sooner, if full.

JOSEPH C. TITTERMARY, Captain.

Philadelphia, August 10, 1861

J. H. Jones & Co., Book and Job Printers, No. 34 Carter's Alley, one door East of the Post Office

Recruiting broadside, 1861. The "California Regiment," formed by Oregon Senator Edward D. Baker, was largely recruited in Philadelphia but "credited to California." After Colonel Baker's death at the Battle of Ball's Bluff in October 1861 the regiment became part of the "Philadelphia Brigade" and its members filled part of Pennsylvania's quota. Note the selectivity implied in the phrase "company of picked men." Library Company of Philadelphia.

vania on independent recruiting missions. Because only full regiments were mustered into federal service, Curtin found himself administering a chaotic recruiting process, with dozens of recruiters competing for volunteers and vying for a handful of spots.[17] In mid-August 1861 an exasperated Curtin wrote directly to Lincoln:

> It appears from the acts of Congress . . . that the President has power to accept volunteers otherwise than through the State authorities only in cases where those authorities refuse or omit to furnish volunteers. . . . On the 26th day of July last a requisition was made on the Executive of this State for ten regiments of infantry in addition to the forty-four regiments already furnished. . . . Active measures were immediately taken to comply with this requisition, but unfortunately the Government of the United States went on to authorize individuals to raise regiments of volunteers in this state. . . . The direct authority of the Government of the United States having been thus set in competition with that of the State . . . the consequence has been much embarrassment, delay, and confusion.[18]

Finally, in late September, the War Department formally handed over control of all Pennsylvania regiments to Curtin.[19] But this did not end the Curtin – Cameron feud; only Cameron's eventual exile to Russia would accomplish that.

How did Philadelphia fit into this evolving military structure? Although the city swarmed with soldiers, Mayor Alexander Henry and the City Council had little to do with sending men to the front.[20] As long as there were more willing recruits than available regiments, the key relationship was between Curtin and the company recruiters. But in the national scheme of things, Philadelphia's size and location guaranteed it a major role.

Henry and the City Council did not sit idly by while others attended to recruiting. The council appropriated $50,000 on April 19 for the city's defense, and requested that each ward form companies for home service. The following day Mayor Henry named Colonel Augustus J. Pleasonton as commander of a newly formed Home Guard, and soon units had formed in most wards. By the close of 1861 the council had spent $138,000 on the Home Guard and other

---

17 Everett, "Pennsylvania Raises an Army," 84–5; Nevins, *The War for the Union*, 1:233–5.
18 U.S. War Department, *Official Records of the Union and Confederate Armies* (Washington, 1880–1901), ser. III, 1:439–41 (hereafter *OR*).
19 *OR*, ser. III, 1:541.
20 Philadelphia's council was made up of a Select Council and a Common Council. I have chosen to refer to the two councils in the singular.

aspects of the city's defense.[21] The council also established a fund to aid the families of local volunteers, spurring recruitment by assuring Philadelphians that their families would be cared for in their absence.[22] Both of these city government initiatives owed their success to private support. Although adopted by the mayor and council, the Home Guard evolved out of meetings held by local businessmen.[23] A committee of citizens administered the fund to aid the families of volunteers, and private subscriptions supplemented the council's appropriations.[24]

The Union recruiting structure was in place by the close of 1861. Federal authorities determined manpower needs; state officials orchestrated regimental organization; city officers appropriated funds and attended to local defenses; private individuals and groups worked both independently and within public institutions. Volunteers often enlisted in groups, responding to ethnic, occupational, social, and geographic ties.[25] This organizational mosaic remained largely intact in response to the war's changing demands.

In the summer of 1862 the Army of the Potomac under General George McClellan failed to take Richmond, and Lincoln was forced to turn to a demoralized North for 300,000 more men.[26] Once again, the War Department gave each state a quota to fill and left recruiting in the governors' hands.[27] This time the North responded sluggishly, and soon talk turned to conscription. Fearing a draft, and "following the unfortunate precedent of other cities," the council allocated $500,000 to a City Bounty Fund to spur enlistment.[28]

21 Philadelphia Select Council, *Journal* 14 (18, 19, April 1861); *Fourth Annual Message of Mayor Alexander Henry and Accompanying Documents* (Philadelphia, 1862), 27. The composition of the Home Guard, like that of the three-month regiments, reflected the associational ties molding Philadelphians' actions. See MacKay, "Philadelphia During the Civil War," 13–14.

22 *Fourth Annual Message of Mayor Alexander Henry*, 27–8; Scharf and Westcott, *History of Philadelphia*, 1:758–60; MacKay, "Philadelphia During the Civil War," 13.

23 MacKay, "Philadelphia During the Civil War," 13. Several Philadelphia merchants offered to contribute their own money to supplement the council's appropriation to defend the city. Select Council, *Journal*, 14 (18 April, 1861).

24 For a detailed analysis of this fund see Chapter 4.

25 For a longer discussion of enlistment along ethnic and occupational lines see Everett, "Pennsylvania Raises an Army," 93–4. For enlisting among laborers see Chapter 9. Young men who aspired to join the elite Anderson Troop were required to pass a special physical examination and furnish letters of recommendation from respected members of the community. Suzanne Colton Wilson, ed., *Column South With the Fifteenth Pennsylvania Cavalry* (Flagstaff, Ariz., 1960), 2–3.

26 McPherson, *Ordeal By Fire*, 244–51.

27 McPherson, *Ordeal By Fire*, 251; OR, ser. III, 2:204–5; James B. Fry, "Final Report to the Secretary of War by the Provost Marshal General," *Journal of the House of Representatives*, 39th Cong., 1st sess., House Executive Document, no. 1, vol. 4 (Washington, 1866), 166 (hereafter PMG "Final Report").

28 *Fifth Annual Message of Mayor Alexander Henry* (Philadelphia, 1863), 27; *Report of the City Bounty Fund Commission.* The allocation was made on July 26, 1862.

The decision to offer bounties placed the city government squarely in the center of the recruiting process. But Philadelphia's bounty fund revealed the persistent role of private initiative. The bounty fund, like the fund for the families of volunteers, was administered by members of Philadelphia's elite.[29] And the impetus behind the fund, like that behind the Home Guard, came from the citizenry. On July 24 Mayor Henry presided over a public meeting at the Board of Trade rooms to discuss means of encouraging enlistment. His audience decided to form a bounty fund and subscribed over $40,000 on the spot. Two days later, after the council added its $500,000 to the cause, thousands of citizens attended a mass meeting at Independence Square to raise more money. By the following day subscriptions totaled nearly $160,000.[30]

Other citizens pursued private initiatives. One doctor offered to give ten recruits $10 each and provide each man's family with free medical care.[31] Philadelphia's Corn Exchange Association voted to "organize and equip a first-class regiment of volunteers."[32] Other groups, ranging from the members of the Philadelphia Bar to an organization of Germans, collected funds to aid the families of volunteers.[33] By September 8 a general committee and various ward committees had collected more than $460,000 for a Citizens' Bounty Fund to supplement the municipal fund.[34] The city government created new institutional responses to wartime demands, but the existing web of voluntary societies did not entirely defer to the new order.

On August 4, 1862, Secretary of War Edwin Stanton called for 300,000 nine-month militiamen, with the provision that states failing to meet that quota would be subject to a militia draft. This move was designed to pressure the states into enthusiastic recruiting. Most states met their quotas without conscription. But the widespread use of bounties engendered persistent controversy, and some areas that held drafts – including parts of western Pennsylvania – saw violent protests.[35]

29 Mayor Henry headed the committee to aid families of volunteers, but the five-man bounty fund committee was made up entirely of private citizens. These included "gentleman" John R. McCurdy, attorney J. G. Rosengarten, and leading merchants Amos R. Little, John Ashhurst, and James Barratt. *Fifth Annual Message*, 27; *Report of the City Bounty Fund Commission*, 1.
30 Evening Bulletin, 23, 25, July 1862 (hereafter *EB*); *PL*, 21, 25, 30 July 1862; Scharf and Westcott, *History of Philadelphia*, 1:799; Taylor, *Philadelphia in the Civil War*, 267–8.
31 *PL*, 30 July 1862.
32 *Ninth Annual Report of the Corn Exchange Association of Philadelphia* (Philadelphia, 1863), 12; Taylor, *Philadelphia in the Civil War*, 349.
33 These activities aided the recruiting effort but I have chosen to consider them in the chapter on voluntarism.
34 Taylor, *Philadelphia in the Civil War*, 268.
35 McPherson, *Ordeal By Fire*, 251–2; Eugene C. Murdock, *One Million Men: The Civil War Draft in the North* (Madison, 1971), 6; See Chapter 7.

Philadelphia filled its 1862 quota without a draft, but only after several apprehensive weeks. On August 8 Curtin reported that volunteers statewide were "coming in rapidly," and on the twentieth the governor wrote that with "the use of the power to draft as an incentive the whole quota of Pennsylvania can be furnished without [conscription]."[36] But a week later Colonel Thomas A. Scott asked Stanton to extend Philadelphia's deadline, assuring the secretary that "[m]any districts, if given a little time, will secure volunteers for their entire quota and thus avoid the draft altogether."[37] On August 29 a crowd of citizens assaulted deputy marshals who had been enrolling men for the draft. But after postponing the deadline, the city filled its quota without conscription.[38]

Hard on the heels of the threatened militia draft of 1862, Philadelphians faced a more pressing danger with General Lee's invasion of Maryland. In early September, following the second Battle of Bull Run, wounded soldiers straggled into Philadelphia and its citizens began to fear that the rebel army might be close behind. On the ninth the Citizens' Bounty Fund Committee wrote an urgent letter to President Lincoln insisting that "the rapid advance of rebel armies . . . renders it absolutely necessary that something should be immediately done to secure the safety of the city." The harried president replied that "while I am not surprised at your anxiety, I do not think you are in any danger."[39] The next day Lincoln received a pressing missive from the presidents of several Philadelphia banks describing "the inadequate organization of local troops" and asking the president to create a military district in Philadelphia with an energetic general assigned to ensure the city's safety.[40] Two days later Mayor Henry telegraphed Washington with a similar request, to which an exasperated Lincoln replied: "Please do not be offended when I assure you that in my confident belief Philadelphia is in no danger."[41]

Unable to divert Union soldiers to Pennsylvania, Henry and Curtin sought to raise emergency troops to defend the state. On September 11 the mayor, responding to Curtin's request to "stir up your population tonight," called on Philadelphians to come to the

36   *OR*, ser. III, 2:330, 422.
37   *OR*, ser. III, 2:476. Scott, the vice-president of the Pennsylvania Railroad, had only recently resigned his post as Assistant Secretary of War. Scharf and Westcott, *History of Philadelphia*, 3:2194.
38   *PL*, 30 August 1862; Scharf and Westcott, *History of Philadelphia*, 1:801–4. For evidence of the public concern over the draft see *EB*, 22, 23, 25 July 1862 and *passim; PL* 11, 15, 30 August 1862 and *passim; Friends' Intelligencer* 26 (6 September 1862): 408–9; and *Germantown Telegraph*, 9, 16, 30 July, 6, 13, August 1862 (hereafter *GT*).
39   *OR*, ser. I, 19 (pt. 2): 230–1.
40   *OR*, ser. I, 19 (pt. 2): 250–1.
41   *OR*, ser. I, 19 (pt. 2): 278.

state's defense. The City Council gave Henry discretionary power to spend $500,000 to bolster the local military. The Committee on City Defense worked feverishly to attract and equip volunteers. These calls yielded much activity but few recruits. Curtin had asked the City of Brotherly Love for 20,000 volunteers and it answered with only 6,000. But on the seventeenth the tension eased as the Union army defeated General Lee in the bloody Battle of Antietam and the rebel forces retreated.[42]

The 50,000 Pennsylvanians who did answer Curtin's call were probably too few and too ill trained to stop the rebels had they won at Antietam. But for those who responded, the two weeks in the field left them with a sense of having helped defend their homes from attack. James Tyndale Mitchell was one Philadelphian who responded to the emergency. His memoir of the crisis typifies the experiences of Philadelphia's emergency troops.[43]

On September 9, 1862, the twenty-eight-year-old Mitchell "commenced drilling with the Washington Grays in view of the invasion of the state." On the twelfth he "joined the Germantown Company . . . to go to Harrisburg on the Governor's call." The Germantown Company drilled three times on the thirteenth, and on the fourteenth the call came and they proceeded to the armory, but after sitting all day they were sent home. The following morning the company marched to Washington Square amidst the cheers of onlookers and young Mitchell wrote: "I never felt jollier in my life . . . and the chafing and restlessness of mind that had been urging me to the war for so long a time were driven away entirely." Finally, after waiting for most of the afternoon, the emergency recruits marched across town and over the Schuylkill into West Philadelphia, where they boarded a train for Harrisburg.

The Germantown Home Guard spent one night in Harrisburg and then caught a train south to Chambersburg. The following morning they marched several miles out of town and spent the day swimming while the cannons at Antietam boomed within earshot.[44] Shortly after midnight on September 18 the company marched a few miles, waited in the rain, and then took a train to Hagerstown, Maryland.

On the nineteenth some of the Germantown Company exchanged gunfire with rebel pickets, but Mitchell's closest brush with death came when he was nearly mistaken for a Confederate soldier

---

42 MacKay, "Philadelphia During the Civil War," 31; Scharf and Westcott, *History of Philadelphia*, 1:802; Taylor, *Philadelphia in the Civil War*, 215–18.

43 Small journal among the Mitchell papers, privately owned. All quotations are from Mitchell's diary or the accompanying special journal.

44 Sharpsburg, the site of the Battle of Antietam, is less than forty miles south of Chambersburg.

by one of Philadelphia's Anderson Troop. The Philadelphians marched across the northern Virginia countryside for several days, safe
from the retreating Southern troops. On September 22 the Germantown Company marched back across the border and boarded a train
bound for West Philadelphia. Upon returning home a self-satisfied
Mitchell wrote: "So ended the campaign of the Germantown militia –
short and bloodless but not without arduous labor and hardship."
Although he had not fired his gun in anger, Mitchell seemed pleased
with having contributed to the cause.

Philadelphia's response to the September 1862 crisis underscores
the continuing role of private initiative in filling the military ranks.
When the Confederate forces neared Pennsylvania, Governor Curtin
and Mayor Henry realized that the home defenses were unprepared
to hold off a rebel assault. In the face of this crisis, both leaders had to
rely on their persuasive powers to field an emergency force. Those
who came forward were responding to a range of associational ties.
The existing Home Guard units and Reserve Regiments provided an
organizational center, and many Philadelphians, like Mitchell, enlisted in one of those established companies. Factory laborers, encouraged by fearful employers, volunteered en masse. Two hundred
employees at Baldwin's Locomotive works formed two independent
companies within hours of Henry's call, and men from the Whitney
Car Works and several other Philadelphia factories soon followed.
The Corn Exchange Association recruited and armed three companies. Other citizens formed the Independent City Guards.[45]

But the Antietam crisis revealed the weaknesses in the loose,
voluntaristic structure underlying the local military establishment.
Curtin and Henry simply had no established power to raise emergency troops. Bandstands and oratory no longer drew the responses of
eighteen months before. Those few who came forward were only
prepared to stay in uniform until the immediate danger had passed.
During the year to come Pennsylvanians would find their home
defenses tested once again – and once again they would be found
lacking.

In June 1863 Lee's troops again pushed north, and Curtin called
for 50,000 six-month volunteers.[46] Philadelphia's City Council
appropriated $500,000 for defense of the state; Henry called out the
Home Guard and issued a proclamation asking local businesses to
close their doors and encourage their employees to enlist in emergen-

45 MacKay "Philadelphia During the Civil War," 31; Scharf and Westcott, *History of Philadelphia*, 1:802; Taylor, *Philadelphia in the Civil War*, 215–18; *Ninth Annual Report of the Corn Exchange Association*, 12–13.
46 Scharf and Westcott, *History of Philadelphia*, 1:808. Curtin later changed this to a call for emergency troops.

cy companies. On June 17 Brigadier General Augustus J. Pleasonton, commander of the Home Guard, telegraphed Stanton requesting three field batteries and supplies to defend the city.[47] For the next two weeks Philadelphians alternated between apathy and activity as contradictory rumors filtered into the city. At first Curtin's call spurred brisk recruiting. By June 19 local volunteers forming one full regiment and several independent militia companies – including many veterans of the September 1862 campaign – had been mustered into the service of the United States.[48] But this fervor subsided when no rebel troops arrived. Then, on the twenty-second, reports began reaching Philadelphia that Lee's forces had set foot on Pennsylvania soil. This news led to renewed recruiting and frantic attempts to improve the city's fortifications.[49]

The War Department created two new military districts within Pennsylvania, with Philadelphia falling in the Department of the Susquehanna under Major General Darius N. Couch. On June 26 Couch sent Major General Napoleon Jackson Dana to Philadelphia to improve the city's defenses.[50] Dana reported that the city was "almost entirely defenseless" with only 400 men on guard, no defense works, and only a few pieces of artillery.[51] Having no fortifications and few men to build them, Dana turned to Henry for 2,000 laborers. Henry responded with 700 men, including 100 volunteer clergymen, and with this small crew Dana set about putting up earthworks.[52]

On June 29 a new set of appeals bombarded the still-sluggish Philadelphians. Henry called on all able-bodied citizens to turn out for the city's defense; Curtin issued a proclamation asking Philadelphia to send 8,000 men to Harrisburg; and Dana, mistakenly warning that "[the rebels'] object is Philadelphia," called on its citizens to "[a]rise now in your might." Later that day the Major General, speaking at Independence Square, asked for 40,000 volunteers to drill for the local defense and to help dig fortifications. On July 1, following the first day of fighting at Gettysburg, Governor Curtin addressed a large crowd from the balcony of the Continental Hotel.[53] But

47 EB, 15, 16, 17 June 1863; William L. Calderhead, "Philadelphia in Crisis: June–July, 1863," Pennsylvania History 28 (April 1961): 143–4; Scharf and Westcott, History of Philadelphia, 1:808; OR, ser. I, 27 (p. 3):188.
48 Taylor, Philadelphia in the Civil War, 247–9; EB, 18, 19, 20 June 1863.
49 Calderhead, "Philadelphia in Crisis," 146–7.
50 Weigley, "The Border City in Civil War," 409.
51 OR, ser. I, 27 (pt. 3):365–6.
52 Weigley, "The Border City in Civil War," 409; Calderhead, "Philadelphia in Crisis," 154–5.
53 Calderhead, "Philadelphia in Crisis," 151–2; EB, 2,3 July 1863; PL, 1, 2, 3 July 1863. Oberholtzer says that Curtin's speech prompted the enlistment of 5,000 new recruits. Philadelphia: A History of the City and its People, 2:378.

despite these appeals, Philadelphia produced neither the manpower nor the fortifications to fend off Lee had he defeated Meade.

By the close of the Gettysburg crisis, the city had sent three regiments and several companies into emergency service for the United States, and nine regiments into the ninety-day state militia. About 2,700 Philadelphians served in the Federal troops and perhaps 7,500 in the state militia.[54] As in 1862, the composition of these emergency regiments reflected the continued role of voluntarism in molding local enlistment. Companies formed for local defense or emergency service included the Bridesburg Guard, staffed, uniformed, and armed at the armory of Alfred Jenks and Sons; the Franklin Guard, composed of clerks from two local railroad companies; the Hatters' Guard; the United States Mint Company; the Engineer Corps, made up of students from the Polytechnic College; two companies of Navy Yard workers; companies formed from the local Baptist churches and the First Presbyterian Church; and a home defense company formed by veterans of the War of 1812.[55] One local manufacturer personally led 100 of his workers into emergency service, and gave $4 to each of the 25 wives left behind.[56]

The 1863 emergency underscored the continuing organizational problems besetting Philadelphia's military forces. At one level the problem was political. The Home Guard Brigade was commanded by General Pleasonton, a strong Democrat, and financed by the heavily Democratic City Council, whereas the city's Republicans preferred to lend their support to the local branches of the state militia.[57] Difficulties also stemmed from the confused system for accepting volunteers. Curtin and Couch had initially hoped to avoid the disorders of 1862 by mustering men into the U.S. service for the duration of the crisis. Some, however, resisted enlisting in Federal rather than state regiments; others feared that Curtin would be slow to declare an end to the emergency. These objections resulted in a compromise under which men who left Philadelphia for Harrisburg fell into two categories. Some were mustered in as emergency militia, serving as part of the U.S. forces for the crisis. Others served as ninety-day state militia, authorized only to protect Pennsylvania from invaders.[58] But fundamentally the problem was that emergency recruiting remained

---

54 Taylor, *Philadelphia in the Civil War*, 247–51. These estimates are based on Taylor's descriptions of Philadelphia's various emergency troops.
55 Taylor, *Philadelphia in the Civil War*, 246–7; Calderhead, "Philadelphia in Crisis," 144; *PL*, 1 July 1863.
56 *GT*, 1 July 1863.
57 Weigley, "The Border City in Civil War," 409.
58 Calderhead, "Philadelphia in Crisis," 146; MacKay, "Philadelphia During the Civil War," 32.

dependent on the persuasive powers of the city's civic and military leaders as well as on the continued pull of voluntaristic ties.

Although many remained idle in response to the June 1863 crisis, James Tyndale Mitchell again offered his services. His experiences reveal the persistent role of personal style and associational links in molding recruiting. On June 15 Mitchell spent the evening "at the armory of the Germantown Company" and on the following day, with the "city full of rumors and absurdly exaggerated reports of invasion," the Germantown Company met and "offered [their] services for thirty days or for the emergency."[59]

On June 17 the Germantown Company prepared to leave Philadelphia, but found that they "could not get transportation [without being] mustered into the U. S. service for six months, which [they] were not prepared to do." The frustrated volunteers telegraphed Curtin requesting permission to enlist for either thirty days or – as they had in 1862 – for the duration of the emergency. On the following day, with no answer from the governor, Mitchell and his comrades took a train to Harrisburg, only to discover that the six-month rule had not been rescinded. Some men argued for staying in Harrisburg to see if the danger increased; in the end, however, they elected to return home, temporarily ending what Mitchell termed "the worst managed affair [in which] I have ever had any . . . part."[60]

With the crisis mounting, Mitchell met with the men on the twenty-seventh "to try to organize a new company for immediate service." He came away disgusted, commenting that "not much [was] done as our officers are inefficient and won't resign." The next day they reconvened but again made little headway, leading Mitchell to conclude: "The prospect . . . is not encouraging as there are so many plans and no one willing to give up his own."

Finally, a disappointed Mitchell and several others from the Germantown Company enlisted in Biddle's Company. Mitchell drilled with the new company on July 1, but became irate at Captain Biddle's "perfect childishness." Biddle tried to convince his men to enlist "for City Service," which "produced a row at once, as we had been recruiting with the distinct understanding that we were for general state service and many of us were not willing to give up our business etc for mere city service." The following day Biddle "declared his inability to go for the three months state service and the company was practically disbanded." A frustrated Mitchell privately blamed Biddle "for breaking up the best company in Philadelphia."[61]

59 Mitchell diary, 15, 16 June 1863.
60 The trip home was particularly annoying because the company initially boarded a westbound train before finally settling on a train headed for Philadelphia. Mitchell diary, 17, 18, 19 June 1863.
61 Mitchell diary, 27, 28, 29 June, 1, 2 July. For an account of the Germantown Home Guard's exploits see *GT*, 24 June 1863.

Responses to conscription

Philadelphia's response to the Gettysburg crisis has been termed an "uninspiring story of a politically divided and doubtful city's response to the threat of invasion."[62] Its experience demonstrated the limits of localized voluntarism. Although the war would carry on for nearly two more years, never again would it try to fill its military ranks through the combined forces of patriotic persuasion and associational ties. As the conflict evolved into an "organized war,"[63] provost marshals and bounty agents came to play key roles in meeting enlistment quotas. In April and July 1861 Philadelphia's recruiters appealed to local patriotism; in September 1862 and June 1863 they mixed that call with a warning of imminent attack. After mid-1863 Philadelphians spoke of bounties and quotas and, above all, of avoiding conscription. But despite these changes, the city's war effort continued to rely on localism and voluntarism as well as on the municipal and state governments.[64]

In early 1863 the North faced a serious manpower shortage and the prospect of another year of bloody fighting. Responding to the lesson learned from the toothless 1862 state militia draft, Congress passed the Enrollment Act of March 3, 1863. This law put all further drafts under federal control, to be administered by Provost Marshal General James B. Fry. Under the new system the 185 northern congressional districts were to be the units for enrolling and drafting, with a federally appointed provost marshal, commissioner, and surgeon presiding over each. The Enrollment Act still left draftees ample room to avoid service. All men deemed physically or mentally unfit were exempt; draftees could furnish a substitute to serve in their place; and those unable to furnish a substitute could pay a $300 commutation fee.[65]

The Enrollment Act sought to pressure citizens into energetic recruiting to avoid the draft. The enrollment boards compiled lists of all eligible men residing in their congressional districts. When Lincoln issued a call for troops, each state was assigned a quota based on its

---

62 Weigley, "The Border City in Civil War," 410.

63 See Nevins, *The War for the Union*, vols. 3, 4, *passim*.

64 For discussions of historians' views on the draft see Peter Levine, "Draft Evasion in the North During the Civil War, 1863–1865," *Journal of American History* (March 1981): 816–34; James W. Geary, "Civil War Conscription in the North: A Historiographical Review," *Civil War History* (September 1986): 208–28.

65 Allen R. Millett and Peter Maslowski, *For the Common Defense: A Military History of the United States of America* (New York 1984), 198; McPherson, *Ordeal By Fire*, 356; Murdock, *One Million Men*, 6–9; Geary, "Civil War Conscription," 208–9. The records of the provost marshal general include extensive material on the activities of the boards of enrollment. For example, see "Proceedings of the Board of Enrollment, First District, Pennsylvania," #2823, Record Group 110, National Archives, Washington, D.C. (hereafter #2823, RG110, NA).

number of enrolled men, and these quotas were distributed among the districts. The provost marshals then announced the district quotas and urged the local citizenry to meet that number in order to avoid a draft. Typically the public response progressed from widespread disinterest to desperate activity as the deadline approached.

If the district failed to fill its quota by draft day, the board held a public drawing and chose enough men to make up the difference. The names were then published and provost agents personally notified each man of his selection. Draftees usually had ten days to pay the commutation fee, produce a suitable substitute, or appear before the draft board. Those seeking medical exemptions could claim any of fifty-one "diseases and infirmities" ranging from club feet to excessive stammering. But before he could prove his case the draftee had to stand in line, sometimes for days, waiting to see the district surgeon.[66]

In the war's final two years Lincoln issued four calls that resulted in drafts in some Union states. In one sense the Enrollment Act was an abject failure. Only 46,000 drafted men served in the Union army and an additional 118,000 men served as substitutes. The draft generated less than 10 percent of the Union's fighting force.[67] But in a larger sense the Enrollment Act worked admirably well. Time after time the fear of conscription induced communities to raise sizable bounty funds to attract more recruits. If the draft did not directly produce many new men, the threat of conscription served as a strong stimulus.[68]

Between April 1861 and December 1864 President Lincoln called for a total of 2,760,000 troops. Pennsylvania's aggregate wartime quota was 386,000, it sent 338,000. The drafts following the calls of July 1863 and March, July, and December 1864 raised a total of 8,615 Pennsylvania conscripts personally held to service and 12,636 substitutes; 2,800 other Pennsylvanians paid commutation fees. The state's total wartime quota was 14 percent of all Union troops called, and the drafts generated nearly 19 percent of the men personally held to service and 17 percent of all Northern substitutes. Pennsylvania's first five congressional districts, encompassing Philadelphia and

---

66 Murdock, *One Million Men*, 8–10; *OR*, ser I, 3: 125–7, 133–9.
67 McPherson, *Ordeal By Fire*, 357. The figure of 164,000 excludes the results of the 1862 militia drafts, but McPherson's estimate of under 10 percent includes all draftees.
68 See *EB*, 2, 3 July 1863, *PL* 5, 10 November 1863; 11 January, 22 February, 5, 22 August, 3 September 1864; 21, 22 February 1865. For a strong defense of the wartime draft efforts see Murdock, *One Million Men*, 333–49.

Bucks County,[69] contained roughly one-fifth of the state's population but accounted for only about 4 percent (373) of Pennsylvania's draftees personally held to service, 25 percent (3,124) of its substitutes, and 4 percent (1,174) of the draftees paying commutation fees.[70] Somehow the city that responded so poorly to invasion managed to raise enough volunteers to minimize the local impact of the draft. How did it do so?

On May 25, 1863, the North's provost marshals began enrolling men in accordance with the Enrollment Act of March 3. In some places these efforts met with organized resistance. In Indiana two men murdered an enrolling officer; Ohio's Governor David Tod asked for armed support to put down disorders; provost marshals in Pennsylvania's Tenth, Eleventh, Sixteenth, and Twenty-fourth districts all reported troubles.[71] In August 1862 a crowd of Philadelphians had attacked the deputy marshals charged with enrolling men for the militia draft,[72] but in 1863 the city's provost marshals completed their duties without incident.[73]

On July 9 Lincoln set the draft wheels in motion by calling for the conscription of 300,000 men to serve for three years. On the fifteenth the draft began in Philadelphia's Fourteenth Ward, and it continued throughout the city for the next three weeks. Across the North, the draft – like the enrollment – sparked a series of violent outbursts.[74] But in Philadelphia a well-prepared police force and a strong military presence combined to spare the city from any serious disturbance.[75]

Even before the president called for a draft, Philadelphians had begun to minimize its consequences. On July 4 the *Public Ledger* printed a list of twenty-five companies and individuals who had donated a total of $8,500 to the Citizens' Bounty Fund.[76] Still greater

69 The draft records are organized by congressional district. Philadelphia encompassed Pennsylvania's first four districts and part of the fifth district, with Bucks County making up the remainder of District Five. In 1860 Philadelphia County's population was 565,529. Bucks County's population was 63,578, or roughly 10 percent of the total population of Districts One though Five. Bureau of the Census, *Eighth Census of the United States, Population* (Washington, 1866).
70 PMG's "Final Report."
71 *OR*, ser. III, 3:338–82, 1047; W. B. Lane, Assistant Acting Provost Marshal General, Eastern Division of Pennsylvania, "Historical Report," National Archives microfilm M1163 (hereafter "Historical Report").
72 Scharf and Westcott, *A History of Philadelphia*, 1:801.
73 Although they reported no organized violence in response to enrollment, Philadelphia's five district provost marshals all acknowledged that many citizens successfully evaded the lists. Provost Marshals, 1st through 5th Districts Pennsylvania, "Historical Report," *passim*.
74 *OR*, ser. III, 3: 488–96, 1049–50.
75 For a detailed discussion of draft disturbances, see Chapter 7.
76 Murdock, *One Million Men*, 162.

fund-raising activity occurred at the ward level. The "Enlistment Association of the Twenty-third Ward" collected $14,474.79 and paid bounties to 316 men, or almost half of the ward's entire quota.[77]

The Citizens' Bounty Fund and the Enlistment Association of the Twenty-third Ward were part of a continuing voluntary effort to encourage recruiting. But their activities were too limited to spare Philadelphia from the draft. That summer the names of nearly 20,000 men in Pennsylvania's first five districts were drawn. Of those chosen, 4,169 (21 percent) were "held to service" – 343 were personally held; 2,667 sent substitutes; 1,162 paid the $300 commutation fee.[78] Combining draftees and substitutes, Philadelphia and Bucks County provided 28.8 percent of the men furnished by the state and 8.4 percent of all Union soldiers generated by the draft. But the city sent only 9.8 percent of Pennsylvania's conscripts and about 3.4 percent of the North's.[79]

Following the first draft, Philadelphians developed an increasingly effective system of draft avoidance. On February 1, 1864, Lincoln announced an increase in the July quotas from 300,000 to 500,000, leaving Philadelphia with an unfilled quota of over 13,000.[80] But the city's recruiting efforts proved so successful that it had a negligible burden in the March 1864 draft. By the time draft day arrived, several wards had overfilled their quotas while others had fallen only slightly short. After inspecting the enlistment returns, a Committee of Councils offered a plan to juggle the figures so that all the wards in districts one through four escaped the draft.[81] Only the Fifth District, encompassing the Twenty-fifth Ward and Bucks County, held a drawing; this resulted in a mere fifteen men held to service.[82]

On July 18, 1864, Lincoln called for another 500,000 men: Philadelphia's quota was 13,778. The city already had a credit of 4,000 men, and all of the wards managed to meet their goals before the September draft.[83] The fourth and final draft followed Lincoln's De-

77 Report of the Enlistment Association of the Twenty-Third Ward (Philadelphia, 1866). The Twenty-third Ward, in the northeastern corner of the city, had a population of 24,000 in 1860 according to Bureau of the Census, Eighth Census of the United States, Population.
78 PMG "Final Report." According to a summary in the Germantown Telegraph, 28 October 1863, Bucks County draftees paid 132 commutation fees and sent 426 substitutes.
79 Of course there is no reason to assume that substitutes for Philadelphia draftees came exclusively from the city.
80 Scharf and Westcott, History of Philadelphia, 1:811.
81 Scharf and Westcott, History of Philadelphia, 1:814.
82 One of these conscripts served personally, two sent substitutes, and the rest paid the commutation fee. PMG "Final Report," 177.
83 Scharf and Westcott, History of Philadelphia, 1:817; PMG "Final Report," 187. Note that these quotas were subject to later negotiation as discussed below.

cember 19, 1864, call for 300,000 new men. After adjustments for its accumulated surplus, Philadelphia's quota was roughly 9,000.[84] Although the president gave the states until the following February to meet the quota, Philadelphia could not dodge this final draft. Between February 23 and 28 the provost marshals ran small drafts in the city's First, Second, and Fifth districts. In the end, 32 men were personally held and 455 sent substitutes.[85]

The last three Northern drafts resulted in 5,143 Pennsylvanians personally held, and 5,683 substitutes. The North as a whole sent 36,466 conscripts and 47,605 substitutes. Philadelphia and Bucks County sent 33 draftees and 457 substitutes. In each of Lincoln's calls Philadelphia's quota was nearly 3 percent of the Northern total; but in the three 1864 drafts Philadelphia sent only .6 percent of all substitutes and conscripts.

What explains Philadelphia's successful avoidance of the draft? Its population composition certainly provides part of the answer. Once recruiting hinged less on patriotism than on financial inducements, urban districts had an advantage over their rural counterparts because they had larger lower-class populations. But this apparent advantage must have been partially offset by the general disinclination to enlist among the largely urban Irish and German Catholics.[86] And even if its population included many men willing to listen to offers of several hundred dollars, Philadelphia's achievement lay in its ability to provide sufficient funds.

Philadelphia filled its 1864 quotas because the city adjusted its traditional array of public and private voluntary institutions to meet a new demand. No single structure emerged to answer Lincoln's calls. Rather, Philadelphians, prompted by self-interest and communal concern, created a successful recruiting machine out of various, often unconnected, cogs.

After Gettysburg, recruiting was increasingly based on an escalating bounty fund system. In each of the last three drafts, communities had ample time to fill their quotas before the scheduled drawing.[87] It was in these months that the bounty machinery worked to its fullest. From October 1863 on the federal government paid a

---

84 Scharf and Westcott, *History of Philadelphia*, 1:820. Again, this quota was later adjusted down even further.
85 Scharf and Westcott, *History of Philadelphia*, 1:821; PMG "Final Report," 201. Commutation fees for all but noncombatants ended in October 1864. Hugh G. Earnhart, "Commutation: Democratic or Undemocratic?" *Civil War History* 12 (June 1966): 133.
86 McPherson, *Ordeal By Fire*, 358; Ella Lonn, *Foreigners in the Union Army and Navy* (Baton Rouge, 1951), 4–5.
87 In the July 1863 draft there was only one week from the official announcement to the day that drawing commenced.

$300 bounty to all three-year volunteers. These bounties, which amounted to $300 million over the course of the war, provided the base figure upon which states and localities grafted additional inducements.[88]

The City Council supplemented the federal bounty with a steady flow of money into the City Bounty Fund. As we have seen, the council appropriated $500,000 to help fill the 1862 quota. By the close of 1862 the five-man committee had distributed $370,000.[89] During the summer of 1863 many Philadelphians crossed the Delaware River to take advantage of Camden's $270 bounty, so in late 1863 Philadelphia's City Council voted a $250 city bounty to compete with their New Jersey neighbor.[90] With conscription posing a continual threat in 1864, the council took out additional bounty loans, distributing nearly $4.3 million. That winter the competition for men pushed city bounties even higher. The council's January 1, 1865, appropriations enabled the City Bounty Commission to pay $100 to one-year volunteers and $450 to three-year men. Two months later three-year enlistees received $600 and two-year men earned $500.[91] By the war's final months recruits could earn over $1,000 in national, city, and local bounties.[92]

The scale of these expenditures is evident when compared to the overall city budget. In 1858, 1859, and 1860 the city treasurer dispensed $5 million, $4.7 million, and $5.5 million respectively. In 1862 that figure rose to $6.3 million, with $657,000 going to the families of volunteers, $81,000 to the city defense, and $367,000 to the City Bounty Fund. In 1864 the treasury paid out $11.2 million, with $4.3 million going to bounties and $624,000 to the families of volunteers. Thus by midwar nearly half of Philadelphia's budget was devoted to war-related items.[93] The council financed these extensive bounties

---

88 McPherson, *Ordeal By Fire*, 356; Murdrock, *One Million Men*, 218; Geary, "Conscription in the North," 212–15.
89 *Fifth Annual Message*, "City Treasury Report."
90 Murdock, *One Million Men*, 162. By the close of 1863 they had paid out an additional $100,000. *Sixth Annual Message of Alexander Henry*, "City Treasury Report" (Philadelphia, 1863).
91 *Seventh Annual Message of Mayor Alexander Henry*, "City Treasury Report" (Philadelphia, 1864); *Twelfth Annual Report of the City Controller* (Philadelphia, 1865): *Report of the City Bounty Fund Commission* (Philadelphia, 1865).
92 Murdock, *One Million Men*, 166.
93 In 1863 the council spent $5.9 million, with $99,000 spent on the City Bounty Fund; in 1865 they spent $10.4 million, with $1,774,000 going to the fund. *Annual Message of Mayor Alexander Henry* (First through Fourth), "City Treasury Reports"; *Report of the City Bounty Fund Commission*.

through a large sinking fund loan rather than, as in the case of many other cities, through some form of direct tax.[94]

Philadelphia's five-man bounty commission distributed a total of 25,500 bounties. It was charged as well with contesting the city's assigned quotas. The commission formed to meet the December 1864 call faced an official quota of 17,514. By January 24, 1865, they had managed to reduce this figure to 10,518, and to 4,457 by March 25. "These successive reductions," the commission explained, "arose from the correction of errors in calculation."[95] After the later drafts the commission successfully lobbied for similar "corrections," which earned the city 12,529 additional credits. In its final report the commission claimed to have provided Philadelphia with 50,866 men – 25,280 bounties and 25,183 "credits secured" – while spending only $12,138 on advertising and other expenses.[96]

Federal and city bounties made up the top two tiers in the Union's bounty structure, but during the winter of 1863–4 Philadelphia's wards began to supplement those bounty sources with their own funds. In early December the citizens of the Twenty-fourth Ward held a mass meeting to raise $15,000 to give supplemental bounties of $50 to all recruits. The Fifth Ward formed precinct committees to raise enough funds to offer each recruit $75; the Sixth Ward countered with $150 per man.[97] Public concern that men from the poorer neighborhoods were flocking to the wealthier wards prompted calls to limit ward bounties. In the fall of 1864 Professor E. D. Saunders, with the support of the *Public Ledger*, waged a passionate citywide campaign to collect money for the low-income First Ward.[98]

Often when draft day approached wards held fund-raising festivals or concerts. Most wards published the names of bounty fund contributors and some promised contributors that they could have

---

94 Murdock, *One Million Men*, 176–7. For details on Philadelphia's sinking funds see the "Treasury Report" in Mayor Henry's Fourth through Seventh *Annual Messages* (1861–1864). The wartime city loans continued to be a budget item into the postwar years. See *First Annual Message of Mayor Morton McMichael*, "Treasury Reports" (Philadelphia, 1867). Philadelphia's banks repeatedly used their funds to buy city loans. See Nicholas B. Wainwright, *The Philadelphia National Bank: A Century and a Half of Philadelphia Banking, 1803–1953* (Philadelphia, 1953), 119.
95 *Report of the City Bounty Fund Commission.* By the time of the final reduction the city had already raised 5,276 men.
96 *Report of the City Bounty Fund Commission.*
97 See Murdock, *One Million Men*, 164; *PL*, 9, 22 December 1863.
98 *PL*, 4 April 1864. In March 1865 the Enrollment Act was amended to require that volunteers should be credited toward their home district's quota. But this vaguely worded amendment came near the close of the war. Lane, "Historical Report," 24–5.

19th WARD

AVOID the DRAFT

At a Meeting of the **BOUNTY FUND COMMITTEE** of the 19th Ward, the following Resolution was adopted:

Resolved, That the Citizens of the Ward pledge themselves not to contribute, directly or indirectly, to any Fund to procure Exemption for any Citizen, in employment and health, who may be Drafted and who has not **CONTRIBUTED** to the **WARD BOUNTY FUND**; and they will also *GUARANTY EXEMPTION* to any Man who may be Drafted, under the present call, who has contributed Twenty Dollars to the Fund.

MASS MEETINGS

WILL BE HELD ON

Friday, Monday & Tuesday Eve'ngs

MARCH 4th, 7th and 8th.

AT TEMPERANCE HALL,

Cor. York and Trenton Avenue.

Rev. FATHER McLAUGHLIN is expected to Address the Meeting on Monday Night

By Order of the Committee,

AND'W J. HOLMAN, Pres.

WM. N. LOCKHART, Sec.

If every Workingman liable to the Draft, will contribute One Day's Labor, the Ward will be Exempt from the Draft, *which will take place on the 10th of March.*

Broadside announcing a March 1864 "Mass Meeting" to be held by the 19th Ward Bounty Fund Committee. After three years of conflict, Philadelphians struggled to raise bounties to fill local quotas before draft day. Library Company of Philadelphia.

their money back if they were drafted.[99] These efforts frequently proved quite successful. After the fall 1864 draft the Eighteenth Ward (which had completely filled its quota) enjoyed an $800 surplus.[100] Between August 8, 1864, and January 12, 1865, the Twelfth Ward Bounty Committee raised $8,293 and paid 90 bounties.[101] In most cases the ward committees depended on extremely widespread participation. The Fourteenth Ward avoided the final draft by collect-

99 Murdock, *One Million Men,* 162–5; *PL,* 13, 14 September 1864; *EB* 28 March 1864.
100 Murdock, *One Million Men,* 164.
101 MacKay, "Philadelphia During the Civil War," 41.

ing almost $20,000 from 1,500 local citizens, with only a handful giving more than $50.[102] In response to the December 1864 call the Twenty-third Ward collected nearly $20,000 from about 1,300 subscribers. Only five of these contributions were for over $25.[103]

Philadelphians managed to minimize the draft burden by successfully bringing a wide range of public and private institutions to bear on the problem. Federally conducted conscription introduced an efficiency that the state militia drafts had generally lacked; and the national bounty provided a major incentive to volunteers. But although the draft reflected the war's powerful centralizing forces, it worked as a recruiting tool because of the energies expended at the local level. As Philadelphia finished its first decade as a consolidated city, the City Council took out extensive loans to fund municipal bounties. However, these new government initiatives did not displace the continued presence of voluntary contributions.[104] Private citizens donated money to the City Bounty Fund, and later served on the Bounty Fund Commission. And from the first draft call, private groups worked alongside the city's organization. The Citizens' Bounty Commission served until July 1864 when it gave way to the Citizens' Volunteer Substitute Commission.[105] At the ward level, hundreds of Philadelphians gave their time and energies to local bounty fund drives; thousands donated money to keep their neighborhoods free from the draft.

Three factors combined to make Philadelphia's bounty collections successful. First, the city managed to develop an organizational mosaic that took advantage of the existing array of public and private institutions and affiliations. In this sense the "organized war" of 1864 and 1865 was merely an evolution from the excited patriotism of April 1861. Second, the draft system allowed ample time for bounty-raising to gather momentum. When Philadelphians became aware that the government was prepared to use conscription, the

---

102 Fourteenth Ward, *Exhibit of Transactions Connected with the Fund Subscribed to Promote Enlistments* . . . (Philadelphia, 1865). About 200 of these contributions were $25 "conditional subscriptions" by men who would have received their money back if drafted. In addition, the ward collected fifty-three $100 contributions in a "special subscription" to be used only if the original fund ran out. Some of the ward's wealthier men put together $61,600 in cash to be used to redeem the city bounty warrants at par, thus protecting the recruits from later discounting.

103 *Report of the Enlistment Association of the Twenty-Third Ward.* In 1860 the Fourteenth Ward had 23,594 white citizens and the Twenty-third Ward had 23,366 white citizens, Bureau of the Census, *Ninth Census of the United States, Population.*

104 And even these loans reflected both localism and voluntarism at work as Philadelphia's banks repeatedly joined together to purchase city loans (while also making substantial donations to the Volunteer Bounty Fund). See Wainwright, *The Philadelphia National Bank,* 118.

105 Murdock, *One Million Men,* 165.

threat of the draft became an important recruiting device.[106] This threat proved more successful in cutting through public apathy than the confused reports of invasion, which resulted only in disappointing emergency recruiting. Finally, the bounty funds allowed for an enormous breadth of participation by allowing Philadelphians to sacrifice as little or as much as they chose.

We have thus far spoken of Philadelphia's recruiting "successes" and "failures" both in absolute terms (it sent a disappointing number of emergency troops in 1863, but nearly avoided the draft in 1864 and 1865) and in relative terms (it tended to "outrecruit" the rest of the state and the North as a whole in filling draft quotas). But we have not compared Philadelphia's performance with that of other urban areas. New York City's example suggests that Philadelphia was not alone in its success. In New York's Fourth through Ninth districts (the city and county of New York) the July 1863 draft left 28 citizens personally held for service, 1,977 sent substitutes, and 351 paid the commutation fee. New York City totally escaped the following two drafts, and sent only three conscripts and 199 substitutes after the December 1864 call. This pattern is generally similar to Philadelphia's, but New York performed slightly better. The provost marshal general's estimates show New York outspending Philadelphia by a substantial amount in 1863. And the final figures indicate that New Yorkers spent about $12 million on bounties compared to roughly $10 million spent in Pennsylvania's first five districts. New York's 1860 population was 813,000 as against Philadelphia's 566,000. Thus it appears that New York was slightly more successful in avoiding the draft, but Philadelphia distributed more bounty money per capita. More important, the North's two largest cities were both more successful than the norm in avoiding the draft.[107]

What explains these urban successes? Further investigation might show that these major cities enjoyed particularly strong associational networks. Or perhaps higher population densities made ward- and precinct-level bounty-raising particularly effective. And the relatively greater wealth stratification in these cities provided a ready pool of men willing to accept the financial inducements. Finally, New York's bloody July 1863 draft riots also might have spurred its citizens into particularly enthusiastic efforts, thus explaining its successful record in the later drafts.[108]

---

106 See EB, 28 March 1864; PL, 4 April 1864.
107 The provost marshal's final tally shows New York's Fourth through Ninth districts credited with 137,183 men; whereas Pennsylvania's first five districts were credited with 77,314. PMG "Final Report," 157.
108 On the New York riots see Chapter 7 and Adrian Cook, The Armies of the Streets: The New York City Draft Riots of 1863 (Lexington, 1974).

Who served?

Several factors make difficult any estimate of the total number of Philadelphians who served during the Civil War. There is the problem of distinguishing between long-term volunteers and emergency troops. Should James Tyndale Mitchell, who donned a uniform in 1862 but saw no fighting, count the same as his Uncle Hector, who served valiantly for several years? We also do not always know where enlistees were from. Early in the war, when Pennsylvania readily filled its alloted regiments, many Philadelphians traveled to New York to enlist. Later volunteers often left home to enlist where the bounties were greatest. This drew Philadelphians into neighboring Delaware, but it also enticed men into the city from the hinterlands. Finally, the aggregate lists count reenlistees twice.

One historian, working from Frank H. Taylor's regimental histories, concluded that Philadelphia units sent between 89,000 and 90,000 men, excluding three-month volunteers. The provost marshal general's final report credited Pennsylvania's first five districts with about 77,000 long-term recruits. Contemporary estimates placed Philadelphia's 1862 emergency volunteers at over 6,000, and more than 8,000 locals responded to the Gettysburg crisis in 1863.[109] It is probably safe to say that between 80,000 and 100,000 Philadelphians served in the army at some point. Is this a large number? Philadelphia's male wartime population was roughly 300,000. About one-quarter of all white men in 1860 were between ages fifteen and twenty-nine. If we assume a similar age distribution in Philadelphia, approximately seventy-five thousand of the city's males were between fifteen and twenty-nine. Three-fourths of all Union volunteers were from that age group. If the same were true of Philadelphia's volunteers, somewhere between sixty-thousand and seventy-five-thousand Philadelphians between ages fifteen and twenty-nine served.[110] These figures indicate that the vast majority of Philadelphia's young men donned the Union uniform.

Civil War historians have frequently asked whether the conflict was a "rich man's war and a poor man's fight." The aggregate data from the North seem to contradict that charge. Two surveys of the composition of the Union army – by the United States Sanitary Commission and by Bell Wiley – found that the distribution of prewar occupations among soldiers conformed fairly closely to the occu-

109 Weigley, "The Border City in the Civil War," 396; PMG, "Final Report," 157; Taylor, *Philadelphia in the Civil War*, 218, 247–51. Presumably many Philadelphians responded to both crises.
110 Roger Lane, *Violent Death in the City* (Cambridge, 1979), 11; Benjamin Apthorp Gould, *Investigations in the Military and Anthropological Statistics of American Soldiers* (New York, 1869), 35; Bureau of the Census, *Historical Statistics of the United States, 1789–1945* (Washington, 1949), 28.

pational breakdown among Northern adult white men in the 1860 census. These findings are particularly striking, given that the census includes a much older population. In fact, James McPherson concluded that "if anything, unskilled workers were underrepresented – partly because of the underrepresentation of Irish Americans" in the Union army.[111]

Apparently the pulls of patriotism, popular pressure, and increasing financial inducements appealed to a goodly portion of young men from all social strata.[112] But what of the unequal burden posed by conscription? As we have seen, the Enrollment Act allowed draftees to purchase their freedom by hiring substitutes or paying a $300 commutation fee.[113] How did such regulations affect Philadelphians?

Many contemporaries leveled charges of class bias. Philadelphia labor leader Jonathan Fincher frequently used the pages of his *Trades' Review* to lobby against the inequity of the conscription laws.[114] "This allowing a citizen to shirk his duty simply because he has means at command," Fincher argued, "is anti-Republican and should be discarded." Rather,

> let every man whose name is drawn, at once take up his position in line, and march to the music of the Union: and should stern fate bring a millionaire's son cheek by jowl with a sturdy mechanic, ere the campaigns are over, perhaps both may be benefitted by the contact.[115]

But other observers defended the commutation fee as an important measure guaranteeing that even humble mechanics could afford to avoid service.[116] One Philadelphia newspaper reckoned that "an industrious mechanic making $10 a week at his trades, could afford to give $300 to release him from a service of three years, equivalent to only $100 a year out of his wages, and still be pecuniarily a large gainer, comparing his wages with the amount the Government gives

---

111 McPherson, *Ordeal By Fire*, 357–9. The two surveys were based on samples of 666,530 and 13,392 men. See McPherson, 637, fn 18. A study of the Confederate army (also summarized by McPherson) yielded similar results. For a study of one New England town see R. J. Rorabaugh, "Who Fought for the North in the Civil War? Concord, Massachusetts, Enlistment," *Journal of American History* (December 1986): 695–701. See also Chapter 9.

112 For a discussion of the forces motivating Union enlistment see Marvin R. Cain, "A 'Face of Battle' Needed: An Assessment of Motive and Men in Civil War Historiography," *Civil War History* (March 1982): 12–13.

113 *OR*, ser. III, 3: 136–9. McPherson, *Ordeal By Fire*, 355–6. The commutation fee, which Congress abolished in July 1864, only exempted the draftee from that particular call-up.

114 *Fincher's Trades' Review*, 13 June, 25 July, 19 December 1863; 25 June 1864; 7 January 1865 (hereafter *FTR*).

115 *FTR*, 19 December 1863.

116 Without such a fee, the logic ran, prices for substitutes would become prohibitive.

in pay, bounties, etc."[117] Although Fincher certainly held the moral high ground in this debate, it remains to be seen how the Enrollment Act's provisions actually affected drafted men.

After each drawing, countless newspaper advertisements offered large inducements for substitutes. Many draftees, hoping to avoid costlier routes, sought to convince the examining surgeon that they suffered from one of the "diseases and infirmities" that merited an exemption.[118] After the 1863 draft the lines grew so long at the surgeon's office that Philadelphia's prospective exemptees took to lining up as soon as the office *closed* to guarantee that they would reach the head of the line by the end of the next day. Some enterprising souls waited in line and then sold their spaces for healthy sums. (One able-bodied draftee earned his commutation fee in this manner.) Others sought exemption as the sole support of widowed mothers, although the truth was that many were young men who actually relied on their parent's income.[119]

For twenty-six-year-old carpet dealer Jacob Elfreth, Jr., the draft was a repeated inconvenience, but not a substantial burden. On August 12, 1862, he wrote:

> I received notice of enrollment in the state militia last evening much to my sorrow. I went round to Jane and she gave me a note to Dr. Littel asking him for a certificate in regard to my eyes. He gave it me, stating therin that in his judgement I was unfit for military duty.[120]

In mid-July 1863, the provost marshals began drafting in Elfreth's ward, and on the twentieth he wrote: "I was drafted today though I do not expect to go my eyes being too sore." On the thirtieth Elfreth visited the provost marshal's office to secure an exemption, but waited in line for two and a half hours without success. The next day he returned but quit the line when the sun began hurting his eyes. A few days later Elfreth wrote that he "went to the Provost today determined to stick it out, sat in the broiling sun 2 1/2 hours . . . when a man came and told me to come early next morning when he would get me through." The next morning he returned, the man was true to his word, and soon Elfreth returned home with his exemption.[121]

Jacob Elfreth, Sr., watched the draft with particular care because

117 Unidentified paper quoted in *FTR*, 19 December 1863.
118 *OR*, ser. III, 3: 136–9.
119 Murdock, *One Million Men*, 70; "Proceedings of the Board of Enrollment, First District, Pennsylvania," #2823, RG110, NA.
120 Jacob Elfreth, Jr., diary, 12, 13 August 1862, Haverford College Library, Haverford, PA.
121 Jacob Elfreth, Jr., diary, 13, 20, 27, 30, 31 July; 3, 4 August 1863. Elfreth did not note whether he had to pay his friend for his assistance, but presumably any "fee" seemed less a burden than the cost of a substitute.

he had four adult sons liable to the call and because, as Quakers, his sons would not pay their way out of service if drafted. On July 24, 1863, he wrote that his son Caleb "seems rather dull and apprehensive he will be drafted as my son Jacob, Jr. was on the 20th of this month. I hope he will not be & if he is he will be exempted on account of his ill health." Soon Elfreth had reason to celebrate, for Caleb escaped the draft, Jacob, Jr., received his exemption certificate ("a great relief to himself and all our family"), and the Camden, New Jersey, community where a third son, Joseph, resided filled its quota without resorting to conscription.[122]

In the February 1865 call Caleb, Jacob, and James (a fourth brother) escaped, but Joseph Elfreth did not. On March 9 Jacob, Jr., reported that "Joseph has not got clear of the draft yet, this is the day he is to report but I trust there will be a way opened for him to escape." His father seemed less concerned when he wrote: "My son Joseph supped with us this evening. I think he is not likely to be much inconvenienced by the Draft." In the end that optimism proved warranted, for Camden again filled its quota without forcing its draftees into service.[123]

Lewis Walker, a thirty-eight-year-old doctor, was vacationing on Cape May in August 1863 when he discovered his name on a list of draftees published in the *Evening Bulletin*. That night several friends advised him that draftees often had very little time to report for duty or make other arrangements. Upon hearing this news Walker "felt [so] excited [that] the perspiration rolled off [his] forehead" and he resolved to return to Philadelphia immediately. On August 13 he arrived home and wrote "I got my *notice* that I had been drafted for *3-years service in the US army* and to report at the Provost Marshalls Office Oct *7th*." Apparently the distant deadline calmed his nerves because Walker wrote nothing more of the draft until late September when he noted: "I paid my $300[,] went to the Provost Marshall & got my exemption from the draft."[124]

Drug merchant George Fahnestock anticipated the stiff competition for substitutes that would follow the 1864 draft, and in early August he "went to hunt a substitute to take my place in the army." Although the call was still a month off, he found that the best he

---

122 Elfreth, Sr., diary, August 1862; 15, 20, 22, 24, 25, 28, 29 July 1863, Haverford College.
123 Elfreth, Sr., diary, 23 February, 9 March 1865; Elfreth, Jr., diary, 23, 25, 28 February, 9, 19 March 1865.
124 Lewis Walker diary, 4, 6, 13 August, 28 September 1863; 9, 27 July 1864, Historical Society of Pennsylvania, Philadelphia (hereafter HSP). In the summer of 1864 a friend of Walker's secured a substitute for $660 and Walker prepared to do the same before discovering that those who had paid a commutation fee were not liable to the current call.

could do was pay $900 through a broker. A few days later he met his substitute – "a good countenanced Irishman" – and spent the morning interviewing the man and then getting him mustered in.[125] Although he could well afford the cost of a substitute, the whole process left a bad taste in Fahnestock's mouth. He seemed content with his replacement, but felt "indignant and sick at the rascality of the brokers and their pimps," and he was sure that "John [the substitute] will be robbed of every dollar before a week."[126]

Some Philadelphians banded together in small insurance societies, in which each man agreed to contribute to the exemption expenses of any of their party who was drafted.[127] Henry Wharton, a lawyer with three young children, made such an agreement with several of his friends. This turned out to be a wise gamble, for when Wharton was chosen in the February 1865 draft, his exemption only cost him $200.[128]

Both Fahnestock and Wharton acted in anticipation of the draft to minimize the financial burden, but each – like Lewis Walker – earned a living that allowed him to cover the necessary costs without hardship. John A. Wilson, a young civil engineer with the Pennsylvania Railroad, found the cost more burdensome. During 1861 and early 1862 Wilson drilled with the Home Guard but he never entered active service. At the start of 1864 Wilson was earning $150 a month, a figure that rose to $200 in April. When the draft lists that summer included his name, Wilson lacked the wherewithal to hire a substitute. But rather than enter the army, Wilson secured a $650 loan from the Pennsylvania Railroad and spent this money – the equivalent of more than three months salary – on a substitute. This young man, who had been married only seven months, preferred to go into debt rather than join the army.[129]

Most in this handful of cases found conscription inconvenient, some seemed to find it sobering, but each adopted some means of avoiding service. But we must still wonder what became of those men of more modest incomes. One way to assess the draft's impact on Philadelphians is to consider the number of locals who were actually forced into service. By this standard the Enrollment Act clearly posed only a minimal burden. One could also consider the machinery created by the Enrollment Act and ask how easy it would have been to

125 By buying a substitute Fahnestock was able to recoup an earlier donation of $250 he had made to the Bounty Fund Committee in hopes of helping to spare his ward from a draft. This example demonstrates the increase in substitute prices following the removal of the commutation fee.
126 George W. Fahnestock diary, 9, 10, 12 August 1864, HSP.
127 Murdock, *One Million Men*, 169–70.
128 Katherine Brinley Wharton diary, 26 February 1864, HSP.
129 John A. Wilson diary and account book, *passim*, HSP.

avoid service. The local enrollment officers rarely met with outright violence; however, their task was difficult and their resulting lists rarely complete. One district marshal complained that "the people resort to all devices to evade [enrollment]."[130] Some gave false names or lied about their age.[131] Others simply moved and did not report their new addresses.[132] As was the case in many aspects of Philadelphia's wartime life, the Enrollment Act depended on voluntary efforts to ensure its success. One marshal noted that "regular appeals were made to the interest, duty and patriotism of the citizens to assist in the work."[133] Where citizens were willing to make sure that their neighbors were enrolled, the system worked well. But in hostile wards lone enrolling officers could accomplish little.

A different approach is to focus on the fates of those whose names were chosen on draft day. What were their chances of escaping service? The evidence indicates that although draftees of substantial means certainly sat in the most comfortable positions, the vast majority of selected men from all classes avoided service. A third (9,007) of all draftees were never examined. Half of these men were from wards that filled their quotas after draft day (3,750) or were "discharged per order" (821) before examination.[134] What of the 4,436 conscripts who "failed to report"?[135] Some officials estimated that half of these men were already in uniform.[136] But clearly several thousand conscripts actively resisted service. As one district provost marshal reported, those who "were unwilling to assist the government by entering the service or furnishing the necessary equivalent left their homes and sought new localities under assumed names."[137] Any draftee willing to make such a sacrifice had a very good chance of staying out of uniform. But whereas Peter Levine has found that

130 William Lehman, First District provost marshal, "Historical Report."
131 In one precinct in 1862 seventeen men said they were forty-four, forty-four said they were forty-three, forty-three claimed to be forty-six (and thus ineligible for conscription). This distribution suggests expected "age heaping" at age forty-five and some intentional draft avoidance by men overstating their age. "Enrollment of the Citizens with the Eighth Precinct of the First Ward, Philadelphia . . . August 9, 1862," #2794, RG110, NA. For a discussion of age heaping see David Hackett Fischer, *Growing Old in America*, expanded ed. (New York, 1978), 82–6.
132 Several district provost marshals reported problems with population mobility. First District provost marshal William Lehman claimed that three-fourths of his district moved every two years. See "Historical Report."
133 Lehman, "Historical Report."
134 PMG, "Final Report."
135 Murdock, *One Million Men*, 10–11. For discussions of draftees who "failed to report" see Levince, "Draft Evasion in the North," 818–34; Geary, "Conscription in the North," 221–3.
136 Second and Third districts provost marshals, "Historical Reports." Provost Marshal General Fry estimated that 30 percent of those who failed to report were not true deserters. See Levine, "Draft Evasion During the Civil War," 820–1.
137 Captain Edwin Palmer, Second District provost marshal, "Historical Report."

"illegal draft evasion became chronic" throughout the North after the March 1864 repeal of the commutation fee (for all but noncombatants), in Philadelphia the vast majority of those who failed to report (3,781 of 4,436) did so during the July 1863 draft.[138]

Of the 17,500 draftees who reported for examination, nearly a third (5,225) received some sort of medical exemption and another 7,600 qualified for one of a long (and fluctuating) list of other exemptions. In sum, Philadelphia's draft boards only held 4,671 of 26,514 draftees to service. Less than one in five men chosen on draft day even had to consider the prospect of paying a commutation fee or purchasing a substitute.[139]

This evidence suggests that most draftees of all classes managed to avoid service, but what of those who could not meet any of the exemption requirements?[140] Did only wealthy men take advantage of the regulations allowing for substitutes and commutation fees? Two Northern studies have addressed this problem.[141] In his district-by-district analysis of the New York State draft, Eugene C. Murdock found no correlation between either commutations purchased or substitutes hired and per capita wealth.[142] In a more detailed essay, Hugh G. Earnhart examined the draft records from four Ohio districts and concluded "that the majority of the draftees from the lower economic groups could pay commutation but could not raise the sum necessary to hire a substitute."[143] But Earnhart's findings demonstrate that men from all occupational strata continued to purchase exemptions throughout the war. Of the drafted "laborers" held for service in these four Ohio counties, 86 percent sent substitutes or paid commutation.[144] Among drafted merchants, 93 percent purchased their exemptions. After the commutation fee had been re-

---

138 Levine, "Draft Evasion," 828. This difference reflects Philadelphia's particularly successful recruiting after the first federal draft.

139 PMG, "Final Report." In fact, nearly as many draftees (4,436) failed to report at all.

140 It is possible that there were class biases underlying the other exemptions as well, but it would seem that these cut both ways. On the one hand, one can well imagine examining surgeons listening more closely to the complaints of a well-dressed gentleman than those of a common laborer; on the other hand, the 1,900 Philadelphians exempted in 1863 as "aliens" were probably disproportionately of the lower classes. Moreover, the very rich were probably content to hire a substitute rather than waste hours in exemption lines.

141 Also see Geary, "Conscription in the North," 220–1.

142 Murdock, "Was it a 'Poor Man's Fight?' " *Civil War History* 10 (September 1964): 241–5.

143 Earnhart, "Commutation: Democratic or Undemocratic?" 134.

144 After Congress removed the commutation fee there was no check on the price of substitutes. Of course the draft hit Philadelphia the hardest in 1863, when the commutation fee was still in effect. All calculations are from Earnhart's tables. Note that he differentiates between "laborers" and "skilled laborers." These calculations only include the former.

Table 2.1. The 1863 Draft in Philadelphia, Fifth District: Distribution of Paid Exemptions
by Occupation

Class	Number	Percent	Bought Substitute	Paid Commutation
1[a]	35	24.8	23	12
2[b]	25	17.7	21	4
3[c]	51	36.2	42	9
4[d]	11	7.8	8	3
5[e]	19	13.5	14	5
Total	141	100.0	108	33

[a] Class 1: merchants, manufacturers, professionals, gentlemen*
[b] Class 2: agents, storekeepers, wealthiest craftsmen, farmers*
[c] Class 3: most types of craftsmen
[d] Class 4: clerks, salesmen, carters
[e] Class 5: unskilled and semiskilled laborers

Classes have been adapted from Stuart Blumin, "Mobility in a Nineteenth Century
American City: Philadelphia, 1820–1860" (Ph.D. diss., University of Pennsylvania, 1968),
Appendix. Occupations marked with * do not appear on Blumin's lists.

Source: Germantown Telegraph, 28 October 1863.

moved, about 75 percent of all laborers held for service sent substitutes as did 82 percent of the merchants.

Although comprehensive occupational data for Philadelphia
draftees are not available, the evidence from one district does shed
light on the matter. On October 28, 1863, the *Germantown Telegraph*
published an "abstract of exemptions granted to drafted persons by
the board of enrollment of the Fifth District of Pennsylvania."[145] This
list included 1076 men from Philadelphia's three northernmost
wards.[146] Of these, 66 (6.1 percent) paid commutation fees, 290 (27
percent) provided substitutes, and the rest met one of the other
exemption requirements. A search of the Philadelphia City Directories of 1861 and 1866 yielded occupations for 141 of the 356 men
purchasing their exemptions. These occupations have been divided
into five categories, based on the rankings used by Stuart Blumin in
his study of Philadelphia's nineteenth-century occupational
mobility.[147] The results are summarized in Table 2.1.

145 *GT*, 28 October 1863.
146 The Twenty-second, Twenty-third, and Twenty-fifth wards.
147 Stuart Blumin, "Mobility in a Nineteenth-Century American City: Philadelphia,
     1820–1860" (Ph.D. diss., University of Pennsylvania, 1968), appendix; Blumin,
     "Mobility and Change in Nineteenth-Century Philadelphia," in *Nineteenth-
     Century Cities: Essays in the New Urban History*, eds. Stephan Thernstrom and
     Richard Sennett (New Haven, 1969), 174. The first category includes merchants,
     manufacturers, professionals, and gentlemen. The second includes farmers,
     agents, storekeepers, and men from the highest ranking crafts (based on mean
     wealth). The third category includes most types of craftsmen. The fourth includes
     clerks, salesmen, and carters. And the last includes various forms of unskilled
     and semiskilled labor.

What can we conclude from this table? First, the data clearly demonstrate that *some* men of all occupational strata bought themselves out of the army. Ten men, for instance, appeared in the directories as common "laborers," an occupational group that in 1860 had a mean wealth of only $180.[148] The fifty-one draftees in class 3 include nine carpenters, seven machinists, four shoemakers, and five butchers and bakers. But the 141 men in this study comprise only about 42 percent of the draftees who paid commutation fees or hired substitutes. How accurately do they represent the rest? Seventy-nine of the "unknowns" are cases where it was impossible to distinguish between several men in the directories with the same name. The remaining 111 cases (33 percent) were men whose names did not appear in either directory. Because city directories offer an economically skewed portrait of the population by concentrating on heads of households, there is reason to believe that the 111 "missing" men came from a less wealthy pool than the 141 in Table 2.1.[149] And matching lists of names to directories – even with rough addresses – is a very imprecise procedure. Since mean wealth among men in the directories was presumably greater than that for all draft-age white men, misidentifying draftees who were not really listed in the directory (listing sons by their fathers' occupations, for instance) probably would have artificially raised the average occupational level described in Table 2.1. In sum, it seems likely that the occupational distribution described in the table was higher than the distribution among all men who purchased substitutes or paid exemptions.[150]

Table 2.2 compares the occupational distribution among men randomly selected from the two directories to the distribution among

148 Blumin, "Mobility and Change," 169. The 1860 mean wealth of men involved in the crafts in class 3 ranged from $1,500 to $4,000. By 1863 inflation had raised this average somewhat; but because all draftees were under forty-five years of age, their mean wealth was probably below that of all men in class 3. Thus, although many presumably had sufficient savings to purchase an exemption, such an expenditure would have represented a substantial portion of their wealth.
149 The assumption here is that, on average, men between ages twenty and forty-five who were heads of households were wealthier than men of the same age cohort who were not heads of household. Moreover, by using directories from 1861 and 1866 the sample is biased in favor of geographically stable men. There is no particular reason to believe that the 79 unidentifiable cases with several men of the same name systematically differed from the 141 identifiable men.
150 In twenty-four cases I chose one man among several with the same name based on street addresses. The distribution of occupations among these twenty-four men – who were probably the most problematic matches – was quite similar to the overall distribution among all 141 cases: 5 in class 1: 7 in class 2: 7 in class 3; 2 in class 4; and 3 in class 5.

Table 2.2. Occupational Distribution of Men Sampled from the 1861 and 1866 City Directories Compared with Occupational Distribution of Exemption-Purchasing Draftees in the Fifth District

| | Draftees | | | Directory Samples | | |
Class	Number	Percent	1861	1866	Total	Percent
1	35	24.8	72	136	208	20
2	25	17.7	61	63	124	12
3	51	36.2	207	183	390	38
4	11	7.8	48	29	77	8
5	19	13.5	122	100	222	22
Total	141	100.0	510	511	1021	100

Note: The directories were sampled by taking the occupation of the first man listed on pages evenly distributed across the directories. Partnership listings were ignored because they were always listed separately as well.
For a definition of classes, see Table 2.1.

Sources: McElroy, *Philadelphia City Directories, 1861 and 1866* (Philadelphia) and Table 2.1.

exemption-purchasing draftees.[151] There was a slight overabundance of exemption-purchasing draftees in the top two categories, and a more substantial underrepresentation of men from the lowest occupational rank. Draftees in classes 3 and 4 (artisans and low-level white-collar workers) purchased exemptions in numbers fairly proportional to their representation in the directory samples. This evidence suggests that craftsmen bought their way out of the army at a rate roughly proportional to their share of the total population, whereas unskilled laborers were somewhat less likely to adopt that route. But actually the mean wealth in Philadelphia's northernmost wards was lower than in the city as a whole.[152] Therefore, the gap between the draftees buying exemptions and the rest of the population is understated in Table 2.2. This analysis of draftees from Philadelphia's northernmost wards generally concurs with what we know of New York and Ohio; that is, at least some men from Philadelphia's lowest occupational groups did pay commutation fees or hire substitutes. And men from occupations above unskilled laborer purchased their exemptions in numbers roughly comparable to their share of the population.

The provisions of the Enrollment Act certainly favored those of

151 The occupational distributions in the two directories apparently differed quite substantially. This probably says more about changing standards of inclusion than actual shifts in the population. I am basing my evaluation on the combined figures from the two directories. One hundred and four of the men in Table 2.1 appeared in the 1861 directory and seventy-nine appeared in the 1866 directory (forty-five appeared in both).
152 Blumin, "Mobility in a Nineteenth-Century American City," 134.

means, but in practice conscription was more complex. Anyone who actively sought to avoid the enrollers had a good chance of escaping service. And while draftees who failed to report were subject to arrest, those willing the flee the district were presumably safe. The men who were most in jeopardy were those who felt the weight of community, family, or patriotism, and thus cooperated with the provost marshals. In Philadelphia only 373 of these conscripts actually served.

Minority experiences

Thus far our discussion of enlistment and the draft has ignored two groups – blacks and Quakers – whose wartime experiences are well documented.[153] In Philadelphia, as elsewhere, these two bodies fought separate, and quite contradictory, battles against the established recruiting structures. Many blacks sought from the outset to serve in uniform, but had to wait two years for the opportunity. The Quakers, in contrast, refused to enlist and became embroiled in heated debates when volunteering gave way to conscription. But despite their differences, both experiences fit snugly into the larger pattern as the federal demand for men produced a complex response involving local voluntary organizations as well as national, state, and city institutions.

The call to arms in the spring of 1861 spoke strongly to many of Philadelphia's 22,000 blacks.[154] On April 20 schoolteacher Alfred M. Green called on the city's blacks to forget "past grievances" and "take up the sword." Soon three companies of black Philadelphians offered their services. But Philadelphia's *Christian Recorder*, the nation's only black newspaper, insisted that "to offer ourselves for military service *now*, is to *abandon self-respect* and *invite insult*." Governor Curtin soon settled the debate by joining the other Northern governors in refusing to accept black volunteers.[155]

The barrier to black enlistment remained until mid-1862, when the possibility of arming Southern freedmen prompted Congress to include a provision in the July Militia Act allowing the president to

153 On blacks, see James M. McPherson, *The Negro's Civil War* (New York, 1965); Philip S. Foner, *History of Black Americans* (Westport, Conn., 1983), vol. 3, *From the Compromise of 1850 to the End of the Civil War*. On Quakers, see Edward Needles Wright, *Conscientious Objectors in the Civil War* (1931; reprint ed., New York, 1961).
154 Bureau of the Census, *Eighth Census, Population.*
155 Foner, *History of Black Americans*, 3:315; Jeffry D. Wert, "Camp William Penn and the Black Soldier," *Pennsylvania History* 46 (October 1979): 337; *Christian Recorder*, 27 April 1861. (hereafter *CR*); William Dusinberre, *Civil War Issues in Philadelphia, 1856–1865*, (Philadelphia, 1965), 161–2. For a good discussion of the differing black views in 1861 see McPherson, *The Negro's Civil War*, 19–36.

receive black volunteers.[156] Some Philadelphians immediately sought to form a black regiment; others set about petitioning Curtin to take advantage of the new regulations. One black resident wrote that these efforts found unusual allies among Philadelphia's Irish, who could not "see exactly why it is that the *Negurs* can't go to the war" rather than drafting local whites.[157] But these early efforts died in the face of white hostility, and Philadelphia's blacks spent another winter as noncombatants.

The following March, after Lincoln's Emancipation Proclamation, a group of white Philadelphians met to discuss the recruitment of a local black regiment. At that first meeting they made plans to distribute 5,000 circulars to Philadelphia's blacks, and named a delegate – James Logan – to go to Washington to secure permission for their venture. That evening they met with an enthusiastic body of blacks who claimed that several companies were already drilling and many more would answer the War Department's call. On the eighteenth the *Germantown Telegraph* reported that the local recruiting stations only awaited an order from Washington to begin operations. But Logan failed to win official authorization for the project, and yet another effort dissolved in disappointment.[158]

Even before Logan's failed visit to Washington, many black Philadelphians had given up on local efforts and enlisted in Massachusetts's new black regiments.[159] In mid-March 1863 Frederick Douglass visited the city, seeking recruits for the Fifty-fourth Massachusetts. The *Christian Recorder* advised its readers to fill the three Massachusetts black regiments rather than listening to self-professed "friends" who spoke of local plans. About 300 Philadelphia blacks enlisted in the Massachusetts regiments, and one company of the Fifty-fourth was raised entirely in Philadelphia.[160]

It appeared in June that Pennsylvania's blacks would finally have the opportunity to serve from their home state. When Curtin responded to Lee's invasion with a call for emergency troops, Philadelphia's black community sprang into action and soon ninety recruits set off for Harrisburg. But Major General Couch refused to accept any but three-year black volunteers, and the dejected company

156 McPherson, *The Negro's Civil War*, 164–5; Foner, *History of Black Americans*, 3:332.
157 Jacob A. White, Jr., to Joseph C. Bustill, 19 August 1862, *Journal of Negro History* 11 (January 1926): 83.
158 Wert, "Camp William Penn," 337–8; *GT*, 18 March 1863.
159 For a good discussion of the Fifty-fourth Massachusetts see Foner, *History of Black Americans*, 3:357–60.
160 White to Bustill, 20 March 1863, *Journal of Negro History* 11 (January 1926): 83; *CR*, 4 April 1863; Wert, "Camp William Penn," 336; Taylor, *Philadelphia in the Civil War*, 187.

returned to Philadelphia.[161] Couch's refusal was only a temporary
barrier to the combined weight of federal initiative and the pressure
of voluntary associations. Major George L. Stearns, fresh from
recruiting blacks in Massachusetts, stepped in as Recruiting Commissioner for U.S. Colored Troops in Pennsylvania. After the Philadelphia troops returned to town, Secretary of War Stanton authorized
Couch to accept all volunteers regardless of race, but advised Stearns
to avoid any controversy.[162] Meantime, the Citizens' Bounty Fund
Committee petitioned Stanton for permission to recruit blacks in
Philadelphia, and formed a twenty-seven member Supervising Committee for Recruiting Colored Troops. Shortly thereafter, the War
Department authorized the committee to raise three regiments in
Philadelphia. These troops, the orders instructed, would enlist for
three years, receive no bounty, and earn only $10 a month.[163] As
Lee's troops moved into Pennsylvania, the military and citizen mech-
anisms for recruiting black soldiers came in place.

A week after the rejected black company returned from Harrisburg, an enthusiastic crowd of black and white Philadelphians met at
Franklin Hall to hear Major Stearns, members of the Supervising
Committee, and several black leaders call for black enlistment.[164]
Soon the city's streets were full of circulars encouraging blacks to
volunteer, and on June 26 the fresh recruits began training at Camp
William Penn, eight miles north of the city.[165] The new enthusiasm
led the *Christian Recorder* to marvel at the "improvement in the public
sentiments" over eighteen months.[166] During the next two years
nearly 11,000 black volunteers, many of them Philadelphians, received their training at Camp William Penn and marched off to serve
the Union.[167]

Several forces joined in successfully putting Philadelphia's blacks
into uniform. Much of the credit must go to Stanton and the War

161 Frederick M. Binder, "Pennsylvania Negro Regiments in the Civil War," *Journal of
     Negro History* 37 (October 1952): 386–7; Foner, *History of Black Americans*, 3:361;
     Harry C. Silcox, "Nineteenth Century Philadelphia Black Militant: Octavius V.
     Catto," *Pennsylvania History* 49 (January 1977): 59–60. Many of the volunteers,
     including Octavio Catto, came from the Institute of Colored Youth. This suggests
     how associational ties within the black community, like those among whites,
     played a key role in generating emergency volunteering.
162 Binder, "Pennsylvania Negro Regiments," 386–7.
163 Wert, "Camp William Penn," 338–9; *OR*, ser. III, 3:404–5.
164 Binder, "Pennsylvania Negro Regiments," 388; Silcox, "Philadelphia Black Mili-
     tant," 60.
165 Taylor, *Philadelphia in the Civil War*, 188; Wert, "Camp William Penn," 340.
166 *CR*, 27 June 1863.
167 Wert, "Camp William Penn," 335; Foner, *History of Black Americans*, 3:361–2;
     George W. Williams, *A History of Negro Troops in the War of the Rebellion, 1861–1865*
     (1888; reprint ed., New York, 1969), 119–22.

Department, with Major Stearns as the military's key emissary to Philadelphia. In a war in which states' rights played a continuously important role, this remained largely a national issue. But though Washington opened the floodgates to black enlistment, the local citizenry guaranteed its success in Philadelphia. Four subcommittees of the Supervisory Committee aided Stearns in all facets of recruitment and training. Committee members raised money, distributed circulars, held rallies, and engaged in all manner of recruiting activities. Once a volunteer had enlisted, the committee was charged with feeding and transporting him until he was formally mustered in at Camp William Penn.[168]

The changed policy toward black recruits also owed much to evolving attitudes in both the white and black community. Many white Philadelphians must have agreed with diarist George Fahnestock: "I only wish we had two hundred thousand [blacks] in our army to save the valuable lives of our white men."[169] Others developed an enthusiasm for the idea when the War Department announced that any black enlistees would be credited against the state's quota, thus helping to avoid a draft.[170] Lincoln's Emancipation Proclamation helped change the minds of many blacks who had counseled against military participation. The African Methodist Episcopal Church held its annual meeting in Philadelphia in late May 1863 and announced that "considered in the light of self-interest and mutual protection, it is the duty of the entire colored people of the North" to support the war with arms.[171] On July 6 Frederick Douglass spoke to "deafening applause" at a recruitment rally at the National Hall. That Saturday and the following week the *Christian Recorder* ran strong editorials urging black enlistment.[172]

Although black military involvement raised distinctive issues, its resolution also followed the larger recruitment pattern in that it com-

168   Binder, "Pennsylvania Negro Regiments," 389–91.
169   Fahnestock diary, 6 June 1863.
170   *OR*, ser. III, 3: 356–7. It is certainly no coincidence that the Supervisory Committee evolved out of the Citizen's Bounty Fund Committee. Taylor says that the black recruits did not actually count toward the state or local quotas because they were mustered into U. S. regiments. See *Philadelphia in the Civil War*, 189.
171   *CR*, 23 May 1863.
172   *CR*, 18 July 1863. The recruiting of black soldiers had a larger impact on race relations within the city. Philadelphia's black leaders, with the support of some whites, used black soldiers and their families as evidence supporting their call for the desegregation of local streetcars. This battle reflected the same sort of associational networks within the black community that contributed to black enlistment. But whereas black soldiers aided the argument, white Philadelphians continued to resist desegregated streetcars into the postwar era. See Philip S. Foner, "The Battle to End Discrimination Against Negroes on Philadelphia Streetcars: (Part I) Background and Beginning of the Battle," *Pennsylvania History* (September 1973):261–90.

bined the efforts of the federal government, a local citizens' committee, and broad-based public support. The chronology of black
recruiting also mirrored the larger wartime picture, but with somewhat altered timing. In the first months after Camp William Penn
opened, Philadelphia's blacks responded with a fervor reminiscent of
white recruiting after Fort Sumter, and by the end of July 1863 the
Third Regiment of U.S. Colored Troops had been filled.[173] But this
enthusiasm did not last long. In early September black Philadelphian
Jacob A. White reported that "recruiting is dull at present"; in October only fifty-four new volunteers reported to Camp William Penn.[174]
In December 1863 black recruiting took another step closer to its white
counterpart when the city began offering a $250 bounty to black
volunteers.[175] In just over a year and a half the forces of military
necessity – channeled through familiar national and local avenues –
had taken the city from a passionate hostility to arming blacks to the
stage where willing black soldiers could earn substantial bounties.

Wartime recruitment posed quite different problems for Quakers, but the means to their resolution were similar. At first the issue
was largely an internal one. When the war began, most Meetings
firmly forbade any military participation by their members. A committee of Philadelphia Friends appointed to consider the military
situation reminded its members that "whatever peculiar circumstances attach to the war which is now waging . . . the testimony of
our religious society has ever been against all war." It went on to
advise that any members who pay a fine or tax "in lieu of personal
service . . . be tenderly dealt with, and if they are not brought to an
acknowledgement of their error, monthly meetings should proceed to
testify against them."[176]

Although many Quakers chose to fight, the Meetings faced no
serious dilemma until the possibility of conscription threatened their
autonomy. In early 1863 the widespread discussion of an impending
federal draft led the Friends to submit a "memorial" to Congress
stressing their pacifist position. That April a bill before the Pennsylvania Legislature proposing fines for noncombatants prompted another special meeting to send a lengthy "Remonstrance" to
Harrisburg.[177] The 1863 draft brought the issue to a head when two

173 Wert, "Camp William Penn," 340–1
174 White to Bustill, 8 September 1863, *Journal of Negro History* 11 (January 1926): 85;
     Binder, "Pennsylvania Negro Regiments," 393.
175 Binder, "Pennsylvania Negro Regiments," 393.
176 William H. S. Wood Collection, Box 1, "Minutes of the Meeting for Sufferings of
     Philadelphia, 1860–1867," Haverford College Archives, Haverford, Penn.
177 Wood Collection, "Minutes of the Meeting for Sufferings of Philadelphia," 23
     February, 6 March 1863.

young West Chester Quakers – Edward and William Smedley – informed the provost marshal that they were unwilling to serve, pay a commutation fee, or furnish a substitute. The two cousins were arrested and confined in the Philadelphia conscript barracks at Wood and Twenty-second streets. Soon they became a *cause célèbre* among Philadelphia's Quakers. A week after their arrest Jacob Elfreth, Sr., wrote that the "young friends . . . have been enduring great hardship & cruel treatment . . . but so far they have carried out the principles they profess of nonresistance and I hope they will be favored to endure."[178]

Edward Smedley's diary tells a somewhat different story.[179] In their first days of confinement the two Friends were forced to wear uniforms and carry knapsacks, but after the first morning Smedley wrote that he had "some conversation with several officers who were rather kind than otherwise." On the second day he noted that "even the rough men among whom we are placed show much respect to us." Within a week of their confinement the two prisoners were given a day's furlough to attend a wedding; ten days later the commanding officer gave them passes that merely required that they report to the barracks each morning for roll-call. About a month later the Smedleys received an honorary discharge from Washington and were freed from any further service.[180]

The Smedleys' release was a product of private benevolence, citizen initiative, and federal decision making. Soon after their incarceration, an anonymous donor paid their commutation fees. Unfortunately, once the conscripts had been mustered into the service (as the Smedleys had been) the commutation fee was no longer legally valid.[181] But after a Committee of Friends journeyed to Washington to visit Stanton, the Secretary of War was happy to free the boys and be rid of the controversy.[182]

In the months to come, government officials and Quaker representatives struggled over the treatment of conscientious objectors. The leading authority on the matter has concluded that most sects "paid the commutation fee whenever they could."[183] But many – including the Philadelphia Meeting – objected to aiding the war effort financially. Stanton thought that he had solved this problem when he

178 Elfreth, Sr., diary, 20 August 1863.
179 "Diary of Edward G. Smedley while at Conscript Barracks in Philadelphia Drafted for War, 1863," Haverford.
180 Wright, *Conscientious Objectors in the Civil War*, 161.
181 Elfreth, Sr., diary, 8 September 1863.
182 Wood Collection, "Minutes of the Meeting for the Sufferings of Philadelphia," 18 September 1863. For a discussion of Stanton's sympathy for the Quakers see Wright, *Conscientious Objectors in the Civil War*, 71–5 and *passim*.
183 Wright, *Conscientious Objectors in the Civil War*, 207.

Table 2.3. Experiences of Drafted Quakers from Philadelphia Yearly Meeting

38	Released, physical disability
1	Released, only son of a widow
2	Released, underage
1	Released, overage
1	Released, "informality in proceedings"
1	Released, nonresident of district
1	Released, without reason
16	Notified but never called
34	Released when others paid the exemption fee ("generally without their . . . consent")
5	Released "by County officers paying for substitutes in their places"
24	Released, paid the $300 fee
7	Released, procured substitutes
4	Went into the army
2	Arrested as deserters but soon paroled
5	Arrested and forced into military service—held in barracks or Camp Philadelphia but paroled within five weeks
3	Sent to Camp Curtin but released on application of Philadelphia friends
1	Sent to army but released after "two months of trial and suffering"
4	"Told provost marshals their scruples and not molested"
150	Total

Source: William H. S. Wood Collection, "Minutes of the Meeting for Sufferings of Philadelphia, 1860–87," April 13, 1866. Haverford College Library, Haverford, Pennsylvania.

suggested that the Friends' commutation fees go to the relief of the freedmen. But the various Yearly Meetings rejected the proposal.[184] In the end, Congress refused to budge from its official position,[185] but Provost Marshal General Fry instructed his provost marshals to follow a lenient policy by which all draftees claiming conscientious opposition to bearing arms were "paroled until called for."[186]

At the war's close the Philadelphia Yearly Meeting reported that 150 of its members had been drafted during the conflict. Table 2.3 summarizes their experiences. Sixty-five managed to avoid service without arrest or violation of their scruples. Thirty-nine were released when an outsider paid their commutation fee or furnished a substitute. Thirty-one violated their Meetings' instructions by purchasing exemptions. Eleven were arrested and spent varying terms in confinement. And four draftees chose to serve in the army. The report

184 Wood, "Minutes of the Meeting for the Sufferings of Philadelphia," 4 December 1863; Murdock, *One Million Men*, 211.
185 The July 1864 amendment abolishing commutation fees included a provision allowing conscientious objectors to continue paying the $300 exemption fee.
186 Murdock, *One Million Men*, 211.

concluded that those young men who paid for their freedom had been disciplined by their monthly meetings.

Those Quakers who failed to earn physical exemptions and who refused to pay commutation or substitution fees fell into three broad categories. In over half of these cases a private citizen or county officer paid the necessary fee or purchased a substitute – in these instances private voluntarism spared the conscientious objector from imprisonment.[187] Thirty-one draftees refused to yield any ground to the authorities: four of these informed the provost marshals of their scruples and "were not molested"; an additional sixteen were "notified but never called." These draftees profited from the unwritten policy of leniency practiced by Fry and his men. The remaining eleven conscripts suffered more tangibly for their scruples. In all but one of these cases, however, the combined weight of private intervention and official action freed them without much hardship.

Conclusion

The Civil War came at a time in American life when the preindustrial was giving way to the industrial era.[188] This "first modern war" was fought with ironclads and railroads, with horses and swords. Its administration reflected the forces of change, but also the tenacity and malleability of tradition. This internal conflict was nowhere more evident than in the raising of troops. If the war was to be a time for nationalization and centralization, its army might certainly be expected to lead the way. And in many senses it did. Men from all over the North fought side by side under generals who took their orders from Washington. When fresh troops failed to fill depleted regiments, presidential proclamations sent federal provost marshals into the states to administer drafts. The North, in short, organized itself to fight as a single entity rather than as a loosely joined federation of states.[189]

But beneath this newly expanded federal military bureaucracy, much remained unchanged. In this "peoples' war," the cities and towns did not abdicate their roles in deference to centralizing forces.[190] Philadelphians responded to the manpower need through

187 The extreme Quaker position considered such actions a violation of their teachings, even if the draftee had no part in raising the money.
188 See Eric Foner, *Politics and Ideology in the Age of the Civil War* (New York, 1980), 20, 32–3.
189 For a discussion of the interplay between conscription and states' rights see Geary, "Conscription in the North," 209–11.
190 Although the war years witnessed various tensions between local initiatives and centralizing forces, these generally did not reflect conflicting policy goals. Rather, the national goals – recruiting, contracting, benevolence – were often best served by decentralized activity.

three interconnected routes: local governmental initiatives, private voluntary institutions, and widespread associational networks. The City Council used its limited financial powers to prepare defenses, encourage recruiting, and aid the families of volunteers; Mayor Henry, armed with little more than the strength of his position, added his voice to Governor Curtin's and President Lincoln's whenever crisis threatened. When public institutions failed, Philadelphia's citizens formed countless recruiting and fund-raising committees. In the case of the city's Quakers, citizen organizations acted to protect Friends from conscription.

Besides these public and private institutional structures, troops were raised and bounties collected in Philadelphia's diverse neighborhoods. Wherever men met – in firehouses, saloons, or clubs; on shop floors or street corners – they spoke of the war. Whether they joined three-year regiments or ninety-day emergency troops, they often enlisted with friends, neighbors, or co-workers. This organizational diversity and breadth of involvement is typical of every aspect of Philadelphia's wartime experiences. As the following chapters will demonstrate, although the war continually challenged Philadelphia's citizens and institutions, the city successfully adjusted to these challenges within the context of its existing social and institutional structures.

3   Kinfolk at war:
Philadelphians' responses
to death and separation

When Philadelphia's recruits left for the battlefield, thousands flocked to railroad depots to watch them go. How did these departures affect those left behind? Philadelphians' diaries and letters were filled with concern for soldiers in the field. Those statements reveal much about the ways in which people on the home front adjusted to wartime separation. These personal writings are, most important, a record of highly individualized responses to the war's pains. But the letters and diaries also suggest how Philadelphians persistently sought to continue their antebellum practices throughout the war years. People at home maintained their relationships with soldiers at the front through frequent letters and occasional furloughs. Citizens who lost loved ones endeavored to maintain traditional mourning rituals despite dramatically unfamiliar circumstances.

Mourning in wartime

Roughly 10,000 Philadelphia soldiers, more than 1.6 percent of the city's 1860 population, died from wounds or disease.[1] What did this loss mean to Philadelphia? In a normal peacetime year, somewhere between 1,200 and 1,400 Philadelphia men between the ages of twenty and forty died.[2] If there had been no war, roughly 5,000 military-age Philadelphia men would have died between April 1861 and 1865. In other words, the war-related deaths alone were about twice the "normal" death rate for this age cohort. And while enlistment reduced the number of young men "at risk" in Philadelphia, home-front deaths among this group certainly continued. Thus deaths

1 This figure is based on information in Frank Taylor, *Philadelphia in the Civil War, 1861–1865* (Philadelphia, 1913). In some cases Taylor only gave aggregate casualties for regiments with only a few Philadelphia companies. In these instances I have estimated Philadelphia's share.

2 In 1860 men aged twenty to forty made up roughly 9 percent of all Pennsylvania deaths. Between 1861 and 1870, Philadelphia deaths ranged from 12,600 to 15,875, with the higher figures occurring during the war years. If we assume that young Philadelphia men died at a rate roughly similar to the statewide figure, between 1,140 and 1,440 died each year. See Joseph C. G. Kennedy, *Preliminary Report on the Eight Census, 1860* (Washington, 1862), 139–142; *Health Officer's Annual Report of Births, Marriages, and Deaths for the City of Philadelphia, 1886* (Philadelphia, 1887), 6.

among men of military age were nearly three times their peacetime rate.

Death was an all-too-familiar experience for early and mid-nineteenth-century Americans. Henry Clay marveled at their "careless and uncalculating indifference about human life." Historian Fred Somkin has noted that "Americans seemed strangely to accept the possibility of violent death on a mass scale."[3] In his analysis of the personal papers of antebellum America's "ordinary people," Lewis O. Saum found "superabundant musings and dotings on death." And Paul C. Rosenblatt's study of grieving among nineteenth-century diarists revealed a "heavy involvement of diarists with dying and the dead [which] makes the preoccupation with death . . . more understandable."[4]

Although nothing in their past prepared Philadelphians for the magnitude of the Civil War's destruction, violent death had always been part of the city's life. In the mid-nineteenth century railroad collisions, steamboat accidents, boiler explosions, and other catastrophes were almost commonplace in the industrializing city.[5] Between 1861 and 1865, 1,753 Philadelphians died in violent accidents.[6] Did Philadelphians who lost friends and relatives on the battlefield view these losses as distinctly different from deaths at home?

After the bloody battle of Antietam, diarist William Eyre described the "deepest sorrow in many households." Anna Ferris added: "many domestic histories are full of tragic interest . . . these humble sufferers are the real martyrs of the war."[7] As May 1863 came to a close, Sarah Richardson wrote: "It has been a sad [month] to many whose sons, brothers, & husbands have been swept away by the ravages of war."[8] Such was the conventional response to wartime

3 Fred Somkin, *Unquiet Eagle: Memory and Desire in the Idea of American Freedom, 1815–1860* (Ithaca, 1967), 40–1. Somkin cites *The Speeches of Henry Clay* ed. Calvin Colton, (New York, 1857), 1:451

4 Lewis Saum, "Death in the Popular Mind of Pre-Civil War America," in *Death in America*, ed. David E. Stannard, (Philadelphia, 1975), 30–48; Paul C. Rosenblatt, *Bitter, Bitter Tears: Nineteenth-Century Diarists and Twentieth-Century Grief Theories* (Minneapolis, 1983), 71. Also see Kent Lancaster, "On the Drama of Dying in Early Nineteenth Century Baltimore," *Maryland Historical Magazine* (Summer 1986), 103–16; Lewis Saum, *The Popular Mood of Pre-Civil War America* (Westport, CT, 1980).

5 For frequent discriptions of such events see J. Thomas Scharf and Thompson Westcott, *History of Philadelphia, 1609–1884*, 3 vols. (Philadelphia, 1884), 1, *passim*.

6 Roger Lane, *Violent Death in the City* (Cambridge, MA, 1979), 11. This figure includes "casualties" (a broad category of accidental deaths), "drownings," and "burns and scalds."

7 William Eyre diary, 12 October 1862, microfilm, Swarthmore College Library, Philadelphia; Anna Ferris diary, 18 October 1862, microfilm, Swarthmore. Ferris was from Wilmington, Delaware, a short distance form Philadelphia. Except where noted, all other diarists were from Philadelphia.

8 Sarah Richarson diary, 31 May 1863, typescript, Swarthmore.

carnage. Those who had not yet felt the personal impact of the war repeatedly turned their thoughts to the sufferings of their fellow citizens.

Before long most Philadelphians felt the war's burden in their own lives; nearly every diarist described the military death of at least one friend or relative. In February 1862 James Tyndale Mitchell spent an evening with friends, but "the whole party felt a little dampened in spirits by Bob Cole's death at Roanoke Island of the Rebel side." In December Mitchell received a letter from Pennsylvania volunteer Frank Shippen, and on the same day heard that Shippen had been killed at Meadville. Eight months later Mitchell described the death and funeral of yet another friend, whom he remembered as "always brave and generous as a boy."[9] On Christmas Day 1862, a distraught Susan Trautwine wrote: "The deep cloud of war with its train of sorrows hanging heavily – Uncle William's death almost undoubted, & Emmie Doer's brother's ascertained – so many breaking hearts in our land today."[10]

For many the overpowering fear was that death's hand would reach closer still, taking a brother, son, or husband. After the safe return of one young soldier, Rebecca Gratz admitted that "he is a brave soldier – but I am a very coward for those I love."[11] When Philadelphia's emergency troops marched off to meet Lee at Gettysburg, three of Mary Ashhurst's nephews were among their number. As news filtered back that Richard's division had suffered heavy losses, Ashhurst wrote: "O God sheild [sic] his & my other dear nephews' heads in the day of battle."[12] Often letters from the field reminded those at home of the dangers. As a battle approached, William Thomas Jones wrote to his father: "If I fall, do not grieve but think, I fell while trying to preserve this Glorious Union. I could not die in a better cause."[13] Corporal J. L. Smith's letter to his mother offered less encouragement: "I write very long letters as we are being killed so fast. This may be my last."[14]

Although her brother Godfrey had long been in the army, Katherine Brinley Wharton remained unprepared for the grimmest realities of war. In August 1862 she learned of the death of a "boyish lover" from her past but wrote:

9   James Tyndale Mitchell diary, 15 February 1862; 12 December 1863; 28 August, 1 September 1864, privately owned.
10   Susan Trautwine MacManus diary, 25 December 1862, Historical Society of Pennsylvania, Philadelphia (hereafter HSP).
11   Rabbi David Philipson, ed., Letters of Rebecca Gratz (Philadelphia, 1929), 432, entry of 14 November 1862.
12   Mary Ashhurst diary, 3 July 1863, HSP. Richard was wounded at Gettysburg.
13   William Thomas Jones to Father, 27 May 1862, Letters of William Thomas Jones, HSP.
14   J. L. Smith to Hannah Smith, 6 June 1864, Letters of J. L. Smith, HSP.

> I can't think of him as a brain-wearied young soldier, another life lost in this dreadful war. . . . How long it is since I have thought of those times. I got bored with him at the time, & did not keep him in mind, but today I have thought of him a good deal.

This death troubled Wharton, but the following June she admitted, "I'm afraid I have grown callous . . . because I have personally suffered nothing." Two months later Wharton's father received a letter from Godfrey, dictated to his captain, from a South Carolina hospital. The letter reported that he was sick but would soon be on his way north; but the captain had added his own postscript, reporting that Godfrey was actually "dangerously ill" and might not survive. Before Mr. Brinley could sail south, a second letter arrived from Captain Winn informing them that Godfrey had died.[15]

Although the number and circumstances of wartime deaths was shockingly new, individual cases suggest strong continuities with peacetime grieving. Paul Rosenblatt explained that nineteenth-century diarists relied on both spiritual strength and family systems in coping with the loss of loved ones. He also found that the diarists deemed presence at the deathbed critical in accomplishing their necessary "grief work."[16] In war, as in peace, Philadelphians turned to their religious beliefs and personal relationships when family members fell on the battlefield. And whenever possible, they sought to learn the details of the death and burial.

The war's losses first touched Rebecca Gratz personally when her brother's youngest son fell in the battle of Wilson's Creek. A few weeks later she wrote to her sister-in-law:

> Thanks . . . for your most kind letters, over which I have wept again, and again – and prayed for my beloved Brother – whose grief I share, but cannot measure even by that which fills my heart – all human sympathy are but drops of comfort, in his great sorrow, but God in *his* mercy will open a fountain of consolation to his mourning spirit.[17]

Thirty years before, Gratz's brother had lost another child, and she had written a very similar letter to her sister-in-law:

> My hearts & thoughts have been with you My dearest Maria in all your afflictions – and tho my pen has been silent . . . now my anxiety can hold out no longer and I must beg either you or My dear Brother to write. I know the God you trust in will not desert

---

15 Katherine Brinley Wharton diary, 1 August 1862; 21 June, 21 August 1863, HSP.

16 Rosenblatt, *Bitter, Bitter Tears*, 122–151, 166. See also Lancaster, "On the Drama of Death."

17 Philipson, ed., *Letters of Rebecca Gratz*, 424–5, Rebecca Gratz to Ann Boswell Gratz, 23 August 1861.

you in your affliction and that as you suffer by his will – he will
visit you with consolation.[18]

In both letters Gratz's efforts to comfort her brother's family coupled
her own words of sympathy with reminders of the need for spiritual
strength. The fact that one nephew died in battle seemed irrelevant to
her response.

But battlefield deaths were a different matter in that relatives
were deprived of the crucial deathbed scenes.[19] Antebellum diarists
in Philadelphia often went into gloomy detail in describing the final
moments of loved ones.[20] Such accounts suggest that they took comfort in witnessing their loved ones' last moments. Sometimes fate
forced survivors to mourn at a distance. When Rebecca Gratz's sister-
in-law died in Kentucky in 1841, she wrote to her brother that "[t]he
distance seems interminable now when one's whole heart and spirit
longs to be near." After Benjamin finally answered his sister's plea for
news, Rebecca responded:

> I thank you My dear Ben, for giving me an account of her last days
> – I longed to know every particular and wrote to Sara Bodley for
> information which I feared would be too painful to relate – I thank
> God that she breathed out her pure spirit calmly – and that her
> bodily sufferings were mitigated – in a little while we shall be
> reunited . . .[21]

Gratz relied on letters to bring her information to assist her grieving.

Wartime Philadelphians often had to depend on letters for details
about the final moments and burials of fallen soldiers. Following the
death of Katherine Brinley Wharton's brother, Godfrey, Captain
Winn wrote a long letter explaining that he had overseen the burial in
South Carolina. Winn followed his careful description of the funeral –
which Wharton recorded in meticulous detail – with a package of
Godfrey's possessions and a final letter describing the twenty-five-
year-old lieutenant's brave service.[22] While the family had to be

18   Philipson, ed., *Letters of Rebecca Gratz*, 116, Rebecca Gratz to Maria Gist Gratz, 11
     October 1830. (Maria was Benjamin Gratz's first wife.)
19   Psychologist John Bowlby has pointed out that several variables may help explain
     "why the mourning of some individuals follows a pathological course." Among
     these variables Bowlby notes the importance of being present when death occurs
     or at least having detailed information of the death to minimize the degree of
     disbelief among those left behind. John Bowlby, *Attachment and Loss* (New York,
     1980), vol. 3, *Loss: Sadness and Depression*, 172, 182.
20   See, for instance, Nicholas B. Wainwright, ed., "The Diary of Samuel Breck,
     1827–1833 *Pennsylvania Magazine of History and Biography* 103 (July 1979): 229–30,
     entry of 25 July 1828; Eliza Cope Harrison, ed., *Philadelphia Merchant: The Diary of
     Thomas P. Cope, 1800–1851* (South Bend, IN, 1978), 538–41, entries of 25 August to 3
     September 1847.
21   Philipson, ed., *Letters of Rebecca Gratz*, 297, Rebecca Gratz to Benjamin Gratz, 19
     November 1841.
22   Wharton diary, 1 September, 14 October 1863.

content with descriptions of Godfrey's burial, Rebecca Gratz hoped that her brother's friends would "be successful in obtaining the dear remains" of Cary Gratz.[23] And as the war came to a close, Lewis Ashhurst noted the successful return of Charles McEven's body, and hoped that "it might be made the instrument of good to his father."[24]

Susan Trautwine's diary provides particularly strong testimony to the persistent fascination with the deathbed. Trautwine, a young, religiously minded woman, began visiting Turner's Lane Hospital in late 1862. In March 1863 she was "shocked" to hear of the death of sixteen-year-old Webster Decatur, a soldier she had been visiting for several months. After Webster's death, Trautwine wrote to the soldier's sister "telling her all I knew about him," adding, "I hope, I feel almost certain that he has gone to God." Two days later she returned to Turner's Lane to say good-bye to Webster's body: "I saw Webster again [,] combed back his hair from his cold forehead, kissed it twice for his mother & sister & cut hiss soft hair for them, keeping a small lock for myself." That August, after sitting with another soldier as he died, Trautwine "closed his clearbrown eyes – laid his head back . . . & kissed his sweet peaceful forehead."[25]

Trautwine's journal reveals the same "powerful intimacy with death" that Saum found in antebellum America.[26] Trautwine also expressed concern for the state of her patients' souls. On visiting Turner's Lane she was "surprised to see what a dearth of religion" existed there. When she learned that one soldier appeared to be dying, Trautwine sent him a short note "urging him to come to Jesus & find rest." Under Webster Decatur's name she recorded: "I saw him very frequently . . . and tried my best to point him to the Lamb of God."[27]

When men died during the Civil War, their loved ones were often deprived of the grieving rituals that might have helped them cope with their loss; but the evidence suggests that the reactions to wartime deaths differed little from those that prevailed before the war. Survivors sought comfort in religion and family, showed specific interest in how their loved ones died, and frequently sought to bring the body home for burial. Hospital volunteers like Susan Trautwine and battlefield comrades like Captain Winn eased the adjustment for

23 Philipson, ed., *Lettters of Rebecca Gratz*, 425, Rebecca Gratz to Ann Boswell Gratz, 23 August 1861.
24 Lewis Ashhurst diary, 4 April 1865.
25 MacManus diary, 3 November 1862; 14, 16 March 1863; 3 August 1863.
26 Saum, "Death in the Popular Mind," 35.
27 MacManus diary, 1 July 1863, Journal on hospital patients, MacManus Papers. Susan Trautwine MacManus's diary includes dozens of references to the spiritual state of her patients.

some soldiers' relatives by writing letters describing deathbed scenes. The war separated families from their dying fathers, brothers, and sons, therefore changing the experience for all. The many miles from the home front to the battlefield presented a physical obstacle, but did not require a concomitant attitudinal change. And although the war forced Trautwine to confront several tragedies, her journal describes grieving that was typical of mid-nineteenth-century America both in its emphasis on the last moments of life and in the profound concern for the spiritual lives of her dying patients.

Responses to separation

The 10,000 Philadelphians killed in the Civil War exacted an enormous toll on the emotions of the city's citizens. But the conflict also claimed other victims. Tens of thousands on the home front suffered daily from the fears and longings that accompanied a loved one's enlistment.

One cold February night Sidney George Fisher wrote that "I can think of nothing but the wounded now lying exposed to the weather on the battlefield."[28] Two winters later, on a "raw inclement evening," George Fahnestock sat in his "warm library" and wrote: "I thank God for his blessings and think of the poor soldiers in the field."[29] For other Philadelphians, the men in the trenches were not so faceless, the trauma of separation not so impersonal.

At the war's outset, Katherine Brinley Wharton had been married less than three years and had one young child. Her husband Henry began drilling with the Home Guards, but promised not to abandon his family except to defend the city. In the fall of 1862 his departure seemed imminent, and Katherine – now with two infants in tow – felt the fear of impending separation. On September 8, with the war news growing grimmer, Henry had a long talk with his wife about the future. Katherine found his words "very comforting," and chided herself for her selfishness: "What am I more than others that I should say I cannot give him up [?]."[30] On the twentieth, after spending all night in town monitoring the latest news, the young lawyer told his anxious wife that "he had made up his mind to go at once in case of our defeat."[31] But despite these tense moments, Henry

28 Nicholas B. Wainwright, ed., *A Philadelphia Perspective: The Diary of Sidney George Fisher* (Philadelphia, 1967), 419, entry of 28 February 1862.
29 George W. Fahnestock diary, 11 December 1863, HSP.
30 Wharton diary, 8 September 1862.
31 Wharton diary, 19 September 1862.

never left home. Like many other Philadelphia husbands and fathers, Wharton concluded that his family obligations barred him from active service.

Personal papers support the view that the war was fought largely by unmarried men and boys. When these Philadelphians considered volunteering, entire families – faced with this first stage of separation – became involved. Mary Ashhurst's June 1863 entry about her nineteen-year-old son Frank hints at the domestic battles behind the decision to enlist:

> alarm in Phila. calls are urgent for men to join. . . . F. has found so many of his companion[s] going it was not to be wondered that he was anxious to go also. Mr. A in excitement was induced to consent but I cannot do so until our news is more reliable & until some organization would protect him.[32]

A week later Mr. Ashhurst had apparently come to his senses, because Mary recorded that "F would be only too glad to join [two enlisting friends] but his father[']s unwillingness prevents him."[33]

Other Philadelphians noted similar family tensions. John M. Hale's son wrote to his father from school reporting the recent enlistment of eight schoolmates, but added "I don't suppose you will give your consent for me to go so I suppose I will have to give up hope."[34] When seventeen-year-old John McKinley volunteered, Jacob Elfreth, Sr., wrote that "it [was] a grief to his mother who is my Niece [sic]. His father also I believe disapproved of it."[35] Shipley Newlin, a Philadelphia Quaker, "went into the war from a real sense of duty & the most patriotic conviction of right," but his stand placed him firmly "at variance with his family."[36]

Many volunteers found that when they entered the army they moved from family battles over enlistment to equally strong conflicts

32 Mary Ashhurst diary, 17 June 1863.
33 Mary Ashhurst diary, 25 June 1863. Interestingly, Lewis Ashhurst's diary does not mention these debates over his youngest son's actions.
34 James Hale to John M. Hale, 17 June, 24 August 1861, John M. Hale Letters, HSP.
35 Jacob Elfreth Sr. diary, 15 August 1862, Haverford College Archives, Haverford, PA. McKinley's family found his enlistment particularly troubling because, as Quakers, they had professed objections to all warfare.
36 Ferris diary, 19 October 1862; 21 October 1864. Also see Harold B. Hancock, ed., "The Civil War Diaries of Anna B. Ferris," *Delaware History* 9 (April 1961): 256, entry of 21 October 1864. For other descriptions of domestic battles over proposed enlistment see Fahnestock diary, 13 September 1862; John W. Lynch to Miss Bessie Mustin, 1 May 1861, John W. Lynch Letters, HSP; Charlotte Erikson, *Invisible Immigrants: The Adaptation of English and Scottish Immigrants in 19th Century America* (London, 1972), 347–49; Mary Dreer diary, 23 July 1864, Papers of Edwin Greble, Manuscripts Division, Library of Congress.

over reenlisting. In the war's first month, many patriotic Philadel-phians joined Colonel Robert Patterson's three-month regiment. They marched off to the tune of enthusiastic cheers, but their loved ones soon grew disillusioned. Word that the regiment had been accepted for three years' service led many to send anxious letters to their menfolk in the field. The unmarried mother of one soldier's child wrote: "I hope that you are not among them that will enlist for that period. That has worried me very much my dear. But I hope you are not so foolish as to do so."[37] Another Philadelphian told her husband: "i hear that your regetiment has gon[e and re-enlisted] for three years but hope you have not done the same."[38]

Perhaps such pleas had some effect. But a letter from one Man-ayunk woman to her brother suggests that many recruits acted just as they pleased: "You say you will list a gaine we would like to see you . . . but you can please you self as you always do."[39] William Thomas Jones seemed equally sure of his own mind. When his storekeeper father wrote suggesting some ruse to terminate his service, the young volunteer replied:

> Your advice is very good and I am very much obliged to you. But I think it is my duty to go back and you can not hire me to stay away. I would never be satisfied to stay home while this wicked Rebelion lasts. I think it is my duty Both to God and my Country. When I enlisted I took an Oath to my country for 3 years and to use no fool means to get out of it.[40]

Parting, like death, was a time for detailed descriptions in private journals. When Jacob Elfreth, Sr., watched a company of Philadel-phians leave for the front, he thought: "poor fellows they appeared . . . to be going 'like sheep to the slaughter.'" As the Washington Grays marched out of town, Katherine Wharton waved good-bye to several friends from her window. But she was most interested in seeing her brother go, and wrote that it was "a great comfort to me" when "G looked up & saw us" as he passed. After her best friend's brother enlisted, Susan Trautwine felt "almost too sad to pray." And when her son Sam left for Nashville, Mary Ashhurst could only write: "Heavenly father watch over him . . ."[41]

37 SWW to Charley, July 1861, Cadwalader Collection, HSP. For selections from the Cadwalader Collection see Edward G. Longacre, " 'Come home soon and dont delay': Letters from the Home Front, July, 1861," *Pennsylvania Magazine of History and Biography* 100 (July 1976): 395–406 (hereafter " 'Come home soon' ").
38 Melvina R. Buckman to George Buckman, 12 July 1861, Cadwalader Collection; Longacre, " 'Come home soon,' " 402.
39 Sister to William H. Collins, 10 July 1861, Cadwalader Collection.
40 William Thomas Jones to Father, 26 November 1862.
41 Elfreth, Sr. diary, 18 May 1861; Wharton diary, 8 May 1861; MacManus diary, 19 April 1861; Mary Ashhurst diary, 20 January 1863. Also see Septunius Winner diary, August 1863. See Chapter 6 for a discussion of the public rituals surround-ing departures for the front.

Soldiers' accounts of their departures generally mixed equal parts of enthusiasm and melancholy, often with a healthy dose of romance as well. In the days before he left for camp in August 1862, Will Colton made the rounds of friends and relatives to say his final good-byes. He seemed most touched with his visit to Lizzie Childs:

> . . . we parted sadly, she with a tearful voice. Said she: " . . . one of my best wishes is that you may have a nice time, and be protected through all dangers, and come back to us safely. And, oh, we'll make a good deal of you when you come home from the war." And then I asked her for a kiss, and she kissed me, lip to lip.[42]

Six weeks later Will and his brother Ball returned home on a four-day furlough. Although she had initially resisted their enlistment, the boys' mother now declared that "she 'would be ashamed to have us at home now and not in the army.' " But soon it was time for a second round of leavetakings:

> Again we bade good-bye to mother, father, brothers and sisters, and I could hardly command my voice to say good-bye and mother made a great effort to control her feelings, but her lips twitched and she could not speak, and sisters were convulsive in their embraces.[43]

That evening the brothers were "settled once more in [their] tent, feeling as though we had been on a visit and were now home again."[44]

Participation in the Union army was so widespread that it was the rare Northerner who knew no one in uniform. In his travels through the North in early 1862, Edward Dicey met a Northern woman who claimed that "till within a year before, she could not recall the name of a single person whom she had ever known in the army, and . . . now she had sixty friends and relatives who were serving in the war."[45] Six weeks after the firing on Fort Sumter, Sarah Butler Wister wrote: "I have but two men friends . . . left in Philadelphia."[46]

Susan Trautwine's detailed diary reveals the dimensions of war-time separation. The war first touched Trautwine only days after it commenced, when her uncle "JDR" and her best friend's brother

42 Suzanne Colton Wilson, *Column South With the Fifteenth Calvary* (Flagstaff AZ, 1960), 3–4, entry of 14 August 1862.
43 Wilson, *Column South*, 29–30, entries of 26, 29 September 1862.
44 Wilson, *Column South*, 30, entry of 29 September 1862.
45 Edward Dicey, *Six Months in the Federal States*, 2 vols. (1863), 2:5.
46 Fanny Kemble Wister, "Sarah Butler Wister's Civil War Diary," *Pennsylvania Magazine of History and Biography* 102 (July 1978): 303, entry of 30 May 1861.

volunteered after Fort Sumter.[47] That July Trautwine went to visit a friend, Mrs. Weidley, whose husband had "gone to the war." The young woman found her friend so sick with anguish that she "scarcely knew what to do with her." In the months to come, Trautwine repeatedly visited the Weidley home to cheer up her lonely companion.[48] On October 29, 1861, Trautwine had tea with a Mr. Yerger who had "just returned . . . from going with his sister Emma in search of her husband – who, we heard today, is a prisoner of war." On another occasion she sent a note to a Mrs. Easler, "much distressed about her husband" who had not written as expected. Soon Mrs. Easler joined Mrs. Weidley on Trautwine's visiting schedule.[49] Such visits suggest how the philanthropically minded Trautwine shifted her busy social schedule to help ease the pain of wartime separations.

But though this adjustment was in response to the war, Trautwine's actions were in keeping with established patterns. Rosenblatt's research supports the intuitive conclusion that "in the nineteenth-century . . . having a shoulder to cry on help[ed] assuage grief." Men and women who had lost loved ones to death or separation repeatedly turned to powerful friendship networks.[50] The war years brought such grief to many of Trautwine's friends, leading the young Philadelphian to unusually energetic activity. But her visits and notes were no different from peacetime measures to support grieving friends.

In late June 1863 Trautwine returned home from a tiring day at the hospital to discover that her brother Willie had enlisted. The following day she was pleased to learn that Charlie MacManus, a close friend, had decided to volunteer with Willie. On June 30 she wrote: "Charlie has just left after bidding me a warm good-bye & receiving permission to write. He has been a good friend to me dear fellow – I hope he may come safely home again."[51] On July 2 the two volunteers left to meet Lee's advance. This parting, it seems, sparked a flame within Trautwine. Although the two soldiers spent only a few weeks in the field, Trautwine sent MacManus several letters, including one six-page missive. After his return, MacManus became a more regular visitor to the Trautwine household.[52]

As the year came to a close, Trautwine's romantic plot thickened as James Clegg, a seemingly casual friend, declared his love for her on

---

47 MacManus diary, 18, 19 April 1861.
48 MacManus diary, 23 July, 31 August, 30 December 1861; 24 January, 30 April, 21 June 1862.
49 MacManus diary, 29 October 1861; 20, 26 September 1862; 28 November, 12 December 1862; 19 February, 19 March 1863.
50 Rosenblatt, *Bitter, Bitter Tears*, 145–9.
51 MacManus diary, 29, 30 June 1863. It appears that MacManus's motive in enlisting was at least partly to look after his young friend.
52 MacManus diary, 2, 10, 17, 28 July 1863 and *passim*.

the day before he was to leave for camp. Trautwine gently deflected her suitor's advances, but felt guilty about sending a man off to war with a broken heart.[53] Three days later Charlie MacManus visited, and although Trautwine (who had yet to acknowledge her feelings for him) valiantly tried to steer her friend away from delicate topics, Charlie announced that he loved her. This left the poor young woman reeling: "I hardly know what to do – two such experiences in one week."[54]

Over the next several years, Trautwine slowly yielded to Charlie's advances, and in 1870 the two were married. But for our purposes, the more interesting relationship is that which developed between Trautwine and James Clegg. In the weeks before he departed, Clegg bid Trautwine farewell on five separate occasions. When Clegg finally left she thought: "May God keep him ever more from all evil." Although she did not share Clegg's love, Trautwine's thoughts often turned to her suitor in the field. In January 1864 Trautwine considered the harsh weather and wrote: "Poor, dear brother, James, must find it rather cool to camp out on such nights as this." News of a major battle in Virginia made her "wonder where my dear brother James is – I think of him continually."[55] The next day, as Trautwine learned more of the bloody Battle of the Wilderness, she added: "I feel very anxious about James Clegg" and, a week later: "[I] wish I could hear from him." Finally, Trautwine received a short letter from her friend informing her that he had been wounded in the shoulder, but she felt "glad that it is not worse." In the next few days Trautwine sent a package and several letters to Clegg at Washington Hospital. For the rest of the war Clegg escaped injury, but his correspondence with Trautwine continued.[56]

Although she did not lose any family members to the war, Susan Trautwine felt the conflict's separation at many levels. Friends with absent loved ones spurred her to small acts of benevolence. Her brother Willie's enlistment brought the pains of separation into her own home. While James Clegg served in the army, Trautwine continually referred to him in terms which suggested his position as an unrequited lover. Rather than writing that his leaving left an emptiness in her life, "brother James" was a "poor, dear . . . precious boy"[57] whom she frequently thought of and felt sorry for. Conversely, her

53 MacManus diary, 1, 2 December 1863.
54 MacManus diary, 4 December 1863.
55 MacManus diary, 23 to 30 December 1863. Trautwine's repeated use of the words "brother James" suggests her discomfort with his role as a suitor.
56 MacManus diary, 2, 5, 19 January, 12 March, 2 April, 7, 8, 13, 14, 16, 18 May 1864; 16 February, 15, 18 April 1865.
57 MacManus diary, 30 December 1863.

diary seems to suggest that Charlie MacManus's brief excursion into the military helped soften her feelings for her hopeful suitor.[58]

Philadelphians' letters and diaries suggest that the emotional chords struck by wartime separation depended largely on the nature of the disrupted relationship. Moreover, frequently those letters indicate that men and women at home and in the camps responded to this wartime "test" by relying on the mails to continue their familiar relationships. While Susan Trautwine corresponded with two suitors in the field, other Philadelphians lost spouses to enlistment. The wives and lovers of men in the Patterson Regiment, suffering through their first months of separation, gave poignant evidence of their loneliness and fear. One unmarried woman wrote to the father of her child:

> I feel so bad to night. I think my heart will break. I worry so much about you. I cannot sleep sound no more. I awaken up at night and lay for hours wondering if I ever shall see my dear Pet again. Oh I hope to God I shall, for I cannot tell you here how dear you are to me. You are my all in this world and without you now my Pet I feel as though I could [not live]. . . . I feel as if I would almost go crazy to see you.[59]

As Independence Day approached, another young mother told her husband:

> we are all well at present time hoping that it may find you in good health to day is Sunday and it is lonesom i wish you was here the next will be the forth and no plesure with out you last forth i had plesure but this forth i have none but when you come home i expect to have my plesure then and i hope it will soon come My Dear Joel[60]

For such separated couples, the burden on the written word was especially great. In early 1863 Richard Lewis Ashhurst wrote home emphasizing "the importance of wives writing cheerful letters." Two officers in his regiment, he reported, "[had] been . . . receiving the most melancholy desponding letters from their wives [which] brought on depression of spirits," leading them to resign their com-

---

58 The link between wartime separation and romance is a persistent subtheme in Philadelphians' personal papers. For instance, young Mary Dreer's love for Ned Greble apparently began when he enlisted in July 1864, blossomed when he returned deathly ill three months later, and resulted in a January 1865 engagement. Mary Dreer diary, Papers of Edwin Greble, volumes for 1864 and 1865 (the 1865 volume is not signed). And Will Colton's romance with Julia Knight also seemed to grow more intense with separation before it was dissolved as the war neared a close. See Wilson, Column South, 325 and passim.

59 SWW to Charley, July 1861; Longacre, " 'Come home soon,' " 400.

60 Sarah Myers to Joel Myers, 30 June 1861, Cadwalader Collection.

missions and return to their families.[61] John Lynch typically took great joy in the letters from his fiancée, but when these notes took on a melancholy tone, he chastized his intended for making his "heart sad."[62] Such letters to wives and lovers helped ease the transition to separation by reinforcing peacetime roles.

These roles centered on shared needs for material, moral, and emotional support. By the nineteenth century middle-class marriages had become partnerships built on love. But each partner was expected to act in a separate sphere. Husbands spent their days in the outside world providing for their families' material comfort, whereas wives, responding to the dictates of True Womanhood, remained at home and acted as the keepers of "piety, purity, submissiveness, and domesticity." Men dominated these relationships, but early nineteenth-century diaries and letters suggest that husbands readily acknowledged the moral superiority of their wives.[63]

What became of these partnerships when circumstances separated men and women for long periods? In the early months of separation, letters did little to ease the pain for the wives and lovers of men in the Patterson Regiment. When Sallie answered her "Dear Charley's" first letter, she "hardly knew what to write." At night she "lay [awake] for hours wondering if I ever shall see my dear Pet again." Sallie's fears for her lover intertwined with her own loneliness. She wrote: "I worry so much about you," but added: "I cannot tell you what a three months this will be to me." Although they were a poor substitute, Sallie recognized the importance of letters. "I feel as if I would almost go crazy to see you," she wrote. "Wont you like a dear good Pet answer this as soon as ever you get it and tell me all the particulars about all that is going on where you are."[64]

Irregular mails during the war's early months threatened the already tenuous relationship of Sarah and Joel Myers. On July 3, 1861, Sarah wrote: "to day I recived you[r letter]. you talk very quear to me. you say if i dont intend to rite i shall let you know. did i say so?

61 Richard Lewis Ashhurst to Wife, 2 March 1863, typescript, R. L. Ashhurst Papers, HSP.
62 Lynch to Mustin, 3 January 1862.
63 Degler, At Odds, 14–31; Barbara Welter, "The Cult of True Womanhood: 1820–1860," American Quarterly (Summer 1966): 151–174; Mary Ryan, Cradle of the Middle Class: The Family in Oneida County, New York, 1790–1865 (New York, 1981), 179–80, 196. In her analysis of working-class women in antebellum New York City, Christine Stansell found that marriages were less affective relationships than "practical household arrangements based on reciprocal obligations." See Stansell, City of Women: Sex and Class in New York, 1789–1860 (Urbana, IL, 1987) 77.
64 SWW to Charley, 11 July 1861, excerpted in Longacre, " 'Come home soon,' " 400–1. The letters in the Cadwalader Collection were sent from various Pennsylvania towns to men in the Patterson Regiment. All of these letters were mailed in early July 1863, and none arrived.

let me know if i did. i said that i was glad to hear of you and anser them [letters] to." Joel's angry tone in his previous letters led Sarah to suspect that "thay are people riting to you a bout me." After defending herself at length she closed with: "I hope you wont refuse me." But this letter, like her earlier notes, never reached the Patterson Regiment.[65]

Melvina Buckman's early letters also failed to reach her husband. But their relationship seemed better prepared to stand the test. On July 12 she wrote:

> My dear husband, i take my pen in hand to let you know that we are all well at present . . . i have not had a letter from you for a week and more and did not know wear to wright. i want to hear from you very bad . . . i have sent three letters to you and put post stamps in them and ten cents and i expect you did not get them or you would wrote to me.[66]

Beyond their strong emotional content, these letters reveal the varied ways in which the war forced adjustment in other marital roles. All three women reminded their men that they had left small children behind. Melvina Buckman, concerned that her husband might reenlist, reported that "saly . . . does nothing but talk about you coming home and cry when eneybody says you are not."[67] Sarah Myers, who signed her letter with her name "and your son William Myers," made a point of telling her husband about all the sewing she had "done sinse you left me in truble."[68]

Sallie was in a particularly difficult position because Charley had left her unwed but with a child to care for. "I think I have had a pretty hard tug of it since you have been gone," she reported. Charley's brother, feeling only minimal responsibility for the mother of his brother's child, had brought her $5 on each of the previous two weeks, but nothing at all before that. Finding Charley's brother unsympathetic, Sallie turned to her landlord, who, she noted, *"has a particular liking for me I am shure."* In this letter Sallie managed to assure Charley that she was "not in want at present" while also giving him ample incentive to attend to her future needs.[69]

These Philadelphians' responses to wartime separation reflect the various aspects of their peacetime marital relationships. During the war's early months the most difficult adjustments were emotional. Although their husbands had only been away for a few weeks,

65 Sarah Myers to Joel Myers, 3 July 1861, excerpted in Longacre, " 'Come home soon,' " 405–6.
66 Longacre, " 'Come home soon,' " 401–2.
67 Longacre, " 'Come home soon,' " 402 and *passim.*
68 Longacre, " 'Come home soon,' " 405–6.
69 SWW to Charley, 11 July 1861; Longacre, " 'Come home soon,' " 401.

each woman seemed almost desperate to see her spouse. All complained of the additional burdens placed on them because their men were not at home performing their roles as fathers and providers. Their concerns suggest, on the one hand, an assumed continuation of traditional marital roles and, on the other hand, an inability to fulfill those roles.

The correspondence between John W. Lynch and his fiancée Bessie Mustin, which continued from May 1861 until late 1863, gives a fuller picture of how men and women adapted to meet wartime circumstances. After he enlisted, Lynch spent several months on duty near Philadelphia at Fort Delaware. In early June Bessie became "heart sick & disheartened" when John "did not come [home on furlough] as . . . expected." Soon Lynch did manage to visit Philadelphia and apparently had such a good time that he overstayed his furlough and was arrested on his return to the fort. As long as Lynch stayed in the vicinity and they could see each other fairly often, the couple did not fully adjust to their separated life.[70] But in the fall of 1861 Lynch joined the 106th Pennsylvania Volunteers, soon leaving for Maryland.[71] It was then that the frequency and content of their letters suggested that they had begun to come to terms with their separation.

Bessie Mustin buttressed Lynch's sagging morale by reminding him that "although so many miles lay between us our hearts are united that nothing could part them." An impassioned Lynch answered that "every throub of my heart respond[s] to those words." But even in his passion, Lynch felt qualms, and asked his loved one never again to mention the name of a "Mr C.," presumably an ex-beau.[72] The pains of separation grew greater when Christmas arrived and Lynch had to rely on his thoughts for comfort: "my darling how my thoughts have been following you all day. I have pictured you in all kind[s] of positions until my imagination has been tired out."

As 1862 began, the strains of separation began to show. Bessie repeatedly chastised her fiancé for failing to obtain a furlough. On January 3 a troubled Lynch answered Bessie's last two letters:

> darling it has made me sad to see the strain of your letters, it would lead one to suppose that you think I have not made any efforts to obtain a furlough & am reluctant to visit the city & do blame me because I have allowed you to hope that I should obtain a furlough

70 Lynch to Mustin, 9 May, 16 June, 1, 13, 24 July 1861.
71 *Official Army Register of the Volunteer Force of the United States Army* (Washington, 1865) 3:941; Lynch to Mustin, 22 October 1861.
72 Lynch to Mustin, 13 December 1861. This letter includes a direct quote from Mustin's previous letter.

– O my darling do not think for one moment that I would be
unwilling to throw myself among those whom I *love* as *dear* as my
own *life* if it was within my power to do so & you are more desirous
of seeing me than what I am to see you. You are surrounded by
those dear ones whose objects alone are to make you happy, how
different is my position, surrounded on all sides by those persons .
. . whose friendship is cultivated only for their own selfish desires .
. . would I under such circumstances hesitate to grasp the opportunity to be with those who are *so dear to me* [?] no! no! no! If I have at
times lead you to hope that I was comming to see you it was the
yearning of my heart . . .[73]

This letter touches on two recurring themes in Bessie Mustin's later
letters. She repeatedly urged Lynch to secure a furlough, often imply-
ing that he was not pursuing that goal with enough vigor;[74] she
feared that Lynch preferred camp life to her own company.

Bessie took her role as defender of Lynch's virtue quite seriously.
On February 2 Lynch casually mentioned that a friend had sent him a
deck of cards. Within days he received a questioning letter leading
him to respond: "Card playing my darling is no *evil virtuously within
itself*, but is like theater going & such amusements. The evil is in the
dangerous associates which they are surrounded by." Bessie also
asked if Lynch did "not feel the Savior very near to [him]" to which he
replied: "I am *sorry* to say such is not the case." Later, when Lynch
spoke of leaving the army because of its poor administration, she
helped talk him out of it, reminding him that people would think ill of
him if he resigned.[75]

Bessie frequently asked John about his health and encouraged
him "not to keep any of [his] troubles big or little from [her]."[76] In his
letters Lynch typically played the role of protector, trying to spare his
love from any heartache. "Do not be dishearten[ed]" he insisted,
"*trust* a *little* more to *him* who 'ruleth all things.' "[77] This protective
instinct outweighed Lynch's professed belief in an openly honest
relationship. For over half a year he concealed debilitating chest pains
from her, not revealing them until he sought a medical discharge.[78]

73 Lynch to Mustin, 3 January 1862.
74 The wives and mothers of men in the Patterson Regiment expressed similar
    sentiments when they unanimously begged their men to not reenlist for another
    three years.
75 Lynch to Mustin, 2, 7 February, 23 November 1862.
76 Lynch to Mustin, 26 March, 6 April 1862.
77 Lynch to Mustin, 23 February, 29 April 1862.
78 Lynch to Mustin, 27 August 1863. In choosing to spare his fiancée, Lynch violated
    the "ethic of openness" that generally ruled mid-nineteenth-century courtship.
    See Ellen K. Rothman, *Hands and Hearts: A History of Courtship in America* (New
    York, 1984), 108–14.

If John Lynch's camp life tested Bessie Mustin's responsibility as a defender of virtue, shifts on the home front caused further adjustments in her gender role. In August 1862 Bessie wrote to her fiancé, asking him what he would think of her visiting the military hospitals. The idea clearly disturbed Lynch. He warned her "that there is a spirit of criticism & I might say sort of *slur* thrown out to those young ladys which attend the Hospitals." But despite these reservations Lynch concluded: "darling do just as you think is your duty." A few months later Bessie seemed hesitant to admit that she had gone to work in her brother's trimmings store. Once again, Lynch responded with an open mind:

> Does Bessie suppose I would think ill of her because she has gone into her brother's store. I hope not but your letter leads me to form such an opinion & has therefore refrained telling me what she considers a secret & would not have done so was she not afraid that I should have been informed by others.

In both of these instances Bessie Mustin seems to have gone beyond what she saw as normally accepted activities because of the war. And in each case she acknowledged that Lynch would very likely disapprove of her desires. But Lynch gave his blessing to both decisions. Although her sense of the social role that she might play was expanded by the war, her relationship with Lynch continued in a traditional mode in that she sought his opinion concerning her activities.[79]

The war forced many shifts in the relationship between John Lynch and Bessie Mustin, but during Lynch's two years in the army the couple persisted in maintaining fairly consistent gender roles. Bessie alternately worried about her fiancé's moral, spiritual, emotional, and physical health, while fearing his responses to her desires to visit the hospital and work in her brother's store. Although not yet a material provider, Lynch sought in his letters to protect Bessie from mental hardship. And both partners used their correspondence to ease the emotional burdens of separation.

Many volunteers left spouses behind, however, many more were unmarried young men whose letters reveal continuing relationships with parents and siblings. Corporal J. L. Smith's letters to his mother demonstrate this persistence. Smith often requested mundane items – food, stamps, paper – suggesting that the eighteen-year-old soldier continued to rely on his mother for daily comforts. In other instances the young volunteer responded to his mother's concern for his morality and health. In early 1863 he assured her: "No, I dont drink whiskey nor use tobacco." When his mother worried about unsavory

79 Lynch to Mustin, 9 August 1862; 2 February 1863.

Southern women, Smith reassured her: "No, I won't fall in love with any of the Rebel girls." And when she expressed concern for his safety he asked: "why do you worry so? I am well and there is no use of worrying over it." Hannah Smith's letters frequently showed a greater concern for her son's comfort than an understanding of the realities of camp life. On one occasion she offered to send her son a cat. Smith advised against this, warning that "the soldiers would mistake him for a rabbit." In other correspondence Mrs. Smith wanted to know if her son sat on the ground, if the military "houses" had windows, and if he would be in danger of freezing in the cold.[80]

Despite the trauma of separation, Hannah Smith sustained a traditional maternal role, expressing concern for her son's safety, morality, and comfort.[81] Certainly some of her fears were peculiar to wartime, but more often her letters suggested ignorance of the harsh realities of war. Corporal Smith also continued in his prewar role. He relied on his mother for material comforts; at the same time many of his letters were aimed at reassuring or protecting her. Smith also carried on his antebellum role as provider, frequently sending small amounts of money to his mother.[82]

William Thomas Jones was seventeen when he enlisted in Birney's Zouaves. In his three years of service Jones fought in several major battles. But through frequent letters home he managed to maintain his prewar relationship to his family. After only a month in uniform, Jones wrote to his brother describing the comforts he had left behind: "I tell you what[,] when we come back we will know how to appreciate our home. I never knew what it was. When it comes to washing your own clothes, and getting coffee without milk and hard . . . bread without Butter." Jones, like Smith, relied on his family for food, clothing, and other items. His frequent requests for goods from home reflected his different relationships with the members of his family. Jones's sister sewed him a pair of gloves, his mother sent food and warm underwear, and he asked his father to mail him a revolver. In one particularly revealing letter to his brother he wrote: "Harry, I tell you what I would like you to do for me. That is, send me down a bottle of Chestnut Grove Whiskey for medicinal purposes." He added: "Don't let the folks know it."[83]

---

80 J. L. Smith to Hannah Smith, 25 January, 11 April, 6 August 1863; 7 April, 24 June, 10 November, 3 December 1864; 23 January 1865.
81 Mary Ryan found that Utica mothers sent their sons everday items such as socks and food and notes "steeped in concern for the character and morality of the young men." See Ryan, *Cradle of the Middle Class*, 175.
82 J. L. Smith to Hannah Smith, *passim*. Joseph Kett has found that nineteenth-century working-class families often depended on teenage boys to supplement the family income. See Kett, *Rites of Passage: Adolescence in America 1790 to the Present* (New York, 1977), 169.
83 Jones letters, 5, 11, 21, 25 October, 1 November, 27 December 1861.

Jones initially thoroughly enjoyed camp life and told his parents that he "wouldnt come back for anything." But even while in the field, he looked forward to returning to his place in his father's dry goods business. As Jones saw it, the war had interrupted, but not permanently changed, his normal life.[84] As 1863 neared a close Jones's letters became increasingly despondent. He was particularly distressed because his sister, Kate, was scheduled to be married and he could not obtain a furlough. On November 18 he wrote: "In about 9 months more – Oh! I wish I could catch Old Mr Time by the Forelock and haul him around a little faster." A month later he claimed that some soldiers who had refused to reenlist had been transferred to black regiments. "They may put me in a Nigger Regiment," he promised "but I will not Re enlist."[85]

Jones's relationships with his siblings are mirrored in the letters of other Philadelphia soldiers. Like Jones, Sergeant Thomas W. Smith relied on his brothers to supply him with whiskey. On one occasion Smith wrote to his brother, Joe, describing an upcoming battle, but asked him not to tell the rest of the family. Later, when his two brothers talked of enlisting, Smith told his sister to "tell Joe and Bob not to go a soldiering unless they are drafted."[86] If these letters suggest a continued "brotherly" relationship, Elizabeth Brown's notes to her brother Andrew suggest a powerful "sisterly" affection. On June 11, 1864, she wrote:

> I wish we could get [a letter] every day from you . . . I hope God
> will take care of you and save you always put your trust in him and
> I hope you will get home safe after what you have come through I
> know you have it awful hard the more you never complain andy
> you ought to try and get in to some thing easeyer then whare you
> are andy fleming says he has got in the hospital and if you were
> some place like that you would have it a great deal better andy

On the twentieth Elizabeth sent her brother another long letter, telling him that "when I get a letter from you there are always half a dozen [of his friends] round me to hear how you are." But this final note was written two days after Andy died at Petersburg.[87]

The letters of Ball Colton and his brother Will reflect a similar range of family relationships. Elder sister Delia served as their chief correspondent, writing each Sunday and providing her brothers with a steady flow of lively anecdotes about family and friends. Younger brother Sabie kidded Ball that the lice problem had cleared up since

---

84 These hopes were nearly dashed in June 1862 when Will was wounded near
    Richmond. See Jones letters, 4 October, 1 November 1861; 2, 16 June 1862.
85 Jones letters, 18 November, 17 December 1863. Despite Jones' fears only white
    officers served in the black regiments.
86 Thomas W. Smith, 15, 28 February, 25 July 1862. Thomas W. Smith Letters, HSP.
87 Andrew Brown, 11, 20 June 1864, Andrew Brown Letters, HSP.

his brother's departure; Ball offered his fourteen-year old sibling advice on ladies: "look for size and [don't] be led away by any little spindle shanks." The boys' father regularly reported his financial misfortunes and various financial ventures, ranging from potato selling, photography, and inventing, to selling life insurance. His sons responded with advice and financial support. Interestingly, their mother never wrote while the boys were away, despite their persistent requests.[88] Perhaps because of his wife's silence, father Sabin took on the role of moral protector so often played by soldiers' mothers. In one letter to Ball he advised: "do your best to tent with men of good moral character, and be very careful lest you be lead away by the numerous temptations incident to camp life."[89]

Each of these cases has unique aspects, reflecting particular familial relationships, but taken as a group they present clear patterns. Soldiers in the camps and on the battlefields maintained their various roles within their families by relying on letters and packages to and from Philadelphia. Frequently the same soldier adopted different attitudes in corresponding with different family members, seemingly reflecting antebellum relationships. And these distinctions were reflected further in the sort of gifts shipped from the home front to soldiers in the field.

Sallie Stokes, a young Germantown girl, kept a remarkable wartime diary devoted largely to the military exploits of her brother Wyn. This journal provides a detailed account of the emotional impact of the separation of a soldier and his younger sister.[90] Soon after the war began, Wyn volunteered and went off to camp. One early morning Sallie awoke when her brother "threw something up at [her] window," and she "went down & opened the door for him & kissed him." The next day Wyn's company marched out of town and Sallie and a friend "went down to the Apple tree and waved [their] handkerchiefs to the soldiers."[91] Two months later an excited Sallie rushed outside to see her brother march through Germantown:

88   Other letters provide ample evidence of Mrs. Colton's love for her sons. Perhaps she found the task of writing too painful. If so, this is stark evidence of the limitations of letters in overcoming separation.

89   Wilson, *Column South*, 54, 57, 58, 76, 77, 83–4, 109–11, 160–1, 163, 248, 272 and *passim*.

90   Sally M. Stokes diary, HSP. The Stokes diary is a single volume of scattered entries, often appearing out of chronological order. Stokes does not record her age, but her entries indicate that she was a teenager during the war years. In early 1864 she took a job as a governess. In 1865 her.father, Wyndham H. Stokes was listed in *McElroy's City Directory* (Philadelphia, 1865) as a secretary working for the Mutual Fire Insurance Company. Her brother, Wyndham, Jr., appeared in the 1865 directory, but with no listed occupation.

91   Stokes diary, 7 May 1861.

> . . . the company marched up the street & Wyn was just on our side
> he looked up & nodded at one of us when Uncle beckoned. Peg & I
> went over and found Wyn & Jack divested of their knapsacks . . .
> and taking his musket he & I walked home.

But soon Wyn was back in uniform and Sallie described another
good-bye in meticulous detail:

> . . . he wore his officer's cap with a bugle wrought in gold on it . . .
> [he] went up stairs & got his things . . . and bid us good-bye in the
> parlor . . . I carried Wyn's canteen, scissors and books . . . Wyn
> kissed me again over in the lawn . . .[92]

After Wyn's second departure, Sallie wrote a poem in her diary:

Wyn

Go in the name of "Him"
Whose arm is strong to save
When the deep cannon roar
Bids thy young heart be brave
Go, dearest brother go,
That sheltering army shall shed
A mightier love than I could yield
To guard thy tented bed

When bearing on the foe
"Charge"! is the onward cry
Raise those to "God" above
Thy mild & earnest eye,
One moment at his throne
Thy soul pour out in prayer
Then with thy hand bear on
Proud or victory's there

May he who shields thy flower
Till the dark storm is past
Guard thee in strife's wild hour
From Southern hate & wrath;
Thy country calls thee go,
Thy mother O'er thee lends
Her angered {?} pinions low
To shield thee to defend
Sallie[93]

For the next fifteen months Sallie's only contact with her brother
was through his regular letters. In March 1863 Sallie's journal entry

92 Stokes diary, 29 July, 7 October 1861.
93 Stokes diary, 5 October 1861.

read: "Wyn came home . . . we jumped out of bed and hurried on some clothes & rushed to see him." For the week of Wyn's furlough Sallie's journal became an intimate record of her brother's actions. On his first day home Sallie made him breakfast and the two went for a long walk as Wyn told of his exploits at Antietam. The following day Sallie gave her brother a handkerchief she had made for him and he told her more war tales. Often the young girl seemed content to silently marvel at her brother's presence. One entry closed with the lines: "How glad we all are to see Wyn. His sword is laying on the piano." Another was devoted to a careful description of the room in which she sat, with Wyn straddling a camp stool nearby and Charlie (a furloughed friend) languishing on a couch.[94]

Wyn's furlough ended all too soon. And as March closed, a lonely Sallie noted that "A week ago today Wyn was sitting here with us."[95] Later, in an undated entry in the middle of her journal, Stokes tried to express the emotions engendered by this second separation:

> He was gone – really gone. I was not even to hear of him for a long time; & when I was to see him God knew alone, I was swept out of his sight; & he out of mine as if we did not belong to each other. There was only the one [?] in heaven or earth, that at the same moment could see him & me. When I thought of that it melted all my heart. . . . God was my link to my brother. There we were near to each other, however else we might be separated. No distance in the world, though it put us for a time out of sight of each other, could put us out of the sight of God.[96]

A few months after Wyn's furlough Sallie wrote:

> I used to feel so awfully about Wyn when he was home. [A]s long as I could employ myself I could control my feelings but as soon as a leisure moment came & I looked at him & thought how soon he would be far away it was all over and my pent up soul would have its way.[97]

What can we conclude from this highly personal wartime diary? The war disrupted Sallie Stokes's relationship with her brother, and the prolonged separations seem to have intensified her emotional attachment to her older sibling. But Wyn's absence did not appear to disrupt Sallie's everyday life. Sallie idolized Wyn as an older brother and though their separation upset her, it did not require a shift in the way in which she perceived their relationship. The spouses of men in the Patterson Regiment ached with a longing that suggested a

94   Stokes diary, 16 to 23 March 1863.
95   Stokes diary, 29 March 1863.
96   Stokes diary, 24 April, no year.
97   Stokes diary, 23 August 1863.

stronger dependence. Their letters portray the pain following the abrupt break of a marital partnership. Stokes's needs seemed fullfilled by Wyn's mere presence, rather than by any role he played in providing her physical or emotional comfort.

James Tyndale Mitchell experienced the war as an occasional participant, but for most of the conflict he remained an interested spectator. This interest was heightened by the military movements of his uncle, Hector Tyndale, and his close friend, Charley Robinson. Mitchell's diary provides glimpses into the impact of wartime separation on male relationships. In the summer of 1861 Mitchell's· Uncle Hector left for Harper's Ferry as a major in the Twenty-eighth Volunteers.[98] That fall and winter Mitchell and Charley Robinson were regular companions, while the diarist kept track of his uncle through letters to his family.[99] In August 1862 Charley Robinson enlisted in the 114th Volunteers, and Mitchell went to Harrisburg to seek a commission. When that failed, he served with the Germantown Home Guards during the Antietam crisis.[100]

At the Battle of Antietam Mitchell's uncle, by then a lieutenant colonel, received a near-fatal head wound.[101] On September 24 Mitchell's company returned from the field and he went immediately to visit his partially paralyzed uncle. For several months Mitchell regularly visited his uncle.[102] During that time Mitchell also drilled with his company and anxiously waited for word from Charley Robinson. When news of the Battle of Fredericksburg reached Philadelphia, Mitchell spent the evening at the Robinsons; he "found them all worried about Charley who was in the battle on Saturday." A few days later a worried Mitchell went with Mrs. Robinson to the Baltimore Depot in hopes of meeting Charley, but his train did not arrive. The next day Robinson did return, and the two friends were once again constant companions.[103] In June 1863 Hector Tyndale reentered active service as a brigadier general. A few months later he was

98 Mitchell diary, 9, 21 June, 21 September 1861. For a detailed account of Hector Tyndale's career, see Hector Tyndale, *A Memoir of Hector Tyndale* (Philadelphia, 1882).
99 Mitchell diary, 26 September, 22 October, 12 December 1861; 15 February 1862. Hector Tyndale to Edward Mitchell, 15 October 1861, letter among Mitchell papers, privately owned.
100 Mitchell diary, 19, 20 August 1862. Robinson's name appears among the 114th PVs in the *Official Army Register*, 3:950. See Chapter 2 for an account of Mitchell's 1862 military adventures.
101 *Memoir of Hector Tyndale*, 13–14. Tyndale's regiment captured seven regimental battle flags during the engagement.
102 Mitchell diary, 24 September, 20 October 1861 and *passim*.
103 Mitchell diary, 19, 20 December 1861 and 16 December 1862, *passim*. The *Official Army Register* 3:950 shows Robinson resigning his commission on April 4, 1863, but Mitchell's diary makes no mention of his returning to service in 1863.

home again on sick leave; but his ailments did not disable General Tyndale for long, and soon he was with his troops in Tennessee. In January 1864 Tyndale came home on furlough and his nephew visited him several times before he returned to the field.[104]

Mitchell's journal provides none of the emotional detail of other diaries, but it does suggest the varied dimensions of wartime separation. When Charley Robinson enlisted, Mitchell temporarily lost his closest friend. Twice that fall Mitchell wrote that he and Charley walked past Colonel Rush's camp to view the troops. One can easily imagine how their conversations turned to their own future decisions. When Mitchell sought a commission a year later, he was answering an urgent call. But he was probably also responding to Robinson's recent enlistment. After Fredericksburg, Mitchell found the Robinsons "all worried about Charley." He neglected to mention his own worry, which drew him to their home and shortly thereafter led him to a futile excursion to the train station. Mitchell tells us little about his thoughts, but his actions suggest a young man who was missing the companionship as well as fearing for the safety of an old friend.

Mitchell's relationship with his uncle also retained its peacetime flavor, although their contact seemed to increase. Before the war, Hector did not figure prominently in Mitchell's day-to-day life. When his uncle was at war, Mitchell wrote of him only occasionally. But whenever Tyndale returned home on leave his nephew was sure to call on him. Again we must surmise from what is left unsaid. Hector was well known in the community, and his exploits probably came up frequently in conversation. In that sense he played a regular role in Mitchell's life. His travels added a particular realism to the young Philadelphian's perceptions of the war. Charley's and Hector's enlistments did not create the void in Mitchell's life that Wyn Stokes's absence left in his sister's world. Although he feared for their safety, Mitchell was better prepared to continue his established relationships with his best friend and his uncle through their letters and visits home than were men and women who lost close relatives to the military ranks.[105]

---

104 *Memoir of Hector Tyndale*, 14–17; Mitchell diary, 24 September 1863; 18 January, 7 February 1864.

105 For an interesting account of one young Philadelphian's relationship with a friend in the army see the diary of Joseph Boggs Beale. On occasion Beale seemed quite irritated by his cousin's ostentatious behavior and his military finery. Beale diary, 20 July, 3, 9, 10, 13, 14, 22, 23 August 1861 and *passim*, HSP. Also see Nicholas B. Wainwright, ed., "Education of an Artist: The Diary Of Joseph Boggs Beale, 1856–1862," *Pennsylvania Magazine of History and Biography* 97 (October 1973): 485–510.

Antebellum separations

The Civil War forced Philadelphians into wide-ranging personal adjustments, as those who stayed behind watched friends and loved ones depart for the battlefield. We have already argued that citizens at home turned to familiar means, aided by detailed letters, to cope with the harshest wartime losses. The evidence from letters and diaries also seems to indicate that many people successfully maintained friendships and family ties despite the distance. Communications with the camps – coupled with the joys of periodic furloughs – eased the pain of separations while allowing soldiers to continue to play their established home roles. This raises a further question: How novel were these coping devices? Were wartime separations merely a continuation, albeit on a grander scale, of familiar experiences?

Departure from the family had long been viewed as a major step in the maturation of young American males. And as the nineteenth century progressed various forces – urban growth, the decline of traditional apprentice systems, early industrialization, rising college enrollments, and the lure of the West – combined to separate increasing numbers of young men from their homes. In a study of nineteenth-century American adolescence and youth, Joseph Kett concludes that the acknowledged transition from childhood to youth typically came when a young man left the home and became a "burgeoning independent."[106] These first years following the break from home were viewed as especially perilous ones, requiring careful preparation and continued supervision.[107] Even when sons of antebellum families went off to college, their correspondence demonstrates that fathers maintained the "paternal vigilance" necessary to mold successful businessmen, while mothers often adopted the moral upbringing of their charges as their special province.[108] Thus there was ample precedent for family separations in the peacetime world, and parents did not abdicate their instructive roles when their sons left home.[109]

---

106 Joseph F. Kett, "Adlescence and Youth in Nineteenth-Century America," in *The Family in History*, eds. Theodore K. Rabb and Robert J. Rotberg (New York, 1971), 105–7.
107 Middle-class families in Utica, NY, took great pains to prepare their young men for independence. See Mary P. Ryan, *Cradle of the Middle Class* (Cambridge, MA, 1981), 167–74.
108 Ryan, *Cradle of the Middle Class*, 173–4; Carl N. Degler, *At Odds: Women and the Family in America from the Revolution to the Present* (Oxford, 1980), 83–5; Joe L. Dubbert, *A Man's Place: Masculinity in Transition* (Englewood Cliffs, NJ, 1979), 17.
109 For an overview of the impact of economic change on family relations see Daniel Blake Smith, "Family," in *Encyclopedia of American Economic History*, ed. Glenn Porter, (New York, 1980) vol. III, 976–84.

Of course young men who left for college or to find jobs in distant cities severed family ties without undergoing the physical risk encountered by Civil War volunteers. Perhaps the traumas of wartime partings were more comparable to the separations when men and women migrated west. Between 1840 and 1860 over a quarter of a million Americans traveled overland to Oregon and California.[110] Although entire families sometimes moved west, the bulk of fortune seekers in the mining towns and farmers on the frontier were young men between ages twenty and forty.[111] In reality the trip west was not particularly dangerous: trail mortality was little more than 4 percent. But rumors of hostile Indians, disease, and violent accidents exaggerated the fears of those left behind.[112] This massive antebellum migration must have left thousands of Easterners better prepared to cope with the loss of young men to the battlefield.

Family members who remained in the East rarely received much information from their migrating relatives. Western travelers were often gone for several years, with only occasional communication with family and friends in the East.[113] Correspondence from western migrants suggests the frustrations of these lengthy separations. In 1849 one man wrote to his wife from California: "Over a month yet must pass before you get this letter. I know your anxiety, your love, your inquietude on my account. How gladly would I, if I could, relieve you by imparting with an electric current the news that I am here alive and well." Sometimes those left behind had to wait over a year to learn that their loved ones had arrived safely.[114] In such circumstances absent family members could hardly maintain their prior relationships with those left behind.

Conversely, Union soldiers were often in regular contact with home. Even when her son was serving in a Nashville hospital, Mary Ashhurst was pleased to report that she was "hear[ing] constantly from dear Sam."[115] In the twenty-nine months that J. L. Smith spent in the army, fruit dealer Hannah Smith received at least 184 letters

---

110 John D. Unruh, Jr., *The Plains Across: The Overland Emigrants and the Trans-Mississippi West, 1840–60* (Chicago, 1979), 120.

111 Jack E. Eblen, "An Analysis of Nineteenth-Century Frontier Populations," *Demography* 2 (1965): 412; John C. Hudson, "The Study of Western Frontier Populations" in *The American West*, ed. Jerome O. Steffen, (Norman, OK, 1979), 43; James Edward Davis, "Demographic Characteristics of the American Frontier, 1800–1840," (Ph. D. diss., University of Michigan, 1971), 230.

112 Unruh, *The Plains Across*, 135–7, 408.

113 For discussions of the slow and unreliable mail service to the west, see Unruh, *The Plains Across*, 239–41, 277; J. S. Holliday, *The World Rushed In: The California Gold Rush Experience* (New York, 1981), 309–11.

114 Holliday, *The World Rushed In*, 309–10; Unruh, *The Plains Across*, 239–40.

115 Mary Ashhurst diary, 27 February 1863.

from her teenaged son.[116] The papers of Sergeant Thomas W. Smith include sixty letters written to his family over a period of thirty months.[117] Perhaps the best evidence of the frequency of communication is the occasional disgruntled comment when expected letters did not arrive. On June 11, 1862, an angry John W. Lynch, encamped near Richmond, wrote to his fiancée Bessie Mustin that "the last letter which I rec'd from you was dated on the 15th of May . . . I am indeed unable to imagine what can be the matter that I do not hear from you – if you were sick I know some one of you [sic] family would write me to that effect. *Then what must I think*[?]"[118] Even allowing for the insecurities of young love, Lynch's near-frantic tone after only three weeks of silence suggests that the mail service between Philadelphia and Virginia must have been quite reliable.[119]

Perhaps we should conclude that although the massive westward movement in the two prewar decades prepared Northerners for wartime leave-takings, the qualitative experience of the antebellum separations was actually in certain ways more difficult.[120] For instance, while Wyn Stokes was in the army, his sister received regular letters from him, and the pair enjoyed several brief reunions. This consistent contact may well have enabled Sallie to maintain an emotional relationship with her brother that would have been impossible had he gone to California a decade earlier. On the other hand, the persistent reminders of her brother's absence, and the repeated homecomings and separations, made Sallie's "grief work" that much more difficult. Rosenblatt found that grief over separation slowly diminished with time, but was often rekindled by letters or reminders of absent loved one.[121] During the Civil War frequent letters and occasional furloughs might have enabled those on the home front to maintain their established relationships with the men in the field, but such contacts also made the renewed separations all the more difficult.

These observations speak to the experiences of young men who left parents, siblings, and sweethearts behind, but what of those who had young wives and children? Was there an antebellum context to these severed relationships? Investigating marital separation during

---

116 J. L. Smith to Hannah Smith, November 1862 to March 1865.
117 Thomas W. Smith, January 1862 to July 1864.
118 The following day, Bessie's letter arrived and Lynch "felt like another person." See Lynch to Mustin, 11, 12 June 1862.
119 For a good description of the quantity of mail to and from the camps see Bell Irvin Wiley, *The Life of Billy Yank* (Baton Rouge, 1952; 1981), 183. The experiences of the aforementioned Patterson Regiment, whose early letters were not delivered, are clearly different in this regard. But such problems were apparently cleared up after the war's first few months.
120 Of course the *fear* for loved ones was presumably more powerful during the war.
121 Rosenblatt, *Bitter, Bitter Tears*, 72–80.

the American Revolution, Mary Beth Norton discovered that many wives found "the experience a positive one" that freed them from their confined marital roles.[122] But similar separations during the mid-nineteenth century revealed a strengthened emotional dependency. "I love my husband so much," wrote a missionary's wife in 1838. "I find it hard to be reconciled to the thought of ever being separated from him." In 1823 a sea captain's wife pleaded with her husband to return home because "everything about seem'd melencholly" when he left.[123]

Separated spouses did what they could to maintain their idealized roles in these new circumstances. In a study of the wives of seagoing men, Tamara Miller found that they struggled persistently to overcome the barriers posed by distance. In the nineteenth century's early decades these young women sought emotional and material support in the homes of relatives. Later, when separations became longer and the ideal of the single-family home grew stronger, the wives of sailors lived alone or chafed at living with others. Miller argues that by mid-century these women were increasingly reluctant to cross the boundaries of their prescribed gender roles. The idealized husband's role was to attend to the family's day-to-day material needs, share in child-rearing duties, and act as a romantic partner. As the gap between expectation and reality widened, couples relied increasingly on detailed letters to carry out their idealized roles. But, Miller tells us, "as voyages became longer and ideals more important . . . it became harder and harder for the ideals to be fullfilled . . . . As a result, wives of seamen became increasingly bitter about separation."[124]

Although letters and periodic furloughs might have left wartime spouses confident of their partner's love, Civil War soldiers, like antebellum seafaring men, could not effectively play their varied roles while in the field. Thus, although frequent contact assured that marital relationships remained distinct, regular correspondence does not appear to have eased the task of coping with separation.

Conclusion

The Civil War took thousands of young Philadelphians from their homes. Some served for a few months, others fought for four years. At one time or another, an enormous percentage of the city's

122 Mary Beth Norton, *Liberty's Daughters: The Revolutionary Experience of American Women, 1750–1800* (Boston, 1980), 214–24.
123 Degler, *At Odds*, 33. For further examples also see 33–41.
124 Tamara G. Miller, " 'Hartsick and Homesick:' Domesticity and Seafaring Life in Nineteenth Century New England," (Unpublished essay, Brandeis University, 1985), 54 and *passim*.

young men donned a uniform. The traumas and challenges of the separations washed over those left behind in waves. First came the concern for friends and acquaintances who had enlisted, and the fear that sons, brothers, and husbands might follow. Then came the separation itself, initially leaving a sharp emotional loneliness, followed by the pain of a more tangible void. And with the emptiness came the fear that a loved one might not return. The war's destruction left no one untouched. Those whose family members were spared watched friends mourn their loved ones.

Americans were unprepared for the scope of these losses. But they did have traditions to cling to to help them cope. Departures at young adulthood were a familiar aspect of young men's experiences. The westward migration of the previous several decades had accustomed many to long separations. Mid-nineteenth century Americans also had a particular familiarity with death. People died at home, surrounded by watchful loved ones, rather than in distant hospitals.

Regardless of precedents, however, the enlistment of Philadelphia's young men presented a strong wartime test, straining relationships with friends and kinfolk left behind. For Philadelphians at home the task was really twofold: (1) to re-create as much as possible what was severed, and (2) to cope with what was irrevocably lost. In coping with their losses they turned to familiar devices. Religious beliefs comforted many who mourned fallen loved ones. Many others joined Sallie Stokes in seeking spiritual strength to withstand the pains of separation. Often visits from family and friends proved vital in coping with both separations and deaths. And, as we shall see, the war spawned numerous public rituals to honor departing troops and fallen heroes. Such events became occasions for acknowledging a shared sense of loss, providing those left behind with yet another means of coping.

In reconstructing their disrupted relationships Philadelphians turned less to past experience than to regular communications. Each passing month in the camps drew the soldiers further from their past lives, widening the gap between citizens and soldiers. This physical and psychological separation could have blurred the distinctions between different roles so that absent brothers, husbands, and sons came to be thought of in similar terms. But the letters and diaries examined here suggest that Philadelphians adjusted to these separations without fully recasting antebellum relationships. This continuity owed much to the evolving efficiency of the military mails that allowed for more regular contact with the soldiers than had been possible with the western mining camps.[125] Often letters brought

125 Wartime Philadelphians also benefited from occasional furloughs, providing them with visits that western migrants did not generally enjoy.

detailed descriptions of the death and burial of relatives and friends or news that loved ones had been captured or wounded, but they usually contained mundane information, whereas packages from home provided the comforts of everyday life. In these small ways, citizens on the home front sustained their peacetime relationships with Philadelphia's military men.

We have focused here on the most personal aspects of the wartime tests. Now we will turn, in the next several chapters, to the ways in which Philadelphians adjusted to the structural challenges posed by the war. We will continue to consider the experiences of individual citizens, and we will also ask how civic rituals and institutions evolved in the face of new circumstances. Once again, it appears that Philadelphia and its citizens responded to the crisis without dramatically altering their world.

4　Old rituals for new causes: Civic celebration at war

In February 1861 president-elect Abraham Lincoln included a whistle-stop tour of the North's major cities on the way to his inauguration. On the twenty-first he arrived in Philadelphia to a thirty-four-gun salute and an enthusiastic crowd. One young Philadelphian described the scene:

> A grand procession . . . was formed, but had no military in it except one company who were on horseback, & in addition to about 300 uniformed police were Lincoln's bodyguard. . . . Mr. Lincoln . . . bowed to the people as they waved their handkerchiefs to him & saluted him with cheers & firing off pistols. The streets of the route of the parade were jammed as full of people as they could be . . . & they cheered & made as much noise as possible, as long as they could see Lincoln. . . .Mr. Lincoln's carriage was followed by 200 or more carriages . . .[1]

Several groups prepared special displays honoring Lincoln's arrival. The William Penn Hose Company fired salutes as the president-elect's barouche passed, and a banner in a window at Sixth and Arch street offered a promise and a warning: "Enforce the laws and the people will sustain you."

Later, Lincoln stood at the head of the stairs in the Continental Hotel while crowds passed through the lobby to catch a glimpse of their new leader. When darkness fell, a fireworks display at Union and Chestnut read: "Abraham Lincoln, The Whole Union." An exhausted Joseph Boggs Beale reported that he "saw Mr Lincoln 8 times today."[2] The next morning a committee of councilmen escorted Lincoln, with the Scott Legion (a local private militia) as an honor guard, to Independence Hall. There Lincoln drew applause by promising that "the Government will not use force unless force is used against it," and then proceeded to raise the city's new flag with an additional star commemorating Kansas's entrance into the Union. Patriotic songs and an artillery salute filled the morning air; by 8:30 A.M.

---

1 Nicholas B. Wainwright, "Education of an Artist: The Diary of Joseph Boggs Beale, 1856–1862," *Pennsylvania Magazine of History and Biography* (October 1973): 498, entry of 21 February 1861.
2 Joseph Boggs Beale diary, 21 February 1861, Historical Society of Pennsylvania, Philadelphia (hereafter HSP).

Lincoln's carriage was on its way to West Philadelphia where a special train waited.[3]

Beale joined the crowds at Independence Hall to hear Lincoln speak and then drifted to the corner of Chestnut and Third to await a grand Parade of Workingmen. The workers, marching under the banners of most of Philadelphia's major industrial establishments, proceeded to National Hall where they joined with delegates from the National Workingmen's convention (which was meeting in the city) to discuss national affairs. The gathering resolved that it was "eminently proper on this anniversary of the birth of George Washington, to consult and advise together in regard to the most proper and effectual measures to be adopted and maintained for the preservation of the Union." The correct course, they concluded, was compromise without coercion.[4]

Elsewhere in the city, "the Anniversary of the Birthday of Washington was more generally observed as a holiday than for many years past." Philadelphians marked the day with a customary array of rituals. After Lincoln's departure, Mayor Henry joined both branches of the council at Independence Hall, where Joseph R. Ingersoll, a prominent Constitutional Unionist, read Washington's Farewell Address. The Veterans of the War of 1812 also met and heard the first president's words of warning, while a large gathering at Mechanics Hall sang stirring hymns and listened to patriotic speeches. That afternoon the city's elite military units followed tradition by parading and playing martial airs.[5]

These two days, coming in the midst of the secession winter, fused the political concerns of the moment with familiar patriotic symbols and modes of celebration. The 1860 election had sparked heated debate in the city – only 52 percent of Philadelphia's vote went to Lincoln.[6] Many rallied to the president-elect's side; however, others feared that the "Black Republican" would threaten the union.[7] When the City Council asked General Robert Patterson to call out the militia to escort Lincoln, the Southern Democrat declined, explaining

---

3 This description of Lincoln's visit has been taken from *Philadelphia Public Ledger*, 21, 22, 23, 25 February 1861, (hereafter *PL*); J. Thomas Scharf and Thompson Westcott, *History of Philadelphia, 1609–1884*, 3 vols. (Philadelphia, 1884), 1:250–1; Joseph George, Jr., "Philadelphians Greet Their President-Elect," *Pennsylvania History* 29 (October 1962): 381–90.

4 Beale diary, 22 February 1861; *PL*, 23 February 1861. See also Chapter 9.

5 *PL*, 23 February 1861.

6 Russell F. Weigley, "The Border City in the Civil War, 1854–1865," in *Philadelphia: A 300-Year History*, ed. Weigley (New York, 1982), 392. Lincoln received 57 percent of the vote statewide.

7 See Nicholas B. Wainwright, *A Philadelphia Perspective: The Diary of Sidney George Fisher* (Philadelphia, 1967), 367–8, entry of 6 November 1860.

that the president-elect was not visiting in an official capacity. The elite First Company Troop joined in this disingenuous refusal, thus depriving the honored guest of the traditional trappings of such a visit.[8] But a mounted police escort, cheering crowds, and fluttering flags provided Lincoln with a sufficiently grand and patriotic entrance into the city. That evening, and again the following morning, Lincoln yoked his goals to Philadelphia's historic past by paying homage to the "consecrated walls wherein the Constitution of the United States and . . . the Declaration of Independence, were originally framed and adopted." Although contemplating the dangers ahead, he assured his listeners that he had "never had a feeling politically that did not spring from the sentiments embodied in the Declaration of Independence."[9] (Yet Philadelphia workers employed the same symbols to call for compromise at any cost.)[10]

February 1861's two intertwined celebrations, honoring Lincoln's visit and George Washington's Birthday, introduced antebellum Philadelphia rituals to a changing social and political climate. During the war years to come both kinds of ritual – traditional celebrations of patriotic holidays and special occasions honoring visiting dignitaries – would survive in familiar forms.

Philadelphia's ritual traditions

Anthropologists often dwell on the importance of ritual in society, and recently a number of historians have emphasized the varied functions of civic rituals and celebrations. Rituals promote change or protect stability; they have been used symbolically by the lower classes to assault their "betters" and by elites to maintain their place in society. Richard Trexler's study of Renaissance Florence calls rituals "an integral part of established urban life," providing the city with an identity and reinforcing relationships within it. Peter Shaw's *American Patriots and the Rituals of Revolution* found public and private rituals playing key roles in easing the transition from royal dominance to independence. In his study of antebellum America's "quest for a definition of self," Fred Somkin noted the importance of a single event – Lafayette's return in 1824–5 – in spawning "a ritual of mass reconciliation," and the continued role of a holiday, Independence

---

8   Scharf and Westcott, *History of Philadelphia*, 1:749–50; George, "Philadelphians Greet Their President-Elect," 385.
9   Arthur Brooks Lapsley, ed., *The Writings of Abraham Lincoln*, 8 vols. (New York, 1906), 5:242–6.
10   *PL*, 23 February 1861.

Day, as a shared occasion for defining the national past through public oratory.[11]

Parades served varied functions and took on many forms in the "street drama" of early nineteenth-century Philadelphia. Many were part of the city's "recurring calendar of festivities"; others commemorated specific events or important visits.[12] There were several different ceremonial traditions, reflecting different social agendas. The city's orderly parades were generally dominated by the elite volunteer militias that used such opportunities to reassert their lofty place in the social order. But Philadelphia also had a "burlesque" tradition of wild, disorderly processions, often mocking the militia. The city's laborers occasionally held spontaneous marches that degenerated into violence, but more often they opted for respectable processions either as part of larger civic ceremonies or as independent parades. Philadelphia's volunteer fire companies also had a long history of parading both separately and in citywide processions.[13]

When Lincoln agreed to include the City of Brotherly Love in his grand tour, Philadelphians could turn to numerous precedents to plan the occasion. Thirty-six years before, the Marquis de Lafayette had entered the city in a grand procession. In 1833 President Andrew Jackson included Philadelphia in a national tour, and thousands of citizens turned out to view the parade honoring the Hero of New Orleans.[14] A decade later Philadelphia received a visit from President John Tyler. Harrison's successor also enjoyed a fine military procession, but bystanders in some parts of the city hissed at him as he passed and one visitor noted that he had "never witnessed a colder reception."[15]

11 Richard C. Trexler, *Public Life in Renaissance Florence* (New York, 1980), xix; Peter Shaw, *American Patriots and the Rituals of Revolution* (Cambridge, MA 1981); Fred Somkin, *Unquiet Eagle* (New York, 1967), 3, 9, 169, 177. For other recent studies that make particularly good use of the importance of rituals, see Rhys Isaac, *The Transformation of Virginia, 1740–1790* (Chapel Hill, 1982); Bertram Wyatt-Brown, *Southern Honor: Ethics and Behavior in the Old South* (New York, 1982).
12 For an excellent study of parades in antebellum Philadelphia see Susan Gray Davis, *Parades and Power: Street Theater in Nineteenth-Century Philadelphia* (Philadelphia, 1986). Quotation is from page 15.
13 Davis, *Parades and Power*, 49–72, 77–84, 113–14, 144–7 and *passim*.
14 Davis, *Parades and Power*, 65–66; Scharf and Westcott, *History of Philadelphia*, 1:636–7. Although Jackson's military reception was grand, public enthusiasm was muted by his controversial battle with the Bank of the United States.
15 Scharf and Westcott, *History of Philadelphia*, 1:662; Philip English Mackey, ed., *A Gentleman of Much Promise: The Diary of Isaac Mickle*, 2 vols. (Philadelphia, 1977), 1:375, entry of 9 June 1843. Jackson and Tyler learned, as Lincoln would in 1861, that the various components of Philadelphia's celebratory world – the militia, officeholders, local dignitaries, firemen, and ordinary citizens – could decline to play their customary role, thus adjusting traditional rituals to meet the political climate.

Like the ceremonies honoring Lincoln, the 1861 celebration of Washington's Birthday relied on long-established rituals. In 1832 the city honored Washington's hundredth birthday with a grand procession of 15,000, including city officials, policemen, several volunteer militia organizations, fire companies, and representatives from more than forty occupations and trades. In other years February 22 was commemorated by military displays, flag raisings, and public readings of Washington's Farewell Address.[16]

Antebellum Philadelphia's Independence Day celebrations generally incorporated a wider range of rituals, involving a number of social levels. The city's respectable classes marked the day with militia parades, private dinners, patriotic oratory, and daylong outings. Elsewhere in the city members of the working classes gathered at parks or in the streets for festive revelry.[17] When darkness fell, organized fireworks displays competed with raucous street celebrations in filling the night air. Often Philadelphia's elite citizens complained of the wild noisemaking that typically marked July Fourth celebrations. In 1849 Sidney George Fisher left the city to "escape the noise, vulgarity and various abominations of 4th of July patriotism." Seven years later Fisher still was complaining about "the incessant firing of pistols & crackers & the ringing of the fire bells."[18] In a testy 1860 Independence Day editorial the *Public Ledger* criticized "Old John Adams" for leaving a legacy of bells, pistol shooting, and fireworks. Despite efforts by "the city authorities . . . to stop the firing of projectiles," the *Public Ledger* noted that four fires, several barroom brawls, and a large battle involving several hundred firemen marked the 1860 celebration.[19]

Although Philadelphia's officeholders often participated in annual celebrations, it appears that the city's antebellum officials balked at spending public funds on such festivities. In 1849, following the conclusion of the Mexican War, a body of citizens petitioned "for an appropriation of money to defray the expense of a public exhibition of

16 *Germantown Telegraph*, 29 February 1832 (hereafter *GT*); Davis, *Parades and Power*, 1–3, 59–60; Nicholas B. Wainwright, "The Age of Nicholas Biddle, 1825–1841," in *Philadelphia*, ed. Weigley, 289–90; Mackey, ed., *The Diary of Isaac Mickle*, 1:32, entry of 22 February 1838.

17 Davis, *Parades and Power*, 40–5, 102–3. From his vantage point across the river, Camden resident Isaac Mickle regularly reported that hordes of Philadelphians crossed the river to celebrate the Fourth in New Jersey. See Mackey, ed., *The Diary of Isaac Mickle*, 1:54, 193, 298, entries of 4 July 1840; 5 July 1841; 4 July 1842.

18 Wainwright, ed., *A Philadelphia Perspective*, 224, 258, entries of 7 July 1849; 5 July 1856. On New Year's Eve 1827 diarist Samuel Breck complained that "The fireing of guns . . . by the vulgar, was incessant all night." Wainwright, ed., "The Diary of Samuel Breck, 1827–1833," *Pennsylvania Magazine of History and Biography* 103 (April 1979): 223.

19 *PL*, 4, 5 July 1860.

fire works on the ensuing fourth of July." The Common Council turned this proposal over to a Committee on Police, which concluded that "at this time it is deemed inexpedient to grant the request."[20]

Don Harrison Doyle has found that in Jacksonville, Illinois, the "Fourth of July procession was the perfect symbol of Jacksonville's new social order," and that both the Fourth and Washington's Birthday were "important community rituals of nationalism." When war came, Jacksonville celebrated Independence Day 1861 with a huge parade, reflecting the unity born of nationalism. But for the next three years the town was too divided to produce a unified celebration. Thus, Doyle concluded, "nationalism [was unable] to overcome internal factionalism during the war." Once victory was firmly in hand, political differences were forgotten and fifteen to twenty thousand citizens crowded into the fairgrounds to celebrate July 4, 1865.[21]

Did the Civil War put an end to such traditional displays, or did Philadelphians continue to mark important patriotic dates? Did new events, peculiar to wartime, force the city to adopt new civic ritual forms? What role did public officials play in wartime rituals? Did they break with tradition and spend city revenues on patriotic civic celebrations? In short, to what degree did the Civil War transform (or fail to transform) this evocative part of the city's life?

Traditional rituals in a wartime world

In early June 1861 a City Council committee presented a detailed program for the upcoming Independence Day celebration. The plan included military displays, boat races, Fire Company competitions, fireworks, illuminated arches, and a grand procession. But many council members objected to the proposed $8,000 price tag. Some argued that it was wrong to spend public money on fireworks when factories were closed and citizens were out of work. Why not let the "citizens, trades, and societies" run the celebration "without cost to the city?" But others pleaded the case for extravagance by noting New York City's ambitious plans and calling on the council to not let Philadelphia be outdone. The committee responded to these criticisms with a cheaper proposal, but not even the amended version passed. The war's first Independence Day had no publicly sponsored events.[22]

20 *Appendix to the Journal of the Common Council* (Philadelphia, 1849), appendix LVII, 217. Davis notes that the City Councils helped fund the Washington Centennial Birthday in 1832. See Davis, *Parades and Power*, 60.
21 Don Harrison Doyle, *The Social Order of a Frontier Community: Jacksonville, Illinois, 1825–1870* (Urbana, IL, 1978), 232, 235–39.
22 *PL*, 7, 11, 13 June 1861; *Journal of the Select Council of the City of Philadelphia*, vol. 14 (15 November 1860 to 27 June 1861), appendix 173.

When the Fourth arrived, Philadelphians celebrated the day in their customary manner.[23] Numerous private groups held banquets; several groups conducted flag-raisings, sword presentations, and other displays that symbolically linked the war effort with the city's patriotic past. That evening Professor Jackson, the city's foremost pyrotechnist, put on an enormous fireworks display near Twenty-first and Arch, whereas other Philadelphians enjoyed a similar show at Fifth and Shippen. Jacob Elfreth, Sr., concluded that the day's fireworks "exceeded anything of the kind I saw before."[24] But with the war still in its first months, many Philadelphians were more interested in the military effort than in idle celebrations. The *Press* noted that "the exigencies of the conflict may prevent many from celebrating the day in their usual manner." But it emphasized that "the outburst of practical patriotism which it has evoked in this period of trial and danger is the most acceptable and conclusive evidence that could be given of the perpetuation of the spirit of '76."[25]

This practical spirit molded the day's dominant celebration: a procession of 5,000 soldiers, including the Home Guard, the Reserve Brigade, and several other local military groups. The parade, called "the finest ever witnessed in Philadelphia," attracted a large crowd of citizens anxious to survey the city's new troops.[26] Patternmaker Washington Penrose went to the corner of Sixteenth and Walnut streets to watch and came away impressed with both the crowd and the soldiers. James Tyndale Mitchell found the number of soldiers substantial, but thought them "not well drilled and very badly officered."[27] Rather than serving merely as an occasion for Philadelphia's elite militia units to symbolically assert their social position, the war's first Independence Day parade gave the city a chance to observe and evaluate the men who might have to defend the city's borders. The city's newspapers expressed the hope that such displays would both improve military organization and stimulate public patriotism.[28]

In September, as the seventy-fourth birthday of the Constitution approached, a petition from more than a hundred leading Phil-

23 The general description of the day's events is from the *Public Ledger*, the *Press*, and the *Evening Bulletin*.
24 Jacob Elfreth, Sr., diary, 4 July 1861, Haverford College Library, Haverford, PA.
25 *Press*, 4 July 1861.
26 *PL*, 6 July 1861.
27 Washington Penrose diary, 4 July 1861, HSP; James Tyndale Mitchell diary, 4 July 1861, privately owned. For more comments on the military procession see Wainwright, ed., "Education of an Artist," 501–2, Jacob Elfreth, Jr., diary, 4 July 1861, Haverford; Jacob Elfreth, Sr., diary, 4 July 1861; Wainwright, ed., *A Philadelphia Perspective*, 395–6.
28 *PL*, 6 July 1861; *Press*, 5 July 1861.

adelphia citizens suggested that this first anniversary of the Constitution's signing "since the commencement of the Great Rebellion, should be observed here in a manner commensurate with the loyal character of the people." The City Council unanimously agreed to the proposal and named a joint commission to carry it out.[29]

The day began with a cannon salute at the Navy Yard, followed by a parade of the Home Guards. The procession stopped at the home of former vice-president and prominent Democrat George M. Dallas, the day's orator, and then proceeded to Independence Square where Republican Mayor Henry spoke, the City Council adopted a series of patriotic resolutions, and Dallas delivered his address.[30] Sidney George Fisher thought the "show was not very grand as a military display," but thought that Dallas's speech was "a good one."

> He paints in strong colors the guilt and folly of those who are attempting to overthrow the Constitution and destroy a government which has produced so much prosperity & happiness and he sustains fully the war, appealing to the people to be united in their efforts to prosecute it with success. As Mr. Dallas is a leading Democrat, his speech will have a good influence throughout the country. It was free from partisan spirit, altho he is a partisan, and from the insidious arts of a demagogue, altho he is one or has been one all his life.[31]

In this instance a bipartisan gathering of Philadelphia's leaders, responding to public pressure, employed a traditional ritual to address contemporary needs. Although they had refused to spend any money on the Independence Day festivities, the City Council appropriated $929.86 for the September 17 celebration.[32] The planners hoped that the celebration would "be recorded in the history of Philadelphia, as a new era in national holidays – a connecting link . . . that will bind our people together more firmly in the bounds of fraternity and patriotism."[33]

In February 1862 Philadelphia's Select Council called for a joint committee to arrange a George Washington's Birthday celebration "in a manner appropriate to the importance of the occasion, the high character of the City for patriotism and loyalty, and the present unhappy state of public affairs."[34] The resulting celebration relied on

29 *Celebration of the 74th Anniversary of the Signing of the Constitution of the United States of America* (Philadelphia, 1861).
30 Scharf and Westcott, *History of Philadelphia*, 1:779–80.
31 Wainwright, ed., *A Philadelphia Perspective*, 404–5, entries of 17, 18 September 1861.
32 *Annual Report of the City Controller exhibiting the Receipts and Expenditures of the City of Philadelphia for the year 1861* (Philadelphia, 1862), 35–6. This figure was roughly $750 less than had been spent on the reception honoring Lincoln.
33 *Celebration of the 74th Anniversary of the Signing of the Constitution.*
34 *Journal of the Select Council,* 16 (18 February 1862); *GT,* 19 February 1862.

traditional ritual forms to commemorate the patriotic holiday as well as the recent triumphs of General Ulysses Grant in Tennessee. The council met Governor Curtin and members of the state legislature at Independence Hall, where the president of the Select Council and the governor delivered addresses. From there the city and state officials proceeded to the Academy of Music to review a milelong procession of Philadelphia volunteers. That evening special guests joined the dignitaries for a banquet highlighted by a reading of Washington's Farewell Address. The entire affair cost the city $1,999.[35]

The day was marked also by numerous smaller activities. Various groups met for formal dinners, many office buildings and private homes displayed transparencies or banners, fire companies and labor unions paraded and fired salutes, and several local churches held special ceremonies.[36] But local diarists seemed most impressed with the military display. Anna Blanchard reported that the procession was "the handsomest I have ever seen." Henry Benners described a "Great Parade of 10,000 men here" and added that there had been "nothing like it [in Philadelphia] since 1832."[37] It would be several years before the city would see another such display.

The summer of 1862 provided an illuminating contrast for America's military observers. On the Rebel side Stonewall Jackson was perfecting his highly mobile tactics in the Shenandoah Valley; in the North a frustrated Lincoln tried to spur a recalcitrant McClellan into his long-promised offensive. In late June an outmanned Lee attacked McClellan east of Richmond. By July 1 the fighting had cost 20,000 Confederate and 16,500 Federal casualties. But if the Union forces had won a numerical victory, they failed to press their advantage while in the shadow of the Rebel capital.[38]

At home Philadelphians viewed the approaching Independence Day in a grim context of battle reports and arriving wounded. In early June 1862 a committee of councils proposed an ambitious Fourth of July celebration, with an estimated price of $3,000. But once again, critics assailed expenditures on fireworks when soldiers were in need. Although the committee pruned back its plan, the opponents were not silenced.[39] And when the Fourth arrived, no public celebration marked the day.

35 Scharf and Westcott, *History of Philadelphia*, 1:793–4; *Journal of the Select Council* 16 (6 January to 3 July 1862), appendix 72; *GT*, 26 February 1862.
36 *PL*, 21, 22, 24 February 1862.
37 Anna Blanchard diary, 22 February 1862, HSP; Henry Benners diary, 22 February 1862, HSP. See also Elfreth, Sr., diary, 22 February 1862.
38 James M. McPherson, *Ordeal By Fire: The Civil War and Reconstruction* (New York, 1982), 239–50.
39 *Journal of the Select Council*, 16 (5 June 1862); *PL*, 9, 12, 17, 19 June , 3 July 1862.

With municipal officials opting for frugality over festivity, it was up to private initiative to maintain Independence Day traditions. On July 3 the *Public Ledger* reported that "Citizens are making very general preparations, and military and fire companies will assist to make the day pass off in the proper manner."[40] The annual Independence Hall meeting and the planned celebration by Colonel Ellmaker's Gray Reserves were canceled because of "the peculiar situation of national affairs," but other bodies held their normal banquets and numerous salutes and flag-raisings marked the afternoon's events. Philadelphia's various fire companies decorated their buildings and spent the day honoring their comrades in the field with speech and song. Citizens who sought lighthearted entertainment picnicked at Fairmount Park or gathered at Jones's Woods for an afternoon of dancing and amusements. The latter included a ritual hanging of Jeff Davis and a balloon ascension depicting the battle between the "Monitor" and the "Merrimack." Because the city cancelled its planned fireworks, an anonymous Philadelphia gentleman stepped forward to finance a massive pyrotechnic display on the Schuylkill River. Mayor Henry had issued an order before the Fourth, forbidding fireworks in the streets. Several observers remarked that the day's festivities were particularly "tame," owing to the "slight reverses to our glorious army." The *Germantown Telegraph* noted the overall "soberness" of the day and added that the Fourth "was never more sensibly observed." But despite the mayoral order, Philadelphia's tradition of street revelry continued alongside her more formal rituals.[41]

Although much of Philadelphia celebrated Independence Day in 1862 with traditional activities, there were others who heeded the *Public Ledger*'s suggestion: "At a time like the present how can our 4th of July be so nobly spent as in arranging and contributing for the relief of the sufferers in the late battles before Richmond?"[42] Several local ladies' groups made special visits to the wounded in the city's hospitals; prominent prowar Democrat Daniel Dougherty delivered patriotic speeches to the men at the Broad Street and Christian Street hospitals; and the children at two local schools presented 100 quarts of ice cream to hospitalized men. These activities suggest that many revelers remained mindful of the war, incorporating its practical demands into the day's rituals.[43]

---

40 *PL*, 3 July 1862.
41 *GT*, 2, 9 July 1862; *PL*, 3, 4, 5 July 1862; *Press*, 4, 5 July 1862; Caleb Wistar diary, 4 July 1862, HSP. The *Public Ledger* reported several fires caused by fireworks and eight cases of boys injured by explosions.
42 *PL*, 4 July 1862.
43 *PL*, 5 July 1862.

In 1863 the City Council spent nearly $800,000 on the Families of Volunteers, the City Bounty Fund, and the City Defense. They also appropriated over $1,700 for receptions honoring the visiting city councils of Cincinnati and Boston. But they failed to devote any funds for the annual Washington's Birthday or July Fourth celebrations.[44] This decision kept local patriotic rituals in private hands for another year.

A heavy snowfall made Washington's Birthday 1863 a "gloomy holiday" and forced most groups to put off their celebrations.[45] On the following day Philadelphians commemorated the occasion with a familiar range of dinners and patriotic addresses. Although one newspaper reported that the day had been "celebrated . . . with a good deal of spirit," it seems to have passed with minimal fanfare. Several military bodies began the day with thirty-four-gun salutes. Later that morning the Provost Guard paraded to Independence Square for a reading of the Farewell Address and then proceeded to their new barracks at Fifth and Buttonwood. Governor Curtin and Mayor Henry were on hand for the grand opening of a new post office building on Chestnut Street.[46]

Some Philadelphians invoked Washington's name in partisan skirmishing. In November 1862 sixteen local gentlemen, disgusted with the pro-Southern sentiments expressed by their fellow "club men," had organized the Union Club of Philadelphia. Soon this social group reconstituted itself into the Union League, a much larger society, including both Republicans and Democrats, dedicated to the defense of the Union. On February 23 the Union League spelled out "Washington" in gas jets above its clubhouse. This display, which linked the Union League's cause with Washington's Birthday, began the League's long tradition of holiday celebrations.[47] Meanwhile the city's Peace Democrats, angered by Lincoln's removal of General McClellan and his January 1 Emancipation Proclamation, had opened their own new headquarters – the Central Democratic Club – on January 8. On February 23 the club held a large, enthusiastic meeting at the Concert Hall to call for "peace and conciliation." The club's president, prominent Copperhead Charles Ingersoll, made a rousing speech in which he discussed Washington's character; the featured

44 Sixth Annual Message of Mayor Alexander Henry, "City Treasury Report" (Philadelphia, 1863); City Controller, "Monthly Appropriations Dispursals, 1863," 86, 202, Philadelphia City Archives.
45 Elfreth, Jr., diary, 23 February 1863; Anna Ferris diary, 22 February 1863, microfilm, Quaker Collection, Swarthmore College Library, Swarthmore, PA.
46 PL, 21, 23, 24 February 1863.
47 Maxwell Whiteman, Gentlemen in Crisis: The First Century of the Union League of Philadelphia, 1862–1962 (Philadelphia, 1975), 18–28, 305, note 8; PL, 23, 24 February 1863.

orator delivered a eulogy to the first president.[48] Whereas the Union League members displayed Washington's name, antiwar Democrats linked his memory to their defense of the Constitution.

That summer the city was faced with more than conflicting rhetoric. On July 1 Lee's troops engaged the Union army at Gettysburg, and for three days Philadelphians anxiously waited for news from the battlefield. Once victory was assured, the city turned its attention to the 10,000 wounded soldiers who poured into local hospitals.[49] The national anniversary came at a particularly difficult, emotionally tense time.

A month before, it had seemed that Philadelphia's Fourth of July celebration would be unusually grand. Twelve committees of citizens and Union League members had worked for weeks on an elaborate Independence Day program to be financed by public subscriptions. The planned celebration was to include an imposing procession featuring league members, city and state dignitaries, several military regiments, delegations from all over the North, and President Lincoln and his cabinet.[50] When the battle began, the Union League called off the grand July Fourth celebration in favor of a smaller display at its clubhouse. On the Fourth the *Press* insisted that "we care little for patriotic words . . . when we know that our sons or brothers are dying by the hundreds." The *Public Ledger* added that "our national anniversary could not be celebrated in a more appropriate and useful manner than by each man doing what he can to swell the numbers of recruits at Harrisburg."[51]

One newspaper reported that the holiday "passed off in a very ordinary manner. Beyond the ringing of salutes, and the discharge of firearms and fireworks, there was not anything to mark the day." But there were other organized patriotic displays. The city's fire companies decorated their houses; the St. Louis Hotel held a fireworks show; some of the warehouses displayed bunting; the Independence City Guards drilled at their armory; and several groups held their

48 Wainwright, "The Loyal Opposition in Philadelphia," *Pennsylvania Magazine of History and Biography* 88 (July 1964): 298–9; *PL*, 24 February 1863; Journal of Anna Mercer LaRoche, 26 February 1863, Columbia University Archives.
49 See Chapter 2. See also William L. Calderhead, "Philadelphia in Crisis: June–July, 1863," *Pennsylvania History* 28 (April 1961): 142–55; Weigley, "The Border City in Civil War," 408–11; Frank H. Taylor, *Philadelphia in the Civil War, 1861–1865* (Philadelphia, 1913), 225.
50 Although the plans stated that "no political device will be allowed to be carried," the Union League and the Democrats could not agree on a single celebration. Since the Democrats had already reserved Independence Square for their annual meeting, the larger celebration was relegated to Fairmount Park. See *GT*, 17, 24 June 1863; *PL*, 6, 8 June 1863.
51 *Press*, 4 July 1863; *PL*, 4 July 1863.

annual meetings.[52] In the evening James Tyndale Mitchell "went up on the roof to see the fire works – but there was not much to see – the invasion of the state and the uncertainty of the result of Meade's battle yesterday and today with Lee – preventing the people from celebrating the day with any spirit." Jacob Elfreth, Sr., agreed that there was "no[t] so much Parade as usual on this Anniversary." But he did note a "great deal of noise to day from the firing of cannon, fire crackers etc."[53] Though the crisis had dampened enthusiasm for a civic celebration, Philadelphia refused to let Independence Day pass totally unacknowledged.[54]

In the early months of 1864 the original three-year enlistments expired, and Philadelphia's volunteer regiments returned to enthusiastic greetings. The *Public Ledger*, discussing "The Celebration of Washington's Birthday," called for a large military procession to celebrate the holiday. It would restore the traditional martial luster of the annual celebration, and give Philadelphians an opportunity to view the men who had been fighting for the nation's defense.[55] This suggestion met with an enthusiastic public response, and plans were soon underway for a display that the *Ledger* predicted would "exceed the parade of the 4th of July, 1861."[56]

Once again, city government chose to leave a major civic celebration in the hands of private citizens. On February 18 the Select Council resolved that:

> In the present state of our country, it becomes our special duty to recall to the citizens the memory of those great founders . . . to whom the doctrines of secession would have been abhorrent . . . [and suggest] [t]hat the citizens, Heads of Departments, and all public officers of the United States, State and City be requested to leave their ordinary avocations, and devote the entire day to the object of doing public honor to the memory of Washington.[57]

But although the city government endorsed the observance of Washington's Birthday, it provided neither direction nor financial support for the proposed parade.

---

52 *GT*, 1 July 1863; *PL*, 3, 4, 6 July 1863; *Press*, 4 July 1863.
53 Mitchell diary, 4 July 1863; Elfreth, Sr., diary, 4 July 1863.
54 Patent medicine dealer H. T. Helmbold created a stir by hiring 20 black musicians and 100 uniformed black marchers to parade on the Fourth, carrying advertising and patriotic placards. But few Philadelphians saw Helmbold's parade because Mayor Henry ordered it stopped after a few blocks. Henry's action demonstrated that although the city government was unwilling to spend money to create patriotic celebrations, it was still prepared to monitor private activities to avoid disturbances. See also *PL*, 6 July 1863; George W. Fahnestock diary, 4 July 1863, HSP.
55 *PL*, 11 February 1864.
56 *PL*, 20 February 1864.
57 *Journal of the Select Council*, 17 (18 February 1864).

When Washington's Birthday arrived, Philadelphia's celebration fused traditional civic rituals with immediate wartime needs. An enormous crowd turned out to watch the furloughed veterans, many carrying tattered battle flags, join with the Reserves, the Invalid Corps, and new recruits in the largest parade of the war. Elsewhere in the city, other groups marked the holiday with traditional meetings and nighttime illuminations. But the martial display was the occasion's central event.[58] In one sense this was traditional: Washington's Birthday had long been an occasion for military pomp. However, now the throng had come to see war-weary veterans rather than ornately clad private militias. And the organizers and paraders were concerned with more than social status. On February 1 President Lincoln had increased the call for the March 1864 draft, forcing recruiters into frantic activity to fill these increased quotas.[59] An exhilarating martial display, they hoped, would stir young men into enlisting and encourage their elders to give generously to the bounty funds.[60] Thus did the city's leaders direct traditional rituals toward a pressing military need.

In the war's final year Philadelphia marked the two civic holidays with familiar festivities but no large displays. On July 4, 1864, the city celebrated in traditional but unspectacular ways.[61] One diarist who "worked all day" simply noted that the "celebration was conducted as usual." The *Public Ledger* observed: "In the absence of any large public demonstration, . . . the Fourth just passed was celebrated with becoming spirit by our citizens." The largest event of the day occurred when 175 sailors paraded from the Navy Yard to the Volunteer Refreshment Saloon. Other military organizations staged smaller processions, and the familiar list of clubs and organizations held their meetings.[62] The "disorderly" portion of Philadelphia's population also observed the war's fourth Independence Day in typical fashion. Several fires, three homicides, and numerous injuries marked the holiday, and the *Press* reported that "there was a continual rattle of small arms" during the day.[63] The cantankerous Sidney George Fisher described the celebration in typical fashion:

58 *PL*, 23 February 1864; Scharf and Westcott, *History of Philadelphia*, 1:813; Diary of Anna Yarnall diary, 2 February 1864, Haverford College Library; Benners diary, 22 February 1864.
59 Scharf and Westcott, *History of Philadelphia*, 1:813. See also Chapter 2.
60 On February 22 the *Public Ledger* ran an editorial encouraging enlistment and throughout the previous weeks advertisements. offering high bounties ran alongside notices of the upcoming parade. See *PL*, February 1864.
61 Of course in 1864 Independence Day came shortly after the city's exhausting Great Sanitary Fair.
62 Benners diary, 4 July 1864; *PL*, 4, 6 July 1864; *Press*, 4, 6 July 1864.
63 *PL*, 6 July 1864; *Press*, 6 July 1864.

It is the great anniversary of the birth of democracy in the western world, & is very appropriately celebrated by license & brute noise – guns, pistols, crackers, & squibs thro the day, fireworks, drunkenness & brawls at night. . . . the constant noise of crackers, etc., is enough to drive a nervous person frantic.[64]

During the previous two months the Army of the Potomac had suffered 64,000 casualties in northern Virginia. But Grant *had* been making progress, and Sherman had begun cutting his swath through the South.[65] The organized rituals on this Independence Day stressed flag-raisings over fireworks, perhaps calling for steadfastness rather than enthusiasm; the street celebrations released pent-up energies in noisy revelry.

By February 1865 the news from the battlefield was quite favorable. On the seventeenth Sherman's troops marched into Columbia, South Carolina, and on the next day the city was in ashes. On the eighteenth the Confederate stronghold of Charleston surrendered after a two-year naval siege.[66] On the twenty-second the newspapers published an announcement from the mayor:

> In conformity with the request of the councils of the City of Philadelphia for the public observance of the Anniversary of the Birthday of George Washington, and for the manifestation of the proper assent to the recent adoption of the Federal Congress of an amendment to the constitution of the United States prohibiting slavery within its borders; and more especially in rejoicing for the glorious successes of our Army and Navy, I do hearby order a national salute to be fired at sunrise, and at noon a salute of one hundred guns and also the ringing of the bell upon Independence Hall; and I do hearby invite the sounding of the church and other public bells, and a general display of the National Colors during the day by the citizens of Philadelphia.[67]

This modest notice was a return to government direction of city ritual. But it revealed also how minor a role public officials continued to play.

The day proceeded according to Henry's suggestions. Banks, public offices, and many private businesses closed; salutes were fired; bells pealed in church steeples and engine houses; and the entire city was bedecked with flags and banners. At nightfall gas jets above the Union League spelled out "Victory," while the Union Club chimed in with "God and Our Country," and dozens of private homes and

---

64 Wainwright, *A Philadelphia Perspective*, 452, entry of 4 July 1864.
65 McPherson, *Ordeal By Fire*, 414–36.
66 McPherson, *Ordeal By Fire*, 471–74.
67 *PL*, 22 February 1862.

businesses were illuminated.[68] On this day victory seemed near. And in that mood Philadelphians chose displays of the sort they had used three years previously, after Fort Henry and Fort Donelson had fallen. Rather than holding parades or displaying fireworks, they opted for bunting, illuminations, and bells. With these symbols they shared a collective feeling of relief rather than exhortatory celebration.

Philadelphia's wartime observances of Washington's Birthday and the Fourth of July included elements both of continuity and adjustment. Each holiday had a long celebratory tradition. Parades, fireworks, flag-raisings, dinners, speeches, and decorations had familiar roles in the city's civic rituals. The war changed little of that. Philadelphia's private organizations continued to hold their holiday meetings as they had for decades. Various military groups staged patriotic parades. Each Independence Day crowds gathered in the streets to fire pistols and explosives. The greatest variations came in citywide events. Sometimes there were large parades or gay illuminations; other times there was little formal recognition. These variations were a barometer of the war's progress. In the worst times, such as the summer of 1863, public ritual was dispensed with. When the city was full of newly arrived wounded, holidays became an occasion for visiting hospitals. When new recruits were needed, the city responded with a large military parade. The victories in Tennessee in 1862 and in South Carolina in 1865 engendered festive decorations.

Philadelphia's ethnic celebrations, like its citywide patriotic holidays, survived the war years in amended forms. On March 18, 1861, the city's Irish population celebrated St. Patrick's Day with a large parade of Irish military regiments. The following year the *Public Ledger* reported that *"St. Patrick's Day* was celebrated in the usual manner in this city, except that there was not any military parade" because most of the Irish companies were in active service. In 1863 the Hibernia Society held its annual dinner and the holiday passed quietly. In 1864 the largely Irish Sixty-ninth Regiment returned and staged a lavish St. Patrick's Day parade that concluded in Independence Square.[69] Philadelphia's Germans also continued their established rituals despite the war. In August 1863 they held a two-day "Volkfest" at Washington Retreat that featured singing, dancing, and a parade of several German voluntary associations. The following

---

68 *PL*, 23 February 1865. Several diaries made particular reference to the bells and flags. See Elfreth, Jr., Elfreth, Sr., Benners, and Beale diaries. See also Amanda Marklee diary, HSP; Isaiah Hacker diary, A. H. Howell Collection, HSP; Francis Jordan diary, Ewing Jordan Collection, HSP.
69 *PL*, 16,18, 19 March 1861; 18 March 1862; 18 March 1863; 18 March 1864; Taylor, *Philadelphia in the Civil War*, 87.

September the German Society of Philadelphia marked its centenary with a festive celebration. In December 1863 Philadelphia's Poles held a banquet celebrating the anniversary of the Polish Revolution. The diners sat beneath a portrait of Washington flanked by the U.S. and Polish flags. They drank toasts to "The Day" and "Poland" but also to "The US President" and "The Union." In this fashion local Poles linked their historic tradition to both America's past and to the Union's cause.[70]

Athough the war affected Philadelphia's established holiday calendar, it neither ended celebrations that existed before the war nor created notably new forms of ritual. The conflict required no new patriotic rituals because the traditional forms already featured military displays and glorified American nationalism. And wartime orators seeking to support the Union could scarcely improve on the Declaration of Independence or Washington's Farewell Address. Nor did the war seriously change the sponsorship of celebrations. Time after time the city government chose not to spend public money on displays that might have stimulated morale. Instead the mayor and council issued periodic proclamations encouraging patriotic celebrations, but left most planning and financing in private hands. Military bodies, patriotic societies, newspaper editors, and individual citizens all stepped forward to sponsor holiday displays. The city, state, and national governments controlled men and arms, but the public remained the able custodian of civic spirit.

Rituals of wartime

Beyond the established calendar of civic celebrations, the Civil War created its own ceremonies. Some of these were carefully planned affairs, celebrating the return of local volunteers or honoring fallen heroes. Others were spontaneous gatherings, often at local military camps or train stations. Taken together, these ceremonies suggest two conclusions: Philadelphians quickly grew accustomed to the war's novel events; most of the ceremonial conventions developed during the war years harkened back to similar antebellum events.

Shortly after the firing on Fort Sumter, Philadelphians filled the streets to watch Union troops passing through the city on their way south. On April 18, 1861, the Sixth Regiment Massachusetts Volunteers marched through to enthusiastic cheers, and on the following day the Eighth Massachusetts paraded to the Girard House, where a large group met them.[71] These impromptu gatherings had no formal

70 *PL*, 24, 25 August 1863; 1 December 1863; 12, 13 September 1864.
71 *PL*, 19, 20 April 1861; Scharf and Westcott, *History of Philadelphia*, 1:759; Taylor, *Philadelphia in the Civil War*, 345; Beale diary, 18 April 1861.

structure, but they satisfied the citizens' thirst for glimpses of uniformed volunteers. They were matched by dozens of flag-raisings at schools, stores, factories, private halls, and public buildings all over Philadelphia.[72] Both spontaneous gatherings and orchestrated ceremonies became familiar parts of Philadelphia's wartime life. Most fell into one of six categories: military departures, military arrivals, military reviews, visiting heroes, funeral processions, and victory celebrations. Each ritual developed its own form, its scale varying depending on the occasion but never shifting in content.

On the morning of May 8, 1861, Colonel Francis E. Patterson's First Artillery Regiment gathered to prepare for its departure to the battlefield. Within a few hours the streets leading from Washington Square to the station were packed with spectators. At 9:00 A.M. a band escorted the regiment to the depot. Along the route fire engines rang their bells and thousands cheered. Friends and relatives said their good-byes, and many followed the slow-moving cars out of the city.[73] Sarah Butler Wister described the departure: "The Washington Grays left this morning . . . crowds of people went to see them, hundreds & hundreds of ladies, the mothers & sisters of many of them; few of them are old enough to be married."[74]

These scenes soon became a routine part of Philadelphia life. Regiments encamped near the city rarely had much advance warning of their departure. Usually they would receive orders to assemble at their armory and from there they would march to the depot. As the volunteers gathered, their friends and relatives lined the procession route or massed at the station. Sometimes a band would be present, but there was rarely a military escort or formal ceremony. Instead the final hours were reserved for last minute leave-takings. At first the sight of troops marching out of Philadelphia attracted careful descriptions in the city's newspapers and regular comments by local diarists. But soon the newspaper reports grew shorter, and diarists only noted the passing of relatives and friends.[75]

The return of troops from the battlefield provided occasions for greater martial pomp and wider public interest. At the end of July 1861 Philadelphia's first ninety-day enlistees began to stream back into the city. On the twenty-third at least 3,000 spectators crowded

---

72 See *PL*, 19, 20, 21 April 1861; Wainwright, "Education of an Artist," 499, entry of 18 April 1861; Beale diary, 24, 25 April 1861.
73 *PL*, 9 May 1861; Scharf and Westcott, *History of Philadelphia*, 1:764.
74 Fanny Kemble Wister, ed., "Sarah Butler Wister's Civil War Diary," *Pennsylvania Magazine of History and Biography* 102 (July 1978), 295, entry of 8 May 1861.
75 For a list of arrivals and departures see Taylor, *Philadelphia in the Civil War*, 345–56. Scharf and Westcott's *History of Philadelphia* describes dozens of these processions. Also see the *Public Ledger*, 13 May, 5 August 1861; 1, 2 September 1862 and *passim*.

into the Baltimore Depot to welcome Colonel Dare's regiment. This arrival had not been publicly announced and no formal body awaited them at the station. But two days later, when Patterson's Regiment arrived, a thirty-four-gun salute heralded the train's appearance and the Gray Reserves served as an official escort. In the next few weeks several more regiments returned to similar receptions. In each instance a military body met the veterans at the depot and escorted them into the city, and thousands of citizens flocked to the station or lined the streets to see the battle-weary volunteers.[76] This pattern, with returning regiments parading alongside military escorts as Philadelphians crowded the streets, remained the norm for the entire war. The only substantial change came when the volunteer refreshment saloons began greeting returning regiments with banquets.

In late December 1863 the Twenty-ninth Pennsylvania Volunteers became Philadelphia's first three-year regiment to return home. Their reception combined the personal and public aspects that had marked the return of the ninety-day recruits. At noon a cannon salute announced the train's arrival. When the 300 tired veterans arrived in West Philadelphia, the station was filled with friends and relatives. After these brief reunions the Twenty-ninth paraded towards the Market Street bridge. Before they crossed into the city they were joined by a band and a large military procession. This escort led them on a festive parade through the city with banners, flags, and cheering crowds lining their route. After the parade Cooper Shop volunteers fed the veterans at the National Guards Hall.[77] All of Philadelphia seemed to repond to the appearance of this small band of men, veterans of ten battles and thirty-one months in the field, who had already reenlisted as a group. George Fahnestock was on Chestnut Street that afternoon and described the parade:

> First came a splendid looking body of armed and uniformed police. Then artillery, which was followed by large bodies of troops of the Invalid Corps and regiments on hospital duty. When the 29th Regt came along a tremendous cheering and waving of hats and handkerchiefs greeted them along the route.[78]

Many observers remarked that three years of war had dramatically changed the faces of the boys who had volunteered. Fahnestock found the young veterans "war worn and stern men."[79] The other three-year regiments returned home that winter to similar receptions,

---

76 *PL*, 24, 26 July 1861; Scharf and Westcott, *History of Philadelphia*, 1:773; Beale diary, 23, 25 July 1861; Penrose diary 26 July 1861; Marklee diary, 27 July 1861.
77 *PL*, 24 December 1863; Scharf and Westcott, *History of Philadelphia*, 1:810.
78 Fahnestock diary, 23 December 1863.
79 Fahnestock diary, 23 December 1863; *PL*, 24 December 1863. See also Katherine Brinley Wharton diary, 27 December 1863, HSP.

but none attracted the attention that the Twenty-ninth had drawn.[80] Like other wartime rituals, the novelty of furloughed troops and torn battle flags soon wore off.

The arrival and departure of troops presented natural occasions for public gatherings, but many citizens also made excursions to the camps to watch the recruits train. In the spring of 1861 Sarah Wister regularly went to the Chestnut Hill barracks to observe the drilling troops.[81] Diarists Anna Blanchard and Katherine Wharton described visits to Colonel Rush's regiment's camp in September 1861.[82] But as the interest in drill parades waned such visits declined, until late 1862 when the arrival of conscripts from eastern Pennsylvania attracted crowds of interested spectators to Camp Philadelphia.[83] In mid-1863 Philadelphia mustered in its first black troops, once again piquing the curiosity of local citizens and drawing them to Camp William Penn.[84] On other occasions the local volunteers staged special drills or flag-raisings for Philadelphia's citizens.[85]

The celebrations honoring Philadelphia's regiments mirrored the associational ties that had molded their formation. The *Germantown Telegraph* frequently reported celebrations honoring local companies; the *Christian Recorder* paid careful attention to the activities of black regiments. Before Colonel Schimmelpfennig's largely German regiment left for the front the "friends of the regiment" held a picnic that attracted hundreds of people from Philadelphia's German community.[86] The August 1864 return of Baxter's Zouaves, a regiment composed of Philadelphia firemen, prompted an enormous procession of volunteer firefighters.[87]

The military displays generated by the war combined the spontaneity of individual emotions with the antebellum tradition of martial pomp. In the war's first month each troop movement attracted widespread attention. But Philadelphia quickly adjusted to these military spectacles and fell into a routine that joined traditional

80 See *PL*, 25 January, 13 February 1864; 1 June 1865; Fahnestock diary, 12 January, 13 February 1864; *GT*, 20, 27 January 1864.
81 Wister, "Sarah Butler Wister's Civil War Diary," 295, 297, 300–01, 306, entries of 9, 12, 22, 27 May, 11 June 1861.
82 Blanchard diary, 30 September 1861; Wharton diary, 23 September 1861.
83 Caleb Cresson Wistar to G. Woolman, 2 November 1862, Caleb Cresson Wistar Papers, F-2, HSP; Fahnestock diary, 14 November 1862.
84 Sarah Richardson diary, 31 July 1863, Quaker Collection, Swarthmore; Beale diary, 10 February 1864; *GT*, 5, 19 August, 23 September 1863.
85 *PL*, 4, 7 December 1861; *GT*, 5 August, 30 September 1863; *PL*, 13 February 1864.
86 *PL*, 16 July 1861; Scharf and Westcott, *History of Philadelphia*, 1:772. The Twenty-seventh and Seventy-fifth PVs received similar receptions from the local Germans. See Scharf and Westcott, *History of Philadelphia*, 1:815; *PL*, 25 January 1864.
87 Scharf and Westcott, *History of Philadelphia*, 1:817; Taylor, *Philadelphia in the Civil War*, 354.

public parades with new private concerns. The war's other civic rituals revealed a similar reliance on antebellum forms, amended to meet new circumstances.

Philadelphians paid painstaking attention to the dramatic events that followed the collapse of the Union. The first weeks of the war saw a number of men elevated to the status of heroes and sometimes martyrs. Heavy casualties soon would dull the senses, but in 1861 there was still room for individuals to capture the public's imagination. Two popular commanders, Fort Sumter's Colonel Robert Anderson and Fort Pickens's Lieutenant Slemmer, visited Philadelphia in the war's first months and received the sort of hero's welcome traditionally reserved for presidents and visiting dignitaries.

On May 10, 1861, a committee of the City Council met Colonel Anderson and his traveling companion, Mrs. Lincoln, at the railroad depot and escorted them to the Continental Hotel. The following morning a military procession escorted Anderson to Independence Hall, where he was formally received by the mayor and City Council. Anderson rode in an open barouche drawn by four white horses, and his route was lined with cheering crowds. Joseph Boggs Beale, ever the parade enthusiast, was on hand and "saw the whole procession & the Major, who was bowing to the people." At Independence Hall Mayor Henry delivered an address, and Anderson responded briefly and signed the visitors' book.[88] A month later Lieutenant Slemmer arrived in Philadelphia, stayed at the Continental Hotel, received a military escort to Independence Hall, was met by Mayor Henry, and signed the visitors' book directly below Anderson's name.[89]

The two visits were nearly identical. The only apparent difference was that Anderson, like his fallen fort, received more public attention.[90] And they were very similar to Lincoln's visit earlier in the year. Philadelphia had an established agenda for greeting heroes and dignitaries and the war did nothing to change that. But in later months these familiar ceremonies were reserved for men of loftier reputations. In July 1861 favorite son George B. McClellan was escorted through the streets; in February 1864 Brigadier General George Meade returned home to a large public reception; and in June 1864 Lincoln returned to attend the Great Central Fair.[91] On each occasion Philadelphia engaged in a ceremonial ritual that Lafayette would have recognized.

88 *PL*, 11, 13 May 1861; Scharf and Westcott, *History of Philadelphia*, 1:765; Wainwright, "Education of an Artist," 500, entry of 11 May 1861.
89 *PL*, 12 June 1861; Scharf and Westcott, *History of Philadelphia*, 1:769.
90 For diaries that mentioned Anderson and not Slemmer see Wharton, Benners, Mitchell, Beale, and Wister.
91 Scharf and Westcott, *History of Philadelphia*, 1:774, 811, 816. For Lincoln's visit see Chapter 4.

Celebrations honoring visiting dignitaries, like those for returning troops, occasionally had strong ethnic components. In August
1862 Brigadier General Michael Corcoran of New York's Irish Brigade
was released from a Confederate prison and began a whistle-stop
tour of the East. When Corcoran and his entourage arrived at Philadelphia's Baltimore depot, they were met by "almost the whole Irish
population" and thousands of other citizens. A large procession escorted the hero of Bull Run to the Cooper Shop Volunteer Refreshment Saloon. There the featured speaker lauded Corcoran's heroics
and concluded that

> when . . . our country shall erect monuments . . . to commemorate
> the bravery and valor of those engaged in this war . . . then will be
> placed on those tablets . . . the names of Corcoran, Shields,
> Meagher, Mulligan, Nugent and a whole host of others, the sons of
> Erin-go-bragh![92]

The war's rituals linked Philadelphia's powerful ethnic associations to
the patriotic sentiments of the time.[93]

When the remains of fallen heroes returned to Philadelphia, their
arrival prompted quite different, but equally familiar, ceremonies.[94]
In late May 1861 the city mourned the death of Colonel Elmer
Ellsworth, the flamboyant young commander of the New York
Zouaves. Ellsworth, who had recently passed through the city, was
shot in Alexandria, Virginia, while tearing down a Confederate flag.
His body arrived at Philadelphia's Baltimore depot on the twenty-
fifth and was escorted across the city to the New York depot by seven
Zouaves. Although the train's arrival was not widely announced, the
Pennsylvania Rangers and Mayor Henry were on hand at the depot
and a large crowd gathered along the procession route.[95]

Before long Philadelphia had its own fallen soldiers to honor. In
June Lieutenant John T. Greble, a member of a prominent Philadelphia family, fell at Big Bethel, Virginia. The young lieutenant's body
was brought home to a private funeral service at his father's home,
after which a Committee of Councils and a military escort

92 James Moore, *History of the Cooper Shop Refreshment Saloon* (Philadelphia, 1866),
    60–84.
93 For a discussion of antebellum Philadelphia's Irish associations see Dennis Clark,
    The Irish in Philadelphia: Ten Generations of Urban Experience (Philadelphia, 1973),
    106–12. Before the war, local officials tried to stop Philadelphia's Irish from public
    parading. Thus, the war seems to have extended the ritual role of the city's Irish.
    See Davis, *Parades and Power*, 157.
94 See Davis, *Parades and Power*, 66–7.
95 Allan Nevins, *The War for the Union*, (New York, 1959) vol. 1, *The Improvised War,
    1861-1862*, 146; *PL*, 27 May 1861, Scharf and Westcott, *History of Philadelphia*, 1:767.
    For a comment on Ellsworth's death see Wister, "Sara Butler Wister's Civil War
    Diary," 300, entry of 24 May 1861.

conveyed the remains to Independence Hall where they were placed in state. Thousands of Philadelphians gathered on Chestnut Street to view the coffin and filed through Independence Hall for several hours. That afternoon a procession of policemen, soldiers, councilmen and 150 high school students escorted the hearse along crowded streets across the Schuylkill to the Woodland Cemetary.[96] Philadelphia staged another major funeral procession in November 1861 when the remains of Colonel E. D. Baker arrived in the city.[97] Once again, a large body of military and political dignitaries escorted the hearse to Independence Hall. There the open coffin was placed on a bier and thousands of citizens streamed through to pay their respects.

The solemnity of wartime funerals was a mirror image of the festivities honoring returning heroes. Each event began at a crowded railroad depot, where a spontaneous gathering and a formal escort met the honored guest or soldier's remains. Whereas Anderson and Slemmer rode in barouches pulled by matching white horses, Baker's hearse followed black horses. And whereas cheering crowds and patriotic banners met the commanders of Sumter and Pickens, equally large crowds of silent and bareheaded mourners honored the deceased soldiers. Each procession culminated in ceremonies at Independence Hall.

Funerals continued to be a regular part of Philadelphia civic life, but grand public obsequies passed from fashion as the death toll mounted. Historian Ellis Paxson Oberholtzer remarked of the procession for Ellsworth's remains: "one now was mourned as thousands were not as the war advanced."[98]

The parades and processions created by the war followed time-honored patterns combining formal ritual roles and spontaneous public displays. News from the battlefield generated similar responses. Word of serious clashes attracted information-hungry crowds to newspaper bulletin boards. These impromptu gatherings often led either to angry discussions of military failures or jubilant celebrations. When Vicksburg fell, the ringing of bells and beating of drums drew an enormous crowd to a "spontaneous demonstration in front of the State House." Elsewhere in the city, homes displayed flags, engine houses rang their bells, and 400 Union League members paraded. That evening saw a general illumination, highlighted by the spelling of "Victory" in gas jets above the Union League, and dozens

96 *PL*, 15 June 1861; Scharf and Westcott, *History of Philadelphia*, 1:769. For a description of the procession see Beale diary, 14 June 1861.
97 Baker, the commander of the California Regiment (composed largely of Philadelphians), fell at Ball's Bluff on October 21.
98 Ellis Paxson Oberholtzer, *Philadelphia: A History of the City and Its People*, 4 vols. (Philadelphia, 1912), 2:363.

of fireworks displays.[99] Each of these ritual forms had long been part of Philadelphia's Independence Day tradition.

Philadelphia's financial outlays underline the importance of the war's rituals. As we have seen, the city government rarely voted to spend public money on holiday celebrations.[100] But in many instances the City Council voted to help pay for war-related ceremonies. When Colonel Anderson came to Philadelphia, the city spent $398 on the reception and an additional $500 on a commemorative sword; Lieutenant Slemmer's reception a month later cost $134; Lieutenant Greble's 1861 funeral procession cost $226. In the next three years the council appropriated $2,170 for military funerals. And when the three-year volunteers returned, the city spent nearly $6,000 on receptions. Over the four war years the City Council allocated roughly $10,000 for war-related rituals.[101] These figures greatly exceeded the amounts spent on traditional patriotic holidays, but they were not a substantial portion of the city's budget: In 1861 the city government spent $4,783,000; by 1865 annual expenditures had risen to over $10 million.[102] They were rather modest, too, by postwar standards. In 1876 the council spent nearly $10,000 on the Centenary Celebration, with half that devoted to fireworks alone.[103] This suggests that the city government's role in financing civic rituals did not expand until after the war.

Philadelphia celebrated the war's end with larger versions of its recurrent wartime rituals. On April 3, 1865, bulletins announced the fall of Richmond, and Philadelphia erupted. Bunting and flags appeared everywhere, and soon every bell rang in celebration. After a spontaneous gathering before Independence Hall, the assembled firemen formed a procession and paraded all over the city. Citizens from the Second Ward and 2,500 navy yard workers formed their own parades. A cannon atop the *Evening Bulletin* building fired salutes all afternoon. That evening the city was lit by bonfires and illuminations; "the night was an admixture of New Year's eve, Christmas eve, and Fourth of July combined." On the following day members of the Union League gathered in front of Independence Hall for formal addresses and prayer. On Sunday the news of Lee's surrender ar-

99 Taylor, *Philadelphia in the Civil War*, 351.
100 The only two such occasions were September 17, 1861, when the council appropriated $930 to commemorate the anniversary of the Constitution's signing, and February 1862, when they spent $2,000 for Washington's Birthday.
101 *Annual Reports of the City Controller* (Philadelphia, 1862, 1863, 1865, 1866, 1867); City Controller, "Monthly Appropriations Dispersals, 1863," Philadelphia City Archives.
102 *Mayor's Fourth Annual Message*, "City Treasury Report" (Philadelphia, 1861); *Annual Report of the City Controller* (1866).
103 *Annual Report of the City Controller* (1876).

LINCOLN LIES SLEEPING

By Nathan Upham.
AIR.—Under the Willow.

Up, from the homes of the land, a cry
Comes from a nation bewailing—
Lincoln, the merciful, doomed to die,
  Ah! merciful e'en to a failing.
    Chorus.—Strike, strike the traitor down!
        Cry of a sad people while weeping;
        Crown, crown, the Martyr crown,
        Weep o'er the grave where he's sleeping!
Lower the Flag of the Nation, now:
  Drape the proud Banner in sorrow;
Sleeping to day in that marble brow—
  He'll waken in Heaven to-morrow!
    Chorus.—Peace, peace, in Union peace!
        His earnest counsel, while living;
        Peace, peace, in Union peace!
        Never a heart so forgiving!
Tearfully, sadly, gaze on the dead,
  While ev'ry bosom is swelling;
Tenderly place him in his last bed,
  And shroud in deep gloom ev'ry dwelling.
    Chorus.—Peace, peace, in Heaven peace!
        Sing a sad people, while weeping;
        Peace, peace, in Heaven peace!
        Jesus that white soul is keeping!
Tenderly, sadly, we lay him down,
  Mourning his murder so gory—
Heaven will find him a golden crown:
  He's gone from Glory to Glory!
    Chorus.—Live, live, the Union live!
        Sing a firm people, while weeping;
        Lord! Lord! the crime forgive,
        The prayer of him who is sleeping!

Johnson, Song Publisher, 7 North Tenth St., Philad'a.
We have Reduced our Wholesale Prices of Songs.

Song sheet for sale in Philadelphia following the assassination of Abraham Lincoln. Library Company of Philadelphia.

rived, and Philadelphians began another round of ecstatic celebration.[104]

But the North would not celebrate for long. On April 15 Philadelphians were rocked by the news of President Lincoln's assassination. One diarist wrote: "I felt as tho I had lost a personal friend."[105] Within hours nearly every public and private building was draped in

104 Scharf and Westcott, *History of Philadelphia*, 1:822–3; Wharton diary, 8 April 1865; Taylor, *Philadelphia in the Civil War*, 311. Scharf and Westcott's account of the celebration of the fall of Richmond consists of a lengthy quotation from the *Public Ledger*.
105 Wainwright, *A Philadelphia Perspective*, 492, entry of 15 April 1865.

black. The City Council postponed its planned victory illumination. Churches held special services and numerous private organizations passed resolutions decrying the act. A large body of local women met and agreed to wear mourning for a month.[106]

On the nineteenth Lincoln's funeral service was held in Washington, and Philadelphians spent the day in fasting and prayer. Three days later the funeral train arrived in the City of Brotherly Love. Thousands of citizens crowded the streets to observe the solemn procession. The remains arrived with a delegation of relatives and national dignitaries, and were escorted to Independence Hall by a large military body. An estimated 120,000 people filed past the body in the twenty hours that it remained in Independence Hall. Then, on the morning of the twenty-fourth, a delegation of soldiers, firemen, and National Union Club members escorted the hearse to the Kensington Depot. As one witness observed: "Never before was there such a universal demonstration of love & of sorrow."[107] The day was marked by unheard-of expenditures by the city government. The council appropriated over $14,000 to "pay the expenses incurred in the obsequies upon the reception of the remains of the Late President of the United States, and for draping the public building in honor of his memory." This far exceeded the expense of any event in the decade since consolidation.[108]

Philadelphia responded to Lincoln's death with an unprecedented show of grief, but that grieving repeated familiar forms. The processions to and from the railroad depots and the endless lines at Independence Hall echoed the ceremonies for fallen wartime heroes. They also mirrored dozens of antebellum funerals. Isaac Mickle's account of Benjamin Harrison's 1841 death provides one such comparison. On Sunday April 4 the young diarist described a solemn sermon for the dying president, reporting that "[m]any were the sad faces in the peaceful streets of Philadelphia" at the news of his passing. The next day flags flew at half-mast and pealing bells honored the deceased leader. On the seventh Harrison was buried in Washington, most Philadelphia businesses closed for the day, and the Navy Yard's cannons fired a salute. Two weeks later the city staged a lengthy procession honoring the late president. "The mili-

---

106 Mary Ashhurst diary, 18 May 1865, HSP. For America's responses to the April 1865 events, see Thomas Reed Turner, *Beware the People Weeping: Public Opinion and the Assassination of Abraham Lincoln*, (Baton Rouge, LA, 1982).

107 Victor Searcher, *The Farewell to Lincoln* (Nashville, 1965), 111–21; Scharf and Westcott, *History of Philadelphia*, 1:824. Hancock, "The Civil War Diaries of Anna M. Ferris," 261, entry of 22 April 1865. Most contemporary diarists recorded lengthy accounts of the events of April 1865.

108 *Annual Report of the City Controller* (1866), 84–9.

"The Funeral of Mr Lincoln, April 22, 1865." Albumen-print stereo-graph by an unidentified photographer. Library Company of Philadelphia.

tary," Mickle wrote, "was splendid. . . . muffled bells sent forth their doleful sounds and many of the fronts of houses were hung with heavy festoons of black crape." The following month the city observed a national day of "fasting and prayer" by closing its shops and holding church services.[109]

The private responses and public procession following Lincoln's death were merely grander versions of Philadelphia's obsequies following Harrison's death or those honoring Washington, Lafayette, Andrew Jackson, or John Quincy Adams.[110] The reactions to Lincoln's assassination also had some of the equivocal elements that marked his 1861 visit. When Lincoln died, Katherine Brinley Wharton was surprised at her own grief. "Little did I suppose I should ever shed tears for him," she admitted. "But horror stricken as I was,"

109 Mackey, ed., *A Gentleman of Much Promise*, 1:143–6, 153–4, 166, entries of 4, 5, 6, 7, 20 April, 14 May 1841.
110 Davis, *Parades and Power*, 66–7.

Wharton added, "I would say that I think things were carried to a ridiculous length."[111] Jacob Elfreth, Sr., took exception to the "parading [of the coffin] from place to place and from city to city, until it becomes a mass of undistinguished humanity."[112] Wealthy Democrat Edward Waln was even less impressed with the display for the president whom he dubbed "the common man, whom Yankee cunning, and trickery have raised into the control of the Government."[113]

After the trials of April 1865 Philadelphians settled down to welcome their volunteers home from the battlefield. On June 10 the city held a grand military review, with General Meade commanding the troops and Governor Curtin, Mayor Henry, and numerous military officers observing from a stand in Penn Square. Delegations of city firefighters escorted each military company. The City Council provided nearly $6,000 for the reception. That afternoon General Grant spent three hours entertaining visitors at the Union League. These and other celebrations brought private organizations, military bodies, civic leaders, and enthusiastic citizens together to greet the furloughed veterans.[114]

This ritual of homecoming borrowed from both antebellum traditions and wartime patterns. At the end of the Mexican War, Philadelphia's Select and Common councils appropriated $1,500 to welcome returning veterans. On July 24, 1848, a large crowd met the First Pennsylvania Regiment at the depot, and a procession led them through flag-lined streets to a magnificent banquet.[115] In 1865 the city engaged in slightly different forms of ritual to welcome its veterans, but both celebrations included contributions by city officials, clubs and societies, firemen, and private citizens.

On July 4, 1866, Philadelphia hosted a grand review of Pennsylvania's veterans as they came together to return the state battle flags. The ceremony formally closed the books on the state's Civil War experience. Like the rituals of the preceding year, this event drew from familiar ceremonial forms but enlarged them. The day began, like other national anniversaries, with the firing of salutes. At 10:00 A.M. the procession of seven divisions formed and marched through

111 Wharton diary, 4 May 1865. Wharton refused to wear the mourning badge donned by many other women.
112 Elfreth, Sr., diary, 23 April 1865. Elfreth's son added that "I do not approve of keeping him out of the ground so long." See Elfreth, Jr., diary, 24 April 1865.
113 Edward Waln diary, 23 April 1865, typescript, HSP. See Chapter 7 for the threats of violence that followed Lincoln's assassination.
114 Scharf and Westcott, History of Philadelphia, 1:825; Taylor, Philadelphia in the Civil War, 313; Twelfth Annual Report of the City Controller, (Philadelphia, 1866), 84–9.
115 Journal of the Select Council for 1847–1848: (6 July 1848), 131; Scharf and Westcott, History of Philadelphia, 1:687; GT, 26 July 1848.

gaily decorated streets to a reception at Independence Square. There General Meade presented Governor Curtin with the flags amidst patriotic fanfare and rhetoric. At the close of the ceremonies various patriotic groups fired salutes all over the city. And when night fell a magnificent fireworks display lit the sky. In this fashion the rituals of war and the city's established patriotic calendar combined in a single dramatic demonstration.[116]

Patriotic pamphleteering

This analysis of Philadelphia's wartime civic rituals leads to several conclusions. First, the city did not do away with its peacetime holiday calendar. (The war's patriotic and nationalistic demands meshed nicely with the traditional images evoked on Independence Day and Washington's Birthday.) Rather, it supplemented that calendar with various rituals created by the war. Second, both the old and the new rituals evolved from antebellum practices. Contemporary demands molded each event, but the organizers and spontaneous revelers chose their actions from an established array of ritual forms.

This last distinction – between planners and street participants – is crucial. As in antebellum Philadelphia, a holiday or an important event during the war years touched the city at several levels. On such occasions thousands massed in the streets and public squares to watch processions or share in impromptu displays; dozens of clubs and societies held private meetings or displayed public decorations and parades; and Philadelphia's elites, whether officeholders or leading citizens, often stepped forward to organize or guide citywide commemorations.

This suggests a final conclusion. There was no wartime agency charged with using ritual and symbol to bolster morale. As long as war widows needed food and firewood, no one was prepared to spend tax dollars on maintaining the public spirit. Philadelphia's heroes – both living and dead – deserved the city's hospitality. But public-financed celebratory (or even hortatory) fireworks had no place in wartime. Privately sponsored flag-raisings, speeches, banners, illuminations, parades, and fireworks displays guaranteed that the patriotic holidays would not be forgotten.

Many Philadelphians promoted patriotism through wartime rituals, but some citizens sought to influence attitudes with a war of

116 Scharf and Westcott, *History of Philadelphia*, 1:828–9; Taylor, *Philadelphia in the Civil War*, 315–19.

words. Political partisans turned to podiums, editorial pages, and privately printed pamphlets to present their cases. Although they often considered revolutionary ideas, their form followed familiar lines.

Lincoln's 1861 suspension of the writ of *habeas corpus* and his subsequent refusal to acknowledge Chief Justice Taney's contradictory ruling drew a number of Philadelphia pamphleteers into heated debates over constitutional interpretations. This battle continued a long Anglo-American tradition of partisan pamphleteering.[117] As the war progressed, pro-Southern Philadelphians grew bolder in their dissent. Charles Ingersoll's *Letter to a Friend in a Slave State* of March 1862 assaulted the Northern war effort, and William B. Reed's series of antiadministration publications, culminating in his *A Paper Containing a Statement and Vindication of Certain Political Opinions* prompted widespread cries of treason.[118] These and similar pamphlets provoked heated discussions in elite households, but they were generally aimed at policymakers and legal thinkers rather than toward a larger common audience.

Philadelphian Charles Janeway Stillé's *How a Free People Conduct a Long War* was a quite different sort of pamphlet in that it sought to raise public confidence rather than debate government policy. Discouraged by Northern failures in late 1862, the historian Stillé turned to England's Peninsular campaign in Spain during the Napoleonic Wars for inspiration. In *How a Free People Conduct a Long War* he argued that the North, like England, was suffering through the inevitable dissension that accompanied a "free people's" involvement in a major war. Stillé argued that victory would be won through patient support of the government and the military rather than through factionalized infighting. At first Stillé only ordered seventy-five copies of his thirty-nine-page pamphlet, but his words struck a popular chord and the pamphlet went through thirteen editions

---

117   For discussions of pamphlets concerning the writ of habeas corpus see William Dusinberre, *Civil War Issues in Philadelphia, 1856–1865* (Philadelphia, 1965), 128–31; Whitemen, *Gentlemen in Crisis*, 10–11; and William H. Riker, "Sidney George Fisher and the Separation of Powers During the Civil War," *Journal of the History of Ideas* 15 (June 1954): 397–412. Horace Binney's *The Privilege of the Writ of Habeas Corpus under the Constitution* and Edward Ingersoll's response, *Personal Liberty and Martial Law: A Review of Some Pamphlets of the Day*, are reprinted in Frank Friedel, ed., *Union Pamphlets of the Civil War, 1861–1865*, 2 vols. (Cambridge, MA., 1967), 1:199–294.

118   Irwin F. Greenberg, "Charles Ingersoll: An Aristocrat as Copperhead," *Pennsylvania Magazine of History and Biography* 93 (April 1969): 197; Schankman (*sic*), "William B. Reed and the Civil War," *Pennsylvania History* 39 (October 1971): 463–4.

and was reprinted in ten newspapers. Historian Allan Nevins judged it worth a "half dozen brigades" to the Union cause.[119]

The use of pamphlets to stir public opinion became widespread in 1863 with the emergence of publication societies. Using techniques perfected by the American Tract Society and various abolitionist groups, these bodies provided the funding for large printings and the direction necessary to target specific audiences. Three publication societies, all formed in February 1863, dominated the field. The pro-war Loyal Publication Society and the Democratic-sponsored Society for the Diffusion of Political Knowledge were established in New York. The third, the Union League's Board of Publication, was based in Philadelphia. The Board of Publication soon boasted a twenty-seven-member board and a $35,000 treasury. During the war's final two years it became actively involved in aiding Governor Curtin's 1863 reelection and Lincoln's 1864 victory over McClellan. But the board's larger objective was to use its substantial resources to support the war effort nationwide. The board distributed pamphlets and broadsides to all corners of the Union, to men at the front, and to several Confederate regiments. During the conflict the Board published 102 pamphlets; in 1864 alone it distributed over 1 million copies. These efforts were often directed at certain interest groups. The board printed fifteen pamphlets and numerous broadsides in German. It distributed speeches by local Irish leaders to counteract the strong Democratic sentiment within the Irish community.[120]

Philadelphia's wartime printed propaganda, like her patriotic rituals, grew out of established traditions. Private pamphleteering had been used in America since before the Revolution, and antebellum reform groups had often used pamphlets to bring their cases to the public.[121] Even the refinement of these methods – specifically the concentration on particular ethnic groups – reflects the persistence of antebellum associational patterns. The continued partisan stances – and financial dependence on political parties – of most of the city's newspapers also mirrored antebellum patterns.[122]

In both their roles as distributors of pamphlets and as sponsors of

119 Joseph George, Jr., "Charles J. Stillé, 'Angels of Consolation,' " *Pennsylvania Magazine of History and Biography* 85 (July 1961): 306–15; Friedel, ed., *Union Pamphlets*, 1:381–403; and William Quentin Maxwell, *Lincoln's Fifth Wheel: The Political History of the United States Sanitary Commission* (New York, 1956), 345. Estimates of the total number of copies printed range from a quarter to a half million.
120 Friedel, ed., *Union Pamphlets*, 1:2–7; Whiteman, *Gentlemen in Crisis*, 29–34, 57–62, 82, 303, fn 57, 306, fn 16.
121 Friedel, ed., *Union Pamplets*, 1:1–3; Whiteman, *Gentlemen in Crisis*, 3.
122 Robinson, "The Dynamics of American Journalism from 1787 to 1865," *Pennsylvania Magazine of History and Biography* 61 (October 1937): 435–45.

civic ritual the members of the Union League pursued tasks traditionally performed by Philadelphia's elite. But though it followed
familiar paths, the league certainly expanded the use of patriotic
propaganda and made its own clubhouse a staple in Philadelphia's
ritual routine. In this sense the Union League is an example of a new
institution that emerged during the war years and remained to play a
prominent part in postwar Philadelphia's public life.

Philadelphia's peacetime rituals typically commemorated important dates, paid tribute to visiting dignitaries, or honored local
heroes. Those who organized and participated in these events generally expressed some version of patriotic nationalism. Although their
agendas may have differed, and citizens from different social strata
may have pursued distinct manners of celebration, these basic values
were shared. This continuity meant that despite the conflict's unique
tests, wartime rituals did not require new forms. And the broadly
shared goals ensured that private citizens would continue to keep the
rituals alive without substantial public direction.

5 *Help from the home front: Wartime voluntarism in Philadelphia*

The soldiers entertain a high regard for Philadelphia. Nowhere else that I have been are soldiers treated with so much consideration and respect as there. If rations are served to us there, it is of a quality good enough for the most fastidious, and that peculiar air, 'Good enough for soldiers,' seems to be entirely wanting among these benevolent people.[1]

All soldiers have a great love for [Philadelphia]. Every tired & hungry regiment that has marched through there, has been rested and fed, and treated with every attention which the kind hearts of the Quaker City could suggest, and this grateful care has been bestowed just as freely after three weary years, as when the first raw recruits passed through. I never have heard a soldier speak of it but with as much affection as he would of his own home.[2]

Such was Philadelphia's reputation among the Union soldiers. Men who marched through the city consistently sang its praises. Tired veterans lauded both Philadelphia's benevolent spirit and the well-oiled organizational machinery that its volunteers brought to their task.[3]

The various aspects of Philadelphia's wartime benevolence reveal the ways in which the conflict molded the city's responses to social need. First we will consider how Philadelphia's peacetime benevolent institutions fared during the war. Did the war's demands sap financial resources from established charities? Then we will turn to Philadelphia's war-related voluntarism. What options were available to benevolent-minded Philadelphians? Did the war push chari-

---

1 Emil Rosenblatt, ed., *Anti-Rebel: The Civil War Letters of Wilbur Fisk*, (Croton-on-Hudson, N.Y., 1983), 56.
2 Christopher Pennell to Migonne, 14 July 1864, Christopher Pennell Papers, Frost Library Archives, Amherst College, Amherst, Mass. Transcribed by Daniel Cohen.
3 See also George T. Stevens, *Three Years in the Sixth Corps*, (1866; reprint ed. Alexandria, Va. 1984), 5–6.

117

table citizens onto new terrain or were old structures merely expanded to meet new requirements? The membership of these benevolent organizations, and the personal histories of a few volunteers, will improve our understanding of how this new organizational web touched life in Philadelphia. The following chapter will expand on these themes by focusing on a single event: the Great Sanitary Fair of 1864.

Peacetime benevolence in crisis

Philadelphia had over seventy benevolent societies on the eve of the war.[4] They varied in organization and funding, thus providing several models for wartime voluntarism. Some were run by a single gender group; others included men and women. Many were self-sufficient, depending on membership dues or patient fees. Others relied on contributions and were frequently buffeted by the winds of fiscal fortune.

Most antebellum organizations had modest aims. The Antediluvian Society's Infants' Clothing Association was limited to twenty women, chosen by election, who met every few weeks to sew clothing for children. The small group, founded in 1814, relied on small membership subscriptions to cover its expenses.[5] The all-male Philadelphia Merchants' Fund Association was founded in 1854 to provide confidential relief for merchants who had fallen on hard times. In 1861 the association had 114 life members who had paid $50 to the fund, and more than 400 annual members who gave $5 annually.[6] These two associations were similar in that they were restricted to a single sex, met infrequently, had carefully circumscribed goals, and sought little outside funding. Other single-gender organizations routinely turned to their counterparts for aid and advice. The women of the Indigent Widows' and Single Women's Society relied on local men for periodic advice and help in fund-raising; the men of the all-male Provident Society acknowledged that Phil-

4 Issac Collins and John Powell, *A List of Some of the Benevolent Institutions of the City of Philadelphia* (Philadelphia, 1859); Eudice Glassberg, "Philadelphians in Need: Client Experiences With Two Philadelphia Benevolent Societies, 1830–1880" (Ph.D diss., University of Pennsylvania, 1979), 4. For a discussion of the various antebellum benevolent societies see Robert H. Bremner, *The Public Good: Philanthropy & Welfare in the Civil War Era* (New York, 1980), 14–34.
5 "Glimpses into our Antediluvian Heritage," (typescript, 1957), Box 3, Papers of the Antediluvian Infants' Clothing Association, Historical Society of Pennsylvania, Philadelphia (hereafter HSP).
6 Philadelphia Merchants' Fund, *Seventh Annual Report* (Philadelphia, 1861).

adelphia's women were best able to identify the most worthy among the city's needy.[7]

The Infant School of Philadelphia, founded in 1827 to educate poor children, had an annual budget of about $1,000. The school was managed by twenty-five elected women, under the direction of five gentlemen.[8] A small body of men overseeing the activities of a group of women characterized many larger Philadelphia benevolent societies. The Union Benevolent Association (UBA), a far more ambitious organization, employed such a gender division. The UBA was a nonsectarian organization established in 1831 to promote moral reform among the needy by distributing material aid and instruction in temperance and industry. The UBA's Ladies' Branch was charged with visiting the poor at home, ascertaining their needs, and providing counsel and relief. The female "visitors" were overseen by an Executive Board of Gentlemen. During the five prewar years the UBA disbursed between $16,000 and $23,000 annually.[9]

Unlike the Benevolent Association, the Philadelphia Society for the Employment and Instruction of the Poor (PSEIP) was directed by a Board of Managers that included both men and women. But the Philadelphia Society, established in 1847 to improve "the conditions of unfortunate persons living in the southern limits of the city and Moyamensing," soon relegated its female managers to a small auxiliary board with strictly limited tasks.[10] In so doing, the PSEIP joined the Infant School and the UBA in defining benevolent roles according to gender.

The Civil War affected both the demands on charitable institutions and the resources available to them. Many changes stemmed from economic fluctuations, others were directly related to the war effort. In the months following secession the North's economy faced a crisis that rivaled the Panic of 1857. This created a sudden increase in Philadelphia's needy poor. Between January 1858 and December 1860, the city's monthly almshouse population never rose above 3,128. In February 1861 that figure jumped to 3,809. In 1861 the almshouse averaged about 300 more persons per month than

---

7 Indigent Widows' and Single Women's Society, *36th Annual Report* (Philadelphia, 1853); Provident Society, *35th Annual Report* (Philadelphia, 1859).
8 Minute Book, Papers of the Infant School of Philadelphia, HSP.
9 *Constitution of the Union Benevolent Association* (Philadelphia, 1831); Glassberg, "Philadelphians in Need," 147–51; Union Benevolent Association, *25th–29th Annual Reports* (Philadelphia, 1856–1860). The UBA also employed a paid agent who attended to administrative needs.
10 *Constitution of the Philadelphia Society for the Employment and Instruction of the Poor* (Philadelphia, 1847, 1852); Glassberg, "Philadelphians in Need,": 258, 272–4.

in the previous three years.[11] The Spring Garden Soup Kitchen, which dispensed food during the winter, had 1,338 applicants in 1860 and 3,054 in 1861.[12]

Even as demands rose, local benevolent institutions faced declining resources. The UBA, dependent on small donations, found that the economic crisis cut into its revenues. In 1861 the women made fewer visits than the year before and dispensed less money than since the mid-1850s. The managers of the Friends' Asylum for the Insane built a new building in 1859, put in gas lighting and did major painting and wallpapering in 1860, but could manage no capital improvements in 1861.[13]

New charitable societies were formed to help Philadelphia's needy through the crisis. In early 1861 a group composed largely of Quakers established the Central Soup Society of Philadelphia to provide for citizens "thrown out of employment by the derangement in . . . business affairs."[14] In Germantown the Women's Employment Society organized to distribute sewing to unemployed women.[15]

Soon the pendulum swung in the other direction; Philadelphia shifted into a wartime boom. Able-bodied workers found jobs readily available, and men of military age could earn increasingly large bounties for going to war. These changes reduced the traditional demands on the city's charities. In early 1862 the managers of the Central Employment Association, a Quaker body that produced work for sewing women, feared that the war would impede donations and increase the number of needy women. But they soon discovered that although donations declined, government jobs reduced the demands for their services.[16] By mid-1863 the monthly almshouse population had dropped below prewar levels, as had the lines at the Spring Garden Soup Society.[17]

During the middle war years, many of Philadelphia's benevolent institutions appeared to be unaffected by events on the battlefield. In February 1862 the Board of Managers of the Magdalen Society (for the reformation of fallen women) reported a budget deficiency of $148 and appealed for more contributions. But the 1863 report opti-

11 Philadelphia Guardians of the Poor, *Statements of Accounts* (Philadelphia, 1859), 12; (1860), 24; (1861), 16; Guardians of the Poor, *Annual Statement* (Philadelphia, 1862), 46, See also Chapter 12.
12 Spring Garden Soup Society, "Registry of Applicants," HSP.
13 UBA, *25th through 30th Annual Reports* (1856 through 1861); Friends' Asylum for the Insane, *43rd through 45th Annual Reports* (1860 through 1862).
14 *Friends' Intelligencer*, 19 January 1861, 712–3 (hereafter *FI*).
15 *Germantown Telegraph*, 26 February, 24 December 1862 (hereafter *GT*).
16 FI, 19 January 1861, 17 January 1863, 713; 714.
17 Guardians of the Poor, *Annual Statement* (1864), 13; Spring Garden Soup Society, "Registry of Applicants."

mistically noted that "amid the many exciting events of the past year the quiet and good order of the family have been preserved."[18] In the same year the Indigent Widows' and Single Women's Society announced that "the storm which has broken over our unhappy country has, as yet, been unfelt within the walls of the Society's Asylum."[19] The UBA's board of managers admitted in October 1862 to a "general uncertainty of the future," but a year later they were pleased to report that "anxious fears for our country . . . have given way to brighter skies."[20]

The war did indirectly disrupt the financial fortunes of some institutions. In late 1862 the UBA's managers attributed declining donations to the competition from war-related voluntarism and the unusual economic pressures on customary donors. In early 1863 the Merchants' Fund blamed the economy for decreasing subscriptions.[21] The managers of the Friends' Asylum for the Insane reported in 1863 that "financial embarrassments arising from the general stagnation of trade" had placed some patients' families behind in their payments. They also warned that the "novelty" of war-related charities "[might shut] out from the view of some, that class of our afflicted fellow creatures for whom we speak."[22]

Although the war subjected Philadelphia's charities to a few tough years, most muddled through successfully. Initially, the Indigent Widows' and Single Women's Society relied on income from investments, which "relieved them from the necessity of urging their claims upon the charitable." But in 1864 the society's managers were forced to reach into their own pockets. In 1865 they reported that the past year had brought "more than ordinary trial," forcing them to spend $4,669 of the society's permanent investments. The society celebrated the war's end and its fiftieth anniversary in 1866 with a fund-raising drive that netted over $7,000.[23] Wartime discomforts had

18 "Minutes of the Board of Managers," Annual Report – February 1862, Box 3, vol. VI, Papers of the Magdalen Society of Philadelphia, HSP; Board of Managers of the Magdalen Society, *Annual Report* (Philadelphia, 1864), 3. (Note: both citations are from the Magdalen Society's annual reports, but only the second was taken from the published version.).
19 Managers of the Indigent Widows' and Single Women's Society of Philadelphia, *47th Annual Report* (Philadelphia, 1864).
20 UBA, *31st Annual Report, 32nd Annual Report* (1862, 1863).
21 UBA, *31st Annual Report* (1862), 5; Philadelphia Merchants' Fund, *Ninth Annual Report* (Philadelphia, 1863), 5–8.
22 Friends' Asylum for the Insane, *46th and 48th Annual Reports* (1863), 20; (1865), 23. The Female Association of Philadelphia for the Relief of the Sick and Infirm Poor with Clothing also complained that money usually earmarked for their organization had "been absorbed in new and more popular charities," forcing them to cut back their activities in the face of increased prices. See *FI*, 16 January 1864, 713.
23 Indigent Widows' and Single Womens' Society, *48th Annual Report, 49th Annual Report* (1865, 1866).

forced a series of progressively radical adjustments, but never led the society to deviate from its established goals and structure.

In early 1865 the managers of the Magdalen Society reported that although "prices are so far above an ordinary level" they had, through "the economical organization of the house," managed to maintain a healthy balance.[24] And as the war's end appeared in sight, John M. Atwood, president of the Merchants' Fund, wrote:

> It may justly be accounted a matter of gratitude to God that in the midst of the terrible Civil War which inflicts our land, our benevolent institutions have been prosecuting their various objects without interruption and that their members may peacefully assemble in their annual meetings, as we do now, to encourage each other for future efforts.[25]

As Atwood implied, the Civil War presented Philadelphia's benevolent institutions with an obstruction to overcome. Any required adjustments were of a financial sort. Donors and volunteers might have divided their energies between established charities and war-related activities, but the city's benevolent institutions generally survived in unaltered form.[26]

Wartime prosperity and military recruitment changed the makeup of Philadelphia's needy population. In her analysis of UBA clients in the Spring Garden District, Eudice Glassberg found a decline in the share of skilled workers among wartime recipients, reflecting the increased availability of skilled jobs but also indicating that those benefits were not shared equally by unskilled workers.[27] The war also kept down the number of needy young men. During the war years only about half of the lodgers in the PSEIP's House of Industry were between seventeen and thirty-six. In the five postwar years that proportion rose to 72 percent.

In early 1861 the managers of the Indigent Widows' and Single Women's Society noted that they had been forced to turn away applicants and predicted that "the numbers of these will increase from among those whose sole support may be taken from them by the casualties of the war." A year later they called for donations, noting that "the calamities of the recent war now render this appeal one as well to patriotism as to benevolence."[29] In the late 1850s about

24 "Minutes of the Board of Managers," Annual Report – January 1865, Papers of the Magdalen Society.
25 Philadelphia Merchants' Fund, *Eleventh Annual Report* (1865), 6.
26 For a discussion of national patterns see Bremner, *The Public Good*, 79–90.
27 Glassberg, "Philadelphians in Need," 206–7.
28 Glassberg, "Philadelphians in Need," 206–7; 303–5. The House of Industry figures include women, who made up about 25 percent of the population between 1861 and 1865.
29 Indigent Widows' and Single Women's Society, *47th Annual Report, 48th Annual Reports* (1864, 1865).

14 percent of the lodgers in the PSEIP's House of Industry were women. During the war that figure rose to 25 percent, but in the five postwar years it plummeted to 5 percent.[30] In 1858 1,594 white male and 970 white female vagrants were incarcerated in the Philadelphia House of Corrections; in 1863 the prison held only 545 white men but 1,152 white women.[31] The war took indigent men off the streets but was a dislocating force for some of the women left behind.

The needy class of dependents created by enlistment led to adjustments by the city's public and private charities.[32] On April 22, 1861, the City Council appropriated $125,000 for the families of volunteers and appointed a commission, composed of Mayor Alexander Henry, the city solicitor, the presidents of the Select and Common councils, and three leading citizens, to administer the fund. By August 1865 the commission had made over a million separate payments totaling $2.6 million.[33] Two days after the initial appropriation, the Benevolent Association voted to offer "the services of the Lady visitors . . . as distributors of the funds now being collected for the families of volunteers."[34] This response to the needs of the families of volunteers was typical of wartime Philadelphia. Although payments per family were small, about $1.50 a week in 1861, they were substantially larger than outdoor relief for other families,[35] reflecting the pull of patriotism and the need to assure potential volunteers that their loved ones would be cared for. The use of leading citizens to help direct the fund, and of the UBA to distribute aid, reveals the government's continued dependence on private institutions.

In addition to its disbursal of public monies, the Commission for the Relief of Families of Volunteers ran a private fund to help meet needs – particularly burial expenses – not covered by the council's appropriation. The commission collected nearly $18,000 from fifty-eight donors for this purpose, including $4,000 from the city's lawyers, $55 from the Second Police District, several hundred dollars from the proceeds of musical entertainments at the Academy of Music, and donations from a number of Philadelphia insurance companies, from the St. George's Society (a body of local Englishmen), and private individuals. This fund, like the bounty fund drives and other war-related charities, succeeded because it tapped into existing

---

30 Glassberg, "Philadelphians in Need," 288, 296–7.
31 Priscilla Ferguson Clement, "The Transformation of the Wandering Poor in Nineteenth-Century Philadelphia," in *Walking to Work: Tramps in America, 1790–1935*, ed. Eric H. Monkkonen (Lincoln, Nebr., 1984), 66.
32 See Bremner, *The Public Good*, 74–6.
33 *Report of the Commision . . . for the Relief of Families of Philadelphia Volunteers* (Philadelphia, 1865); J. Thomas Scharf and Thompson Westcott, 3 vols., *History of Philadelphia* (Philadelphia, 1884), 1:762.
34 UBA, Minutes, 24 April 1861, HSP.
35 Glassberg, "Philadelphians in Need," 117.

associational links and familiar fund-raising methods. Although the war created new causes, it did not require new organizational solutions.[36]

Other individuals and groups created their own institutions to aid the families of volunteers. In the war's first weeks the city's Germans met and formed a fifty-person committee to solicit contributions for the families of German volunteers. Jenks and Sons, a major Philadelphia manufacturer, offered to provide for the families of any of its employees who enlisted. On April 22, a Germantown druggist announced that he would give free medicine to the families of local volunteers. These and similar organizations, reflecting the continued pull of ethnic, religious, occupational, and neighborhood ties, typified later efforts to care for the volunteers and their families.[37]

The slaves freed by the Union army placed further demands on the North's benevolent citizens.[38] In early 1862 Philadelphia's Quakers joined groups in Boston and New York to collect money for freed blacks in Port Royal, South Carolina. That spring, ninety of the "contrabands" arrived from Harper's Ferry and dozens of Philadelphians offered them homes and jobs.[39] When Washington, D. C., abolished slavery, the *Friends' Intelligencer* declared that "it behooves the people of the North who have suffered the least in the past from the degrading system" to help the freedmen develop their "new latent capacities."[40]

Anna Ferris's response to the new refugees embodies local attitudes:

> Went [to Philadelphia] this afternoon [March 11, 1862] to Ann Wharton's "Contraband party" to sew for the fugitive slaves at Port Royal . . . Everybody seems willing to respond to the appeal made by these helpless outcasts, for aid & succor of every kind, & I hope something available may be done for their physical & moral improvement [41]

Several local groups arose to aid former slaves. One of these, the Women's Association of Philadelphia for the Relief of the Freedman,

36 "Account book," Fund for the Relief of the Families of the Philadelphia Volunteers, Papers of Peter Williamson, Treasurer, HSP; Scharf and Westcott, *History of Philadelphia*, 1:762.
37 Scharf and Westcott, *History of Philadelphia*, 1:762; PL, 22 April 1861.
38 Bremner, *The Public Good*, 91–110.
39 FI, 29 March 1862; GT, 2 April 1862; Scharf and Westcott, *History of Philadelphia*, 1:795–6. For a discussion of Philadelphia's role in the Port Royal experiment see James M. McPherson, *The Struggle for Equality* (Princeton, 1964), 160–9.
40 FI, 26 April 1862, 105.
41 Harold B. Hancock, ed., "The Civil War Diaries of Anna M. Ferris," *Delaware History* 9 (April 1961): 235.

was organized in April 1862 to sew clothing and raise money. In 1864 the Friends' group collected more than $10,000 and supplied thirty-four sewing circles.[42] In December 1863 three to four hundred Philadelphia Quakers formed the Friends' Association for the Aid and Elevation of the Freedmen that collected funds to distribute to other groups and also sent teachers to the South.[43]

When benevolent whites began to form aid societies in 1862, the *Christian Recorder*, Philadelphia's leading black newspaper, encouraged its readers to "give to this cause . . . We recommend our people and churches to take hold of this matter, and appoint good and efficient committees who may be responsible."[44] The members of the Mother Bethel Church created a Contraband Committee to answer this call. On February 24, 1863, a large group of Philadelphia blacks met at the Oak Square Baptist Church and formed the Union Freedman's Relief Association of West Philadelphia.[45]

Before the Civil War a wide range of private benevolent organizations aided Philadelphia's needy. The economic dislocation brought on by the war posed problems for many benevolent societies. Charities had to compete with war-related organizations for decreasing donations, inflation raised operating expenses, and families of patients had trouble meeting hospital payments. Some groups temporarily curtailed their activities or turned to new fund-raising devices, but the traditional array of charitable societies survived the conflict unchanged.

The war also changed the makeup of the needy population. Fewer men required aid, but enlistment left many women unprovided for. Wartime dislocations also produced hundreds of needy refugees and freed slaves. The older charities adjusted to meet part of this changing demand. New organizations formed to fill specific requirements. These were often private initiatives, following familiar models. And where the city government became involved, as in the Committee for the Relief of Families of Volunteers, private citizens still played important roles in collecting and distributing monies. In

42 *FI*, 10 January 1863, 695; 17 January 1863, 713–14; 9 May 1863, 137–8; 5 November 1864, 553; 23 April 1864, 105.
43 After two years of cooperation, these organizations merged in December 1865 under the Friends' Association name. *FI*, 9 January 1864, 696; 16 January 1864, 212; 3 June 1865, 196–8; 25 November 1865, 606.
44 James M. McPherson, *The Negro's Civil War* (New York, 1965), 133. Quoting the *Christian Recorder*, 22 March 1862.
45 McPherson, *The Negro's Civil War*, 135; *Christian Recorder*, 7 March 1863. For a good discussion of wartime aid to "refugees, Contrabands, and freedmen" see Bremner, *The Public Good*, 91–110.

short, Philadelphia's complex benevolent system successfully evolved to meet the citizenry's changing needs.[46]

Benevolence and the war effort

The Civil War soldier faced a greater danger from disease than from enemy bullets. In the war's first months members of New York City society, led by Unitarian minister Henry W. Bellows, recognized this danger and organized the United States Sanitary Commission (USSC). Although military authorities initially disapproved of civilians on the battlefield, the Sanitary Commission soon gained official recognition and blossomed into an enormous national organization, bringing clothing and medical supplies to Union field hospitals. A sick or wounded soldier was also fair game for other national benevolent organizations, the most important being the YMCA-sponsored United States Christian Commission (USCC). From its formation in November 1861 the Christian Commission rivaled the Sanitary Commission. The USSC was strongly conservative and militantly secular; the Christian Commission's volunteers dispensed Bibles and evangelical enthusiasm with their blankets and bandages.[47]

As national organizations formed to meet wartime demands, these two benevolent commissions lend support to the view that the conflict helped "centralize" life. But most of the actual fund-raising was accomplished by fairly autonomous local units. In the winter of 1862–3 a handful of Philadelphia women formed the Pennsylvania Branch of the Sanitary Commission, replacing the more confined Philadelphia Sanitary Commission. During the next two years they established 350 affiliates across the state and collected nearly $300,000 worth of cash and supplies.[48] Although these smaller groups worked as part of a national structure, their actions were quite localized, depending on traditional ties for their success.

46 Often the war's victims benefited from spontaneous benevolence without any formal structure. In March 1865 George Stuart, president of the USCC, collected $1,000 from eleven leading Philadelphians to aid a Columbia, SC, woman "having lost all her property and having been very loyal and kind to our prisoners." See "Subscription Book," George Hay Stuart Papers, Manuscript Room, Library of Congress, MMC-3248.

47 See George M. Fredrickson, *The Inner Civil War: Northern Intellectuals and the Crisis of the Union* (New York, 1965, 1968), 98–112; Robert H. Bremner, "The Impact of the Civil War on Philanthropy and Social Welfare," *Civil War History* 12 (September 1966): 293–307; Bremner, *The Public Good*, 39–46, 54–62; William Q. Maxwell, *Lincoln's Fifth Wheel: The Sanitary Commission* (New York, 1956); [Linus Pierpont Brockett], *The Philanthropic Results of the War in America* (New York, 1864), 33–76, 96–164.

48 Linus Pierpont Brockett and Mary C. Vaughan, *Women's Work in the Civil War: A Record of Heroism, Patriots and Patience* (Philadelphia, 1867), 596–606.

Even though the two national relief commissions played the most important roles in directing aid to the front, dozens of unaffiliated groups also collected money and goods to be distributed by their own representatives.[49] A number of such organizations were formed in Philadelphia. The Ladies Association for Soldiers' Relief ("Soldiers' Aid") began operations in July 1862, when a group of West Philadelphia women banded together to help wounded soldiers in nearby Satterlee Hospital. The organization grew into a large body, with affiliate societies across the state and representatives in the field for most of the war.[50] The Ladies' Aid Society began with an April 1861 meeting at Reverend H. G. Boardman's church. After the first battle of Bull Run they sent Mrs. John Harris to the front to deliver articles they had collected, and for the next four years Mrs. Harris was a familiar face to Pennsylvania volunteers on dozens of battlefields.[51]

Other groups concentrated on the large military population at home. Soldiers bound for the South entered Philadelphia's Navy Yard by steamboat and waited at the foot of Washington Avenue for railroad cars to take them on their journey. In the early days of the war, families from the area worked in small groups to provide the waiting men with refreshments. These efforts blossomed into the carefully orchestrated "Refreshment Saloon Movement" that provided 1,300,000 meals to hungry soldiers.[52]

Wilbur Fisk, a Vermont volunteer fresh from the Virginia battlefields, described a September 1863 trip through Philadelphia:

> It was near midnight when we got to Philadelphia. At the Cooper Shop Volunteer Refreshment Saloon we found a glorious supper prepared expressly for us. Bread of an excellent quality, butter and cheese, pickles, hot coffee, and all that a hungry soldier need ask. It was not soldiers' living at all; it was good enough for a first class hotel. This is the first place of the kind that has been opened since the war broke out, and I doubt if any more modern, can surpass it.[53]

Nearly two years later, these Vermont soldiers returned to Philadelphia, and the correspondent had the opportunity to sample the city's other refreshment saloon:

49 Bremner, *The Public Good*, 65–9.
50 Ladies' Association for Soldiers' Relief, *First and Second Annual Reports* (Philadelphia, 1864) (bound in a single volume); Frank Moore, *Women of the War: Their Heroism and Self-Sacrifice* (Hartford, 1866), 38–41, 585.
51 Moore, *Women of the War*, 176–7; Scharf and Westcott, *History of Philadelphia*, 1:762; [Brockett], *Philanthropic Results*, 85–6.
52 Frank H. Taylor, *Philadelphia in the Civil War, 1861–1865* (Philadelphia, 1913), 206–12.
53 Rosenblatt, ed., *Anti-Rebel*, 152, letter dated 25 September 1863.

The Cooper Shop Volunteer Refreshment Saloon. Detail of chromo-lithograph by M. H. Traubel, 1862. Library Company of Philadelphia.

Interior of the Union Volunteer Refreshment Saloon. Albumen-print stereograph by Robert Newell. Library Company of Philadelphia.

. . . the regiment arrived at Philadelphia, where we were treated to another excellent meal at the Union Volunteer Refreshment Saloon, – a place that many a soldier will hold in grateful remembrance. The boys think there is no place for a soldier like Philadelphia, and indeed, we have good reason to think so, for there is nothing in the world that will make a hungry man so grateful as to give him a good dinner. . . . We are usually tired enough and hungry when we get to Philadelphia . . . to appreciate to the fullest extent, the kindness of the ladies and gentlemen who have, during all this war, contributed so bountifully for the comfort of the soldiers passing through there.[54]

Fisk observed that "Americans may well be proud of their nation when the common people show a spirit like this, through a long relentless war."[55]

The Union Volunteer Refreshment Saloon was born in May 1861 when Barzilini S. Brown, a coffee and fruit dealer, leased a boat shop on Swanson Street to serve as a central distribution point. Under its fifty-six member-committee, the Union expanded until it could feed a full regiment at a time.[56] While Brown and his companions fed soldiers at the Union, an equally enthusiastic group performed the same task at an old cooper shop on Otsego Street, a short distance away. The Cooper Shop Refreshment Saloon, which also began in May 1861, first entertained soldiers at a long, roughly made table, but the enterprise grew quickly and could soon feed 1,000 soldiers in an hour. The two refreshment saloons remained fiercely independent, seeking no city or state funds and refusing to combine their operations. But they did agree to coordinate their efforts so that incoming troops were evenly divided between the two groups.[57]

Between fifty and sixty men and women were active in each refreshment saloon; dozens more contributed to a lesser degree.[58] But these efforts were only the tip of the iceberg. In 1862 a group of citizens observed that Philadelphia was filling up with recuperating soldiers and established the Soldiers' Reading Room. This organization restored a dilapidated building near Twentieth and Market and stocked it with nearly 2,000 books and periodicals. Soon they added a kitchen. Later, volunteers taught night school.[59]

54 Rosenblatt, ed., *Anti-Rebel*, 340.
55 Rosenblatt, ed., *Anti-Rebel*, 341.
56 Taylor, *Philadelphia in the Civil War*, 108.
57 James Moore, *History of the Cooper Shop Volunteer Refreshment Saloon*, (Philadelphia, 1866), 13–20, 24–26; [Brockett], *Philanthropic Results*, 28–31; "Scrapbook," Manuscript Room, Library of Congress, MMC-2446.
58 Taylor, *Philadelphia in the Civil War*, 207, 211.
59 Soldiers' Reading Room, *First and Second Annual Reports* (Philadelphia, 1863, 1864).

As new needs arose, the Cooper Shop expanded. Finding that many soldiers were too ill to travel, the Refreshment Committee opened a small hospital. Later, responding to the needs of the growing population of disabled veterans, the managers built the Cooper Shop Soldiers Home.[60] In late 1862 another group of men and women established the Citizens' Volunteer Hospital Association to greet soldiers bound for Philadelphia's hospitals. In its first year it received 30,000 men; in the second year, with kitchen facilities available, it provided over 125,000 meals.[61]

In the course of the war 157,000 soldiers and sailors were treated in Philadelphia's hospitals. The city's hospital system, like its other voluntary activities, evolved slowly, combining public and private initiatives. The 11-bed Cooper Shop Hospital and the 400-bed Citizens' Volunteer Hospital were privately run institutions that filled gaps in an established system of nearly two dozen military hospitals with roughly 6,000 beds. These military hospitals emerged as soon as casualties began streaming into Philadelphia. Some had been private hospitals before the war, others were built to meet the demand. In many cases military and civil authorities and private citizens combined their energies to convert warehouses, taverns, and public halls into temporary hospitals.[62] In Germantown the local Home Guard financed the transformation of the Town Hall into a hospital.[63] Soon the war's centralizing forces came into play. In June 1862 a new 2,860-bed hospital opened its doors in West Philadelphia; Chestnut Hill's 4,000-bed Mower U. S. General Hospital followed in January 1863. With the emergence of these large government institutions, most of the smaller hospitals closed or returned to private care.

As the hospital wards filled, women's groups formed to bring food, clothing, and comfort to the patients. The Soldiers' Aid and Ladies' Aid societies were particularly active, both locally and in the field. The Quakers' Penn Relief Association of Philadelphia, formed in July 1862, quickly expanded into a substantial organization serving at least fifteen local hospitals and sending clothing, supplies, and occasional representatives to Southern hospitals and to the Union's

60 Moore, *History of the Cooper Shop*, 36–59, 94–6; Cooper Shop Soldiers Home of Philadelphia, *First Report* (Philadelphia, 1865).
61 Citizens' Volunteer Hospital Association, *1st Annual Report, 2nd Annual Report, 3rd Annual Report* (Philadelphia, 1863, 1864, 1865); [Brockett], *Philanthropic Results*, 89–92.
62 Taylor, *Philadelphia in the Civil War*, 224–35. See *GT,* 2 July 1862 for a long list of such adjustments.
63 For the remainder of the war the *Germantown Telegraph* published frequent reports on its progress, reflecting a widely shared community interest in their benevolent institutions See *GT,* 25 June 1862 and *passim*.

The Citizens' Volunteer Hospital. Photograph by Frederick Gutekunst, c. 1864. Library Company of Philadelphia.

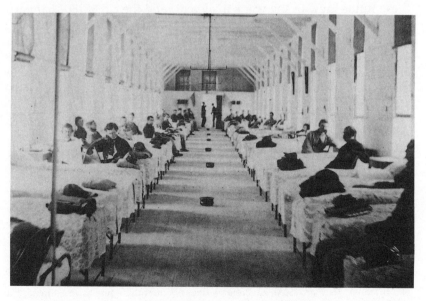

"A Ward," Chestnut Hill Army Hospital (Mower). Photograph by John Moran, c. 1862. Library Company of Phildelphia.

"floating hospitals."[64] Other smaller bodies formed around specific hospitals. The ladies of the Cheltenham Episcopal Church established their own society in 1862 to attend to the eighty patients in nearby Kensington Hospital.[65] This web of voluntary associations distributed hundreds of volunteers, mostly women, through Philadelphia's hospital system, assuring that private benevolence would have a hand in even the largest government hospitals.[66]

It is impossible to measure the amount of money donated to the various wartime voluntary societies. In 1864 Linus P. Brockett estimated that $24 million had been contributed for the "care and comfort of soldiers" and over $1 million more to funds for freedmen, refugees, and "sufferers abroad" who had felt the weight of the Civil War. Of the $24 million in aid to soldiers, Brockett estimated that $8.2 million went to the Sanitary and Christian Commissions; $4 million to supplies sent west, $425,000 to various religious organizations; and $160,000 to old soldiers' homes. Individual donations directly to soldiers accounted for another $2.5 million in money and supplies. Philadelphians took part in each of these benevolent concerns, but there is no way to determine the City of Brotherly Love's exact share.

Brockett also estimated that by 1864 Philadelphia's two refreshment saloons had taken in roughly $112,000; the Ladies' Aid Society had earned $229,000; the local branch of the Sanitary Commission, $135,000; and the Volunteer Hospital Association, $23,000.[67] Each of these funds grew in the war's final year, and the city's 1864 Sanitary Fair added more than $1 million to that total. By war's end these local efforts, excluding the fair, had probably netted close to $1 per capita (Philadelphia's population in 1864 was slightly over 600,000). The receipts from the fair nearly doubled that amount. Donations directly to the various national organizations probably raised the figure substantially.

Robert Bremner has noted that there are "[n]o reliable estimates of . . . private gifts and bequests to religious, charitable, and benevolent causes" during the antebellum years. He went on to offer the purely "conjectural" figure of $1 per capita for the 1850s.[68] Mea-

---

64 Penn Relief Association, *Semiannual Report* (Philadelphia, 1862); *1st Annual Report, 2nd Annual Report, 3rd Annual Report* (Philadelphia, 1863, 1864, 1865). These are stored in a bound volume of printed pamphlets at the HSP under the title, *Reports of the Penn Relief Association of Philadelphia.*
65 *GT,* 27 August 1862.
66 One estimate has $2.2 million in supplies donated to the hospitals in New York, Philadelphia, and Washington, D.C. [Brockett], *Philanthropic Results,* 89.
67 [Brockett], *Philanthropic Results,* 156–60.
68 Bremner, *The Public Good,* 23. Bremner does not offer this figure as an estimate, but as a point of comparison with public expenditures.

sured against such a standard, Philadelphia's war-related fund-raising was quite successful, especially when we remember that the city's older charities also managed to survive the conflict. But the city's greatest benevolent contribution cannot be measured by returns on ledger sheets, but by the long hours devoted to sewing clothing, cooking food, and ministering to wounded soldiers.

Continuity and change in wartime benevolence

Although the war years witnessed a dramatic increase in the level of voluntary activity, the fundamental form of Philadelphia's phil-anthropic organizations did not change. Antebellum America's be-nevolent structure included both national and local organizations, reflected both religious and nonsectarian goals, and addressed both immediate and long-term needs.[69] War-related activities exhibited a similar diversity. The wartime societies' memberships, organizational structures, and financing also followed established patterns.

As Northern men flocked to fill volunteer regiments or to man Home Guard companies, the women left behind dominated the war-related voluntary societies.[70] Anne Firor Scott has argued that their "long apprenticeship in [antebellum] voluntary associations" left women better prepared to orchestrate affairs on the home front than their male counterparts were to fight on the battlefield.[71] The evi-dence from Philadelphia generally supports the conclusion that the war provided women with new benevolent outlets. But it does not suggest that female volunteers enjoyed a concomitant rise in author-ity within these voluntary societies.

As in the prewar years, many wartime organizations were small bodies staffed exclusively by women. The bylaws of the Ladies' Association for Soldiers Relief specifically stated that aside from their Honorary Secretary its members were to be women. Like the peace-time women's groups, each volunteer was to pay a small fee to help finance the association's activities.[72] Other womens' societies were more substantial. The membership of the Penn Relief Association had seven officers and an eighteen-woman executive committee.[73] The Ladies' Aid Society and Germantown's Field Hospital Association

69 Bremner, *The Public Good,* 14–22.
70 See Mary Elizabeth Massey, *Bonnet Brigades* (New York, 1966); Agatha Young, *The Women and the Crisis* (New York, 1959); Moore, *Women of the War.*
71 Anne Firor Scott, "On Seeing and Not Seeing: A Case of Historical Invisibility," *Journal of American History* 71 (June 1984):12.
72 Ladies' Association for Soldiers' Relief, *First and Second Annual Reports* (1884).
73 Penn Relief Association, *Semiannual Report* (1862).

were also exclusively women's organizations, although the latter relied on male agents to help distribute goods to the front.[74]

Other organizations followed the pattern of the UBA, relying on female volunteers directed by a male board of managers. Both the Sanitary and Christian Commissions used female volunteers, but men held the dominant national and local positions.[75] Philadelphia's Citizens' Volunteer Hospital Association had 110 "lady members" who visited the hospital and 25 male managers.[76] Men and women were equally active in establishing the two refreshment saloons, but the officers of both bodies were exclusively male.[77]

As wartime demands on Philadelphia's benevolence grew, the city's women played an enlarged role, and perhaps there was a concomitant expansion in the public perception of that role.[78] But most of the larger new local and national societies followed antebellum practices by placing a corps of female volunteers under the supervision of a handful of male directors.[79] These structures suggest that although wartime benevolence drew attention to the North's charitable women, it did little to change established gender roles.[80]

The Civil War brought Philadelphians from varied social strata into the voluntaristic fold. The men and women in Philadelphia's peacetime philanthropic societies generally came from the city's leisure classes. The officers and male managers of both the Union Benevolent Association and the Philadelphia Society were almost all merchants, manufacturers, and professionals from Philadelphia's "benevolent society complex," and the women in these organizations typically were married to men of the same class.[81] The war years saw

74 Moore, *Women of the War*, 176–7; *GT*, 29 July 1863. The Ladies' Aid Society sent Mrs. John Harris into the field.
75 Scott, "On Seeing and Not Seeing," 12.
76 Citizens' Volunteer Hospital Association, *2nd Annual Report* (1864).
77 Moore, *History of the Cooper Shop*, 14–15.
78 See Septima M. Collis, *A Woman's War Record, 1861–1865* (New York, 1889), 12–13. Several contemporary books highlighted the sacrifices of Northern women. See L. P. Brockett and Mary C. Vaughan, *Women's Work in the Civil War: A Record of Heroism, Patriotism, and Patience* (Philadelphia, 1867); Moore, *Women of the War*; [Brockett], *Philanthropic Results*.
79 In addition to those already noted, the Cooper Shop Soldiers Home distinguished between "managers" and "lady managers" and the male volunteers at the Sixteenth and Filbert Street Soldiers' Home were called the "Board of Officers" and the female workers were called the "Board of Lady Visitors." See Taylor, *Philadelphia in the Civil War*, 213–15.
80 This issue will be pursued more fully in Chapter 6.
81 The twenty-six officers and managers of the UBA at the 20 October 1863 annual meeting included eight merchants, six attorneys and doctors, three executives, and one gentleman, broker, shipper, conveyancer, notary, apothecary, and sawmaker. Two managers could not be matched against the city directory. Minutes, UBA; *McElroy's City Directory*. For a more detailed analysis of the UBA's managerial body and a similar study of the PSEIP see Eudice Glassberg, "Philadelphians in Need," 153–6, 269–70, 370–4.

a continuation of this pattern. The men who directed the Sanitary Commission were "members of the highest social class."[82] The Philadelphians who staffed the local organizations, like antebellum philanthropic leaders, came from the city's elite. The seventeen-man Committee for the Relief of Families of Volunteers included Mayor Henry, the city solicitor, four "gentlemen," two attorneys, and famed locomotive builder M. W. Baldwin. The City Bounty Commission consisted of three merchants, one attorney, and one gentleman. Local commissions followed the same pattern – the Twenty-third Ward Enlistment Association was headed by a publisher, a flour merchant, and a coal and wood dealer.[83]

But the men and women who worked at the refreshment saloons and hospitals were a more diverse lot. Some of the women in the Penn Relief Association were married to men from prestigious professions. But the twenty husbands (out of twenty-five) who could be identified included three small retailers, a machinist, a bricklayer, a salesman, and two clerks.[84] The Cooper Shop Refreshment Saloon volunteers were an even more varied body. Of fifty-eight identifiable men, three were gentlemen, nine were manufacturers or merchants, five were executives, doctors, attorneys, or religious leaders, one was a shipbuilder, and one an importer. At the other end of the spectrum, four of the Cooper Shop volunteers were clerks and bookkeepers and twenty were skilled craftsmen.[85]

The Southwark refreshment saloons evolved out of one of the many associational links that tied mid-nineteenth-century Philadelphia together: the neighborhood. The small church groups that sent visitors and gifts to local hospitals combined religious and community ties. Even the membership of the citywide Penn Relief Association came from a relatively circumscribed section of Philadelphia. Eighteen of twenty-six officers and managers lived in the city's Twelfth, Thirteenth, or Fourteenth wards to the north and the rest lived nearby.[86] In this fashion Philadelphia's wartime benevolent bodies joined recruiting drives and ward bounty fund commissions in relying on neighborhood associational ties to spur voluntarism.

82 Fredrickson, *Inner Civil War*, 99.
83 Commission for the Relief of Families of Philadelphia Volunteers, *Report*; City Bounty Fund Commission, *Report* (Philadelphia, 1865); Enlistment Association of the Twenty-third Ward, *Report* (Philadelphia, 1866); McElroy's City Directories (1861, 1866).
84 Penn Relief Association, *Semiannual Report* (1862); *McElroy's City Directories* (1861, 1866). Two of the initial officers and executive committee members were married to gentlemen, five to merchants, two to wool brokers, and one each to an attorney, a publisher, and a foundry owner.
85 Moore, *History of the Cooper Shop*, *passim*; *McElroy's City Directories*, (1861, 1866).
86 Penn Relief Association, *Semiannual Report* (1862).

The benevolent activities of a small segment of the Philadelphia community – the Jewish population – suggests the range of wartime voluntarism. At the outset of the conflict many Jewish women's groups formed their own independent bodies to sew, roll bandages, or collect money for soldiers. Established organizations, such as the Female Hebrew Benevolent Society and the Hebrew Relief Association, collected funds and supplies to be distributed to the families of Philadelphia's Jewish volunteers. The women of the Mikveh Israel Congregation established the 250-member Ladies Hebrew Association for the Relief of Sick and Wounded Soldiers to support the Sanitary Commission. And when the Sanitary Commission held its Great Central Fair in 1864, a handful of Jewish women formed a sewing circle to prepare needlework for sale.

Jewish Philadelphians thus worked through independent emergency organizations, prewar benevolent groups, a separate committee affiliated with a national organization, and independent bodies aiding the Central Fair. What was more, Philadelphia's Jewish groups donated money to the volunteer refreshment saloons and other wartime charities.[87] Even those Philadelphians who chose to volunteer with their coreligionists found a wide array of options open to them. Philadelphia blacks also acted both through larger organizations and their own bodies. In June 1863 the Union Volunteer Refreshment Saloon invited the black community to visit its buildings for a fund-raising drive. Later, black women in West Philadelphia collected money to buy food for black soldiers at the Summit House Hospital.[88]

The wartime benevolent societies also employed familiar funding practices. Peacetime charitable organizations generally relied on a combination of membership fees, voluntary subscriptions, and charges to clients. Often they solicited voluntary donations indirectly, through festive fund-raising events. According to Robert Bremner, "in good times and bad, charitable groups sponsored fairs, festivals, balls, and benefit concerts." Catherine Clinton adds that during the war "women used many of the innovations developed during the antislavery days, such as the sponsoring of fairs and bazaars, to raise funds."[89]

---

87 Bertram W. Korn, *American Jewry and the Civil War* (New York, 1951), 100–8.
88 CR, 13 June 1863, 3 September 1864.
89 Bremner, *The Public Good*, 20; Catherine Clinton, *The Other Civil War: American Women in the Nineteenth Century* (New York, 1984), 81. For a good account of an 1842 fund-raising fair see Isaac Mickle, *A Gentleman of Much Promise: The Diary of Isaac Mickle, 1837–1845*, ed. Philip English Mackey, 2 vols. (Philadelphia, 1977), 2:254, 291, 293–5. See also Lori Ginzberg, "Women and the Work of Benevolence: Morality and Politics in the Northern United States, 1820–1885," (Ph.D diss., Yale University, 1985), 81.

Philadelphia's wartime benevolent societies continued to rely on contributions. Local businessmen frequently volunteered lumber or empty buildings to provide emergency establishments. And in the first feverish months of the war donations came easily to supplement what the volunteers themselves provided. But soon fairs of all descriptions dotted the city's calendar. In June 1862 the Cooper's Shop Hospital and Soldiers' Home held a fair at Philadelphia's Concert Hall. A few weeks later a group of Spring Alley children raised $80 for the Refreshment Saloon Hospital at a "fair of fruit, flowers, etc." In September several young Germantown ladies earned $105 for the local hospital, and for the next few months other small bodies followed suit, earning money for various voluntary organizations. The following spring a women's group announced a series of "grand demonstrations in behalf of the invalided soldiers." In June 1863 several Grand Floral fairs were held, the largest raising over $10,000.[90]

In its first year the Penn Relief Association collected $3,768, largely in gifts of under $25, and earned $210 from two small fairs. The next year the association took in only 120 new contributions (as compared to more than 320 gifts the previous year) but it raised over $3,500 – or well over half of the year's returns – from two large fairs. The receipts from these two events kept the association in operation through the end of the war, as new donations dropped off dramatically.[91] The Cooper Shop Soldiers' Home relied almost exclusively on fairs to finance its first two years of operation.[92] The Citizens' Volunteer Hospital Association's first year's receipts included 29 gifts from institutions, 400 donations from individuals, and returns from 115 fairs. In the war's final seven months the association collected only forty-five donations but took in $3,352 from a single fair.[93] The Soldiers' Reading Room supplemented small donations of money and books with the proceeds from several concerts.[94]

These fund-raising patterns reflect an evolution in Philadelphia's wartime benevolent institutions. During the war's early years, hundreds of citizens were willing to donate small sums. This reliance on

90 GT, 5, 18, June 3, 17, September, October 1862; 25 March, 15 April, 27 May, 10 June 1863; Letter from S. Montgomery Bond to W. P. Cresson, Box 21, Cresson Papers, HSP. See also "Scrapbook," Manuscript room, Library of Congress; Mary Dreer diary, 16 August 1865, Papers of Edwin Greble, Manuscript room, Library of Congress.
91 Penn Relief Association, *1st–3rd Annual Reports* (1863, 1864, 1865). In its third year the Association received only 140 gifts totaling $1,800.
92 Cooper Shop Soldiers' Home, *First Report* (1865).
93 Citizens' Volunteer Hospital Association, *3rd Annual Report* (1865).
94 Soldiers' Reading Room, *First Annual Report* (1863). The soldiers also paid small sums for their meals.

small gifts mirrored the experiences of the major peacetime charities.[95] But when the patriotic wave subsided, charitable institutions could no longer rely on small donations. This led wartime philanthropies to adopt the familiar peacetime fund-raising devices of fairs and concerts. The conflict did not require that Philadelphians create new fund-raising techniques. But it did lead them to rely more heavily on festive affairs that would stir the patriotic sentiments of a war-weary citizenry.

Benevolent Philadelphians

A wide array of voluntary opportunities was open to Civil War Philadelphians. National and local organizations collected money to buy supplies. Local groups fed soldiers passing through and cared for the wounded who stayed behind. Philadelphians also could choose from among dozens of more personal avenues ranging from sewing for friends and relatives at the front to dropping off a bushel basket of oranges at the nearest hospital. How did Philadelphians respond to this "web of opportunity"?

Philadelphia's volunteers included a handful of self-sacrificing "angels of mercy." Mrs. John Harris was the sickly wife of a Philadelphia doctor who served in the field for over three years. Mrs. Mary Morris Husband, the wife of a wealthy lawyer, cooked for soldiers at the Wood Street Hospital until one of her two soldier sons was wounded. For the next three years she tended to the wounded in the field. The Soldiers' Aid Society was represented on the battlefields by Mrs. Mary A. Brady, an Irish-born mother of five who made five long trips with the army before she died in 1864. Anna Marie Ross, an elderly woman when the war began, served as an active volunteer at the Cooper Shop and later became the Principal of the refreshment saloon's hospital.[96]

Other Philadelphians aided the cause in smaller ways. Sarah Butler Wister's brief wartime diary reveals how one young woman's excitement was translated into voluntaristic activity. The outbreak of

95 In 1850–1 the UBA took in $158.60 in gifts of under $5, 246 gifts of between $5 and $29, and only three donations of over $100; in 1857–8 339 of 417 gifts received by the PSEIP were for under $25. See Glassberg, "Philadelphians in Need," 160, 280.
96 In the summer of 1863 Ross began collecting money for a Soldiers' Home, but she died on the day the new home was dedicated. See Brockett and Vaughan, *Women's Work*, 149–60, 287–98; F. Moore, *Women of the War*, 37–53, 176–212, 313–32, 342–6; J. Moore, *History of the Cooper Shop*, 36–59. For a detailed discussion of Annie Wharton, one of the war's benevolent martyrs, see Fisher, *A Philadelphia Perspective*, 464, entry of 30 December 1863.

hostilities divided Sarah from her Copperhead father, Pierce Butler, and many of her other pro-Southern friends and relatives.[97] On April 20, 1861, her husband Owen began drilling with a local company, while Sarah wondered if her father, who was in the South, had enlisted in the Confederacy. On the twenty-second, with patriotic fervor absorbing her attention, Sarah "stopped to see Mrs. [Alexander] Henry about the sewing for the soldiers, but nothing [had] been set on foot yet."

A few days later, as more and more of her male friends joined the military ranks, this mother of an infant son went "to the room where the ladies were sewing for the soldiers." She reported that "[t]hey had been a week endeavoring to get up some organizations & held three meetings, & finally given it up being told that there were more hands than were wanted." But "some more energetic than the rest . . . went to town . . . saw the Quarter Master, & got a quantity of coats & haversacks & the girls were busy upon them all day." Sarah "found them in the Temperance Hall . . . some forty or fifty, all as busy as bees" and "sewed for a couple of hours." That afternoon she "went again for an hour . . . to the sewing room" and on April 29 she "went up to the Sewing Room . . . & sewed for about two hours."

During the next few months Wister continued to aid various voluntary causes. On May 13 she "went up to the room where the ladies [were] sewing for Miss Dix's Hospital Department." There a volunteer "set [her] at sewing pillowcases." The following week Sarah and her husband drove to Germantown to deliver a $50 subscription for Missouri and Kentucky Volunteers "who will fight for the Union but have neither arms [n]or clothing."[98]

Sarah Wister's diary suggests how a socially active, upper-class woman incorporated voluntarism into her everyday routine. The first months of the war disrupted, but did not shatter, her ordinary life. Although her husband's drilling and newspaper accounts from the field were the subjects of many of her diary entries, she devoted most of her energy to running her household, visiting friends, writing letters, and other familiar tasks. But frequently in those early months she found time to sew for the soldiers. Like many of Philadelphia's fashionable women, Sarah Wister helped only sporadically rather than making a substantial commitment.

---

97 See Fanny Kemble Wister, "Sarah Butler Wister's Civil War Diary," *Pennsylvania Magazine of History and Biography* 102 (July 1978): 271–327.
98 Wister, "Sarah Butler Wister's Civil War Diary," 280–1, entries of 20, 21 April 1861, 287–8, 26 April 1861, 290, 29 April 1861, 297–8, 13 May 1861, 299, 20, 21 May 1861.

But other volunteers made benevolent activities a major part of their lives. When the war began Susan R. Trautwine was an unmarried young woman who spent her days sewing, reading, and visiting friends.[99] Her diary rarely looked beyond the bounds of her own world until, after Lincoln's inauguration in March 1861, she expressed "great hope" that the new president would prove "a blessing to this distracted people."[100] A month later, as the crisis at Fort Sumter reached its climax, national concerns played a far more important role in Trautwine's daily record. When a group of ladies met to discuss "some arrangements for working with the soldiers," she joined them.[101] Nothing seemed to come from those efforts so she returned to her familiar routine. But by February 1862 she had begun sewing for military hospitals, and on one occasion collected "articles for the soldiers who are wounded . . . near Ft. Donelson."[102]

From these tentative beginnings, Susan slowly expanded her voluntary activity. In June 1862 she joined a group of ladies at her church who were "going to work for the Hospitals." From then on, sewing meetings became a part of Susan's weekly schedule. In late July she went with her aunt to deliver clothing to a local military hospital, "seeing the inside of one for the first time." In early October the Sunday School where she taught held a fair "for the relief of sick & wounded soldiers."[103]

Until this time, Susan Trautwine's contributions to the cause had been from a distance; her volunteer hours had been spent sewing with friends. In November 1862 she visited Turner's Lane Hospital, embarking on a new chapter in her philanthropic history. For the next two and a half years she visited Turner's Lane every week to teach Bible class, lead prayer meetings, or simply talk with wounded soldiers.[104] Susan Trautwine's Monday visits to Turner's Lane and her weekly sewing circle did not satisfy her; she "sh'd like to be engaged in some more extended work of usefulness." To this end she added occasional visits to the Soldiers' Reading Room, Chestnut Hill Hospital, and Filbert Hospital to her busy schedule. She frequently took special interest in a single patient, returning to his bedside several times a week to improve his English or discuss religion. In

99   Susan R. Trautwine MacManus diary, HSP. The diary gives no age, but her best friend turned twenty on June 25, 1861.
100 MacManus diary, 4 March 1861.
101 MacManus diary, 6, 9 May 1861.
102 MacManus diary, 18 February 1862.
103 MacManus diary, 20 June, 11, 25 July, 8, 9, 16 September, 1, 2, 3, 8 October, 3 November 1862.
104 MacManus diary, 18 November 1862.

June 1863 she added a Wednesday shift at Turner's Lane to her weekly routine.[105]

The following March Trautwine "attended a business meeting . . . on the Retail Dry Goods branch of the great Sanitary Fair to be held in June." For the next several months she and her best friend, Lizzie, made regular excursions "seeking subscriptions for their branch." But this short-term activity did not detract from Susan's regular hospital work. And at least twice in May she and Lizzie attended meetings of the "Ladies' Christian Commission, auxiliary to the Christian Commission."[106]

During the last year of the war Susan continued her many voluntary activities. In early May 1865 the Turner's Lane Monday Committee held its last meeting: "We gave away our pictures – and sadly came away – For two & a half years we have worked together so pleasantly. Could I have known how soon all would end I would have worked twice as hard while I had the chance." But this did not end her philanthropic work. In June she visited the Episcopal Hospital and in the next several weeks she returned to the wards about three times a week.[107]

Susan Trautwine's wartime benevolent work evolved from attendance at an occasional meeting to a nearly full-time occupation. These activities reflected both her desire to become involved in the events of the day and her strong religious convictions that found an ideal outlet in the hospital wards.

Trautwine's enthusiastic voluntarism owed much to her position as an unmarried woman with few responsibilities. Other Philadelphians accommodated their wartime voluntarism into more crowded personal schedules. For the first two years of the war Amanda Marklee, an independent businesswoman, divided her memorandum book in two. The left side of each page was reserved for war news, the right side for comments on her personal life and business fortunes. As a reporter of large events, she took note of visits by local women to the battlefield: "Who could Minister to them so well as women? Oh *women* this is thy sphere." But in her private world Marklee remained concerned with more mundane matters, noting that "business is still dull" or that "cotton and woolen goods have advanced very much."[108]

105 MacManus diary, 6, 31 January, 11 February, 9 May, 10 June 1863 and *passim*. In October 1864 Trautwine added Thursday afternoon Bible classes at the Filbert Street Hospital to her schedule. See her entry of 19 October 1864. Also see Chapter 3 for a discussion of Trautwine's relationships with several of her patients.
106 MacManus diary, 31 March, 16, 19, 20 April, 4, 31 May 1864.
107 MacManus diary, 8 May, 20 June 1865 and *passim*.
108 Amanda Marklee diary, 23 July, 17 August, 8 October 1861, HSP.

The split between the "left" and "right" sides of Marklee's wartime consciousness was temporarily bridged in early 1862. On February 13 she recorded that "[s]everal hundred sick soldiers have been
brought to the city and are comfortably attended by suitable nurses."
A few days later, the personal side of her diary tells us, Marklee
found her "sympathy very much aroused for the sick," and she began
collecting items for the wounded volunteers. This venture was followed by twice-weekly sewing meetings held at her home. On March
7 the newly active Marklee visited the Ladies' Aid Society and the
Cooper Shop, and came away "delighted with the arrangements."[109]
    Marklee's interest in aiding the soldiers survived into the early
spring of 1863. A March 15 visit to the hospital at Twenty-second and
Wood touched her greatly – she "wept" when she saw "these Poor
men throw[n] in to such a Home." The following week she had
another "Ladies meeting to sew for the soldiers." But thereafter,
whereas the "public" side of her journal carefully recorded the war
news, the other side became an irregular record of personal melancholy and sickness with no further reference to voluntarism.[110]
    Whereas Miss Marklee came slowly to voluntarism and
apparently sustained her efforts only for a short time, Katherine
Brinley Wharton was involved in relief efforts throughout the war,
perhaps spurred on by the actions of her husband and brother. The
wife of prominent attorney Henry Wharton and the mother of three
young children by war's end, she was raised in a world where
political discussions were a male province. In late January 1861 she
recorded in her diary that Henry sat her down and "gave [her] a long
political lect[ure]." During the following year she began setting down
national events and local responses.[111] The war soon took on more
personal meaning when her brother Godfrey departed with the
Washington Grays and her husband began drilling with the Home
Guard.[112]
    In the summer of 1861, following the birth to her second child,
Mrs. Wharton "went to the room where they do army work" to pick
up material to sew for the soldiers.[113] That September, after Henry
told her that he might soon enter active service, she visited the
Soldiers' Relief Association where she "[worked] as desperately as
[she] could, to get some of the weight off [her] heart."[114] When

109 Marklee diary, 13 February, 7 March 1862.
110 Marklee diary, 15, 20 November 1862.
111 See Chapter 1.
112 Katherine Brinley Wharton diary, 23 January, 10, 20 April, 6 May 1861, HSP. See
     Chapter 3 for a discussion of Henry's and Godfrey's military activities.
113 Wharton diary, 19 June 1862.
114 Wharton diary, 19 September 1862.

brother Godfrey home on a twenty-day leave, Katherine went to the organizational meeting of the Sanitary Commission's Pennsylvania Branch and signed up for a Wednesday sewing circle and as a Thursday Volunteer Aid. She commented: "I hope I shall have time for both. I am very anxious to be useful in this way."[115] In the months to come she regularly visited the "Sanitary," where she sewed, packed boxes, or made out lists. But these quietly useful tasks did not satisfy her, for in late June 1863 – with Lee's troops threatening – she wrote: "Oh how I wish I were a man & able to do something – it is so hard to wait & do nothing."[116]

That winter Katherine Wharton had her third child. She took an extended break from her diary and, one supposes, from her voluntary activities. But by late 1864 she had returned to a regular pattern of relief work, including meetings of the Soldiers' Aid Society, visits to the local hospital, and volunteer work at the soldiers' reading room.[117] Like Susan Trautwine, Katherine Wharton pursued several forms of wartime voluntary work. However Katherine had to incorporate her activities into a more crowded home life.

Many Philadelphia diarists devoted long hours to soldiers' relief. Some only mentioned their activities in passing, or for just a few months. Often their actions responded to pressing needs. Long after the war one German immigrant remembered how news of the 1862 invasion left her "good mama . . . [so] entirely beside herself with anxiety" that she "decided to go with [her] sewing maid to the Hospital at Turner's Lane with victuals for the soldiers' there."[118] In July 1863 Sarah Richardson took a day off from her wax flower business to go down to the "Hall" to aid the "Poor sick and wounded soldiers" who had just arrived from recent battles.[119] Mary Ashhurst was not a regular volunteer but on Thanksgiving Day 1864 she finished her own meal and joined her daughter in helping serve a special dinner at the Soldiers' Reading Room. When wounded troops arrived in the city in April 1865, Mrs. Ashhurst spent a few hours in one of the hospitals.[120]

Many Philadelphians, and Quakers in particular, split their energies between aiding soldiers and assisting the growing number of escaped slaves or "contrabands." Sarah Richardson first noted that

115 Wharton diary, 19 February 1863.
116 Wharton diary, 23 September 1862; 7, 18 May; 29 June 1863.
117 Wharton diary, 14, 31 October, 11, 29 December 1863.
118 But as the woman "stood in front of the second bed, that of a German soldier, she suffered a stroke from which she . . . never fully recovered." Memoirs of Ernestine Hochgesang Schaeffer," typescript translation by Alice Rodman Ecroyd, HSP.
119 Sarah Richardson diary, 30 July 1863, Quaker Collection, Swarthmore College Library, Swarthmore, PA.
120 Mary Ashhurst diary, 24 December 1864; 3 April 1865.

she had been "sewing for the Aid Society" in the summer of 1862. In the next four months she returned to the Soldiers' Aid six times, sewed clothing for a "poor colored family," and provided shelter for a homeless contraband. In the following years her diary included periodic mention of afternoons spent sewing for soldiers or contrabands.[121] Young housewife Anna Spencer had little time for benevolent activities. But on one afternoon she "packed up [a] box for the soldiers" and on another occasion she "went to sew at the Ladies Aid Society." In late 1863 the Quaker woman became heavily involved in sewing clothing for escaped slaves, and through most of the following summer she made weekly visits to a sewing circle set up for them.[122]

Patriotic voluntary activities helped to instill a sense of civic pride, even among those who personally sacrificed nothing. Curious Philadelphians frequently visited the city's hospitals and refreshment saloons. When two guests arrived for a few days, patternmaker Washington Penrose took them to visit the military hospital at Sixth and Master.[123] In February 1863 young Sallie Stokes went with several of her girl friends to see the Chestnut Hill Hospital.[124] After a monthly meeting, Mrs. Caleb Wistar and her Quaker neighbor went "to look through the Broad Street Hospital," and came away satisfied that "they were all comfortably clean."[125] In June 1862 Joseph Boggs Beale went to a Fair "in aid of the Cooper Shop Refreshment Committee & some hospital for the soldiers." The following day he attended a concert at the Academy of Music "in aid of the soldiers." Later he spent the day at a "strawberry & Floral Fair at the Union Refreshment Saloon."[126] Such festive events kept the voluntary societies in the public eye while filling their coffers for future activities.

121 Richardson diary, 30 April, 24 July, 12, 14 August, 18 September, 21, 30 October, 13 November, 4 December 1862; 18 February, 28 May 1863; 2, 3, 30 March 1864. For at least a short time in 1864 Richardson belonged to a weekly sewing circle for freedmen.
122 Anna Spencer diary, 4 March 1862; 14 February 1863 and *passim*, Haverford College Library, Haverford, PA. Quakers William Eyre and Jacob Elfreth, Jr., apparently did not become involved in any war-related philanthropy, but they both attended 1864 meetings to aid the contrabands. See William Eyre diary, 4, 17 February 1864, Haverford; Jacob Elfreth, Jr., diary, 19 April 1864, Haverford.
123 Washington Penrose diary, 26 January 1863, HSP.
124 Sallie Stokes diary, 4 February 1863; HSP.
125 Mrs. Wistar to Caleb Cresson Wistar, 4 March 1862, Caleb Cresson Wistar Papers, Box 2, F-2, HSP. See also Joseph Boggs Beale diary, 11 September 1862, HSP.
126 Beale diary, 9, 10, 19, June 1862.

Conclusions

The philanthropic challenges posed by the Civil War pushed charitable Philadelphians into numerous institutional and personal adjustments. But the long peacetime benevolent tradition left the city well prepared to respond to the new demands. Aid to traveling volunteers, wounded soldiers, families of volunteers, homeless contrabands, and other needy victims followed patterns established in the antebellum years. Although the new demand, grafted as it was on enduring benevolent requirements, expanded the burden, it did not produce a concomitant shift toward new methods or centralized structures. When concerned Philadelphians gathered in churches or meeting halls to plan war-related charitable ventures, they formed new societies, but they usually followed familiar organizational lines. And when turning to the public for financial assistance, they relied on traditional fund-raising methods. Many of these local societies drew their support from specific geographic or institutional subsets of Philadelphia's population. However, this pattern changed in the spring of 1864, when the entire city came together to hold its Great Central Fair. The next chapter will examine how that enormous event fit into Philadelphia's benevolent tradition.

6 The great sanitary fair of 1864: Exercise in civic voluntarism

Between June 7 and June 28, 1864 Philadelphia held its Great Central Fair, which raised over a million dollars to renew the Sanitary Commission's dwindling funds. In the process its citizens recapitulated their previous home front activities, but on a much grander scale. Some individuals threw themselves into the fair from its planning stages; others contributed mightily but irregularly; still more made a small donation to the effort; and finally, thousands "contributed" by paying their admission fee.

The Sanitary Commission's "Fair Movement" began in the fall of 1863 with a ten-day fund-raising fair for its Northwestern Branch. This event earned nearly $80,000, a figure that was almost doubled a month later in Boston. Soon Cincinnati, Cleveland, Albany, Brooklyn, and St. Louis followed suit. New York's Metropolitan Fair, which cleared $1,183,505 in April 1864, was the most successful of these ventures, topping Philadelphia's total by about $150,000.[1] By the end of the war roughly thirty Sanitary Fairs had been held, earning about $4.4 million. Some raised money for regional branches of the USSC; others collected funds for supplies to be sent to the home troops through Sanitary Commission channels. Over 80 percent of the $2.7 million funneled directly into the USSC's coffers came from the New York and Philadelphia fairs.

The Great Central Fair extended established practices. As we have seen, fairs had long been a favorite fund-raising device for civic charities. The Sanitary Fairs melded entertainment and benevolence in events that eclipsed anything in antebellum America's experience in both scope and design. Like London's Great Exhibition of 1851, these fairs enticed their visitors with a wide array of manufacturing and artistic exhibits displaying local accomplishments and foreign curiosities. But whereas Prince Albert conceived of the Crystal Palace to showcase the marvels of industrial progress, the Sanitary Fairs' organizers devoted their ingenuity to creating diverse methods for extracting money from their guests' pockets. And whereas the Crys-

---

1 For a good general background on the "Fair Movement" see William Y. Thompson, "Sanitary Fairs of the Civil War," *Civil War History* 4 (March 1958): 51–67. Also see Philadelphia's official fair newspaper, *Our Daily Fare, passim* (hereafter *ODF*).

tal Palace survived as a monument to England's achievements, Philadelphia tore down its fair buildings as soon as they had performed their patriotic purpose.[2]

The initial impetus for Philadelphia's fair came from the Union League, which passed a resolution on January 11, 1864, asking the Philadelphia Associates of the Sanitary Commission to join the nationwide fair movement. Two weeks later the Philadelphia Associates voted to put on a fair under the supervision of an executive committee headed by prominent merchant John Welsh.[3] On February 20 the Committee announced the coming fair in the city's newspapers. Its open letter set the tone for the ensuing months:

> We call on every workshop, factory, and mill for a specimen of the best thing it can turn out; on every artist, great and small, for one of his creations; on all loyal women for the exercise of their taste and industry; on farmers, for the products of their fields and dairies. The miner, the naturalist, the man of science, the traveler, can each send something that can at the very least be converted into a blanket that will warm, and may save from death, some one soldier who the government supplies have failed to reach.

The organizers sought to touch everyone by emphasizing that no gift would be too small.[4]

The Philadelphia Central Fair's organizational structure was enormously complex, with nearly a hundred different committees ranging from the 5-member Committee on Gas Fixtures to the roughly 330-strong Committee on Schools.[5] Most committees were organized around a particular craft or branch of manufacturing. A member visited each of the city's establishments in search of donations of cash or goods to be sold at the fair. Other committees solicited flowers, fruit, handmade items, or "Relics, Curiosities, and Autographs." Tea merchant L. Montgomery Bond's Committee on Labor, Income, and Revenue adopted a massive advertising campaign encouraging all Philadelphians to donate the proceeds of a day's work to the fair.[6] The Ladies' Central Committee on Musical

---

2   Thompson, "Sanitary Fairs of the Civil War," 51–67; R. K. Webb, *Modern England* (New York, 1968), 278.
3   *ODF*, 20 June 1864.
4   Furness Scrapbook, Box 1, H. H. Furness Papers, Historical Society of Pennsylvania, Philadelphia (hereafter HSP).
5   *List of Committee Members of the Great Central Fair for the U.S. Sanitary Commission held in Philadelphia* (Philadelphia, 1864). A copy of this pamphlet is in Box 5, F-1, Furness Papers.
6   *ODF*, 11 September 1865. This particular appeal, which netted $247,500, seems to have been a Philadelphia innovation. For a good description of Bond's visit to the Manayunk woolen mills see *Germantown Telegraph*, 15 June 1864 (hereafter *GT*).

"Buildings of the Great Central Fair, In aid of the U.S. Sanitary Commission, Logan Square." Lithograph by P. S. Duval & Son after James Queen, 1864. Library Company of Philadelphia.

Entertainment followed a more familiar route by holding a series of small concerts. The fair itself generated money in various ways. Ticket sales earned nearly $180,000. Many visitors purchased items on sale at the committees' tables. Others spent $2 to vote on the recipient of one of the elegant gifts donated to the fair.[7]

The 15,000 Philadelphians who attended the fair's opening ceremonies on June 7 viewed a scene that was "possibly the most imposing ever witnessed in Philadelphia." The procession to the speaker's stand consisted of the Executive Committee, which included many of Philadelphia's most prominent citizens; Mayor Alexander Henry; Bishop Matthew Simpson of the Methodist Episcopal Church, who represented President Lincoln during the ceremonies; selected clergy; the governors of Pennsylvania, Delaware, and New Jersey; General George Cadwalader and other military officers; members of the Select and Common Councils; and several committee chairmen.[8] The inauguration was marred by the sudden collapse of a hastily installed platform for the choir, but after a few moments of confusion the program continued.[9] In his welcoming speech Mayor Henry applauded the work of both national relief commissions that jointly provided "wide channels through which the oil and wine of soothing kindness and of strengthening cheer may flow." Governor Andrew

7 These included a sword valued at $2,500, presented to a Union general; a silver trumpet for the most popular fire company; and a bonnet for the city's favorite general's wife. See *ODF, passim*.
8 *ODF*, 8 June 1864. The inaugural ceremonies were actually less crowded than on later days because the admission price was doubled to $2 for the day.
9 *Evening Bulletin*, 8 June 1864 (hereafter *EB*).

"Union Avenue, Great Central Fair." Albumen-print stereograph by
A. Watson, 1864. Library Company of Philadelphia.

Curtin added that "the work before this great nation is big enough for
all."[10]

   The visitor to the fair who made his way to the center of the
Logan Square buildings found his senses assaulted by the smells from
two large, canvas-domed rotundas housing the restaurant and the
Horticultural Department.[11] From that central location Union Avenue
presented a crowded display of tables and flags for half a block in
each direction. On the far side of the Horticultural Department stood

10   *ODF*, 8 June 1864.
11   This description of the fair is from a combination of newspaper and diary accounts,
     ODF, and *Godey's Lady's Book*, August 1864, 179, September, 1864, 262. A map of
     the fairgrounds is on the frontispiece of the bound collection of *ODF* printed
     immediately following the fair.

the 500-foot Art Gallery, featuring what was repeatedly referred to as the greatest collection of its kind in the nation's history.[12]

If the guest walked down Union Avenue, towards the Eighteenth Street exit, she passed displays of items such as umbrellas, glassware, and shoes, and hallways on either side housed the exhibits built by the city's public and private schools and the popular arms and trophies room. At the end of Union Avenue she could choose between the Delaware display to her right and the New Jersey effort on the left. If she chose to turn around and meander back up Union Avenue, she found some of the most crowded exhibits, including the Pennsylvania Kitchen, the William Penn Parlor, the machinery and shipbuilding display, and a wide assortment of sewing machines. To do the fair justice required several days, and many Philadelphians returned frequently during the fair's three weeks.

On June 16 President and Mrs. Abraham Lincoln visited the city. Their short stay brought together public officeholders, civic leaders, and spontaneous crowds in a series of celebrations that reflected the complexity of both the war's rituals and its voluntarism. The Lincolns' carriage rolled down Broad Street toward the Continental Hotel amidst cheering throngs, enjoying a general business holiday, massed on both sides.[13] The Union League House rippled with flags, and League members played a key role in welcoming the recently renominated president. In the afternoon several members joined the City Council at the Continental to escort Lincoln to the fair. The president pleased the throng by vowing to fight for three more years if necessary and by applauding all the "voluntary contributions, given freely, zealously, and earnestly, on top of all the disturbances of business, the taxation, and burdens [of] the war." That evening Lincoln visited the Union League and the National Union Club, before returning to the Continental around midnight. There he found more crowds, a band, and a fireworks display.[14]

The fair's doors stayed open for a week after Lincoln's visit, but some of the novelty had worn off and many of the best displays had been picked clean. On June 27 and 28 the committee lowered ticket prices from $1 to $.25, but still the turnout remained low. By the time

12 Nicholas B. Wainwright, ed., A Philadelphia Perspective: the Diary of Sidney George Fisher (Philadelphia, 1967), 474, entry of 12 June 1864.
13 For descriptions of Lincoln's visit see ODF, 17, 18 June 1864; Maxwell Whiteman, Gentlemen in Crisis: The First Century of the Union League of Philadelphia, 1862–1962 (Philadelphia, 1975), 71–6; EB, 16, 17, 18 June 1864; and Kenneth A. Bernard, Lincoln and the Music of the Civil War (Caldwell, Idaho, 1966), 216–18.
14 EB, 16, 17 June 1864; Bernard, Lincoln and the Music, 217. For diarists' responses to Lincoln's visit, see Jacob Elfreth, Jr., diary, 17, 18 June 1864, Haverford, College Library, Haverford, Pa.; Anna Mercer LaRoche diary, undated, Rare Books Collection, Columbia University.

the fair closed 253,924 ticketholders had made an estimated 442,658 visits, an average of 29,510 each day.[15]

Committees and volunteers

The Sanitary Fair's administrative structure, with over 3,000 members in nearly a hundred committees, was both a continuation and an expansion of established patterns of benevolent organization. One of the first orders of business for the Executive Committee was to recruit committee chairs. The burden of chairing a committee was great, and more than forty nominees refused to serve.[16] Nevertheless, the Executive Committee enlisted many of Philadelphia's business leaders. J. B. Lippincott headed up the Committee on Book Publishers, Booksellers, and Bookbinders; David S. Brown, one of the region's largest textile manufacturers, chaired the Wholesale Dry Goods Committee; William J. Horstmann, the proprietor of the city's foremost military uniform and regalia establishment, led the Committee on Military Goods.[17]

It was up to the chairs to form their own committees.[18] In a letter to Mrs. Thomas P. James, the chairwoman of the Relics, Curiosities, and Autographs' Committee of Women, Emily G. Vaux declined to serve but revealed something of the process of committee formation:

> Do not think me wanting in patriotism . . . but you will doubtless be surprised to hear that I do not intend to take any active part in the Fair; I feel that I am entirely unsuited to the various duties which an acceptance of an appointment involves – and while many ladies are 'dying' to be nominated, it would be wrong for me to take the place of those who could be of *real* use![19]

The individual committees adopted quite different structures. The members of the Ladies' Committee on Boots, Shoes, and Leather visited stores individually, only meeting periodically to report their progress and to discuss plans for decorating their display. The official list includes twenty-six women on the committee, but the minutes show that only three came to all six meetings, thirteen came to four or more, and two never attended.[20] The minutes of the Women's Com-

15 *EB*, 25 June 1864; *ODF*, 11 September 1865.
16 Furness Papers.
17 *List of Committee Members*.
18 For a good description of the experiences of a committee chairman see the "Autobiography of William F. Miskey," 58, HSP.
19 Vaux added that she had already refused similar offers from several other committees. Emily Vaux to Mrs. James, Box 1, F-1, USSC and Fair Papers, HSP.
20 Ladies' Committee of Boots, Shoes, and Leather–Account Book and Minutes, Box 1, Furness Papers. Despite this poor attendance record, the committee collected $1,517.15 in cash, 12 morocco skins, and a wide assortment of shoes.

THE GREAT CENTRAL FAIR

To be held in Philadelphia, June 1864

COMMITTEE ON BOOTS, SHOES AND LEATHER.

WE, the undersigned, in making an appeal to all Boot and Shoe Manufacturers and Dealers, for contributions in material or money to the GREAT CENTRAL FAIR to be held early in June, feel that it is only necessary to allude to the wants of the SANITARY COMMISSION, in order to secure your generous and hearty co-operation.

The sufferings of our gallant soldiers in the field will, in all probability, be greatly increased during the coming summer campaign, and will demand the most energetic and unceasing efforts on the part of those whose privilege it is to live under a Government so nobly sustained.

Let each one then, do his or her part right generously, and by liberal donations, not only show a deep gratitude for so many past blessings in the security of life, home, and property, but help to make this Department of the FAIR one of the most profitable as well as useful.

Personal applications will be made as early as possible by the Committee, and it is earnestly hoped that they will meet with a cordial response. It is requested that all contributions shall be accompanied by an invoice of the goods, in order that they may be promptly acknowledged. Goods of all kinds should be sent to

SAMUEL BAUGH,

Care of A. R. McHENRY, No. 112 Walnut Street,

marked with the contributor's name and the price at which they are to be sold.

SAMUEL BAUGH, *Chairman.*

129 South Second Street.

LADIES' COMMITTEE.

MISS NIXON, *Chairman of Ladies' Committee,* 1703 Spruce Street.
MISS N. DUNLAP, *Secretary,* 218 Washington Square.
MRS. F. GREEN, *Treasurer,* 106 South Delaware Avenue.

MRS. WILLIAM CROTHERS, 1015 Arch St.	MRS. J. L. BISPHAM, 411 South 8th St.
MRS. S. E. STOKES, 832 Pine St.	MRS. A. C. CATTELL, 32 North Third St.
MISS A. H. STOKES, "	MRS. HENRY REED, 1706 Pine St.
MRS. SAMUEL BAUGH, 2025 Chestnut St.	MRS. M. A. TRIMBLE, 727 South 10th St.
MRS. DR. CONDIE, 237 Catharine St.	MISS JAMES, 110 South 21st St.
MRS. J. V. VANDERBILT, 2006 Wallace St.	MRS. W. POWELL, Second St.
MRS. HENRY DAVIS, 1436 Poplar St.	MISS STARR, 1414 Arch St.
MISS A. NIXON, 1703 Spruce St.	MRS. JUDSON, 1135 Spruce St.
MRS. HUGH DAVIDS, 261 South 4th St.	MISS BRINGHURST, 1704 Chestnut St.
MISS M. A. WETHERILL, 348 South 4th St.	MRS. A. G. GAW, 3303 Arch St.

MRS. W. W. PAUL, 1821 Chestnut St.

GENTLEMEN'S COMMITTEE.

CHARLES D. REED, 438 Market St.	PAUL GRAFF, 426 Market St.
W. W. PAUL, 623 Market St.	JOHN SAUNDERS, 34 North Fourth St.
EDWIN A. HENDRY, 55 North 3d St.	THOMAS MILES, 49 South Fourth St.
ANTHONY SEIBERLICH, 224 Carters Alley.	LEONARD BENKERT, 716 Chestnut St.
CHARLES K. THAYER, 417 Commerce St.	A. A. SHUMWAY, 221 Market St.
SAMUEL B. JONES, 429 North Third St.	MICHAEL G. PEIPER, 31 North 3d St.

HENRY WIREMAN, S. W. cor. 6th and Buttonwood St.

Broadside distributed by the Great Central Fair's Committee on Boots, Shoes and Leather. Most committees produces similar announcements. Library Company of Philadelphia.

mittee of the Children's Department of Toys and Small Wares reveal a far more complex infrastructure. Initially, this group of thirty-three women split into six subcommittees to visit local dealers. Later, they formed seven topical subcommittees, which met separately (each keeping its own minutes) for the next month.[21] The all-male Wholesale Dry Goods Committee also had poor attendance at com-

21   "Minute Book of the Children's Department of Toys & Small Wares–Great Central Fair, 1864," Minute Book, HSP.

mittee meetings, with most of the serious work accomplished in smaller subcommittees.[22]

As with the peacetime organizations, the fair's committee structure divided men and women into separate but parallel bodies. Although the women's committees enjoyed substantial autonomy, their tasks often reflected different concerns and circumscribed gender roles. The Wholesale Dry Goods Committee voted to leave the designing of a suitable badge to their ladies' committee; the women's committee of the Children's Department of Toys and Small Wares left the construction of a Maypole to their male affiliates. Both of the aforementioned women's committees devoted special attention to the appropriate apparel for committee members at the fair.

On occasion the female committee members became objects of derision. One male committee member wrote: "[w]e have agreed with every female member of our committees on every suggestion that they have made, and when you consider the variety of the suggestions, and their utter inconsistency . . . you may imagine the mental strain upon us." Another Philadelphian insisted on turning over his gift to a man because "[a] woman is a woman" and should not be trusted with "property."[23]

Even those who applauded the ladies' efforts often treated those contributions as stereotypically feminine. *Our Daily Fare* spoke condescendingly of female volunteers, who were "sending palpitations to the masculine heart" while selling their wares. One observer described how enthusiastic committee women ignored all the "formalities of social intercourse" and, on occasion, bullied men like "accomplished overseer[s]." Still, *Our Daily Fare* proudly declared that "young ladies of the highest social position . . . [had successfully] sustained the part of amateur sales-women" and "shown that ladies can do 'a'most anything'."[24] The fair, like other wartime voluntarism, showcased women in active, patriotic roles. But the reins of power remained in male hands.

Despite its enormous scale, the Great Central Fair was a notably decentralized event. At each level individuals sought to mold the fair to their own desires. Much of recording secretary H. H. Furness's time was devoted to sorting out squabbles among committee heads.

22 Minute Book of the "Wholesale Dry Goods Department–Sanitary Commission Fair," HSP. The minutes of the Newspaper Committee and the Sword Committee reveal similar patterns of procedure with various tasks being turned over to subcommittees while the committee as a whole met less frequently. See Society Misc. Collection, Leland Papers, HSP.
23 *ODF*, 9 June 1864, 12; 11 June 1864, 32.
24 *ODF*, 9 June 1864, 13; 10 June 1864, 20; 11 June 1864, 29; 11 September 1864, 95.

These battles reflected the difficulties inherent in forcing independent-minded volunteers into a large cooperative structure.

Mrs. George Plitt, secretary of the Committee of Women and chair of the Women's Committee on Internal Arrangements, peppered the Executive Committee with notes on a wide range of issues. On March 15 she suggested to Furness that a Miss Blanche Howell should be removed from the published list because she was too young. Later she insisted on removing a woman's name from a chairwomanship because "no lady should be published as [chair] of 2 [committees]." As opening day approached, Mrs. Plitt suggested a Turkish Department to Mr. Welsh, demanded more stamps from Mr. Furness, and continued her efforts at "keeping the names of *sweet young girls* from the public eye" by excluding them from published committee lists.[25]

Whereas Mrs. Plitt sought to have a hand in all of the fair's activities, other committee chairs were directing their groups like well-drilled armies, battling for territory. The most violent controversy swirled around S. Montgomery Bond and his Labor, Income, and Revenue Committee. This group used extensive newspaper advertising and personal visitation to solicit one day's wages or profits from every Philadelphian. By definition this committee overlapped with nearly every other. When rival chairs accused Bond of stealing their thunder, he complained that he was being victimized by "the carpings of others," but maintained that his methods earned more and that he left certain territories alone when asked to do so.[26]

Bond's usurpations led Alexander R. McHenry, the chairman of the Oil Committee, to dissolve that committee.[27] Soon after, McHenry wrote to the Executive Committee, this time wearing the hat of the Chairman of the Receiving Committee, to complain of further indignities. His committee had recently sold a gift of several dozen eggs and placed the receipts in the general funds rather than passing the profits on to the Restaurant Committee. The chair of the Restaurant Committee complained so bitterly about this slight that the Executive Committee passed a resolution barring similar actions in the future. McHenry became furious at the implication behind this decision and wrote: "I will not consent to be placed in an unpleasant position again – I had enough of this in Mr. Bond's case." Although the Executive Committee rescinded what McHenry termed the "vote of censure,"

25 Furness Papers.
26 S. Montgomery Bond to Furness, 18, 19 April 1864, Furness Papers.
27 Alexander R. McHenry to Furness, 22 April 1864, Furness Papers.

the damage was done. He kept his formal position, but McHenry refused to reenter the fair grounds.[28]

These battles suggest that within the fair's hierarchical structure committees enjoyed a wide latitude and chairpersons acted as individuals, not as cogs in a patriotic machine. Similarly, many Philadelphians who were outside the fair's administrative structure viewed the event as their own. Both Executive Committee Chairman Welsh and Recording Secretary Furness received regular letters from townspeople suggesting ways to improve the fair. One inventive writer argued that the Executive Committee should send a wagon through the city to collect rags, old shoes, and newspapers. He believed that such a venture "would raise $20,000 to $30,000." Another citizen took note of the annual infestation in Logan Square's trees and suggested that "a *committee on worms* is very much wanted." A third correspondent, fresh from two days at Brooklyn's fair, wrote that Philadelphia's version should have more seats and better food.[29] These people took their fair seriously and sought to do their part, however small, to make it a success.

In her diary entry for April 4, 1864, Anna Ferris reported the opening of New York's Metropolitan Fair, noting that "every effort will be made to equal it in Phila. & everybody is at work to do what they can for the cause." She added that "the unselfish devotion to a great purpose makes life better."[30] Anna Blanchard shared Ferris's selflessness. As a member of the Restaurant Committee, she worked six-hour shifts and usually stayed late, "always finding there was something to be done."[31] Joseph Harrison, businessman and inventor, chaired the Fine Arts Committee that put together the fair's Art Gallery. Several weeks before the fair opened Harrison explained to a neglected business associate that "I have *much* to do in arranging my department of the Fair." A few days before opening day he could only manage a hurried note to his friend while sitting in the middle of the Art Gallery, surrounded by busy workers. Soon Harrison put aside business entirely, explaining that "my time has been so much taken up with the Sanitary Fair . . . that I [have] little time to think of or do anything else." But the results lightened his burden because

---

28 McHenry to Welsh, 7, 9 May 1864; Welsh to McHenry, 5 May 1864; McHenry to Furness 23 May 1864, Furness Papers.

29 Unsigned to Furness, 28 April 1864, Box 7, F-2; Susan R. Barton to Furness, 23 March 1864, Box 7, F-1; Caleb P. Jones to Furness, 27 May 1864, Box 8, F-2, Furness Papers.

30 Anna Ferris diary, 4 April 1864, microfilm, Swarthmore College Library, Swarthmore, PA.

31 Anna Blanchard diary, June 1864, Anna Day Papers, HSP. This diary has no name on it and is not identified by the HSP. I was able to attribute it to Anna Blanchard because of her position on the Restaurant Committee.

"The Picture Gallery of the Great Central Fair." Albumen-print stereograph by John Moran, 1864. Library Company of Philadelphia.

Harrison found the fair "a great success, particularly the Art Gallery, which has never been equalled in modern times."[32]

Whereas Harrison and Blanchard devoted long hours to the fair, others offered special talents to the cause. Dr. S. M. Landis volunteered to serve as a lecturer on phrenology, and Jonathan M. Thompson made his bookkeeping skills available.[33] Joseph Boggs Beale contributed his artistic talents by drawing an eagle for the Boys Central High School Display.[34] James Tyndale Mitchell lent his time to the Music Commitee and his voice to several fund-raising concerts.[35]

On April 23 William D. Forten and Ebenezer Bassett wrote to Welsh because "an anxiety has been manifested by the better class of our community to render some substantial aid in the benevolent enterprise of which you are the directive head." Consequently, they "respectfully solicit[ed] permission to represent [their] interest by having in the fair a table furnished and attended by the ladies among us whose fathers, brothers, sons and fathers have shared the bles-

32 Joseph Harrison to Thomas Luders, 17 May,-, 21 June 1864, Harrison Letterbook, HSP.
33 S. M. Landis to Furness, undated, Box 5, F-1, Furness Papers; Jonathan M. Thompson to Furness, 16 March 1864, Box 7, F-1, Furness Papers.
34 Joseph Boggs Beale diary, 3 June 1864, HSP.
35 James Tyndale Mitchell diary, 1864, *passim*, privately owned.

sings of the Sanitary Commission's fostering care." Welsh thanked the gentlemen for their offer, but informed them that "whilst through our existing organizations whatever you and your friends may have to contribute to the Fair will be most thankfully received our arrangements do not contemplate private tables." All citizens were welcome to join the Fair effort; however no group could function strictly on its own.[36]

Contributions and contributors

Like other wartime relief organizations, the fair relied on donations of money and goods. In some cases the gift entailed only a small sacrifice, but in other instances the offering was – to the giver – quite significant. Individuals flooded the Receiving Department with all manner of heirlooms, trinkets, handicrafts, and farm products. One Union League member donated a deed to a downtown plot of land valued at $500, another man offered to share in the proceeds from a $1,500 holding in Iowa. A Wilmington inventor wanted to raffle off his patent for coal oil burners (splitting the profits with the Sanitary Commission), and a second inventor hoped to display his new gas stove. If these gifts appeared partly self-serving, the same could not be said for the man who sent pieces of wood he had collected at Gettysburg or the New Yorker who contributed five gallons of water from the Amazon River.[37]

Perhaps the most interesting assortment of gifts came to the Department of Singing Birds and Pet Animals. One poor woman wrote that since her husband would not give her any money she was sending six kittens. The offerings from the countryside included a pet donkey that purportedly served in the War of 1812, and two white mice from China. One ten-year-old boy had only his black terrier to offer; the committee chairwoman gratefully accepted the donation, bought it herself, and returned it to its young owner. Finally, the chairwoman reported, there were "thirty-six parrots, well accustomed to low company," with vocabularies befitting their background.[38]

Numerous organizations and labor groups sent contributions to the fair. The employees of John Bromley's Carpet Factory gave $41.50; the city's policemen donated over $1,000 in wages; the men aboard

36 William D. Forten and Ebenezer Bassett to Welsh, 23 April 1864; Welsh to Forten and Bassett 24 April 1864, Box 7, F-2, Furness Papers.
37 ODF, 11 June 1864; unsigned letters, 22 June 1864, Box 8, F-2; 6 May 1864, Box 8, F-2; undated, Box 7, F-2, all Furness Papers; U.S.S.C. and Fair Papers, Box 1, F-2; Box 1, F-3.
38 ODF, 11 June 1864.

the steamer *Ladona* offered a day's pay; members of Philadelphia's Anderson Troop collected items in the field; and the officers and crew of the ship of war *Constellation* sent $842.75, all the way from Italy.[39] The fair also enjoyed one day's profits from an all-star baseball game, a traveling circus, the Chestnut Street Theater, several local railways, and Bird's Billiard Saloon.[40] Small businesspeople, such as dressmaker Mrs. E. C. Tilton and grocer Joshua Wright, offered part of their revenues. The Great Valley Association for the Detection of Horse Thieves sent $30.[41] The range of donations was limited only by the reach of citizens' imaginations. The Carpenters and Bricklayers helped construct the Logan Square buildings; and representatives of various fire departments agreed to work together to protect the fair from fire.[42]

Many businesses used the festivities for publicity. Newspapers reported on a fierce competition between sewing machine companies seeking to be the most generous establishment in the city. The Singer Sewing Machine Company donated $300; three days later Florence Sewing Machine Company matched that figure. The American Button Hole Machine Company gave two of its machines (valued at $650) *and* $50 in cash, which the *Bulletin* acknowledged as "the largest contribution of any sewing machine company so far."[43]

The evidence of contemporary diaries suggests that nearly every Philadelphian was aware of the fair, most visited it, and almost all were strongly enthusiastic. As early as March 10 Anna Blanchard wrote "the town is in excitement in relation to [the] Great Central for the Sanitary." A month later Henry Benners noted that the fair buildings were progressing rapidly and that workers in his glass factory had given a day's wages to the cause.[44]

Some were less pleased. George W. Fahnestock, who had already refused to serve as a committee member, complained bitterly of being "beset with circulars begging for everything," claiming – rather ironically – that "of course we need no such reminder of incentive to duty." Later he visited the fair buildings, recording his view that the whole affair seemed like "childs play particularly when the Sanitary Commission do not need the money." After he visited

39 *EB,* 4 June 1864; Furness Scrapbook, Furness Papers; Suzanne Colton Wilson, ed., *Column South with the Fifteenth Pennsylvania Cavalry* (Flagstaff, Ariz., 1960), 162; *EB* 13 June 1864.
40 Philadelphia *Press,* 25, 30 May 1864; Furness Scrapbook.
41 *Press,* 2, 3 May 1864; *EB,* 13 June 1864.
42 *Press,* 7 May 1864; Furness Scrapbook.
43 *Press,* 28, 31 May 1864; *EB,* 3 June 1864.
44 Blanchard diary, 10 March 1864; Henry B. Benners diary, 12 April 1864, HSP. For an excellent first-hand account in a published form see Wilson, ed., *Column South,* 163–4.

the fair, Fahnestock's litany of dissatisfaction included the crowds, the high prices, the "uncouth dances" of the "savages" at the Indian display, and the quality of the horticultural exhibit. But even this great cynic found himself swept up in the enthusiasm, and four days later he returned for four evening hours.[45] Another nay-sayer, seventy-five-year-old Jacob Elfreth, Sr., dismissed the whole fair as a "waste of money." But although he never went himself, Elfreth's son and daughter were regular visitors and he soon admitted that it "appears to be very attractive."[46]

Most Philadelphians needed no convincing. Joseph Boggs Beale visited the fair at least ten times, Susan Trautwine mentioned four visits, James Tyndale Mitchell went almost every day, Mary Dreer often went twice a day. Sydney George Fisher called the event a "miracle of American spirit, energy, & beauty." Anna Ferris added that it was "the most wonderful display of everything under the sun." It was certainly, as Anna Blanchard put it, "an Exhibition of which [Philadelphia] may well be proud."[47]

Philadelphia's Great Central Fair was important on several levels. Most significantly, it generated over a million dollars in relief funds. It also involved Philadelphians in an event of great magnitude, with a wide range of opportunities for participation; one that they could cheerfully attend and in that indirect way, too, contribute to the cause.

Over 250,000 people bought tickets to the fair.[48] There were roughly 608,000 Philadelphians in 1864.[49] Even allowing for thousands of visitors from out of town, the fair attracted a large proportion of the city's population. Most accounts of the Great Central Fair stress that all segments of Philadelphia society combined to make it a success. Two months before the fair began George Fahnestock wrote: "Everybody is working for it, talking about it, begging for it. The newspapers are full of it – advertising columns and all – and everybody in town, male and female, is on some committee – self appointed or otherwise."[50] The *North American and United States Gazette* marveled at "how thoroughly this Great Fair has worked into the popular sympathy," and the *Bulletin* noted the "thousands of men, women and children" who worked for its success, and the further

45 George W. Fahnestock diary, 1864, *passim*, HSP.
46 Jacob Elfreth, Sr., diary, 7, 11 June 1864, Haverford College Library, Haverford, PA.
47 Wainwright, ed., *A Philadelphia Perspective*, 473, entry of 7 June 1864; Ferris diary, 9 June 1864; Blanchard diary, June 1864.
48 *ODF*, 11 September 1864, 104.
49 Roger Lane, *Violent Death in the City: Suicide, Accident and Murder in 19th Century Philadelphia* (Cambridge, MA, 1979), 11.
50 Fahnestock diary, 5 April 1864.

"thousands who contributed money, labor, time, gifts or loans."[51]
Forney's War Press made the case even more directly:

> There is not one man, woman, or child out of a hundred within the
> limits of the city, who is not directly interested in the Great Central
> Fair, who has not given it at least one day's labor, and a month's
> sympathy and earnest aid.[52]

When the rules concerning tickets were first announced, it
appeared – mistakenly so – that city inhabitants would have to buy
season tickets for $5 rather than the $1 single-day tickets that would
be available to outsiders. This misunderstanding led a Philadelphia
"Workingman" to write an angry letter to the *Press*:

> I had understood that the Great Fair . . . was to be the spontaneous
> offering of all our citizens, rich and poor, to those brave men who
> are now engaged in upholding our Government . . . with this
> understanding, I and thousands more such as I, gave my mite
> cheerfully – gave as much as I could to a cause with which I
> sympathize so fully.

He went on to object to the prohibitive season ticket prices, which he
felt would exclude workingmen like himself.[53]

The committees clearly embraced the ideal of widespread
participation. Each group followed the lead of the Executive Committee's initial announcement in calling on all classes to do their part.
Bond's Committee on Labor, Income, and Revenue aimed its first
circular at "the working men and women of the city," calling on them
to give a day's earnings or a day's labor. In mid-June Bond visited a
Manayunk woolen mill where the proprietors stopped work so that
he could address the workers, who "manifested a great desire to
contribute." The flyer distributed by the Committee on Looking
Glasses, Picture Frames and Gilt Ornaments was typical in insisting
that "no one [should], on account of its apparent triviality, hesitate to
send any small article." The Committee on Sewing Women explained
that they did not want "to tax heavily those whose livelihood de-
pends upon the needle" but to ensure "that all may be included in
this natural ovation," for "[in] a moral scale 'the widow's mite' will
outweight a Prince's diadem."[54]

51 *North American and United States Gazette,* 4 June 1864; *EB,* 4, 25 June 1864.
52 *Forney's War Press,* 11 June 1864, in Furness scrapbook.
53 *Press,* 17 May 1864. On the fair's last two days, ticket prices were reduced to 25
    cents.
54 *GT,* 15 June 1864; Circular of the Committee on Labor, Income, and Revenue,
    dated 28 March 1864; *GT,* 18 June 1864; Circular of the Committee on Looking
    Glasses, Picture Frames and Gilt Ornaments, dated 15 March 1864; Circular of the
    Committee on Sewing Women, undated. All circulars in the Great Sanitary Fair–
    Misc File, HSP.

Appeals for contributions usually stressed the twin pulls of patriotism and benevolence. In an editorial on a benefit opera performance for the fair the *Ledger* observed that "Patriotism dictates a general attendance." The *Press* argued that "our only tribute to the fallen must be our care for the living." *Our Daily Fare* continually emphasized the good works of the Sanitary Commission and saw the fair as the latest expression of the war's "ongoing tide of benevolence." After the first day, the *Bulletin* concluded that "this scene of wonderful beauty has arisen at the call of the noblest instincts of the human heart – patriotism and humanity."[55]

Beneath the surface patriotism there were other motivations. The committee chairs often used the profit motive to their advantage, reminding businesspeople of the good will a donation could purchase. A circular aimed at the Oil Refiners of Western Pennsylvania argued that by providing the fair with a good display, "contributors whilst aiding the soldiers of the Union, will at the same time, advertise their respective establishments." The Committee on Labor, Income, and Revenue appealed to the pride of the city's shoemakers by announcing that it "had full confidence that the contributions from that branch will be in proportion as liberal as from any source from which it applies."[56] Bond's committee assured that no benevolent light would be hidden by taking out regular newspaper ads listing all the latest donations.

Beyond the profits it brought to the Sanitary Commission, the Great Central Fair temporarily freed Philadelphia from the gloom of war. One writer in *Our Daily Fare* argued that even if the fair earned no money at all, it performed a useful function in spurring the local economy and in taking people's minds off the conflict.[57] The fair made Philadelphians proud of themselves and of their city. Much of the prefair boosterism challenged the local citizenry to top New York's effort. The *Bulletin* predicted that Philadelphia would outdo New York in size, variety, artwork, and proceeds. This, it said, "affords additional proof that the cause of patriotism is more liberally sustained in money as well as men in the City of Brotherly Love than in any other city in the Union."[58] The Committee on Labor, Income, and Revenue knew exactly which strings to pull when it announced:

55 *Philadelphia Public Ledger*, 6 May 1864 (hereafter *PL*); *Press*, 12 May 1864; *ODF*, 8 June 1864; *EB*, 10 June 1864. See also the *PL*, 7 June 1864 and numerous other newspaper editorials for discussion of patriotism and the fair.
56 Furness Papers; *EB*, 2 June 1864.
57 *ODF*, 13 June 1864.
58 *EB*, 18 June 1864. Also see *PL*, 14 May 1864; *EB*, 3 June 1864. In a speech to the committee chairmen, the Sanitary Commission's Dr. Henry Bellows challenged the Philadelphians to beat the standard established by other Northern cities. See "Miskey Autobiography," 58.

When this mighty war, waged by the ambition of disappointed men, shall have passed into history, the humblest citizen will be proud of the record of his deeds of devotion, if not in the defence of the nation's flag, at least in assisting the sufferings of its defenders.[59]

The Great Central Fair and Philadelphia's benevolent traditions

The fair, like the war itself, presented Philadelphia with challenges on a new scale. Mustering committee members and collecting donations, like raising troops and bounty funds, required sophisticated organization and widespread cooperation. The organizers followed the path trod by earlier voluntary activities in relying on antebellum organizational forms and preexisting associational ties. The fair's grand scale made it different, but only in degree.

Committee memberships suggest the importance of these associational ties. Most committees were organized around particular trades. The eight men on the Committee on Boots, Shoes and Leather included two tanners, four leather and skins dealers, and two merchants. The twenty-six members of the associated Committee of Women were mainly relatives of men in the leather trades. All of the Hardware Committee members were hardware dealers, saddlers, or merchants. The Ships and Shipbuilding Committee recognized that it was responsible for collecting from men of varied occupations by forming subcommittees of shipbuilders, joiners, sailmakers, shipsmiths, spar makers, block makers, and riggers.[60]

Those committees not organized around trades followed the antebellum pattern of paternalistic benevolence. The fifty-six men and women on the Restaurant Committee included nine gentlemen and gentlewomen; seven manufacturers or wives of manufacturers; five attorneys, doctors, and executives or their wives; a major shipper; and the wife of a judge. But the Restaurant Committee was not exclusively the province of elites. It also included several storekeepers, a cashier, a bookkeeper, and a carpenter's wife. The thirty-six-man Executive Committee knew no such diversity. This body was composed of gentlemen, professionals, manufacturers, and leading merchants and traders. Its rolls included prominent attorneys Theodore Cuyler, Charles J. Stillé, and Horace Howard Furness, foundry owner Samuel V. Merrick, manufacturer Joseph Harrison, Jr., and wealthy gentleman Caleb Cope.

59 EB, 6/13/64.
60 List of Committee Members. The occupations were taken from McElroy's City Directory. The same pattern holds true for the Bakers Committee and presumably for the other committees organized around trades.

Other committees were formed explicitly around geographic associations. These included the Eighteenth Ward Committee, the West Philadelphia Committee, and the independently run Department of the State of Delaware. The Restaurant Department had special chairwomen for subcommittees representing Germantown, Chestnut Hill, West Chester, Mount Holly, and Roxborough. The extremely large Schools Committee included representatives from the city's various public and private schools, many of which held their own activities to support the fair.

The Civil War tested Philadelphia's philanthropic energies and institutions most profoundly when the city staged its Great Central Fair. But even this great challenge did not force Philadelphians from familiar paths. We have seen that in prefair fund-raising and at the fair tables Philadelphia women continued their antebellum role as the city's dominant benevolent force. And we have also seen that the fair's hierarchy, like that of the other large voluntary societies, placed men in the leading positions. Nor did the fair expand the powers of public institutions or push forward the centralization of city life. The city government's role in wartime benevolence had been largely limited to aiding the families of volunteers. The Sanitary Fair, like other wartime efforts, received no benefit from public funds or any official support from the military. And although the receipts went to the Sanitary Commission, that organization did no more than provide its Philadelphia associates with minor financial support in the fair's organizing stages. The fair was exclusively a local event; more, it was essentially a grass-roots effort. The Executive Committee watched over the activities, but most of the important work was performed in small subcommittees or by individual volunteers. In this sense, too, the Great Central Fair succeeded within the existing structure of Philadelphia society.

The mosaic of organized benevolence spawned by the war helped to maximize public involvement. The various institutions appealed to Philadelphians through a wide range of established associational ties. Citizens could aid the cause through geographic, occupational, or religious groups. What was more, the numerous opportunities for involvement allowed Philadelphians to do as little or as much as they chose. Organizations were so varied and so fluid that an individual could give a small donation, spend a day sewing every few months, or become almost completely consumed by work in a dozen societies. Finally, voluntary involvement did not necessarily imply support for the war or for the Lincoln administration. People who cared for wounded soldiers need not have embraced the decisions that led the men to the battlefield. And Quakers, who rejected all military-related activity, found an ample outlet for their charitable energies in aiding the contrabands.

Philadelphia's war-related voluntarism clearly resembled peace-time benevolence. But its enormous success depended on taking advantage of the patriotic fervor brought on by the Civil War.[61] Thus voluntary organizations opted for fund-raising techniques that capitalized on this enthusiasm. Although fairs and concerts had been familiar prewar tools, the war years saw an increased reliance on such popular events to turn patriotic excitement into financial gains.

The Great Central Fair took Philadelphia's wartime voluntarism to its logical extreme. If hundreds of small fund-raising events had financed the myriad of war-related societies, why not rely on a single enormous fair to aid the Sanitary Commission? The fair's success followed the established formula. Contributors could volunteer as much or as little as they chose; committees solicited funds through established associational ties; thousands mixed pleasure or profits with their contributions.

In his study of Northern intellectuals during the Civil War, George M. Fredrickson argues that the Sanitary Commission's founders embraced a "conservative, basically nonhumanitarian philosophy." These men sought to impose order and discipline in American society by centralizing philanthropy and by ridding it of the sentimental and individualistic aspects that characterized antebellum charities.[62] The commissioners succeeded in their task in that they directed a large share of the North's benevolent funds toward "suitable" activities. But Philadelphia's experience suggests that these representatives of the nation's elite did not meet their larger goals. Numerous other local and national charities provided the humanitarianism and individualism that the Sanitary Commission rejected. Rather than a highly centralized structure, wartime benevolence took a chaotic form reminiscent of antebellum America. Even within the Sanitary Commission's ranks, rigidity gave way to passion as individuals insisted on exercising their autonomy. The Sanitary Commission, like the war itself, was a nationalizing force. Soldiers on hundreds of battlefields came to recognize the USSC's familiar agents and packages; the national structure linked distant cities and a common concern. But on the home front, grandiose ideas

---

61 In his study of World War II America, Richard Polenberg concluded that "the belief that everybody had to do his share strengthened each person's sense of his own worth." Such was the attitude among many Civil War Philadelphians. See Polenberg, *War and Society: The United States, 1941–1945* (Philadelphia, 1972), 133.

62 George M. Fredrickson, *The Inner Civil War: Northern Intellectuals and the Crisis of the Union* (New York, 1965), 98–112.

of order and discipline gave way to traditional methods and familiar ties.[63]

As the war neared its close, Philadelphians marveled at their own voluntaristic spirit. In September 1864 John J. Thompson wrote to his cousin:

> The progress of our war . . . has developed an amount of sympathy, active, earnest and working, with suffering sick & wounded soldiers, such as has no parallel in the history of the world - The amount of volunteer labor on the battle fields, and in the Hospitals, has been extraordinary and the voluntary contributions by our citizens through the Sanitary Commissions amount to many millions of dollars in money & hundreds of tons in merchandize etc![64]

Although the degree of voluntarism in the city was indeed "extraordinary," the nature of that activity was not new. As one French traveler through wartime Philadelphia reported: "Philadelphia has not lost her religious character; she remains equally faithful to her philanthropic traditions."[65]

The philanthropic legacy of the Civil War

We have seen that Philadelphia's benevolent traditions persisted through the war years. Long established philanthropies as well as war-related institutions survived the conflict without altering familiar organizational forms, gender differentiation, and fund-raising methods. Moreover, even widely shared goals did not push the city's benevolent network into a single, centralized structure.[66] These findings support the larger conclusion that the "machinery" already in place in 1860 enabled Philadelphia to master the Civil War's challenges without abrupt changes. But what of the war's aftermath? Although this study focuses on the survival of antebellum practices in

63 In her study of benevolent women, Lori Ginzberg accepts Fredrickson's argument that the USSC dominated wartime giving and acted as a force for both efficiency and centralization. See Ginzberg, "Women and the Work of Benevolence," (Ph. D. diss., Yale University, 1984), Chapter 5 *passim.*
64 John J. Thompson to (Cousin) John Thompson, 26 September 1864, Society Misc. Collection, HSP.
65 Auguste Laugel, *The United States During the Civil War,* ed. Allan Nevins (1866; Bloomington, 1961), 177.
66 Although Americans also relied on voluntarism to further the World War I war effort, much had changed in a half century. Most important, the critical Civil War task–care for soldiers at home and in the field–remained largely a governmental concern in the later conflict. Moreover, though government planners during World War I recognized the value of local organizing, the level of federal direction in such activities clearly exceeded the Civil War standard. See David M. Kennedy, *Over Here: The First World War and American Society* (New York, 1980), 142–3.

the face of wartime challenges, a brief survey of the postwar years reveals that the sort of shift commonly associated with the Civil War – specifically expanded roles for women and increased centralization — did not emerge until roughly a decade after Appomatox.[67] Several indices point to strong continuities through the early 1870s followed by clear shifts in both established bodies and newly formed institutions.

In many senses the Depression of 1873–4 presented benevolent Philadelphians with the same sort of benevolent challenges that they had faced in 1857 and again in 1861. Established institutions, such as the UBA and the PSEIP, reported particular economic challenges during the depression much as they had in the face of the two earlier crises.[68] Other Philadelphians followed tradition by forming emergency relief associations. Like their antebellum and wartime counterparts, these groups typically organized at emergency meetings to meet local needs. In most wards male officers and managers directed the local relief association and female visitors distributed relief to the needy. Thus these new organizations formed eight years after the war turned to traditional gender differentiation as well as decentralized control in response to crisis.[69]

But if Philadelphia's benevolent world in 1873 looked much as it had in 1860, the next several years saw signs of change. Although the established organizations did not alter their practices, the annual reports reveal slight shifts in the recognition of women's activities. For instance, in 1874 the PSEIP's report introduced a new page listing the "Ladies' Auxiliary Committees" and a separate "Report of the Ladies' Board of Managers." The society's next two annual reports

67 On postwar centralization of benevolence see Fredrickson, *Inner Civil War*. On the war's role in increasing the benevolent activities of women see Anne Firor Scott, "Women's Voluntary Associations in the Forming of American Society," *Making the Invisible Woman Visible* (Urbana, Ill., 1984), 281–2; Scott, "On Seeing and Not Seeing: A Case for Historical Invisibility," *Journal of American History* 71 (June 1984), 12–13; Agatha Young, *The Women and the Crisis* (Obolensky, N.Y., 1959), 349–51 and *passim*. On Southern women see Suzanne Lebsock, *The Free Women of Petersburg* (New York, 1984), 239–49, 309 fn 4. For discussions of the war's impact on the ideology of female activists see Lori Ginzberg, "Women and the Work of Benevolence," 223, Chapter 6 *passim*; Nancy A. Hewitt, *Women's Activism and Social Change: Rochester, New York, 1822–1872* (Ithaca, N.Y., 1984), 192–215.

68 Union Benevolent Association, *26th Annual Report, 27th Annual Report, 30th Annual Report, 42nd Annual Report, 43rd Annual Report* (Philadelphia, 1857, 1858, 1861, 1873, 1874; Philadelphia Society for the Employment and Instruction of the Poor, *11th Annual Report, 15th Annual Report, 27th Annual Report* (Philadelphia, 1858, 1862, 1874).

69 See *Report of the Tenth Ward Citizens' Association* (Philadelphia, 1874); *Report of the Executive Committee of the 14th Ward Relief Association* (Philadelphia, 1874); *The Germantown Relief Society* (Philadelphia, 1875) (this is a four-page pamphlet describing the society's aims); *Fourth Annual Report of the Board of Managers of the Germantown Relief Society* (Philadelphia, 1877).

continued these new features and took care to acknowledge the efforts of the Ladies' Branch.[70] The UBA's male managers dispensed with their report in 1874, deferring instead to the Ladies' reports. The following year the managers' reports ran a short page and a half whereas the Ladies' report covered thirteen pages. Again this shift from established practice seemed to be an acknowledgment of the critical role of female volunteers.[71]

The PSEIP's lists of managers also indicates continuity through the war decade and then a shift in the mid-1870s. Of twenty-one "Lady Managers" in 1871, five had been managers since before the war, ten had served since at least 1863, and only one woman had been a manager for less than four years. Four years later, in 1875, only one of these twenty-one Lady Managers remained on the PSEIP's rolls. Among the society's twenty-two "Male Managers" in 1871, ten had joined the ranks by 1863 and fourteen had served for four years or more. But whereas the female membership turned over almost completely between 1871 and 1875, fourteen male managers remained by the middle of the decade.[72] Were the PSEIP's new Lady Managers veterans of Civil War benevolence? None appear among the extensive committee lists for the 1864 Sanitary Fair. Perhaps they were active among the rank and file but deemed too young to have their names published.[73]

The greatest evidence for evolution is not in the records of established bodies but in the nature of organizations formed after 1875. In January 1877 Eighth Ward women responded to the wintertime suffering of local sewing women by forming a relief association designed much like the ward groups of three years earlier. In a sense this group acted like a traditional small, single-gender society, but its

---

70 PSEIP, *27th Annual Report, 28th Annual Report* (Philadelphia, 1875), *29th Annual Report* (Philadelphia, 1876). In 1878 the managers of the Provident Society also took particular care to note "the valuable cooperation of benevolent women." See Provident Society, *54th Annual Report* (Philadelphia, 1878).
71 UBA, *43rd Annual Report, 44th Annual Report* (Philadelphia, 1875). Of course this slight shift in the annual reports does not suggest a movement toward balanced gender roles in the UBA or the PSEIP.
72 PSEIP, *4th through 28th Annual Reports* (Philadelphia, 1851 through 1875).
73 Seventeen of the PSEIP's twenty-two Lady Managers in 1875 were unmarried. Thus, their absence from the Sanitary Fair committee lists does not merely reflect postwar name changes through marriage. The wartime committee lists did include younger women, but the correspondence suggests that younger girls were sometimes kept off the lists. The membership lists of the all-female Indigent Widows' and Single Womens' Society also suggest strong continuities over the war decade. Twenty of twenty-four officers and managers in 1859 were still serving in 1866 (two others were unmarried in 1859 and might have appeared in 1866 under married names). By 1873 fourteen of the 1859 officers and managers remained. See *42nd Annual Report, 49th Annual Report, 55th Annual Report* (Philadelphia, 1859, 1866, 1873).

breadth of activities and budget in excess of $5,300 was more ambitious than its antebellum counterparts.[74]

In 1879 the formation of the Philadelphia Society for Organizing Charitable Relief and Repressing Medicancy (PSOCR) marked a major milestone in the city's benevolent history. The organization, which formed following an 1878 meeting designed to eliminate the evils of overlapping philanthropy, gave Philadelphia charities the centralized agency that the war years lacked. The PSOCR's complicated structure included a wide array of subcommittees and an all-male Board of Directors that supervised the activities of affiliated organizations in each ward. Each ward association organized charities in its own area, but their individual bylaws tended to follow a blueprint suggested by the parent organization.[75]

The PSOCR and its ward associations introduced greater efficiency and organization into Philadelphia's benevolent world and also reflected an increased recognition of the role of charitable women. The original plan followed tradition by placing women in circumscribed roles such as visitation, sewing classes, and day nurseries, whereas men served in the highest offices and controlled the funds. But the *2nd Annual Report* included a call for increased "Cooperation of Men and Women Workers." The letter implied that male directors had become isolated from the needy poor yet persisted in overruling the "Lady Visitors" who had the critical knowledge but lacked the concomitant power. It recommended special meetings between the local Boards of Directors and the female visitors and it even suggested that "in some wards women had been placed on the Board of Directors."[76] By 1884 the Eighth Ward Association had five male and five female directors; in 1888 the combined Thirteenth and Fourteenth Wards Association reported an evenly balanced board of directors and a woman superintendent.[77]

It seems clear that by the end of the 1870s Philadelphia's charities were increasingly centralized and efficient as well as more open to

74 *Report of the Eighth Ward Relief Association* (Philadelphia, 1877). The association's treasurer was the only male member.
75 Philadelphia Society for Organizing Charitable Relief and Repressing Mendicancy, *1st Annual Report* (Philadelphia, 1879), *Suggested By-Laws for Ward Associations* (Philadelphia, 1878).
76 PSOCR, *2nd Annual Report* (Philadelphia, 1880).
77 Eighth Ward Association of the Philadelphia Society for Organizing Charity, *6th Annual Report* (Philadelphia, 1884); 13th and 14th Wards Association of the Philadelphia Society for Organizing Charity, *8th Annual Report* (Philadelphia, 1888). The evidence is too spotty to detect a shift in the practices of any particular ward association, but in 1881 the Tenth Ward Association reported a more traditional structure with men serving as officers and directors and women acting as officers of their own "Corps of Visitors," *3rd Annual Report*.

leadership roles of women.[78] The timing of these shifts certainly does not indicate that the Civil War was directly responsible. Rather, it appears that benevolence in the City of Brotherly Love looked much the same in 1875 as it had twenty years before.[79]

78   But gender differentiation did persist. The women in the Society for Organizing Charitable Relief still did the bulk of the visiting, much as they had for decades in the UBA. In 1881 the ladies of the Indigent Widows' and Single Women's Society reported extensive repairs to their building "under the wise direction of an efficient committee of gentlemen." Twenty-eight years before they thanked a similar body of gentlemen for almost identical assistance. See *64th Annual Report* (Philadelphia, 1881), *36th Annual Report* (Philadelphia, 1853).
79   For a discussion of the differences between the 1864 Sanitary Fair and the Centennial Exhibition of 1876 see Chapter 13.

7 Preserving the peace: Order and disorder

April 1861

The news of the April 12, 1861, firing on Fort Sumter shocked Philadelphians into activity. Thousands responded to Lincoln's call for troops, and soon the city took "on the appearance of a great armed camp." Excited crowds congregated in the streets to hear and debate the latest reports, and "[e]veryone who hinted any sympathy with the secessionists was made to take an unequivocal stand." One citizen's ill-advised comments on April 14 attracted a substantial mob, forcing him to hide in a Chestnut Street drugstore until the police arrived. Later that evening an intoxicated man courted fate by declaring himself a Southern sympathizer. "A rush was made when the secessionist apologized, and stated that he was a Philadelphian and a Union man. 'Well, then,' was the rejoinder, 'take off your hat and give three cheers for the thirty United States,' and he did so to the delight of the crowd."[1]

On the morning of the fifteenth, the crowd ripped the clothes from one supposed secessionist's back, put another man's head in a noose, and roughed up various other victims.[2] But such actions were only incidental to the mob's larger agenda. Before noon, crowds began gathering in front of the Chestnut Street office of the pro-Southern *Palmetto Flag*. When the mob "swelled to many hundreds," Mayor Alexander Henry sent the chief of police and members of the Reserve Corps to the scene. As the crowd clamored for a patriotic display, Henry appeared at one of the newspaper's windows, waving a small flag. His performance was received with cheers, and the popular leader deftly calmed the excited masses:

> Your devotion to the flag of your country satisfies me that you are equally devoted to the maintenance of the laws, and the preservation of order. (cheers) I see that there are no traitors among you,

---

1 Ellis Paxson Oberholtzer, *Philadelphia: A History of Its People*, 4 vols., (Philadelphia, 1912), 2:360; *Philadelphia Public Ledger*, 15 April 1861 (hereafter *PL*); J. Thomas Scharf and Thompson Westcott, *History of Philadelphia, 1609–1884*, 3 vols., (Philadelphia, 1884), 1:753.
2 William Dusinberre, *Civil War Issues in Philadelphia, 1856–1865* (Philadelphia, 1965), 118.

and I rejoice to know that treason cannot rear its head in this city. The flag is an emblem of the Government, and I hope that all citizens who feel loyal to it will show their respect for it and the laws and retire to their respective homes.[3]

The crowd responded with more cheers for the mayor and for the flag. They did not, however, go home.

The assault on Philadelphia's institutions did not stop with the *Palmetto Flag*. For two days crowds moved around the city insisting that hotels, colleges, and newspaper offices display some sign of pro-Union sentiments.[4] One local newspaper contributed to the incendiary spirit by publishing the names and addresses of several wealthy Southerners. Armed with this information, the crowd marched through the streets demanding shows of patriotism at the homes thus targeted. Colonel Robert Patterson's house was mobbed and its windows smashed; Robert Tyler, the former Democratic State chairman, took refuge in the Court House; and Customs Collector Joseph Baker, a Buchanan appointee, was forced to show the flag. One Southerner, General George Cadwalader, quieted the crowd by offering to lead the rioters South to fight the Confederacy.[5]

On the second day of rioting, Mayor Henry again silenced the crowd. This time they had gathered at the Walnut Street home of prominent Democrat William Reed. When the mayor promised that the police would shoot to kill to maintain order, the mob dispersed.[6] The next morning's newspapers featured a short proclamation from the mayor asking citizens to identify any persons suspected of aiding the enemy. The document went on to "require and command that all persons shall refrain from assembly in the highways of the city, unlawfully, riotously, or tumultuously, warning them that the same will be at their peril." The mayor had established that the pursuit of order would lead both to the arrest of active secessionists and the possible shooting of riotous antisecessionists. Henry's statement met with strong approval from the *Public Ledger*: "the object of the war is

3 *PL*, 16 April 1861.
4 *PL*, 16 April 1861; Dusinberre, *Civil War Issues*, 117–18; Joseph Boggs Beale diary, 15 April 1861, Historical Society of Pennsylvania, Philadelphia (hereafter HSP); J. A. Culley letter, 15 April 1861, Manuscript Room, Library of Congress (hereafter LC). When the proprietors of the American Hotel accidentally flew their flag upside down, a large crowd gathered on the scene and threatened violence. See Scharf and Westcott, *History of Philadelphia*, 1:753; *PL*, 15 April 1861.
5 Dusinberre, *Civil War Issues*, 117–18; Russell F. Weigley, "The Border City in Civil War, 1854–1865," in *Philadelphia: A 300-Year History*, ed. Weigley (New York, 1982), 344.
6 *PL*, 17 April 1861; Dusinberre, *Civil War Issues*, 117–19; Arnold Schankman [sic], "William B. Reed and the Civil War," *Pennsylvania History* 39 (October 1971): 461–2. The crowd apparently assaulted several Walnut Street houses.

to establish the authority of the laws over the land. How can we establish this if we begin by a disregard of it at home?"[7]

The news from the South probably drew thousands of Philadelphians into the streets. The *Public Ledger* described a group of "many hundreds" at the *Palmetto Flag* office as "mostly . . . boys and young men"; the group at William Reed's house was "composed chiefly of minors." One diarist wrote that "a tremendous crowd of 200 or 300 men & big boys of the roughest fighting order & better ones carrying the American flag were running through the streets" throughout the fifteenth, and that by that evening – despite driving rain – the group had swelled to five or six hundred.[8] Sarah Butler Wister described an even more frenzied scene:

> There was the most tremendous excitement. Thousands assembled furious at the news of the surrender, & swearing revenge on all disunionists or disaffected. They marched through the streets their numbers swelling as they went, & visited the houses, stores & offices of some of the leading Loco Focos who of course have been especially odious in the last few days.

On April 16th "[t]he mob went to uncle George [Cadwalader]'s, Gen. Patterson's, . . . Wm. B. Reed's, & was finally dispersed authoritatively by Mayor Henry with a strong body of police." Wister added that "[t]hey were the most moderate, mannerly mob ever heard of, but in reality they were in the utmost state of excitement & the least thing would have fired them, & then riots must have followed."[9]

When he went into town on April 18, Sidney George Fisher found "the streets all a flutter with flags" and confidently reported that "we are not likely to suffer from the greater evil of partisan war among ourselves."[10] The publishers of the *Palmetto Flag* had announced that they would not subject the city to more rioting in order to publish their views.[11] Some Southern sympathizers left town immediately; the rest joined the *Palmetto Flag* in judicious silence and decorated their homes and offices with flags. Sarah Wister described one doctor who had been "scared into eating his own words by the threat of a mob." As Fisher put it: "It is at the risk of any man's life

7 *PL*, 16, 17 April 1861.
8 *PL*, 16, 17 April 1861; Beale diary, 15 April 1861 (see #4). J. A. Culley used very similar language in his letter of 15 April 1861.
9 Fanny Kemble Wister, "Sarah Butler Wister's Civil War Diary," *Pennsylvania Magazine of History and Biography* 102 (July 1978): 274–6, entries of 15, 16 April 1861. Dusinberre wrote that the crowd at Colonel Patterson's house was several thousand strong. See Dusinberre, *Civil War Issues*, 117.
10 Nicholas B. Wainwright, ed., *A Philadelphia Perspective: The Diary of Sidney George Fisher* (Philadelphia, 1967), 387, entry of 16 April 1861.
11 *PL*, 16 April 1861.

that he utters publicly a sentiment in favor of secession or the South." Although the streets were clear, several Democrats received threatening notes.[12]

In April 1861 political tensions threatened to erupt in massive violence. But on this occasion, and over the course of the next four years, large scale disorder did not reign. This chapter will attempt to explain why the City of Brotherly Love weathered the storms brought on by the war, conscription, emancipation and inflation without experiencing the bloody disruptions that wracked other cities. Did new forces emerge to successfully combat the rising tensions, or did the means used during the war's first days – an aggressive mayor, a visible police force, and an active citizenry – keep disorder in check throughout the war years?

Philadelphia's disorderly traditions

The period from 1835 to 1850 has been called "the most violent in Philadelphia's history."[13] On several occasions antiblack, antiabolitionist, or antiIrish rage tore the city apart; the depressed economy of the late 1830s and early 1840s sent Philadelphia's handloom weavers on several violent rampages; and large-scale battles between fire companies or youth gangs were commonplace.[14]

Philadelphia's most violent mobs roamed the streets during the 1844 riots that stemmed from rising hostilities toward the city's Irish. The first altercation, in May, followed the disruption of a Native American Party meeting in the heart of Irish-dominated Kensington. Three days of fighting and incendiarism left at least six dead, as many as fifty wounded, and over $250,000 in property destroyed. In July 1844 the Irish arming of a Southwark church sparked a violent nativist response. The militia had been reluctant to act in May; this time they

---

12 Wister, "Sarah Butler Wister's Civil War Diary," 280–1, entry of 20 April 1861; Wainwright, ed., *A Philadelphia Perspective*, 385, entry of 18 April 1861; Dusinberre, *Civil War Issues*, 119; Edward G. Everett, "Contraband and Rebel Sympathizers in Pennsylvania in 1861," *Western Pennsylvania Historical Magazine* 41 (Spring 1958): 35.

13 Michael Jay Feldberg, "Urbanization as a Cause of Violence: Philadelphia as a Test Case," in *The Peoples of Philadelphia: A History of Ethnic Groups and Lower Class Life, 1790–1940*, eds. Allen F. Davis and Mark H. Haller (Philadelphia, 1978), 56.

14 See Elizabeth M. Geffen, "Violence in Philadelphia in the 1840's and 1850's," *Pennsylvania History* 36 (October 1969): 381–410; David R. Johnson, "Crime Patterns in Philadelphia, 1840–1870," in *The Peoples of Philadelphia*, 89–110; Bruce Laurie, "Fire Companies and Gangs in Southwark: The 1840's," in *The Peoples of Philadelphia*, 71–87; Michael Jay Feldberg, "The Philadelphia Riots of 1844: A Social History" (Ph.D. diss., University of Rochester, 1970); John C. Schneider, "Mob Violence and Public Order in the American City, 1830–1865" (Ph.D. diss., University of Minnesota, 1971), 81–111; Richard Alan McLeod, "The Philadelphia Artisan, 1828–1850" (Ph.D. diss., University of Missouri–Columbia, 1971), 165–76.

moved decisively but foolishly. Several times General George Cadwalader's troops upset a precarious balance, leading to greater bloodshed. In the end, ten rioters were dead and twenty were injured; the militia suffered two dead and twenty-three wounded.[15]

Compared to the 1844 riots, the April 1861 disturbances seem subdued. Although accused secessionists were harassed, there was little or no bloodshed. After Fort Sumter, crowds visited selected citizens to demand displays of patriotism; in 1844 nativists burned down Irish homes. Why did these outbursts yield such differing results? The answer lies in part in the varied nature of the disorders, but more so in the character of the city's mechanisms for maintaining control.

Following the nativist riots, the sobering effect of the loss of life created a strong antirioting backlash. On July 11, 1844, thousands of Philadelphians joined in a mass meeting in the State House Yard to promote civil order. During the next fifteen years a Philadelphia police force took form to further that end. In 1850 the legislature replaced the inefficient system of sheriffs and constabulary by a daytime "Marshal's Police" with jurisdiction over all of Philadelphia County. Four years later the City Council of the newly consolidated city created the first Philadelphia Police Department.[16] When Alexander Henry became mayor in 1858, one of his top priorities was an improved police force. In his first years in office Henry appointed a citizen board to oversee appointments, organized a special Detective Department, and put his force into new uniforms. By 1861 Philadelphians enjoyed a far more structured and efficient police force than during the riotous 1840s.[17]

John Schneider argues that mid-nineteenth century mayors rarely demonstrated the "quick action and decisiveness demanded in a crisis situation." Their traditional role as a " 'moral' power . . . was becoming increasingly irrelevant to the growing cities of the nineteenth century," while the enlarged scale of the city meant that "there could be no guarantee that [the mayor] could always be in the

---

15 Feldberg, "The Philadelphia Riots of 1844," 77–109, 151–82; Michael Jay Feldberg, *The Turbulent Era: Riot and Disorder in Jacksonian America* (New York, 1980), 9–32.
16 Feldberg, "The Philadelphia Riots of 1844," 186–99; Feldberg, *The Turbulent Era*, 115.
17 Howard O. Sprogle, *The Philadelphia Police, Past and Present* (Philadelphia, 1887), 114–23; Alexander Henry *1st through 3rd Annual Messages* (Philadelphia, 1859, 1860, 1861); Schneider, "Mob Violence and Public Order," 30–51. For an excellent discussion of the persistent links between the pursuit of law and order and Philadelphia politics between 1854 and 1865 see Russell F. Weigley, " 'A Peaceful City': Public Order in Philadelphia from Consolidation Through the Civil War," in *The Peoples of Philadelphia*, 155–73.

right place at the right time."[18] But in the days after Sumter, Henry managed to combine the traditional mayor's position as moral leader with his new role as director of the police force. Armed only with a small flag, he dispersed the crowd at the *Palmetto Flag* office. On the following day he threatened police violence to maintain control at William Reed's house.

The Jacksonian riots also differed from the April 1861 disturbances in their degree of resistance. As Feldberg explains: "In riots where there was little or no resistance to the rioters, there were usually no fatalities and few injuries."[19] It was only after rioters "met resistance and a return of force" that bloodshed occurred. Even if the mobs in the streets following Fort Sumter were as angry as their 1840s counterparts, their victims did nothing to provoke them to violence.

Civil War rioting in other cities

America's cities were frequently disturbed by Civil War rioting. In July 1861 British diarist William Howard Russell witnessed a pitched battle in New York City between the New York Zouaves, angry at the murder of one of their number, and a militia patrol called out to quell the rioters.[20] A year later, Irish stevedores in Cincinnati battled blacks in bloody street fighting touched off by the bitter struggle for jobs.[21] The 1862 militia draft precipitated violent incidents nationwide. In Port Washington, Wisconsin, a large crowd of Luxembourgers disrupted the scheduled November 10 draft and then pillaged the town.[22] Detroit erupted in racial violence in early 1863 when rising job competition between blacks and whites, Lincoln's Emancipation Proclamation, and news of the new draft law providing for $300 exemption fees created a powder keg that was ignited by the arrest of a local mulatto for molesting two girls, one white and one black.[23]

The worst rioting accompanied the Union drafts of the summer of 1863. In New York mobs of primarily Irish workers burned the draft office, attacked the homes of leading Republicans, and assaulted local blacks in four days of rioting that left roughly 120 dead and over

18 Schneider, "Mob Violence and Public Order," p. 170-171.
19 Feldberg, "The Philadelphia Riots", 171; Feldberg, *The Turbulent Era*, 50.
20 William Howard Russell, *My Diary North and South* (Boston, 1863), 390.
21 Leonard Harding, "The Cincinnati Riots of 1862," *Bulletin of the Cincinnati Historical Society* 25 (October 1967): 229–39.
22 *Official Records*, ser. III, 2:903 (hereafter *OR*); Lawrence H. Larsen, "Draft Riot in Wisconsin," *Civil War History* 7 (December 1961): 421–7.
23 John C. Schneider, "Detroit and the Problem of Disorder: The Riot of 1863," *Michigan History* 38 (Spring 1974): 4–24.

200 seriously wounded.[24] Dozens of provost marshals elsewhere reported violent draft resistance.[25] On July 14, 1863, the provost marshal of Detroit's First District estimated that 1,500 men were prepared to resist. In Roundout, New York, Irish women stopped the enrolling officer from performing his task. The provost marshal in Kingston, New York, claimed that he would need 500 armed men to enforce the draft.[26] In March 1864, Charleston, Illinois Copperheads, angry at the proposed draft and incensed at repeated indignities at the hands of hostile soldiers, assaulted a body of unarmed volunteers.[27] That summer most Illinois districts experienced "open resistance" to the draft enrollment, and in several areas violence broke out.[28] In Pennsylvania five draft enrollers were killed in 1864 while trying to arrest deserters; several others were shot at or threatened.[29] In the Confederacy food shortages often precipitated violent outbursts. The most famous Southern bread riot occurred in Richmond in April 1863, involving as many as a thousand women. That spring similar outbreaks rocked several other Southern cities.[30]

The large body of literature on Civil War riots paints a complex picture in which violence was precipitated by some combination of wartime concerns, but particular outbreaks reflected antebellum frictions. Shortages of food or jobs, unpopular draft laws, or political or ethnic antagonisms generally brought tensions to a head. Usually the catalyst was a minor incident: an angry exchange in Charleston, an unlucky drawing in New York, a volatile court case in Detroit. But when the fighting began it generally pitted traditional adversaries against each other.

Philadelphia's April 1861 riots differed from these other wartime disturbances – as they differed from the city's antebellum violence – in that they resulted in very little damage and few injuries. Indeed a

24 Adrian Cook, *The Armies of the Streets: The New York City Draft Riots of 1863* (Lexington, KY., 1974). The casualty figures are from pages 194–5.
25 In Boston's North End, angry crowds assaulted two assistant provost marshals and forced local policemen to retreat into their stationhouse. See Roger Lane, *Policing the City: Boston, 1822–1885* (New York, 1975), 133.
26 OR, ser. III, 3:488–96, 518; Cook, *The Armies of the Streets*, 52. Pennsylvania experienced widespread resistance to the 1863 and 1864 drafts. See Arnold Shankman, "Draft Resistance in Civil War Pennsylvania," *Pennsylvania Magazine of History and Biography* (April 1977): 194; OR, ser. III, 3:324–5, 330–2, 351–2, 357, 382.
27 The rioting left ten dead and a dozen injured. See Charles H. Coleman and Paul H. Spence, "The Charleston Riot, March 28, 1864," *Journal of the Illinois State Historical Society* 33 (March 1940): 7–56.
28 Robert E. Sterling, "Civil War Draft Resistance in Illinois," *Journal of the Illinois State Historical Society* 64 (Autumn 1971): 244–66.
29 Shankman, "Draft Resistance in Civil War Pennsylvania," 200.
30 Michael Chesson, "Harlots or Heroines? A New Look at the Richmond Bread Riot," *The Virginia Magazine of History and Biography* 92 (April 1984): 131–75; Emory M. Thomas, *The Confederate Nation: 1861–1865* (New York, 1979), 202–5.

state of relative calm characterized the City of Brotherly Love during the course of the war. Although tensions often mounted and angry crowds occasionally collected, the forces of order consistently prevailed.

To understand this relative calm we must return to the descriptions of the other wartime riots. Whereas scholars generally concentrate on the underlying *causes* of each disturbance, most narratives repeatedly note that local police forces were inadequately prepared and poorly directed. The Cincinnati police force quickly stopped the initial outburst, but greater violence followed when the City Council sent 120 of 160 available officers out of town to help stop the famed Confederate raider John Hunt Morgan. When crowds massed at the Port Washington, Wisconsin, courthouse in November 1862, a draft commissioner stepped forward to speak to them. But the commissioner, a German Protestant, was himself objectionable to the rioters. The county sheriff for Coles County, Illinois, was in the courthouse when the shooting began in Charleston. He immediately joined his fellow Copperheads in firing on the soldiers. The Detroit authorities anticipated trouble in March 1863 and sent the city's Provost Guard to escort the convicted black rapist to jail. But then the guards left to put down a draftee uprising, leaving the mob free to wander the streets burning and pillaging.[31]

After a calm first day of drafting, the New York City officials did not anticipate any disturbances. On the following day, when the men of the Black Joke Engine Company led an assault on the draft office, there was only a small police force on hand. The mob quickly overcame the police and then easily defeated the members of the Invalid Corps who arrived as reinforcements. Once the rioting had started, a much larger armed force was required to restore order.[32]

When the Richmond Bread Riots of April 1863 broke out, "Old Joe" Mayo, the sixty-eight-year-old mayor, stood atop a makeshift platform and read the riot act aloud. But the women continued looting. Several other local leaders also spoke to the rioters to little effect. The disturbances only halted after Governor John Letcher

---

31 Coleman and Spence, "The Charleston Riot," 51; Larsen, "Draft Riot in Wisconsin," 422–4; Harding, "The Cincinnati Riots," 231. John C. Schneider has noted that Detroit had no regular police force, but he blames the uncontrolled rioting on poor decision making rather than inadequate manpower. See Schneider, "The Detroit Riot of 1863," 16–8, 23–4.

32 Cook, *Armies of the Streets*, 55–63, 199. Boston's Mayor Frederick Lincoln and his police force were an exception to this pattern in that they acted courageously and effectively in putting down that city's July 1863 draft riot. But although Lincoln's men performed well once the violence had begun, it appears that the Boston forces were poorly prepared (and armed) given New York City's example a few days earlier. See Lane, *Policing the City*, 133–4.

called out the Public Guard.[33] This riot was yet another example of the tendency of wartime leaders to fail to utilize their resources in anticipation of trouble and to mount feeble persuasive efforts that failed to maintain order.[34]

Peaceful Philadelphia

Although Philadelphia was often divided during the war, it rarely experienced mob rioting and never experienced prolonged political violence. Large shows of force generally quieted disorderly crowds. And when tensions did flare up, their potential damage was usually muted by the combination of an aggressive police force and a passive victim. A chronological survey reveals repeated moments when violence *could* have erupted, but only rare occasions when much damage was done.

During the first months of the war, the threat of violence silenced most of the city's pro-Southerners. Thomas Young's experience suggests the prevailing atmosphere. In June 1861 Young publicly declared that captured privateers should be treated as prisoners of war and not as pirates. He went on to defend the shooting of Colonel Elmer Ellsworth in Alexandria, Virginia. These comments enraged Young's listeners who chased the apparent disunionist into a nearby home. Fortunately for Young, a police detachment arrived and the officers took him to the station house. The next day the crowd trailed the prisoner's carriage to the Mayor's office where he was questioned. Henry discharged the prisoner, concluding that Young's words were imprudent and unpopular but not sufficient to justify arrest.[35]

On July 19, 1861, with rumors of fighting in Virginia filtering into the city, a drunken Georgian "took occasion to openly express secessionist sentiments" on the streets. These words attracted a crowd, and an elderly man knocked the Southerner to the ground. Just as the other bystanders were preparing to join in the beating, several police officers intervened. The Georgian spent the night in jail; in the morning an alderman fined him for his drunkenness and lectured him on

---

33 Chesson, "Harlots or Heroines?" 143–51. The small Richmond police force was not on the scene.

34 In November 1864 the Union army deployed a large force around lower Manhattan in response to rumors that the Confederates would try to disrupt New York City's election day. This example demonstrates the value of preemptive measures in maintaining order. See Edward G. Longacre, "The Union Army Occupation of New York City, November 1864," *New York History* 65 (April 1984): 133–58.

35 *PL*, 16 June 1861.

his "treasonable folly." In both of these incidents the public proved intolerant, the police protective, and city officials benign.[36]

Sometimes citizens' activities threatened to go beyond these spontaneous outbursts. In the wake of McDowell's defeat at Bull Run, several leading Republicans discussed "[a] plan to bring social opinion to bear upon those who expressed sentiments hostile to the government and the war." Sidney George Fisher, who participated in these discussions, privately expressed his own fear of "mob law."[37] Occasionally secret messages warned particularly odious citizens out of Philadelphia. One suspected spy received the following note:

> You are hereby notified that your presence in Philadelphia is obnoxious to the "Knights of the Blue Gauntlet," and that at a general convocation held this night beneath the folds of the starry Banner it was determined to notify you of the fact, and to give you ten days from date to place yourself without the pale of our jurisdiction.[38]

In May 1861 Sarah Wister reported that there had been "a great excitment in Philadelphia [when] some miserable little merchant [who] had been sending arms to the South . . . barely escaped the indignation of the mob, after which for several days ropes & nooses dangled ominously from the lampposts."[39]

Government agents began to pursue suspected Rebel sympathizers in August 1861. On the nineteenth, prominent Philadelphian Pierce Butler, recently returned from a stay in the Confederacy, was arrested for openly championing the Southern cause.[40] A few days later, federal marshals in Philadelphia, acting on Lincoln's orders, seized several New York newspapers critical of the government, and shut down operations at the offices of the *Christian Observer*, Philadelphia's only strongly antiadministration newspaper.[41] In the week following Butler's incarceration the marshals arrested six more accused Southern sympathizers. But all were soon released.[42] William H. Winder was not so fortunate. This longtime Philadelphian of an

36 *Philadelphia Evening Bulletin*, 20 July 1861 (hereafter *EB*).
37 Wainwright, *A Philadelphia Perspective*, 401, entry of 21 August 1861.
38 Everett, "Contraband and Rebel Sympathizers," 35–6. Everett cites an undated 1861 letter in the Henry Papers.
39 Wister, "Sarah Butler Wister's Civil War Diary," 298, entry of 16 May 1861.
40 *OR*, ser. II, 2:504–9; Dusinberre, *Civil War Issues*, 128. For contemporary accounts see Wister, "Sarah Butler Wister's Civil War Diary," 321–7; and Wainwright, *A Philadelphia Perspective*, 400, entry of 20 August 1861.
41 Scharf and Westcott, *History of Philadelphia*, 1:777; Dusinberre, *Civil War Issues*, 128.
42 Dusinberre, *Civil War Issues*, 128; Scharf and Westcott, *History of Philadelphia*, 1:777–8, 781; Everett, "Contraband and Rebel Sympathizers," 35; *OR*, ser. II, 2:132–3, 295, 505, 772, 829–57. Butler was freed on September 24.

old Maryland family authored several antiwar newspaper articles, and on September 10, 1861, he was seized as a disunionist. On several occasions Winder refused to sign loyalty oaths; he languished in jail until December 1862.[43]

The city's legal thinkers debated the constitutional implications of Lincoln's actions, but Philadelphia enjoyed a respite from political arrests or mob action in late 1861 and much of 1862.[44] As the administration's policies took on abolitionist tones, however, a portion of the city's Democratic elite became more openly pro-Southern.[45] By the end of the summer of 1862, political discord and the threat of a draft had brought the city to new heights of tension.

On July 21, 1862, Governor Curtin, responding to Lincoln's call for troops, announced that Philadelphia's military quota would be 5,000 men. Philadelphians soon met to encourage enlistment, spurred by the president's announcement that a state militia draft would be used to fill the quotas. On August 8 the War Department ordered the detention of anyone suspected of trying to discourage enlistment or evade the draft.[46] Within a week the Provost Guard removed several draft evaders from a ship bound for Londonderry, and the deputy marshal arrested a Democratic ward politician for discouraging enlistment.[47]

In August Philadelphia's Democrats held their first mass meeting of the war. Most of the speeches were pro-Union, but strongly antiabolitionist and opposed to arbitrary arrests. On the following day Provost Marshal William Kerns arrested Charles Ingersoll for his spirited attack on the administration.[48] The Ingersoll name was well respected in Philadelphia, and the controversy surrounding this arrest became a source of embarrassment for the government. Within a few days the administration ordered the fiery Democrat released.[49]

43 John A. Marshall, *American Bastille: A History of Illegal Arrests and Imprisonment of American Citizens During the Late Civil War* (Philadelphia, 1870), 268–89; *OR*, ser. II, 2:721–47.
44 Dusinberre, *Civil War Issues*, 128–31. This conclusion as to the apparent absence of political arrests and violence is based on a complete reading of the *Philadelphia Public Ledger*, extensive reading in several other local newspapers and in the *Official Records*, and a survey of the secondary literature.
45 Dusinberre, *Civil War Issues*, 135–7.
46 *OR*, ser. III, 2:321–2, 348–9.
47 Scharf and Westcott, *History of Philadelphia*, 1:799–800; *Germantown Telegraph*, 20 August 1862 (hereafter *GT*); Marshall, *American Bastille*, 400–2.
48 Kerns turned Ingersoll over to U.S. Marshal Millward because the arrest had been made under the War Department's August 8 order authorizing U.S. marshals to arrest people for disloyal acts. See Irwin F. Greenberg, "Charles Ingersoll: The Aristocrat as Copperhead," *Pennsylvania Magazine of History and Biography* 93 (April 1969): 199.
49 Greenberg, "Charles Ingersoll," 198–201; Dusinberre, *Civil War Issues*, 141–2; *GT*, 27 August 1862; Wainwright, *A Philadelphia Perspective*, 435–537; Weigley, "The Border City in the Civil War," 405.

During the following weeks the tensions boiled to the surface. The *Public Ledger* reported an August 23 knife fight in West Philadelphia following an angry discussion of "war matters." Two days later the Provost Guard arrested a man who had attracted an excited crowd by "uttering secessionist sentiments." The next evening six men broke up a Third Ward Democratic convention and assaulted several of its members.[50] On August 29 a deputy marshal, who had been enrolling men for a possible draft, was pelted with stones when he arrested one resister.[51] In the month after Ingersoll's release several other local men were arrested for discouraging enlistment.[52]

August 1862 ended with the Confederate army routing the Federal troops at the second Battle of Bull Run. The New York *Tribune* printed incorrect rumors that General Banks's army had been destroyed and that Lincoln had denounced General McClellan as a traitor. When these stories appeared on Philadelphia's bulletin boards, McClellan's supporters attempted to tear them down, "causing quarrels & fighting in the streets."[53] The *Public Ledger* reported that one "unfortunate individual derisively proposed three cheers for Greeley, and this being taken in earnest, the proposer was knocked down and afterwards compelled to run to escape severe punishment." When a second man called McClellan a traitor a Zouave d'Afrique "knocked him down. The crowd cheered and when the anti-McClellan man ran, the crowd followed, giving him an occasional kick. A policeman finally took him from further abuse."[54] The government silenced the rumors by temporarily suppressing the *Tribune*, thus once again opting for civic order over free speech.

On September 7 a scuffle broke out in the Continental Hotel when a customs inspector attacked a broker who had called Horace Greeley a traitor. The following month supporters of Democratic mayoral candidate Daniel M. Fox brawled with partisans of Alexander Henry, but police broke up this row, and the election itself was an orderly affair resulting in an easy Henry victory. A week later a man

---

50 *PL*, 25, 26, 29 August, 12 September 1862.
51 The marshal later returned with a squad of soldiers and dispersed the assembled mob. See *PL*, 30 August 1862; Scharf and Westcott, *History of Philadelphia*, 1:801.
52 Dusinberre reports three arrests (all three were quickly released) in the month following Ingersoll's arrest. See Dusinberre, *Civil War Issues*, 145. John H. Cook was arrested on September 20, 1862 and released on a *writ of habeas corpus*. See *Annual Cyclopedia* (1862), 513; Jesse C. Thomas was arrested the next week on the same charge and also soon released. See Scharf and Westcott, *History of Philadelphia*, 1:803.
53 Scharf and Westcott, *History of Philadelphia*, 1:802; Jacob Elfreth, Sr., diary, 1 September 1862, Haverford College Library, Haverford, Pa.
54 *PL*, 2 September 1862.

was badly beaten in a Chestnut Street lager beer saloon for loudly cheering the reelected mayor.[55]

The conflicts of late July and August 1862 were quite similar to those during the months surrounding the first Battle of Bull Run a year before. There was a handful of violent incidents, but nothing that the police force could not handle; the government arrested a few troublemakers and silenced a dangerous publication; the sum total of public discord was actually quite minimal. Unlike 1861, by August 1862 the Democrats were openly in dissent. But despite rumors of mob action, their mass meetings proceeded unmolested. Even at the height of dissension public and private forces combined to maintain order in the city.

Lincoln's January 1, 1863, Emancipation Proclamation fueled antiadministration feeling in Philadelphia. Some who had heretofore stood by the president refused to support a war to end slavery. The Democratic *Evening Journal* published an editorial comparing Lincoln unfavorably with Jefferson Davis. Major General Robert C. Schenck, commander of the troops in Baltimore, immediately ordered the arrest of Albert Boileau, the *Journal*'s editor, and the suppression of the offending newspaper. This action raised a strong outcry among the city's Democrats. But their anger was soon defused when Boileau wrote an apologetic letter promising to moderate his paper's stances, and was subsequently freed.[56]

Boileau's arrest prompted widespread questioning of the legality and wisdom of arbitrary arrests. Sidney Fisher found the action "a bold step to take in the face of recent Democratic triumphs," adding that he "should not be surprised if trouble grew out of this act." On January 31, George Fahnestock surveyed the situation and concluded: "we are bordering upon anarchy." The firebrand Copperheads, anxious for a martyr to their cause, attacked Boileau's "cringing, whining" apology, that took the wind from their sails.[57] Although the Emancipation Proclamation and Boileau's arrest again raised the level of political tension in Philadelphia, there was no concomitant wave of violence or preemptive arrests.

55 All incidents reported in the *Public Ledger*; Scharf and Westcott, *History of Philadelphia*, 1:803.
56 Shankman, "Freedom of the Press During the Civil War: The Case of Albert D. Boileau," *Pennsylvania History* 42 (October 1975): 305–15; Elwyn Burns Robinson, "The Public Press in Philadelphia During the Civil War" (Ph.D. diss., Western Reserve University, 1936), 170–2; Dusinberre, *Civil War Issues*, 154–8; Scharf and Westcott, *History of Philadelphia*, 1:806.
57 Wainwright, *A Philadelphia Perspective*, 447, entry of 29 January 1863; George W. Fahnestock diary, 31 January 1863, HSP; Shankman, "The Case of Albert D. Boileau," 314.

A month after Boileau's seizure Ohio Congressman Clement Vallandigham, the nation's leading antiwar Democrat, visited Philadelphia. A partisan crowd gathered at the Girard House, but his speech was repeatedly interrupted by hostile jeering.[58] Violence did not mar Vallandigham's stay; however, increasing support for the Peace Democrats did fuel mounting antagonisms in Philadelphia.

In March 1863 police confiscated a stock of pictures of Confederate generals from an Arch Street store. Members of the newly formed Young Democratic Club took to wearing old copper pennies with the head of Liberty facing outward, thus transferring the perjorative appellation "Copperhead" into a symbol of freedom. At one Democratic meeting members openly cheered Jefferson Davis. In April the Provost Guard arrested a man on Chestnut Street who had been drinking to Davis and other Southern leaders. Young Anna LaRoche reflected the combative view of the Peace Democrats: "They threaten us with a military force in our city to keep those down who oppose the Administration in its tyrannies."[59]

March also saw the launching of a new opposition newspaper, the *Age*, committed to the restoration of the Union "as it was."[60] The paper's offices soon became a regular scene of commotion. On May 2, one diarist reported, the building was "threatened by a mob."[61] On the 8 the *Age* posted headlines proclaiming the "Illegal arrest of Mr. Vallandigham" and the defeat of General Hooker at Chancellorsville. A large crowd gathered, a soldier ripped down the notice, and rioters shattered the newspaper's windows. As in April 1861, Mayor Henry, accompanied by a large police force, appeared personally to quell the mob.[62] The openly antiwar *Age* outraged a people reeling from news of recent Confederate victories. These were, Fahnestock wrote, "no times for trifling." The day after the riot, Dr. LaRoche braved an angry mob to attend a meeting of the Democratic Club. The lecturer enraged the crowd outside by advocating immediate peace and permanent slavery, but the police once again managed to protect the Democrats from violence. Sidney Fisher wrote that "the people are becoming very indignant at the men who so openly sympathize with the South."[63]

58 Scharf and Westcott, *History of Philadelphia*, 1:807; Oberholtzer, *Philadelphia*, 2:377.
59 Anna LaRoche diary, 15, 25 March 1863, Columbia University Archives; Frank H. Taylor, *Philadelphia in the Civil War, 1861–1865* (Philadelphia, 1913), 350; PL, 22 April 1863.
60 Robinson, "The Public Press," 176–7.
61 Henry Benners diary, 2 May 1863, HSP; Robinson, "The Public Press," 184.
62 PL, 9 May 1863; Dusinberre, *Civil War Issues*, 158; Wainwright, *A Philadelphia Perspective*, 451, entry of 8 May 1863.
63 Fahnestock diary, 8 May 1863; LaRoche diary, 10 May 1863; Dusinberre, *Civil War Issues*, 159; Wainwright, *A Philadelphia Perspective*, 451, entry of 18 May 1863.

In late May the Democrats resolved to hold a mass meeting to protest Vallandigham's arrest for treason. On June 1, the morning of the meeting, Fisher spoke with a friend who feared that hostile mobs would break up the affair and assault "the abominable clique who persistently denounce the war." But despite popular fears, a strong show of police and militia force protected the Copperheads yet again.[64]

The first months of 1863 seemed to be a time when Philadelphia could easily have erupted in violence. The Emancipation Proclamation, the recent military setbacks, and the continued policy of arbitrary arrests created an increasingly tense atmosphere. As we have seen, other Civil War riots often developed from small sparks. Between March and June Philadelphia experienced many likely catalysts, but Philadelphians did not riot. Much of the credit must go to Mayor Henry and his police force. Officers continued to arrest intemperate citizens before angry crowds could do serious damage. Henry's presence at the *Age* office reiterated his skillful use of persuasion and force. Most important, city officials anticipated possible trouble spots and dispatched large forces *ahead* of time, successfully dissuading violence-minded citizens.

Lee's 1863 invasion of Pennsylvania, culminating in the Battle of Gettysburg, underscored the Union's growing manpower needs. This spurred the use of black soldiers: on July 3 black troops paraded in Philadelphia.[65] On July 9 the president called for a draft of 300,000 men. The Democrats, with their twin planks of white supremacy and personal freedom, were faced with black troops and conscription. These two developments further spurred clashes of public opinion.

In this strained atmosphere abolitionist orators fanned the flames by demanding black equality and suffrage, sentiments that Fisher found both "absurd" and "dangerous."[66] Philadelphia's black community eyed these developments with growing concern. The previous August soldiers had burned down the Harrisburg home of a black man. It was rumored that hostile Philadelphia whites had prepared lists of leading black citizens destined for similar treatment.[67] Following the March 1863 antiblack rioting in Detroit, the *Christian Recorder* reported that "[e]ven here, in the city of Philadelphia, in many places it is almost impossible for a respectable colored person to walk the

---

64 Wainwright, *A Philadelphia Perspective*, 453. Dusinberre, *Civil War Issues*, 159–60; LaRoche diary, 2 June 1863.
65 Taylor, *Philadelphia in the Civil War*, 188; Dusinberre, *Civil War Issues*, 171.
66 Wainwright, *A Philadelphia Perspective*, 456, entry of 8 July 1863.
67 "Documents," Jacob A. White to Joseph C. Bustill, 19 August 1862, *Journal of Negro History* 11 (January 1926): 83; Frederick M. Binder, "Pennsylvania Negro Regiments in the Civil War," *Journal of Negro History* 37 (October 1952): 396.

streets without being assaulted."[68] Then in July, with Philadelphia's draft only a few days away, New York City erupted into massive antidraft and antiblack rioting. Philadelphians read the news with horror, fearing for their own city. The *Christian Recorder*'s black readers felt the dangers most acutely:

> Our citizens are expecting every day that a mob will break out here, in Philadelphia. And if so, it is thought, they will not only resist the draft, but will pounce upon the colored people as they did in New York, and elsewhere, and if so, we have only to say this to colored citizens of Philadelphia and vicinity: Have plenty of powder and ball in your houses, and use it with effect, if necessary, in the protection of your wives and children.[69]

Despite this charged atmosphere, Philadelphia's July 1863 draft passed peacefully.

Yet again, Philadelphia avoided draft riots by carefully positioning police and troops in potential trouble spots. On July 14, 1863, on the basis of reported troubles in several Northern cities, Mayor Henry asked Lieutenant Colonel William D. Whipple, the military commander in charge of Philadelphia, to postpone the local draft. Whipple telegraphed Provost Marshal General James B. Fry: "I think it had better go on, being satisfied that I can quell a riot." The first day's drafting proceeded without disturbance, but Colonel Richard H. Rush sent Fry an urgent telegram:

> I have means of hearing from various sources what has caused me to believe that there will be serious resistance to the draft in [Philadelphia] and under pretext of that the mob will endeavor to take possession of the U. S. property in that city. . . . I have seen the telegram in which Colonel Whipple thinks he can carry out the draft with the force he has. I beg leave to differ with him, and would strongly urge that the draft be not attempted in Philadelphia until the resistance to it elsewhere has been put down by force, and then execute it in Philadelphia under the presence of an efficient force of 1,500 to 2,000 reliable troops.[70]

On the sixteenth Major General D. N. Couch sent two regiments from his Harrisburg command to reinforce the troops in Philadelphia. Secretary of War Stanton, noting that a Philadelphia "district where disturbance is apprehended" was to draft conscripts on the seventeenth, ordered Major General Napoleon Jackson Tecumseh Dana to Philadelphia. The following morning Adjutant General Lorenzo Thomas informed Stanton that he had inspected Whipple's pre-

68 *Christian Recorder*, 4 March 1863 (hereafter *CR*).
69 *CR*, 25 July 1863.
70 *OR*, ser. III, 3:491, 497, 499.

parations and judged that the combined force of "five regiments of infantry, three batteries of artillery, one company of cavalry[, and the] Union Battery of this city . . . with the city police, will be ample." But Provost Marshal Fry sent Whipple another regiment of infantry and two batteries of artillery.[71]

First District Provost Marshal William E. Lehman, unsatisfied with the "Municipal and Military force now in the City," asked Fry for permission to hire fifty special agents. "I suggest," Lehman wrote, "That the distribution of such a force in *citizen's dress* in the crowd that may assemble . . . might be of signal service in suppressing disturbance." Lehman went on to point out that "the 4th ward, part of the first district, has an historical reputation for bold & infamous outrages on public law."[72] On the eighteenth, Whipple – now acting as Dana's Chief of Staff – advised Fry against any postponements. That afternoon Fry ordered Lieutenant Colonel Bomford, the Acting Assistant Provost Marshal General in Harrisburg, to "[l]et the draft go on in Philadelphia."[73]

Even with a large armed force in place, Philadelphia's leading citizens were not satisfied. Ever since the first news of Lee's invasion, they had been clamoring for Lincoln to put General George Cadwalader, the hero of the 1844 riots, in charge of the city. Finally, after drafting had already begun, the president consented and replaced Dana, an unpopular New Englander, with Cadwalader, the old Philadelphia Democrat. Together, Cadwalader and Henry deftly maneuvered their forces to guarantee a quiet draft.[74]

On July 29, about a week before the city's draft was scheduled to end, Bomford reported to Fry that "the draft is so well advanced in Philadelphia" that it would be possible to move troops to Pottsville where they were more needed.[75] On the final day of drafting the *Evening Bulletin* expressed its pride in Philadelphia for having withstood the draft with order and good humor.[76]

The final reports of the district provost marshals agreed that the draft ran smoothly. Captain Lehman of the First District noted that

71 *OR*, ser. III, 3:518–9.
72 Letter from William E. Lehman, Provost Marshal, First District to Colonel James Fry, Provost Marshal General, 17 July 1863, #2816, RG110, National Archives (hereafter NA). Permission to hire these secret agents was apparently not granted.
73 *OR*, ser. III, 3:543
74 Roy P. Basler, ed., *The Collected Works of Abraham Lincoln*, 8 vols. (New Brunswick, 1953), 6:279, Letter from Lincoln to Horace Binney, Jr., 16 June 1863; *OR*, ser. III, 3:573; Weigley, "The Border City in Civil War," 409, 411; Dusinberre, *Civil War Issues*, 170.
75 *OR*, ser. III, 3:590.
76 *EB*, 4 August 1863. Scharf and Westcott say that the draft was "never interrupted by the slightest disturbance." See Scharf and Westcott, *History of Philadelphia*, 1:809. The *Public Ledger* only reported one arrest. See *PL*, 21 July 1863.

"[t]he people of the district are impulsive and being mostly laboring men the draft fell hard upon them, yet nothing unpleasant occurred." The provost marshal for the Second District reported that "[e]verything passed off in perfect order." In the Fourth District a large crowd witnessed the drawing, and when it was over cheered the government. Although the enrolling officers ran into trouble in some wards and the provost marshals frequently had difficulties serving draft notices, Philadelphia had no major violent incidents associated with the draft.[77]

Two factors help explain Philadelphia's relatively trouble-free drafts. First, as we have seen, Philadelphia's recruitment system was so successful that the city was not forced to bear a burdensome draft. Most quotas were met by enticing enlistees with large bounties. Second, the rioting in New York City led city, state, and national officials to take serious measures to avoid similar violence in Philadelphia.[78]

In the summer of 1863 Philadelphia weathered the political tensions brought on by race, invasion, and conscription without widespread disorder. That fall the Democrats remained active, holding a mass meeting on Constitution Day, but they were soundly beaten in the October elections.[79] Still, newspaper reports suggest that politically charged arguments continued to be perilous: In August a taverner called two marines "nigger lovers," shooting one in the ensuing brawl; in October two men fought in a Broad Street public house when one called the other a "Copperhead."[80]

But although Copperheads spoke freely in private homes,[81] public discretion was still advised. In May 1864 a drunken man stumbled around Central Station assaulting anyone who made disparaging comments about the government or the army. In mid-July crowds gathered in Chestnut Street for military news. When one man suggested three cheers for Jefferson Davis, a soldier knocked him down.

77 Provost Marshals, Pennsylvania Districts One – Five, "Historical Reports," entry of 6 September 1865, microfilm M1163, reel #4, NA.
78 See Elfreth, Sr., diary, 15, 20, 22, 29 July 1863 for comments about the military's role in maintaining calm. Also see Dusinberre, *Civil War Issues*, 170. Of course Boston also drafted after New York City but suffered through serious rioting. Lane, *Policing the City*, 134.
79 Nicholas B. Wainwright, "The Loyal Opposition in Civil War Philadelphia," *Pennsylvania Magazine of History and Biography* 88 (July 1964): 307–8. The provost marshals also took care to involve Democrats and Republicans in the procedures, thus avoiding inflammatory charges of partisanship. See "Proceedings of the Board of Enrollment, First District, Pennsylvania," entries of 27, 28 July 1863, #2823, RG 110, NA.
80 *PL*, 31 August, 20 October 1863.
81 For Sidney George Fisher's comments on quarrels with antiwar relatives see Wainwright, *A Philadelphia Perspective*, 468, 470, entries of 16 March, 10 April 1864.

The crowd was about to join in the assault, but the man ran and hid until a policeman came and escorted him to the station. In August the police arrested a Richmond native for treasonable language.[82] These incidents reiterated the two messages of 1861. Although the Copperheads had become strong enough to attack the war in public forums, they uttered such sentiments in the streets at their peril. And if a disunionist found himself in a dangerous position the city's police force would act quickly to preserve order.

The strongest upsurge of Democratic fervor – and the greatest threat to Philadelphia's wartime public order – occurred in the weeks before the 1864 elections. The Democrats campaigned on a platform of negotiated peace without tampering with slavery.[83] On September 26 the *Public Ledger* warned:

> Political excitement and partisan feeling are so high that, unless cool judgement is sprinkled over this passion, the contending parties are likely to come into serious collision at every public assemblage. The torchlight procession on Saturday night ended in a row, during which the Democratic head-quarters on Chestnut Street was stoned and the transparencies injured. It is said that an assault was first committed upon the procession from the house. If this was so, it is no excuse for a riot.[84]

From mid-September to early November torchlight processions lit Philadelphia's nights. On October 11 the National Union Party swept the state and county elections, paving the way for Lincoln's November presidential bid.[85] One group of men, enraged that their votes had been declared illegal, sought solace in a lager beer saloon where they took pot shots at passing soldiers. This resulted in a brawl that "pretty well gutted" the building before a squad of police broke it up. In another incident a man was shot at the Nineteenth Ward polling place. The following day a brief scuffle broke out when crowds gathered to read the election returns. That afternoon a "political disturbance" at the Frankford Road public house degenerated into a large row in which a furloughed soldier was shot and killed.[86]

---

82 *Press*, 16 May 1864; *EB*, 10 June 1864; *PL*, 13 July, 15 August 1864.
83 Wainwright, "Loyal Opposition," 311–12.
84 *PL*, 26 September 1864.
85 Scharf and Westcott, *History of Philadelphia*, 1:818; Beale diary, *passim*; James Tyndale Mitchell diary, 8 October 1864, privately owned. For a discussion of the elections of 1864 see Erwin Stanley Bradley, *The Triumph of Militant Republicanism: A Study of Pennsylvania and Presidential Politics, 1860–1872* (Philadelphia, 1964), Chapter 5. For a European's description of Philadelphia's October 8, 1864, Republican procession see David C. Rankin, ed., "Political Parades and American Democracy: Jean-Charles Houzeau on Lincoln's 1864 Reelection Campaign," *Civil War History* (December 1984), 328–9.
86 *PL*, 12, 13 October 1864.

On October 29 the Democrats held the largest torchlight procession the city had ever seen.[87] When the Democrats passed the Republican headquarters on Chestnut Street, members of the two parties fought and hurled missiles. One bystander was killed by an object reportedly thrown by a man sporting a McClellan button.[88] From a window at the *Age* office, Anna LaRoche watched the parade and saw a Democrat attacked. That evening the LaRoches heard shots and Anna wrote: "we dread blood in the streets." Several Democratic homes were attacked that night, but a kindly Republican talked the mob out of assaulting the LaRoche household.[89]

After the October violence, the Philadelphia Democrats were soundly beaten in the November election.[90] The events leading to the vote revealed widepread dissatisfaction with Lincoln and his party. But given the prevailing animosity and the scope of the political demonstrations, these altercations added up to very little. Once again, the city's police regularly appeared on the scene to keep incendiary situations in check.

The Democrats' electoral defeat and the Union army's successes helped limit tensions during the winter of 1864 and into the spring of 1865. The February draft proceeded smoothly, with Mayor Henry ordering ample police protection. In March the city held its final draft, and the provost marshal again requested a police detail, this time adding: "I have no reason to anticipate a breach of the peace."[91]

The news of Lee's surrender launched Philadelphians into a week of celebration, but Lincoln's assassination a week later posed a stern test to civic order. Although the *Public Ledger* reported that "past political differences were forgotten," the newspaper noted that anyone who expressed joy at the president's death was immediately the target of angry citizens. Diarist Isaiah Hacker commented that "[i]t is almost as much as a man's life is worth if he dare . . . to show any joy at our country's loss." In more than one instance policemen stepped in to protect loose-tongued Southern sympathizers. Although some feared serious violence, the police soon succeeded in clearing the streets and calming the crowds.[92]

---

87 See Auguste Laugel, *The United States During the Civil War*, ed. Allan Nevins (1866; Bloomington, IN, 1961), 71–2.

88 In the weeks to come, Campbell, the only Philadelphian to die during wartime rioting, became a celebrated figure. Scharf and Westcott, *History of Philadelphia*, 1:819; *PL*, 31 October, 2, 4, 7, 19 November 1864.

89 LaRoche diary, 31 October 1864; Elfreth, Sr., diary, 31 October 1864.

90 Wainwright, "The Loyal Opposition," 312.

91 "Proceedings of the Board of Enrollment, First District," entries of 23, 24 February 1865; Provost Marshal to Henry, 21 February, 17 March 1865, F-5, Henry Letters, HSP.

92 *PL*, 17 April 1865; Isaiah Hacker diary, 16 April 1865, HSP.

As he had for the previous four years, Mayor Henry played a key role in maintaining order following the assassination. The *Public Ledger* noted his "personal efforts" in controlling the streets, but he also acted behind the scenes, using both his police power and his persuasive skills. Immediately after the assassination, the editors of the *Age* wrote to the mayor seeking police protection from "causeless and unprovoked assaults."[93] The mob did attack the *Age* office, but the police provided adequate protection. Henry also recognized the limits of the police force: He sent notes to prominent Democrats, advising them to display mourning bows in their windows. His advice was well heeded, and Copperhead homes escaped un-scathed.[94]

On the evening of the assassination Edward Ingersoll delivered a particularly strong speech in New York in which he vowed his contin-ued support for the South. The *Evening Bulletin* described Ingersoll's speech and asked "shall such a *traitor* be allowed to dwell with and among us of Philadelphia?"[95] A few days later, Ingersoll entered a morning train to cries of "traitor." When the train stopped, a soldier demanded that he retract his statements. Ingersoll told the soldier to "go to hell" and the two fought with their canes before a growing crowd. After breaking his cane Ingersoll drew out a pistol, but before he could fire two police officers intervened. With Ingersoll behind bars, irate citizens massed outside the heavily guarded station house. When Charles Ingersoll arrived to visit his brother, the mob beat him quite badly before the guards stepped in. The next day Ingersoll's lawyers secured his release and he retreated to a country home.[96] For a final time the city had successfully navigated the dangerous shoals of wartime dissent without suffering serious casualties.

Preserving the peace

Although secession, military failures, conscription, black recruits, and political conflicts produced numerous tense moments, Phil-

---

93 Glossman and Welch (editors of the *Age*) to Henry, 15 April 1865, F-2, Henry Letters. On April 15 Sidney Fisher wrote that an assault on the *Age* seemed "very likely" and perhaps even justified. See Wainwright, *A Philadelphia Perspective*, 493.

94 Wainwright, *A Philadelphia Perspective*, 493, entry of 17 April 1865; Wainwright, "The Loyal Opposition," 314. Pierce Butler did not bow his windows and only escaped the mob when a neighboring abolitionist quieted a crowd of "laboring men" who had planned an assault. See Wainwright, *A Philadelphia Perspective*, 497, entry of 5 May 1865.

95 Greenberg, "The Aristocrat as Copperhead," 211; Dusinberre, *Civil War Issues*, 174; *EB*, 26 April 1865. See also *GT*, 26 April 1865, for an account of the speech.

96 *PL*, 27 April 1865; Wainwright, *A Philadelphia Perspective*, 495–6, entries of 27, 28, 29 April 1865; Greenberg, "The Aristocrat as Copperhead," 211–12. George Wharton told Fisher that the police were slow to act, but Fisher credited them with stepping in even though they agreed with the sentiments of the crowd.

adelphia never faced the large-scale rioting that ravaged other Northern cities. Part of the explanation lies in the nature of the specific conflicts. Most spontaneous flareups involved a single Southern sympathizer accosted by dozens of militant unionists. Dissent may have been widespread, but the pro-Union forces ruled the streets.

Much of the credit must go to Mayor Henry and his police force. In 1844 troops were used first tentatively and then ineffectively. Throughout the course of the Civil War Henry employed several tools to control his city. Police officers regularly squelched street incidents by arresting the offending party and dispersing the mob. When large crowds formed and ran the risk of getting out of control, Henry repeatedly appeared in person to promote calm and order. And when a Democratic meeting or planned military draft threatened Philadelphia's order, the mayor and military officers arranged shows of force to dissuade troublemakers.

In his annual reports Henry consistently credited his police force with preserving calm. In January 1862 he wrote:

> In reviewing the Police during the unprecedented occurrences and excitements of the past year, I deem it an act of merited justice to express my hearty appreciation of their general efficiency and zeal, and to attribute, in no small degree, the almost uninterrupted order and quiet of the city to their prompt and vigilant efforts.[97]

The following year he took note of "the continued favor of Almighty God towards the city in preserving it from tumult," but added his confidence that the "police [are] fully adequate to quell any riot or outbreak of lawless violence." After Gettysburg and the 1863 draft, Henry proudly observed that "[t]he excitement of popular commotion has never subverted the good order of the city." And in the war's final month the mayor declared that "[t]he deserved confidence of this community in the efficiency of the police force has been conservative of public quiet in recent times of general excitement."[98]

The "public quiet" that Henry took such pride in should not be confused with civic harmony. The police force assembled in the mid-1850s "battled" disorder quite literally. Henry's predecessors had filled the force with tough veterans of Philadelphia's street gangs who were quick to use familiar strong-arm tactics to maintain the peace.[99]

97 Alexander Henry, Fourth Annual Report (Philadelphia, 1862), 26.
98 Henry, Fifth Annual Report (Philadelphia, 1863), 5, 23; Henry, Sixth Annual Report (Philadelphia, 1864), 29; Henry, Seventh Annual Report (Philadelphia, 1865), 29.
99 Weigley, "The Border City in Civil War," 370; David R. Johnson, Policing the Urban Underworld (Philadelphia, 1979), 139–40; Johnson, "Crime Patterns in Philadelphia," 102.

Thus when the mayor threatened violence his audience knew he could back up his words. And if the police force maintained order through intimidation, the citizenry certainly followed a similar formula. The mobs that demanded shows of patriotism in April 1861 and again four years later performed their own form of civic ritual, enhancing group solidarity while forcing community standards on perceived enemies.[100] Such demonstrations, coupled with the occasional street corner assaults on vocal Rebel sympathizers,[101] ensured relative order even when individual feelings ran high.

Philadelphia did not erupt into violence during the Civil War because its people and institutions successfully adjusted to meet the tests posed by wartime tensions. For four years a web of private and public forces combined to ensure order and stability. At one level, these "forces" were highly individualized. In private homes citizens kept violent arguments in check by mutual agreement. In saloons and on street corners only those made brave with drink dared utter pro-Southern sentiments. At the other end of the spectrum, federal initiatives maintained order in Philadelphia. U. S. marshals arrested suspected disloyalists and seized inflammatory newspapers; federal troops helped guarantee a peaceful draft.

But Mayor Henry and his police force deserve the bulk of the responsibility for maintaining calm. Had the war occurred a decade earlier, the unconsolidated city would have been ill prepared to meet the challenge, and repetitions of the 1844 carnage might have ensued. And if Henry had not consistently anticipated troubles and defused them with careful planning, spirited oratory, and a strong-armed police force, the police could not have accomplished their task without greater violence.

The system that Philadelphia had in place in April 1861 proved sufficient to control its citizens for the next four years. Thus two possible war-related changes did not occur. First, the various wartime tensions never produced substantial disorder. Second, despite the

100 For an analysis of "street theater" in antebellum Philadelphia see Susan Gray Davis, *Parades and Power: Street Theater in Nineteenth-Century Philadelphia* (Philadelphia, 1986). For an extensive discussion of the use of intimidation and violence to promote community standards see Bertram Wyatt-Brown, *Southern Honor: Ethics and Behavior in the Old South* (New York, 1982), 435–61 and *passim*. Although the crowds that formed in Philadelphia in April 1861 and April 1865 did not follow any clearly defined ritual patterns, their use of public street displays at the homes of suspected secessionists (and later Copperheads) shared much in common with the burlesques described by Davis and the Southern charivaris portrayed by Wyatt-Brown.

101 Although the evidence is thin, the crowds that followed arrested Southern sympathizers to jail or later to court seemed to follow a pattern that might suggest another form of spontaneous "street theater."

activities of federal marshals, the goal of silencing dangerous dissent did not push power very far toward the center. In a sense Philadelphia's menacing mobs suggest that even censorship remained largely in private hands. But the war also added a new, potentially disruptive, element to Philadelphia life. Shortly after the firing on Fort Sumter, the city filled with uniformed men. The next chapter will discuss how Philadelphia dealt with this new disorderly force.

8 Soldiers in the city: The military challenge to public order

We have seen that the tensions caused by the Civil War did not result in frequent outbreaks of large-scale violence in Philadelphia. But the aggregate impact of the war on crime and violence remains unclear. It could have been that the conflict's violence and destruction changed the atmosphere at home, making local bloodshed more commonplace. Or the influx of young soldiers might have disrupted the city's equilibrium, raising the level of disorder. On the other hand, the army absorbed a large percentage of Philadelphia's young men, including many of its unruly firemen. Could this have made Philadelphia a calmer place?[1] In the previous chapter we asked how wartime tensions disrupted life in Philadelphia; in this chapter we will examine patterns of crime and violence, and consider the role of military movements in disturbing public order.

Arrests and military movements

The existing scholarship on crime during the Civil War offers no consensus. We know, for instance, that jail commitments in Massachusetts declined during the war, as did incarcerations for crimes against persons.[2] And Edith Abbott found evidence of declining male state prison populations in her survey of several Northern states.[3] But another study found a "sharp increase in interpersonal violence" in Franklin County, Ohio.[4] And a survey of "true bill" indictments in Lancaster County, Pennsylvania, concluded that county-wide "crime did not become a more serious problem over the course of the Civil War," but "interpersonal crime . . . rose steadily" in Lancaster City.[5]

1 In a search for references to gangs in the *Philadelphia Public Ledger*, David R. Johnson found six incidents from 1855 to 1859, five in 1860, five from 1868 to 1871, and none during the war years. Perhaps this indicated a disbanding "for the duration." See Johnson, *Policing the Urban Underworld* (Philadelphia, 1979), Appendix I, 189–91.
2 Michael Hindus, *Prison and Plantation* (Chapel Hill, N. C., 1980), 71–2.
3 Edith Abbott, "The Civil War and the Crime Wave of 1865–1870," *The Social Science Review* 1 (June 1927): 216–19.
4 Eric H. Monkkonen, *The Dangerous Class: Crime and Poverty in Columbus, Ohio, 1860–1885* (New York, 1975), 53.
5 Robert L. Hampel and Charles W. Ormsby, Jr., "Crime and Punishment on the Civil War Homefront," *Pennsylvania Magazine of History and Biography* (April 1982): 226–7, 237–8.

194

Eric Monkkonen, in the best systematic analysis of wartime crime, found that urban arrests peaked in 1862, but arrests for crimes with victims did not rise until 1865. Monkkonen ascribes the 1862 "crime wave" to clashes between young men chafing at restrictive social norms and newly created urban police forces seeking to hold them in check. The late-war decline in arrests, he explains, was due to the removal of young men from society by the army. Monkkonen suggests that those responsible for the 1865 peak in crimes with victims were generally older men who would not have been drafted into the service. Monkkonen holds that the postwar crime wave did not reach its high point until 1870, but he shares the common belief that the postwar disruptions resulted from the return of men "incapable of civilian order" into a socially and economically demoralized society.[6] Monkkonen also measured arrest rates for drunk and disorderly conduct in twenty-three cities and found a particularly "high degree of public disorder" during the Civil War. Although the "aggressive draft policy . . . removed just those people one would expect to produce drunken and disorderly behavior," the dislocation of army life placed such men in public places, where they were more likely to run afoul of the law, rather than in homes, out of sight of the police.[7]

The difficulty in assessing this literature is that each body of evidence measures a different reflection of disorder, and none gauges disorder itself. Nevertheless, the evidence clearly indicates that the outbreak of the war did not precipitate a four-year-long increase in crime. Indeed, the worst "crime wave" seems to have occurred in the postwar years, when returning veterans came home to a stagnant economy.[8]

Philadelphia's monthly arrest records allow us to measure wartime patterns of crime and disorder. Monthly arrest figures from 1857 to 1867 (summarized in Table 8.1) show four substantial shifts. Total arrests rose dramatically in mid-1858, declined in the war's first months, surpassed antebellum levels in early 1863, and rose rapidly between 1864 and 1866.[9] Some of these changes were probably due to alterations in Philadelphia's police. Soon after Mayor Henry's May 1858 election, he began to improve his police force. More than 16,000 of the 22,367 arrests in 1858 occurred after June 1, when this

6 Monkkonen, *Police in Urban America, 1860–1920* (New York 1981), 78–82.
7 Monkkonen, "A Disorderly People? Urban Order in the Nineteenth and Twentieth Centuries," *Journal of American History* (December 1981): 540–6.
8 See, for instance, Abbott, "The Civil War and the Crime Wave of 1865–1870."
9 Of course much of the fluctuation in the monthly arrest figures reflects persistent shifts. The decline in arrests after March 1861 is most apparent when compared with the monthly figures for 1860.

Table 8.1. Monthly Arrests in Philadelphia, 1857–67

	1857	1858	1859	1860	1861	1862	1863	1864	1865	1866	1867
January	1,646	1,569	2,416	2,212	2,180	1,710	2,647	2,380	—	2,633	2,414
February	1,830	1,115	2,108	2,144	2,107	1,746	2,260	2,712	—	2,795	2,875
March	2,058	1,209	2,545	2,436	2,502	2,101	2,831	2,818	—	3,629	3,092
April	1,964	1,015	2,512	1,963	2,037	2,093	2,717	2,683	—	3,574	3,689
May	1,971	1,078	2,627	2,588	2,168	2,179	3,048	2,979	—	3,792	3,539
June	2,293	1,558	2,727	2,919	2,229	2,490	3,044	2,471	—	3,713	3,974
July	2,190	2,570	3,161	3,219	2,304	2,871	2,690	3,199	—	4,052	4,114
August	1,281	2,533	3,059	3,054	2,737	2,748	3,113	3,380	—	3,724	4,181
September	1,726	2,554	2,862	3,014	2,472	2,541	3,420	3,067	—	4,163	4,482
October	1,512	2,397	2,753	2,964	2,286	2,114	2,838	3,145	—	3,710	4,300
November	1,543	2,246	2,936	2,893	1,952	2,530	2,755	2,772	—	3,792	3,455
December	1,523	2,523	3,519	2,645	2,309	2,453	2,687	2,615	—	3,644	2,848
Total	21,537	22,367	33,225	32,051	27,283	27,576	34,050	34,221	39,315	43,226	42,963

Note: Monthly figures for 1866 add up to 43,221, but total in Mayor's Report is 43,226. No monthly data available for 1865.

Source: Mayor's *Annual Reports.*

reorganization began.[10] The postwar jump in arrests followed the February 1865 introduction of 100 new police officers, bringing the total to 831.[11] But the decline in arrests in the early years of the war and the subsequent increase in 1863 apparently stemmed from real changes in the rate of wartime crime.

The decline in arrests beginning in May 1861 followed the first wave of enlistments, which removed large numbers of young men from the city's streets.[12] But the return to prewar arrest levels in late 1862 does not seem to be related to military developments. The three-year volunteers did not begin to return home until December 1863, and they continued to pour into the city through the spring of 1864. These arrivals did not coincide with any expansion in arrests over the previous year.

The 1863 rise in arrests followed an increase in political tensions, and perhaps it reflected efforts by the police to maintain control. But the midwar increase in arrests was probably also related to economic shifts. Philadelphia's arrest rates began to rise at just about the same time that organized demands arose from the city's labor force for pay increases to offset declining real wages.[13] Specific events explain the unusual *decline* in arrests in July 1863.[14] Nearly a hundred Philadelphia police officers joined the "Henry Guards" during the military emergency, serving from June 17 to July 21.[15] Those who stayed home had to divide their time between normal duties and helping to maintain calm during the draft.

The postwar increase in arrests also had several possible causes (other than the expanded police force). In March 1867 Mayor Morton McMichael attributed the rising crime rate to population growth.[16] But given that the city's population increased only from about 608,000 in 1864 to about 630,000 in 1866, this hardly explains the substantial jump in arrests.[17] When the war ended, thousands of war-hardened veterans returned to a city with a newly energetic police force, a

10 Henry makes this point in the *Second Annual Message* (Philadelphia, 1860), 27.
11 This shift does not entirely explain the increase in arrests. The police force expanded less than 14 percent in 1865, but the total arrests increased about 25 percent from 1864 to 1866.
12 On December 5, 1861, the *Germantown Telegraph* (hereafter *GT*) noted that "[f]rom the commencement of the war to the present time the twenty-second ward has been unusually free of crimes of every kind." See *GT*, 5 December 1861.
13 See Chapter 9.
14 Note that this decline (Table 8.1) is particularly noteworthy when compared with the standard increase in arrests between June and July.
15 Frank H. Taylor, *Philadelphia in the Civil War, 1861–1865* (Philadelphia, 1913), 248.
16 Morton McMichael, *First Annual Report* (Philadelphia, 1867), 12–13.
17 Roger Lane, *Violent Death in the City: Suicide, Accident and Murder in 19th Century Philadelphia* (Cambridge, Mass. 1979), 11.

declining postwar economy, and a high unemployment rate. Perhaps this explains the substantial postwar increase in arrests.

Table 8.2 breaks down arrests by type of offense and then combines them into three major groups: violent crimes, property crimes, and public disorder. Table 8.3 presents this annual arrest data as percentages of all arrests. Fluctuations in wartime arrests were the result of some combination of three factors: changing patterns of public disorder, shifts in the demographic makeup of the city, and changed police activities. A breakdown of arrests by type of crime may help distinguish among these three factors.

The outbreak of war does not seem to have made the city more violent. Between 1860 and 1862 assault and murder arrests declined both in absolute terms and as a share of all arrests. The 1862 to 1863 rise in arrests includes a notably large increase in these violent crimes, but the total share still did not exceed the prewar levels. In 1865, when according to Monkkonen crimes with victims reached their peak, assaults in Philadelphia increased slightly, but declined as a share of all arrests. Arrests for murder, which Monkkonen described as peaking between 1861 and 1863, were particularly low in Philadelphia during the war. There were fewer homicide indictments per capita in the city between 1860 and 1866 than in the previous seven years or any subsequent seven-year period.[18]

Arrests for disorderly conduct added up to nearly three-quarters of all arrests. The annual shifts in this category generally followed the pattern for all arrests, except in the years from 1861 to 1863 when disorderly conduct charges took an increased share of all arrests. This growth, which preceded the massive return of troops, probably owed more to vigorous efforts by the police force to maintain control of a population under political and economic pressure than to changes in the military component. In fact arrests for disorderly conduct declined in 1864, the year of the largest troop returns.

Property crimes made up a relatively small percentage of all arrests, and changed little during the war. The increases in 1862 and in 1863 might be tied to declining real wages, but the shifts are not very pronounced. These totals do not include the arrests made by the Detective Department, which concentrated on professional thiefs. If we add the arrests for property crimes made by the detectives to those made by the regular police force, we find a slightly more marked increase from 1861 to 1863.[19]

18 Lane, *Violent Death in the City*, 60.
19 In 1861 the Detective Department made 261 arrests for property crimes; by 1863 that figure had risen to 343. See James M. Gallman, "Mastering Wartime: A Social History of Philadelphia During the Civil War" (Ph.D. diss., Brandeis University, 1986), Table 8.4.

Table 8.2. Philadelphia Arrests for Selected Crimes, 1857–67

	1857	1858	1859	1860	1861	1862	1863	1864	1865	1866	1867
Assault	1,480	1,271	1,805	1,847	1,510	1,429	2,208	2,272	2,418	2,264	2,273
Assault with intent to kill	62	112	198	152	103	96	108	91	–	110	162
Assaulting police officer	203	172	212	195	137	91	57	67	–	103	96
Murder	8	20	54	31	16	28	14	11	21	19	25
Riot and inciting riot	147	332	292	216	123	57	90	114	102	274	86
Interfering with police	225	132	171	163	152	103	127	103	69	179	208
Breach of peace	3,978	2,309	4,085	4,034	4,514	4,023	5,677	4,792	5,609	6,006	5,664
Breach of ordinance	117	75	100	83	117	216	487	629	454	537	725
Corner lounging	542	303	466	397	228	152	170	201	362	715	812
Concealed weapons	55	85	106	84	51	37	34	112	–	121	105
Disorderly house	69	78	166	127	125	169	223	251	265	135	114
Desertion	22	5	47	50	172	305	416	829	–	99	86
Intoxication	4,231	4,453	7,182	8,645	6,275	6,380	8,782	8,972	8,809	9,732	10,365
Intox and disord conduct	6,554	8,834	11,497	10,453	9,023	10,070	11,147	11,228	14,481	16,347	15,431
Insulting women	71	41	67	41	26	27	24	16	–	48	64
Vagrancy	1,298	1,352	2,167	2,236	1,788	1,260	1,040	625	–	1,339	1,516
Misdemeanors	549	640	683	540	461	485	735	1,076	1,238	1,259	1,356
Indecent exposure	43	29	67	57	67	56	24	35	–	141	176
Burglary and attempted burg	23	61	98	104	61	60	38	43	–	81	91
Larceny	814	1,004	1,464	1,334	1,228	1,435	1,660	1,738	–	2,159	1,969
Robbery	27	93	86	103	58	57	51	23	–	104	114
Total arrests	21,537	22,367	32,225	32,051	27,283	27,576	34,050	34,221	39,315	43,226	42,963
Total violent crimes[a]	1,753	1,575	2,269	2,225	1,766	1,644	2,387	2,441	–	2,496	2,556
Total disorderly conduct[b]	14,763	15,596	22,764	23,132	19,812	20,473	25,606	24,992	–	32,085	31,460
Total property crimes[c]	864	1,158	1,648	1,541	1,347	1,552	1,749	1,804	–	2,344	2,174

[a]Violent crimes include assault, assault with intent to kill, assaulting police officer, and murder.
[b]Disorderly conduct includes breach of peace, intoxication, and intoxication and disorderly conduct.
[c]Property crimes include burglary, larceny, and robbery.
Source: Mayor's Annual Reports.

Table 8.3. Share of All Arrests for Selected Crimes, 1857–67

	1857 %	1858 %	1859 %	1860 %	1861 %	1862 %	1863 %	1864 %	1865 %	1866 %	1867 %
Assault	6.9	5.7	5.6	5.8	5.5	5.2	6.5	6.6	6.2	5.2	5.3
Assault with intent to kill	0.3	0.5	0.6	0.5	0.4	0.3	0.3	0.3	—	0.3	0.4
Assaulting police officer	0.9	0.8	0.7	0.6	0.5	0.3	0.2	0.2	—	0.2	0.2
Murder	0.04	0.09	0.17	0.10	0.06	0.10	0.04	0.03	0.05	0.04	0.06
Riot and inciting riot	0.7	1.5	0.9	0.7	0.5	0.2	0.3	0.3	0.3	0.6	0.2
Interfering with police	1.0	0.6	0.5	0.5	0.6	0.4	0.4	0.3	0.2	0.4	0.5
Breach of peace	18.5	10.3	12.7	12.6	16.5	14.6	16.7	14.0	14.3	13.9	13.2
Breach of ordinance	0.5	0.3	0.3	0.3	0.4	0.8	1.4	1.8	1.2	1.2	1.7
Corner lounging	2.5	1.4	1.4	1.2	0.8	0.6	0.5	0.6	0.9	1.7	1.9
Concealed weapons	0.3	0.4	0.3	0.3	0.2	0.1	0.1	0.3	—	0.3	0.2
Disorderly house	0.3	0.3	0.5	0.4	0.5	0.6	0.7	0.7	0.7	0.3	0.3
Desertion	0.1	0.02	0.1	0.2	0.6	1.1	1.2	2.4	—	0.2	0.2
Intoxication	19.6	19.9	22.3	27.0	23.0	23.1	25.8	26.2	22.4	22.5	24.1
Intox and disord conduct	30.4	39.5	35.7	32.6	33.1	36.5	32.7	32.8	36.8	37.8	35.9
Insulting women	0.3	0.2	0.2	0.1	0.1	0.1	0.1	0.0	—	0.1	0.1
Vagrancy	6.0	6.0	6.7	7.0	6.6	4.6	3.1	1.8	—	3.1	3.5
Misdemeanors	2.5	2.9	2.1	1.7	1.7	1.8	2.2	3.1	3.1	2.9	3.2
Indecent exposure	0.2	0.1	0.2	0.2	0.2	0.2	0.1	0.1	—	0.3	0.4
Burglary and attempted burg	0.1	0.3	0.3	0.3	0.2	0.2	0.1	0.1	—	0.2	0.2
Larceny	3.8	4.5	4.5	4.2	4.5	5.2	4.9	5.1	—	5.0	4.6
Robbery	0.1	0.4	0.3	0.3	0.2	0.2	0.1	0.1	—	0.2	0.3
Total violent crimes	8.1	7.0	7.0	6.9	6.5	6.0	7.0	7.1	6.2	5.8	5.9
Total disorderly conduct	68.5	69.7	70.6	72.2	72.6	74.2	75.2	73.0	73.5	74.2	73.2
Total property crimes	4.0	5.2	5.1	4.8	4.9	5.6	5.1	5.3	—	5.4	5.1

Note: This table converts the numbers in table 8.2 into percentage shares of all arrests for each year.

Source: Mayor's *Annual Reports.*

A few of the crimes enumerated in Tables 8.2 and 8.3 reveal the impact of the war on certain forms of disorder. Arrests for vagrancy, corner lounging, and insulting women all dropped off substantially. This is evidence that energetic wartime recruitment (perhaps combined with high employment rates) cut down the number of men who spent their days idle on Philadelphia's street corners. The large decline in arrests for riot and inciting riot reinforces the earlier conclusion that the war's tensions rarely spilled out onto the streets.[20] Charges for carrying concealed weapons declined when the war began but then tripled in 1864 when furloughed veterans returned home. And arrests for keeping disorderly houses went up rapidly in the midwar years, probably suggesting adjustments to meet the new military demand.

Philadelphia's arrest data also indicate the age, gender, and race of the culprits.[21] This material, summarized in Table 8.4, permits further speculation as to the changing nature of wartime crime. The fluctuation of arrests of white men suggests that recruitment reduced arrests at home: between 1860 and 1861 total arrests declined by 4,768, almost all of which were in this group. White men made up a smaller share of all arrests between 1861 and 1864 than they had in 1859 and 1860. The fact that white men shared about equally in the increase in arrests between 1862 and 1863 supports the argument that this shift had less to do with troop movements than with the changing climate of wartime life. In 1866 and 1867, after the soldiers had returned home, nearly 10,000 more white men were arrested annually than in 1864 or 1860, and nearly 15,000 more than in the war's first two years.

Arrests of white women and blacks were relatively less important than those of white men, and their fluctuations less dramatic. In the first year of the war arrests of white women barely decreased. During the next three years, as the war's dislocating effects left an increasing number of women indigent, more white women were arrested. After the war the arrests totals of white women actually declined. Arrests of black men increased substantially (in number and as a share of all arrests) from 1860 to 1863, before declining in 1864. Arrests of black women increased from 1859 until 1864, and then dropped dramatically by 1866. To summarize: Arrests of white women and blacks did not decrease when the war began and did not increase when it ended; however, these groups did share equally in the midwar arrest wave. This reinforces the conclusion that the 1861 and 1865 shifts at least

20 In October 1864, forty Philadelphians were arrested for rioting and inciting to riot. Some of these disturbances were probably associated with the elections.
21 The published summaries do not break down individual crimes by these variables.

Table 8.4. Arrests by Race and Age of Offender

	1859	1860	1861	1862	1863	1864	1866	1867
All arrests	32,225	32,051	27,283	27,576	34,050	34,221	43,226	42,963
Whites	30,147	30,009	25,189	25,233	31,003	31,107	40,505	39,289
White men	24,737	24,529	19,767	19,423	24,233	24,120	34,027	33,263
% of total	76.8	76.5	72.5	70.4	71.2	70.5	78.7	77.4
White women	5,409	5,479	5,421	5,809	6,769	6,987	6,477	6,025
% of total	16.8	17.1	19.9	21.1	19.9	20.4	15.0	14.0
Blacks	2,079	2,043	2,095	2,344	3,048	3,114	2,722	3,675
Black men	1,381	1,312	1,353	1,538	2,079	1,890	2,048	2,553
% of total	4.3	4.1	5.0	5.6	6.1	5.5	4.7	5.9
Black women	698	731	742	806	969	1,224	674	1,122
% of total	2.2	2.3	2.7	2.9	2.8	3.6	1.6	2.6
Whites by Age								
10–20	4,046	3,642	3,248	3,600	4,560	4,299	2,796	2,624
20–30	11,737	11,683	9,616	9,104	10,000	10,523	12,787	14,173
30–40	9,022	9,044	7,520	7,297	9,340	9,100	11,461	11,417
40–50	3,671	3,971	3,280	3,582	4,429	4,434	6,536	4,937
50–60	1,191	1,220	1,109	1,209	1,895	1,982	5,001	4,363
60–70	341	324	285	244	541	527	1,714	1,584
Over 70	69	52	35	31	107	93	119	74
Percentage Share of Whites by Age								
10–20	13.4	12.1	12.9	14.3	14.7	13.8	6.9	6.7
20–30	38.9	38.9	38.2	36.1	32.3	33.8	31.6	36.1
30–40	29.9	30.1	29.9	28.9	30.1	29.3	28.3	29.1
40–50	12.2	13.2	13.0	14.2	14.3	14.3	16.1	12.6
50–60	4.0	4.1	4.4	4.8	6.1	6.4	12.3	11.1
60–70	1.1	1.1	1.1	1.0	1.7	1.7	4.2	4.0
Over 70	0.2	0.2	0.1	0.1	0.3	0.3	0.3	0.2
All white men	82.1	81.7	78.5	77.0	78.2	77.5	84.0	84.7

Source: Mayor's Annual Reports.

partially reflected troop movements whereas the midwar increase was a product of larger forces.

What do the fluctuations in white arrests by age cohorts tell us about the effects of enlistment and the draft on order and disorder in Philadelphia?[22] Between 1860 and 1861 arrests of whites between the ages of twenty and forty declined by almost 3,500. This drop, which accounts for about 70 percent of the entire decrease, might suggest that the removal of men of military age caused the dip in arrests. But arrests of military-aged whites did not decline much faster than arrests of whites of all ages. This would seem to indicate that at least part of the early war decline in arrests stemmed from more general causes.

The midwar increase in arrests also seems to owe less to military movements than to other sources. Between 1862 and 1863 arrests of all whites increased, but the share of arrests of whites aged twenty to thirty dropped by 3.8 percent whereas the share for all other age cohorts rose, suggesting that furloughed men were not responsible for the jump in arrests. If soldiers in Philadelphia disrupted life in the city, they did so without turning up on police ledgers in disproportionate numbers.

Public perceptions and military disorder

Although the arrest data apparently clear soldiers of the charge of causing the wartime arrest wave, this hardly proves that they were not a disorderly presence. In some cases unruly volunteers were not arrested. In other instances soldiers' indiscretions attracted disproportionate publicity, perhaps lending a particular air of tension to the home front. Diaries and newspaper accounts will help flesh out our understanding of the importance of soldiers in disrupting Philadelphia.

During the war, military camps, arsenals, refreshment saloons, and hospitals dotted Philadelphia's cityscape. Volunteers filled barracks at Camp Cadwalader to the north; draftees were housed in Camp Philadelphia to the west, across the Schuylkill; when Philadelphia began raising its first black regiments, the new enlistees rendezvoused at Camp William Penn, north of the city.[23] Did this martial presence disrupt life in Philadelphia? How did its citizens respond when their abstract patriotism came into conflict with the

22 These figures include both men and women, but because men made up over 80 percent of all arrests, any dramatic shifts in arrests of military-age men should show up quite clearly.
23 Taylor, *Philadelphia in the Civil War*, 270.

flesh and blood of a sometimes unruly soldiery? Diarists who visited the military camps revealed enthusiasm for these novel scenes. But some Philadelphians were not pleased with what they saw. At one campground Anna Ferris noted that:

> The little white tents look very pretty, in the green grass . . . the Zouaves looked very picturesque . . . but they are very undesirable neighbors & interfere seriously with the quiet & comfort of every day life – they attract the rabble of the city & their own habits are not, I suppose, very regular or moral – & it is not very encouraging to our patriotic hope to see much of these men whom we are depending to fight our battles.[24]

In February 1863 the Provost Guard moved to new quarters, and Jacob Elfreth, Sr. privately applauded their removal from the vicinity of his office because "it was unpleasant to see & hear so much of them as I did."[25] In early 1864 Henry Benners noted the crowds of soldiers on the streets, observing that there were "almost too many . . . for peaceful people."[26] Over the course of the war, this attitude was shared by more and more Philadelphians.

Table 8.5 summarizes the violent incidents recorded in the *Public Ledger* between January 1860 and June 1866. These range from small fistfights to large brawls to the shooting of deserters. The fluctuations in the number of reported incidents generally followed local arrest patterns, with a substantial decline in the second half of 1861, an increase in the middle of the war, and a large postwar rise. The data in Table 8.5 differ from the arrest totals in two respects. First, the midwar increase in incidents did not begin until 1864 and the dramatic climb did not occur until the middle of that year. Second, the number of reported incidents roughly doubled between early 1861 and late 1865 whereas arrests for violent crimes did not rise quite so rapidly.

Violence reported in the *Public Ledger* also helps us to identify the disruptive role of the military (see Table 8.6). During the four years following Fort Sumter, ninety-nine violent incidents, nearly a quarter of all reported cases, involved soldiers or veterans.[27] In the course of the first eight months of the war soldiers were involved in about a third of all reported incidents. But during the next eighteen months (January 1862 to July 1863) they took part in only 20 of 127 reported

---

24 Anna Ferris diary, 18 August 1861, microfilm, Swarthmore College Library, Swarthmore, PA.
25 Elfreth, Sr., diary, 23 February 1863, Haverford College Library, Haverford, PA.
26 Henry Benners diary, 1 January 1864, Historical Society of Pennsylvania, Philadelphia (hereafter HSP).
27 Note that this figure excludes incidents that occurred between July and December 1865.

Table 8.5. Violent Incidents Reported in the *Public Ledger*

Dates	Incidents
January–July 1860	(66)[a]
July–December 1860	(62)[a]
January–June 1861	53
July–December 1861	34
January–June 1862	36
July–December 1862	51
January–June 1863	40
July–December 1863	40
January–June 1864	50
July–December 1864	80
January–June 1865	78
July–December 1865	107
January–June 1866	(90)[a]

[a]The numbers in parentheses refer to periods when only alternate months were read. These numbers have been doubled to allow for comparisons with the other six-month periods.

Source: This material comes from a complete reading of the *Public Ledger* from 1861 through 1865 and a complete reading of every other month in 1860 and in the first half of 1866. Any case involving intentional violence (except suicides) was included if the incident occurred in Philadelphia.

cases. After mid-1863 the total number of incidents rose, but those involving soldiers consistently made up slightly less than a quarter of all cases.

Violent clashes involving soldiers often came in bunches, when the city was most crowded with uniformed men. On April 24, 1861, one volunteer stabbed another at the Baltimore depot.[28] In the next two weeks over a dozen soldiers were involved in five reported shootings, stabbings, and brawls. On August 1, 1861, as soldiers returned from Bull Run, several volunteers battled at a West Philadelphia picnic, leaving one man badly beaten. That same day a returned volunteer stabbed a man, and a marine passing through the city with his company assaulted a police officer at the Baltimore Depot. A few days later, a military captain killed a young civilian. On New Year's Day 1862 a local newspaper reported that "[t]roops continue almost daily to pass through Philadelphia on their way to the seat of war."[29] In less than two months the *Ledger* reported nine violent incidents involving these men.

Although most altercations involving soldiers did not attract much attention, some incidents were particularly newsworthy. In August 1861 a half dozen picnickers at Girard Park became involved

28 All incidents are taken from the *Philadelphia Public Ledger* (hereafter *PL*).
29 *GT*, 1 January 1862. See also Joseph Boggs Beale diary, 1 January 1862, HSP.

Table 8.6. Military Involvement in Reported Violence

Dates	Soldiers Involved	No Soldiers Involved
April–June 1861	9	19
July–December 1861	12	22
January–June 1862	9	27
July–December 1862	7	44
January–June 1863	4	36
July–December 1863	11	29
January–June 1864	11	39
July–December 1864	18	62
January–June 1865	18	60
July–December 1865	11	96
Total	110	434

Source: Public Ledger.

in a large tavern brawl. When Colonel John F. Ballier of the Ninety-eighth Infantry Regiment went to investigate, a flying beer glass struck him under the eye. This brought a wave of enraged German soldiers down upon the battling citizens.[30] By the war's third year Philadelphians living near the camps began losing patience with their new neighbors. In August 1863 a *Public Ledger* editorial raised a series of objections to military camps. They became "the resort of the abandoned women of the town;" the soldiers camped near the city's waterworks created a health hazard; and undisciplined men were apt to steal firewood or fruit and vegetables.[31] In 1863 farmers near Camp Philadelphia formed nighttime patrols to protect their crops. On one occasion such a patrol accosted three soldiers cutting through a cornfield: one private was shot in the face with a load of buckshot and then badly beaten.[32] An adjutant from the 118th Pennsylvania Volunteers rescued the private and later returned with twelve men to arrest the farmers. Seven men surrendered, but one young farmer tried to run and a member of the guard fired, fatally wounding him. That August, a few months after the city's black troops first rendezvoused at Camp William Penn, a nervous sentry shot and killed a sightseeing Philadelphian who refused to leave the camp's perimeter.[33]

---

30 The Ninety-eighth was a primarily German regiment. See Taylor, *Philadelphia in the Civil War*, 116–17; *PL*, 21 August 1861.
31 *PL*, 11 August 1863.
32 *PL*, 31 August 1863.
33 The sentry fired when he mistook the flippant words of an off-duty corporal ("shoot him then") as orders from the corporal of the guard. See *PL*, 10, 20 August 1863; *GT*, 12, 19 August 1863; Jeffry D. Wert, "Camp William Penn and the Black Soldier," *Pennsylvania History* 46 (October 1979): 343–4.

Published reports of violence inside camps were not common, but occasionally Philadelphians got a glimpse of this new form of disruption. In October 1863 the *Public Ledger* described a drunken brawl among substitutes in the Twenty-second and Wood streets barracks that left one man dead. On another occasion the officer of the guard at Camp Graef shot and killed a private who had been "running the guard" to go into town for liquor. In March 1864 a Camp William Penn guard killed an imprisoned deserter who had drawn a knife in the guard house. In a later episode guards shot a civilian as he ran from Camp Cadwalader when he was caught selling passes to the soldiers.[34]

Stories such as these helped foster the sense that the military had its unsavory elements. But soldiers were most disruptive when their violence spilled over into Philadelphia's public places. Sometimes units battled over turf, such as when two companies fought with bayonets for the right to drill in Spring Garden Hall, or when members of competing regiments fought over disputed recruits.[35] Constant troop movement occasionally turned railway stations into battlegrounds. In September 1862 men from two companies in transit from New York to Washington became involved in a "serious row," with several dozen soldiers wielding swords, blocks of wood, and pieces of iron.[36] In other incidents soldiers recuperating in the city's hospitals found their way into nearby taverns and ended up in serious brawls.[37]

As the war progressed, Philadelphians regularly expressed concern over morality within the military. A May 1861 *Public Ledger* editorial on the "Character of Good Soldiers" argued that a worthy cause demanded worthy combatants, not drunk and riotous men.[38] In July 1864 Sidney Fisher complained to Mayor Henry about a "miserable hovel" in his neighborhood that had become the base for several prostitutes:

> The place has for some time been the resort of convalescent soldiers from the neighboring hospital. . . . These soldiers & other rowdies . . . have been for months the pests of the neighborhood. I hear from several that they rob gardens & poultry houses in all directions, they have attacked & beaten unoffending men on the roads, & some days ago a squad of them broke into Cowperthwaite's house . . . & robbed it in broad day.

34 *PL*, 13 October, 16 November 1863; 16 September 1864; Philadelphia *Evening Bulletin*, 31 March 1864 (hereafter *EB*).
35 *Press*, 6 July 1861; *PL*, 1, 2 October 1861; *EB*, 2 October 1861.
36 *PL*, 24 September 1862; J. Thomas Scharf and Thompson Westcott, *History of Philadelphia, 1609–1884*, 3 vols. (Philadelphia, 1884), 1:803.
37 *PL*, 21 December 1862; 22 February 1865.
38 *PL*, 11 May 1862.

The following day the police came to the offending house and arrested its owner.[39] A month later the *Public Ledger* reported that a "disorderly dance house" on Islington Lane near Camp Cadwalader, where soldiers were regularly lured and then encouraged to desert, was often the scene of fights and disorder.[40] Arrest statistics seem to support these complaints. In May 1864 alone, the police made seventy-two arrests for running disorderly houses.[41]

The rest of the city, too, had to put up with ill-mannered military men. In the fall of 1863 "An Old Subscriber" wrote to the *Public Ledger* to complain about cavalrymen riding at full speed through the streets endangering citizens.[42] Sometimes this rudeness was less dangerous than distasteful. During the first months of 1865 a *Public Ledger* editorial complained that decent Philadelphians were being subjected to theater floors "flooded with tobacco spit" and boisterous conversations dotted with "open and loud profanity of speech." The newspaper insisted that "a man can be a soldier and a gentleman."[43]

When soldiers brought their horses, tobacco, drink, and foul language from the fields into Philadelphia's streets, they offended genteel citizens. When they brought their firearms with them the stakes rose. The *Public Ledger* reported in August 1862:

> There has been considerable recklessness shown by some of the returning volunteers in the discharge of firearms in the streets, and the authorities should put a stop to it. Yesterday, a lad was much injured by a musket ball striking him in the head which had been fired in the air, by one of the volunteers. The injuries to the lad were such that it was thought that he could not recover.[44]

The next afternoon the paper recorded that a young boy had been mortally wounded by another errant shot.[45] In late 1864 the *Public Ledger* called for a more vigorous enforcement of laws banning concealed weapons. Soldiers, it explained, were in the habit of carrying their guns into taverns and then using them freely in drunken fights. The newspaper concluded that "the war has undoubtedly lessened the sacredness with which life has been regarded and protected."[46] In October and November 1864 the police made forty-five arrests for carrying concealed weapons; in all of 1863 they had made only thirty-four.

39 Nicholas B. Wainwright, ed., *A Philadelphia Perspective: The Diary of Sidney George Fisher* (Philadelphia, 1967), 80 entries of 27, 29 July 1864.
40 *PL*, 31 August 1864.
41 In 1860 127 such arrests were made during the entire year.
42 *PL*, 10 May 1863.
43 *PL*, 12 January 1865.
44 *PL*, 2 August 1862.
45 *PL*, 3 August 1862.
46 *PL*, 17 November 1864.

Although the army brought violence and disruption to Northern cities, it also developed its own tools for maintaining order. The task of policing a sometimes rambunctious soldiery fell to provost marshals. The wartime provost marshal system began in July 1861 when General McDowell detailed men to protect citizens' property during his Virginia campaign. After Bull Run General McClellan placed Colonel Andrew Porter in charge of restoring discipline to the troops stationed in Washington, D. C. Porter named a Provost Guard and implemented a pass system, a strict curfew, and regular patrols. In February 1862 McClellan created the Provost Marshal's Department with Porter as Provost Marshal General. The duties of the provost marshals included the "suppression of gambling houses, bar-rooms & brothels . . . and of all brawls and disturbances beyond the limits of the camps. . . . Searches, seizures, and arrests. . . . .Enforcement of orders involving the sale of intoxicating liquors . . . [Distribution of] Passes to citizens . . . [and investigation of] Complaints of citizens as to the conduct of the soldiers."[47]

In Philadelphia the duty of arresting disloyal citizens first fell to U. S. Marshal William Millward; the responsibility for policing the troops remained initially in the hands of their commanding officers.[48] Local police were expected to cooperate with the military authorities in maintaining order and arresting persons discouraging enlistment.[49] Philadelphia did not receive a provost marshal until June 1862, when Captain William H. Kerns was named to the post. Within a week after his appointment, the *Germantown Telegraph* reported that Kerns had been

> after [the] loafers in uniform with a sharp stick [enforcing] an order
> from the War Department that hereafter all volunteers clad in the
> United States uniform . . . shall be arrested by the Provost Guard,
> and obliged either to show evidence of discharge or some docu-
> ment proving their right to be absent from their regiment.[50]

For the rest of the war, military provost guards patrolled Philadelphia's streets, looking for deserters and arresting disorderly soldiers.[51]

47 Wilton P. Moore, "Union Army Provost Marshals in the Eastern Theater," *Military Affairs* 26 (Fall 1962): 122–3. Moore cites *Official Register*, ser. II, 5:30 for the provost marshals' duties. Moore's "The Provost Marshal Goes to War," *Civil War History* 5 (March 1959): 62–71, covers almost exactly the same ground. For a discussion of the civilian provost marshals appointed in 1862 to enforce the draft, see Benjamin P. Thomas and Harold M. Hyman, *Stanton: The Life and Times of Lincoln's Secretary of War* (New York, 1962), 248–9, 279–83.
48 *OR*, ser. II, 2:7.
49 *OR*, ser. II, 2:136; ser. III, 2:321.
50 *GT*, 18, 25 June 1862.
51 See, for instance, "Proceedings of the Board of Enrollment, First District, Penna.," #2834 and "Descriptive List of Deserters and Persons Arrested in the First District, Pa.," #2834, RG 110, National Archives (hereafter NA).

Although these efforts helped to maintain order, they sometimes exacerbated existing tensions. A particularly controversial incident occurred one night in November 1862 in front of the Kossuth Exchange Saloon. A military party sought to enter the saloon in search of a suspected deserter but the ticket agent "got excited and swore that there had been enough trouble with the ———— soldiers that night and no more should go in without pay." The agent called a policeman, who pushed the company sergeant out into the street, followed by a large crowd from the saloon. In the subsequent riot the sergeant, Ulrich Reazor, was badly beaten and died the next morning. This homicide, which was reported on the front page of the *Public Ledger* for three successive days, revealed the intensity of civilian–military hostility.[52] A second sensational incident in the following month was very similar. On this occasion nineteen-year-old James Devine of the Seventy-first Pennsylvania Infantry shot James McCawley, a newly arrived Scotch sailor, at a dance house in the southeastern corner of the city. Devine, who had been captured at Balls Bluff and only recently paroled, entered the dance hall with several members of a Provost Guard detail who were checking military passes. The guard members became involved in an altercation with a soldier who was slow to show his pass, when McCawley and his companions got up to leave. Devine blocked their way and after an angry exchange the soldier emptied his revolver into McCawley's abdomen.[53]

In each of these incidents military squads were on the scene to police their own men, but their actions disrupted civilian life and precipitated violence. Sometimes the provost marshals' zeal created unusual friction. In 1863 a party of cavalrymen searched used clothing stores on Shippen Street for illicit traders in government clothing. After confiscating uniforms from several stores, the cavalry were accosted by a drunken "cripple." His actions so angered one soldier that he dragged the handicapped civilian into the street and threatened to take him back to camp for punishment. A crowd immediately formed, taking the helpless victim's side and forcing the soldier to mount his horse and ride off.[54] In another incident Major R. J. Falls had tavern keeper Charles Westcott arrested and held in irons for passing a counterfeit note. Westcott was subsequently freed and Falls was charged with assault and battery for confining the Philadelphian for twelve hours before turning him over to the civil authorities. The *Public Ledger* called the affair "one of those cases

52 *PL*, 17, 18, 19 November 1862.
53 *PL*, 8 December 1862.
54 *PL*, 13 October 1863.

which gives to the disaffected and the malcontents in our midst an opportunity to rail against the Government."[55] A few months later a colonel in the Fifty-sixth Massachusetts Volunteers arrested Henry Brown, a Philadelphia tavern keeper, for getting one of the Massachusetts soldiers drunk. The colonel took Brown and a second man with him to Baltimore, where the provost marshal ordered their release. Once again the *Public Ledger* railed against the "arbitrary conduct" of the colonel.[56] By late 1863 military officers in Philadelphia had taken to using extremely firm measures to enforce order. If these tactics had their merits, they also cast officers in an unfavorable light.

The provost marshals' prime responsibility was to capture men who tried to avoid service.[57] In April 1863 the Provost Guard barracks at Fifth and Buttonwood housed 193 deserters, 162 stragglers, 81 men who had overstayed their furloughs, and 2 soldiers arrested for forging discharge papers.[58] From late 1863 until the end of the war, the army became more energetic and efficient in its efforts at checking desertion. By 1864 the armies in the field were publicly executing runaways on an almost daily basis. At home, armed marshals guarded draftees and bountied enlistees.[59]

The provost marshals hired special agents to pursue deserters, but most of Philadelphia's runaway soldiers were arrested by private citizens. The Enrolment Act of March 1863 provided for a $5 reward for each captured deserter. Four months later the provost marshal general increased the reward to $10, and in late September he increased it again to $30.[60] Between September 9, 1863, when the Eastern Division of Pennsylvania's provost marshal's office opened, and the end of the war, a total of 2,674 deserters were arrested in Pennsylvania's first five districts.[61] The provost marshal for Pennsylvania's Second District credited "the police of the city and citizens at

55 *PL*, 12 January 1864.
56 *PL*, 24 March 1864.
57 *OR*, ser. III, 3:37–8.
58 *GT*, 8 April 1863.
59 Ella Lonn, *Desertion During the Civil War* (1928; reprinted, Gloucester, Ma, 1966), 143–6, 181–2, 163; "Board of Enrollment, First District Penna – Letters Sent," #2813, RG 110; "Proceedings of the Board of Enrollment, First District, Penna."
60 W. B. Lane, Acting Assistant Provost Marshal General, Eastern Divison of Pennsylvania, "Historical Report," 27–30, microfilm M1163, roll #4, NA. Until late 1863, the provost marshals' special agents were paid a monthly salary as well as the reward for delivery of deserters, but a November 4 order announced that they would have to choose one or the other. See *OR*, ser. I, 34: 408. See also "Board of Enrollment, First District Penna – Letters Sent," letters of 31 March, 15 April, 10 June, 22 October 1864; "Proceedings of the Board of Enrollment, First District, Penna," entries of 29, 31 July, 21 September 1863 and *passim*.
61 Lane, "Historical Report," 60. Only 124 of these men were arrested in the Fifth District, which included Bucks County. The reports submitted by the district provost marshals gave slightly different totals.

large [with] many arrests of deserters." Once the number of special agents in the Third District was reduced, deserters were "generally arrested by persons who were interested in getting the reward." In his final report the Fourth District's Captain Lane noted that of 807 deserters arrested in his district, 712 were captured by citizens who were paid rewards and only 95 were caught by special agents.[62] Thus once again, a federal task owed much of its success to private cooperation.

Although many of Philadelphia's citizens were happy to cooperate in catching deserters, the provost guard's techniques often led to friction. When Isaac Grant, a deserting substitute, was shot after jumping off a wharf into the Delaware, the *Public Ledger* asked: "Is an officer justified in having a man escaping shot to death when it could be prevented by means which would not take his life?"[63] The *Germantown Telegraph* seemed less alarmed about the shooting of deserters. In August it reported that a substitute had been shot and seriously wounded while escaping from the barracks at Twenty-second and Wood. "A few more of such examples" the paper noted, "will make desertion a risky business."[64] In 1863 such scenes were still noteworthy. But similar occurrences quickly became almost routine. Twenty-six of the violent incidents reported in Table 8.6 involved soldiers who were performing their duty. Fifteen were cases where soldiers shot at suspected deserters.[65]

Philadelphians did occasionally object to the public shooting of deserters, but a much louder outcry was heard when soldiers fired at runaways and accidentally hit citizens. On July 21, 1864, a surgeon at the Fifth and Buttonwood barracks fired his pistol at a fleeing soldier on Callowhill Street. The bullets bounced off a house and struck a small boy in the back.[66] In the spring of 1865 a similar mishap occurred in the same area when a corporal of the provost guard shot at an escaping man and mortally wounded a nearby woman. The *Public Ledger* angrily declared that "[t]he practice of firing at deserters in the city where it is almost impossible to shoot without injury to someone, cannot be too strongly condemned. Several persons have

---

62 Provost Marshals, Pennsylvania's Second, Third, and Fourth Districts, "Historical Reports," 17; 23; and 11.
63 *PL*, 10 August 1863.
64 *GT*, 19 August 1863.
65 The reported shootings probably underestimate the problem. After a sailor was shot while swimming from his ship, only the second reported case since March, the *Public Ledger* observed: "Deserting both on ship and shore is getting to be a dangerous business." See *PL*, 9 August 1864. For other reported desertions see *EB*, 28 March 1864; 23 March 1864; 12 April 1865; *GT*, 27 April 1864.
66 *PL*, 21 July 1864.

been seriously injured in that way, and near ten deaths have resulted from it."[67] Within two weeks the issue again became a public concern when a guard shooting at a deserter mortally wounded a thirteen-year-old boy near the Broad and Washington station.[68]

During the Civil War uniformed men in the streets of Philadelphia served as a reminder of the conflict outside. The city and its environs became a training ground, a depot, a medical haven, and a source of entertainment. This military presence brought various forms of disruption into Philadelphia's normal routine. In some cases irate citizens joined to combat disruptive soldiers. In other instances police officers shut down disorderly houses and arrested men for carrying concealed weapons. This disorder also brought new instruments of order. Military details roamed the streets seeking out soldiers without passes. If on occasion these excursions led to violence, one can only guess at the incidents that their efforts curtailed. Sometimes, though, the military's interests conflicted with the local ideals of order. Officers harrassed citizens without just cause or due process. Guards fired at deserters to discourage prospective runaways, but their actions brought the random violence of war into Philadelphia's most traveled streets.

The soldiers' return

When the war ended, thousands of discharged soldiers descended on Philadelphia just as the city fell into a postwar economic decline. How did these veterans fit into a world that no longer had provost guard patrols to keep them in check?

Philadelphia's police made 9,005 more arrests in 1866 than they had two years before (see Table 8.2). The five crimes – intoxication and disorderly conduct, breach of peace, intoxication, vagrancy, corner lounging – with the greatest increases in arrests between 1864 and 1866 were all victimless offenses. Arrests for these five crimes increased by 8,321 between 1864 and 1866, accounting for almost all of the postwar "crime wave." This suggests that the postwar arrest boom was caused less by crimes against individuals than by a com-

---

67 *PL*, 14 March 1865. It is unclear what this figure refers to. It is doubtful that nine other civilians were killed in similar, but unreported, circumstances. In fact, my reading of the *PL* only turned up four cases where a deserter was killed (although others may have died from their wounds).

68 This case was particularly upsetting because the shooting occurred after dark and the guards who fired were allowed to continue with their recruits. See *PL*, 27 March 1865.

bination of increased public disorder and greater police vigilance. Soon after the troops returned home the *Public Ledger* was pleased to observe:

> They are, as a general rule, more law-abiding than any one could reasonably expect, when the fact of their long camp life is taken into consideration. Occasionally we meet with small parties who 'fight their battles o'er again' over a mug of beer, but there is nothing like the amount of intoxification which was so generally predicted, would ensue upon the disbanding of the armies. . . . The American soldier . . . is essentially a gentleman.[69]

Arrest totals seem to confirm that judgment. Between 1864 and 1866 arrests of all white age cohorts older than age twenty increased. But despite the veterans' return arrests of whites aged twenty to thirty and thirty to forty declined as a share of all white arrests. Although military-aged men took part in the postwar arrest boom, whites aged forty to seventy were responsible for a surprisingly large share of that increase. Arrests of whites between fifty to seventy, hardly a cohort that included many returned veterans, jumped from 2,500 in 1864 to 6,700 in 1866. At the other end of the age spectrum, arrests of whites between ten and twenty declined from about 4,300 to 2,800.

What explains these shifts? The decline in arrests of young whites coupled with the increased arrests of older Philadelphians suggests that the expanded police force shifted its focus. Mayor Morton McMichael's First Annual Report of 1867 paid particular attention to the recent increase in arrests for "corner lounging."[70] Perhaps these new efforts resulted in the arrest of more older men. Of course this should not denigrate the disruptive roles played by the returning veterans and the declining postwar economy. Between 1866 and 1867 Philadelphia's total number of arrests declined slightly, but veterans seem to have played a larger role in crime. During this time arrests of whites aged twenty to thirty rose by about 1,400, and that age cohort increased its share of all white arrests by 4.5 percent. This would seem to support Monkkonen's contention that the postwar crime wave created by the veterans did not occur until several years after the war. But in Philadelphia the "arrest wave" preceded the increased role by military-aged whites. And even in 1867 whites aged twenty to thirty had a smaller share of all arrests than they had in 1859 and 1860.

69 *PL*, 21 July 1865.
70 Howard O. Sprogle, *The Philadelphia Police, Past and Present* (1887; reprinted N.Y., 1971) p. 128.

Conclusion

The political tensions created by the Civil War, and the continual presence of thousands of furloughed, encamped, hospitalized, and in-transit soldiers combined to pose multiple threats to Philadelphia's social order. The previous two chapters have enumerated a long list of violent incidents provoked by these forces. In various ways the conflict brought dozens of fistfights, brawls, stabbings, shootings, and angry mobs into Philadelphia's wartime life. But measured by any yardstick, these incidents add up to very little. The occasional political disturbances seem trivial when compared with antebellum Philadelphia or other wartime cities. Arrests rates rose during the war, but do not suggest a city undergoing widespread disruption. Philadelphia's newspapers and diarists frequently predicted uncontrolled street rioting, but these fears were never realized. And though military violence in the city outraged citizens, even the handful of street shootings did not substantially upset Philadelphia's equilibrium.

We have seen that a complex web of forces – Mayor Henry, the police, federal agents, private citizens – kept Philadelphia's political tensions from spilling out into uncontrolled violence. When soldiers or veterans threatened to disrupt order in Philadelphia's streets, provost marshals and police officers combined their energies to keep the peace. Sometimes these men stepped in to stop violent outbreaks, but more often they acted in anticipation of problems. Provost details patroled at night checking passes and apprehending deserters; policemen broke up disorderly houses and arrested men who carried concealed weapons. These actions mirrored the preemptive measures employed to curtail political violence and draft-day disruptions.

In most senses the transformation to wartime life was smooth, reflecting the adaptability of Philadelphia. The war did not leave the city unchanged, however. The police force, for instance, expanded in size and apparently shifted its focus between 1861 and 1867. But the critical centralizing process began before the conflict started. Between the riots of the 1830s and 1840s and the onset of the Civil War, Philadelphia's police department had evolved into a potent, and sometimes violent, force. With the war's outbreak Mayor Henry and his officers were ready to handle the new threats to public order. The war produced new forms of disorder, but also new mechanisms to keep them in check. The most important, the Provost Guard, was primarily responsible for controlling the military forces that the war brought into the city. But even this body, which suggests a rising federal role, was most effective when the provost marshals hired civilian guards and agents and worked with a cooperative citizenry and police force.[71]

The institutions and circumstances that spared Philadelphia from serious wartime disorder did not signal an end to disruption in the City of Brotherly Love. In the decade after the war Philadelphians repeatedly complained of disorderly streets, riotous fire companies, and violent elections.[72] Philadelphia's 1871 election day riots, in which mobs sought to keep newly enfranchised blacks from the polls, were far more bloody than the worst wartime episodes.[73] Such problems led to new waves of reform: In December 1870 the City Council created a paid fire department, and William Stokely further strengthened the police force after his election to the mayoralty in 1871.[74] How did the Civil War mold these events? Certainly the postwar dominance of the city's Republicans was one of the conflict's legacies. And the acceleration in black political rights (and the concomitant tensions) was another. But it seems most accurate to see the postwar disturbances as part of a continuous process of expansion and evolution. As Philadelphia grew, old tensions persisted and new conflicts emerged. The balance of forces that maintained relative calm during the war years did not assure a legacy of order.[75]

71 In the summer of 1864 Philadelphia's First District provost marshal hired civilian guards to replace (and later supplement) the military Provost Guard. Provost Marshal William Lehman reported to Fry that "this arrangement works well, & recruits & property are much safer than with a military guard." See "Proceedings of the Board of Enrollment," entries of 11 August, 26 September 1864 and *passim;* "Board of Enrollment, First District – Letters Sent," letters of 31 August, 10 October, 10 November 1864. Quotation from letter from Lehman to Fry, 10 October 1864.
72 See Dorothy Gondos Beers, "The Centennial City, 1865–1876," in *Philadelphia: A 300-Year History,* ed. Russell Weigley (New York, 1982), 437, 438, 440; Scharf and Westcott, *History of Philadelphia,* 1: 834, 836–7.
73 Beers, "The Centennial City," 438, Scharf and Westcott, *History of Philadelphia,* 1: 837.
74 Beers, "The Centennial City," 438, 440; Scharf and Westcott, *History of Philadelphia,* 1: 836.
75 These issues are discussed more fully in Chapter 13.

9   *Philadelphia's workers in wartime*

Philadelphians did not respond to the Civil War's challenges as an undifferentiated mass. Numerous characteristics – gender, race, religion, wealth, occupation – set citizens apart, creating a wide range of wartime experiences. Thus far we have argued that Philadelphia was a city of interlocking "systems," each of which adjusted to the war's new circumstances. Workers took part in each of these systems. But they also had their own set of institutions, formed to defend their economic interests. How did wage earners fare during the war?[1] This question has several facets. What was labor's contribution to Philadelphia's various war-related activities? How did the war's economic fluctuations affect the city's workers? What became of labor unions during the conflict? How did the military's demand for supplies change the work force?

Workers and the war effort

Philadelphians joined in the growing sectional conflict cautiously and reluctantly. As the threat of war grew, and its economic consequences became apparent, Philadelphia's laborers threw their weight behind the growing call for compromise. In late December 1860 workers in Louisville, Kentucky, held a mass meeting to declare their support for the Union and the Constitution. Philadelphia's William H. Sylvis, the national treasurer of the molders' union, played a key role in the Louisville meetings and was then instrumental in launching a similar movement in Philadelphia. On January 11, 1861, the Philadelphia's Industrial Works employees held a large pro-union meeting, and in the ensuing weeks employee groups throughout the city chose delegates for a citywide meeting of workingmen. These delegates met, passed resolutions calling for the preservation of the Union, and made plans for a mass meeting of workers.[2]

---

1 For the purpose of this chapter, I will use the terms "laborers," "workers," and "wage earners" interchangeably. My goal is not to suggest a single labor experience, but to consider how the war affected those Philadelphians who could afford its cost least and who felt its inflation most.

2 *Philadelphia Public Ledger*, 12 through 21 January 1861 (hereafter *PL*); *Germantown Telegraph*, 16 January 1861 (hereafter *GT*); J. Thomas Scharf and Thompson Westcott, *A History of Philadelphia, 1609–1884* 3 vols., (Philadelphia, 1884), 1:748–9.

Although a snowstorm limited the turnout, several hundred workers representing many of the city's foremost establishments congregated at Independence Square on January 26. They heard speakers call for repeal of any legislation obnoxious to the South and for the adoption of the Crittenden Compromise. But though the prevailing mood was anxious, the laborers resolved to support the government in whatever course it took. The workers elected thirty-three delegates to deliver their resolutions to the legislatures in Harrisburg and Washington.[3]

On the afternoon before Washington's Birthday 1861, Philadelphians greeted president-elect Abraham Lincoln, who made a brief stop on his way to Washington. Several representatives of the workingmen's Committee of Thirty-three sought an audience with the new president, but they waited several hours in vain. The next day Lincoln joined city officials in celebrating the holiday, and Philadelphia's laborers held their own grand procession culminating in a mass meeting and more proconciliation resolutions. On the twenty-third, delegations from Maryland, Virginia, Kentucky, Tennessee, Indiana, Ohio, and Delaware joined the Pennsylvania representatives at Wetherill House for another round of speeches and resolutions.[4] In the weeks to come workers from Philadelphia's various industrial branches chose delegates for a March 4 meeting that, in turn, selected representatives to a proposed national convention in Louisville. Two weeks later, the Executive Committee, which had been elected at the February National Convention, reiterated its call for the preservation of the Union.[5]

In a few short months Philadelphia's workers had responded to the national crisis by creating a citywide organization and electing representatives to a national labor body. For three decades the ethno-cultural appeals of the mass political parties had kept the nation's workers divided.[6] But as the threat of war challenged their economic well-being, American workers joined in a brief political movement for peaceful conciliation. Philadelphia's parade for Washington's Birth-

---

3 *PL*, 2 February 1861; Scharf and Westcott, *History of Philadelphia*, 1:749.
4 See Chapter 6.
5 *PL*, 16, 19, 21, 22, 23, 24, 25 February 1861; Scharf and Westcott, *History of Philadelphia*, 1:750–2. For other descriptions of these events see: Philip S. Foner, *History of the Labor Movement in the United States*, 4 vols., (New York, 1947–65), 1:298–306; John R. Commons et al, *History of Labour in the United States*, 4 vols. (New York, 1918–35), 2:10–11; David Montgomery, *Beyond Equality* (New York, 1967), 92; James C. Sylvis, *The Life, Speeches, Labors and Essays of William H. Sylvis* (1872; New York, 1968), 42–6; Jonathan Grossman, *William Sylvis, Pioneer of American Labor* (New York, 1945), 45–7.
6 For a good brief account of this period see David Brody, "Labor Movement," in *Encyclopedia of American Political History*, ed. Jack P. Greene (New York, 1984), 711–13.

day suggests the flavor of that movement. The city's artisans marched by crafts, with some following tradition by carrying the fruits of their labors.[7] Local factory workers, lacking the citywide ties of their more skilled counterparts, joined together by workshop and marched under banners identifying their places of employment. The marchers gathered in the northern part of the city, at Broad and Brown streets, and started marching through Spring Garden, a largely working-class section. They then proceeded east through Northern Liberties and marched down Second and Third streets to Pine Street, at the southeastern corner of the old city. From there the procession moved into the heart of Philadelphia, adopting a path that took them past each of the city's four "squares" before concluding at National Hall. This route took the workers from their home territory, through the city's wealthiest neighborhoods, and into the center of downtown Philadelphia. For a brief moment, the workers spoke with a single voice, calling on all Philadelphians to join them in supporting reconciliation.[8]

Even though Philadelphia's workers initially called for compromise, they responded with enthusiasm when the time came to fight. Shortly after the firing on Fort Sumter, about a hundred workmen from the North, Chase and Company Stove Works marched through the streets, declaring that they "were willing to lay down [to] take up arms for the defense of the Federal Government."[9] The secretary of one local union recorded: "it having been resolved to enlist with Uncle Sam for the war, this Union stands adjourned until the Union is safe or we are whipped."[10] Robert Keen, the leader of the local tailors' union, joined the Twenty-second Pennsylvania at the war's onset, reenlisted in the Ninety-ninth Pennsylvania when his three months' service ended, and was severely wounded at Fredericksburg.[11] William Sylvis actively opposed the movement toward war, but accepted a lieutenancy in a new company when the

7 The glassblowers, for instance, displayed thirty-four glass globes, each bearing the name of a state.
8 PL, 19, 21 February 1861; Sylvis, William H. Sylvis, 44. For a discussion of Philadelphia workers' parading traditions, see Susan Gray Davis, Parades and Power: Street Theater in Nineteenth-Century Philadelphia (Philadelphia, 1986), 113–54.
9 Mayor Henry answered this premature offer with a patriotic speech, encouraging the men to return home until they were called for. See PL, 18 April 1861.
10 Terrence V. Powderly, Thirty Years of Labor, 1859 to 1889, (New York, 1967), 57. This single sentence, describing an unidentified Philadelphia union, has done yeoman's service in labor historiography. See, for instance, Montgomery, Beyond Equality, 93; Foner, History of the Labor Movement, 1:308; and, most recently, Philip Shaw Paludan, "A People's Contest": The Union and the Civil War, 1861–1865 (New York, 1988), 177.
11 Foner, History of the Labor Movement, 1:309.

call came for troops.[12] Many Philadelphia volunteers enlisted with their fellow workers. In September 1861 diarist Henry Benners recorded that eleven men from his glass factory had signed up in Baxter's Zouaves.[13] Sylvis's first company was made up of men from the Molders' Union, and when he went into the field at Antietam he marched with his co-workers at the Liebrandt & McDowell foundry. Within hours after Mayor Henry's September 12, 1862, call for emergency troops, two companies enlisted from the Baldwin Locomotive Works. Soon workers from other local establishments followed suit. The call for local defense in June 1863 attracted companies from several of Philadelphia's prominent industrial works and railroad companies.[14]

Philip S. Foner has argued that Northern workers served in "a ratio greatly out of proportion to their number." He based this conclusion on the findings of a postwar Senate report, which calculated that over 500,000 (of about 940,000) Northern industrial workers served in the military, and B. A. Gould's 1869 study of Northern soldiers, which estimated that the North had nearly 5 million white men of military age (eighteen to forty-five) and that about 1.9 million, or less than 40 percent, served at some point.[15] But other surveys indicate that the occupational distribution among white Union soldiers was quite similar to that of the nation as a whole.[16]

One source casts light on enlistment rates among Philadelphia's skilled workers. The local branch of the National Typographical Union (NTU #2) had 16 of 641 members in service at the beginning of 1862. Nine months later that figure had risen to 91 of 704 members; in the next two years between 73 and 85 brothers were in the army. Thus after the first year of the war the NTU had roughly 10 percent of its membership in uniform at any given time.[17] Gould estimated that in the year following July 1, 1863, 895,000 of 4,731,000 military-aged men (17 percent) served in the army.[18] The NTU's membership cer-

---

12 Although this company did not survive beyond the planning stage, Sylvis later served as an orderly sergeant in the local militia. See Sylvis, *William H. Sylvis*, 42–50; Grossman, *William Sylvis*, 48.
13 Henry Benners diary, 24 September 1861, Historical Society of Pennsylvania, Philadelphia (hereafter HSP).
14 Grossman, *William Sylvis*, 48; Frank H. Taylor, *Philadelphia in the Civil War, 1861–1865* (Philadelphia, 1913), 216, 244–7; *PL*, 1 July 1863. For a discussion of the various associational ties reflected in Philadelphia's recruiting patterns see Chapter 2.
15 Foner, *History of the Labor Movement* 1:307; Benjamin A Gould, *Investigations in Military and Anthropological Statistics of American Soldiers* (New York, 1869), 13.
16 James M. McPherson, *Ordeal By Fire: The Civil War and Reconstruction* (New York, 1982), 359; Also see Chapter 2.
17 National Typographical Union #2 Papers (hereafter NTU), microfilm, Lamont Library, Harvard University.
18 Gould, *Investigations*, 13.

tainly included men who were not of military age, but it seems that members of this skilled Philadelphia trade did not serve in disproportionate numbers.

Although Philadelphia workers joined in the early enthusiasm for enlistment, they objected when city and federal policies placed unfair burdens on their shoulders. When Lee's troops threatened in June 1863, the city's manufacturers agreed to keep their establishments open half days so their employees could divide their time between working and drilling.[19] The manufacturers claimed to be taking patriotic steps, but *Fincher's Trades' Review*, a Philadelphia-based labor weekly, claimed that the employers had merely acted to save their own property at the expense of their workers, who were sent off to shoulder arms while forfeiting half their normal wages.[20]

Fincher and Sylvis threw their weight behind the idea of forced military service, arguing that a properly run draft was the most equitable way of filling the ranks.[21] The paper termed the state's meager home defense a "national blemish," holding that "every citizen, rich or poor . . . [should] be compelled to do military duty."[22] After the Gettysburg crisis demonstrated the inadequacy of the local recruiting apparatus, the draft finally came to Philadelphia. But although the idea pleased *Fincher's*, the ultimate form, with its $300 commutation fee, reeked of class favoritism.[23]

Dissatisfaction with the commutation system was probably widespread among Philadelphia's workers. But as we have seen, several forces combined to keep dissent from turning to violence. Local bounty fund drives helped minimize the draft's burden. Many of the poorer workers moved so frequently that they escaped the enrollers' lists. And when hostility to the draft might have turned to violence, shows of police force effectively removed the danger.[24]

19 *PL*, 1 July 1863. One mining company offered to continue the wages of any employee who enlisted. See Jacob Elfreth, Sr., diary, 29 June, 1 July 1863, Haverford College Library, Haverford, PA.
20 *Fincher's Trades' Review* (hereafter *FTR*), 15 August 1863.
21 *FTR*, 13 June 1863; Grossman, *William Sylvis*, 54. Also see Foner, *History of the Labor Movement*, 1:321 and Montgomery, *Beyond Equality*, 107.
22 *FTR*, 27 June 1863.
23 *FTR*, 25 July, 19 December 1863; 16 January, 25 June 1864; 7 January 1865. For further discussion of labor and the draft see Foner, *History of the Labor Movement*, 1:321–4; Montgomery, *Beyond Equality*, 103–7; Grossman, *William Sylvis*, 50–4. Also see Chapter 2.
24 The provost marshals' reports suggest that in some working-class communities the residents thwarted the enrollers' efforts through noncooperation or violent threats. See Provost Marshal's "Historical Report," First District Pennsylvania, 2, 4, 7; Second District Pennsylvania, 14; Fifth District Pennsylvania, 13–14, all microfilm M1163, roll #4, National Archives. The district reports indicate that most draft days were actually very quiet. See Chapters 2 and 7.

We have seen that although Philadelphia's elites generally dominated the war's benevolent organizations, citizens from all classes took part in wartime voluntarism.[25] But whereas donations were often solicited through workplaces, the city's labor organizations were apparently rather uninvolved in voluntarism. Although the other local newspapers reported the Sanitary Fair's progress with painstaking care, *Fincher's* did not print a word encouraging contributions to the event.[26] Early in the war, the Typographical Union voted to waive monthly dues for any member who joined the army. But an August 1862 resolution to offer $25 to brothers who enlisted was voted down and replaced by a fund to aid the families of members who had volunteered. The initial resolution had called for a $5 per man assessment to cover the added costs; the adopted proposal, however, only created a structure for distributing voluntary donations. In the months to come the union's five-man relief committee distributed small monthly payments of $5 to $25 to needy families. In February 1863 the committee reported that only a third of the employed members had contributed to the fund. In March 1864 the union discharged the relief committee when it appeared that no more donations would be forthcoming. In seventeen months the committee received and distributed less than $1,300, or less than $2 per member.[27]

In their military and benevolent activities Philadelphia's workers followed the more general citywide pattern. Most joined in the initial distaste for war with the South, as well as in the surge of patriotism when the fighting began. When the war came close to home, the city's workers, like its other citizens, responded slowly (though a segment eventually acted energetically). And although Philadelphia's elite continued their peacetime dominance of the major charitable societies, its laborers claimed a role in the voluntaristic proceedings.

During the secession crisis the North's workers banded together to support the Crittenden Compromise; however, once the war began labor did not speak with a single political voice. David Montgomery has demonstrated that even though conscription, emancipation, and inflation strained the relationship between wage earners and the administration, these issues did not push most workers into the Peace Democrats' camp. Even when they disapproved of Lincoln's

25 This was particularly true of the Sanitary Fair. See Chaper 6.
26 It ran only one short editorial praising "the brilliant display of mechanical art" at the fair, and taking note of the president's visit. See *FTR*, 25 June 1864.
27 This relief committee was the only war-related voluntarism mentioned in the union's minutes. See NTU minutes, 11 May 1861; 9 August, 13 September, 8 November 1862; 14 February, 13 March 1864. In March 1864 the NTU had 680 members with 407 listed in "good standing."

methods and turned to the Democratic Party, laborers staunchly approved of the Union cause and rejected "copperheadism."[28] And although they objected to the draft laws, organized labor's leaders strongly criticized the New York City draft riots.[29] Rather than venture into the political arena, Fincher devoted his pages to the cause of organizing to protect wages. He did not specifically discourage his readers from involvement in partisan politics and public affairs, but he warned of the danger of any "diversion from duty."[30]

Like other Philadelphians, the war touched laborers through various affiliations. Sometimes they responded individually or with family members; in other instances they acted as members of an ethnic group or a neighborhood. Perhaps most often, laborers contributed to the war effort through the workplace: enlisting, drilling, or donating money with their fellow journeymen or machinists. The organizers of the Sanitary Fair chose not to divide the city geographically or ethnically, but by types of enterprise, so that the workers who banded together under their factory banners in the peace march of February 1861 were also similarly grouped when the newspapers listed their contributions to the Sanitary Commission in June 1864.

Workers and the wartime economy

When Philadelphia's laborers participated in the war effort, their status as workers affected their actions. Financial constraints limited their donations to benevolent societies and enhanced the lure of enlistment bounties. Later the class-biased conscription law drew their ire, and fears of competition from freed slaves led some to question Lincoln's call for emancipation. But for laborers, the conflict's greatest challenge had little to do with aiding the cause. In the five years following the secession winter, Philadelphia's working-class families had to contend with unemployment, inflation, and government contractors.

The South's secession unleashed an economic crisis that left the North reeling. Many factories halted production and hundreds of weaker establishments failed, as the economy slowly ground to a halt.[31] Northern workers, who had been enjoying a brief period of high employment, suddenly faced major layoffs. In June 1861 a "Laborer" wrote to the *Public Ledger* reporting that "there is hardly a factory running in the city," and called on the council to provide aid

28 Montgomery, *Beyond Equality*, 91–2, 101–2, 113.
29 Montgomery, *Beyond Equality*, 107; FTR, 25 July 1863.
30 *FTR*, 1 July 1864.
31 The larger economic forces summarized in this section are all discussed more fully in Chapters 10 and 11.

for the unemployed.[32] In early July the city's unemployed mechanics asked the council for appropriations to provide jobs. But the City Council voted down a proposal to spend $733,500 for public works, and tabled two committee recommendations suggesting smaller direct expenditures for city improvements.[33]

Soon government contracting and renewed confidence turned the economy around, and those workers who did not join the army enjoyed an increasingly favorable labor market. But for some, wartime economic changes affected the nature of their work. The most dramatic shift took place in Philadelphia's textile manufacturing sector, which turned to woolen goods when the supply of southern cotton ran dry. Some local manufactories adjusted their operations to meet military demands. Foundries turned to the production of shot and shell, pitchfork factories began producing bayonets, and carpet makers specialized in army tents. Still others only adjusted slightly to profit from the war. Shipyards started placing armor plating on their vessels, boot and shoe manufacturers (who had lost the demand for cheap slave's shoes) began making army footwear, and clothiers branched out into uniforms and regalia.

In most cases workers shared in this boom. In early September 1861 the *Public Ledger* reported that between three and four hundred hands were making shot and shell at the North, Chase and North foundry, men at the Bush Hill Iron Works were manufacturing Dahlgren shell guns, and Bement & Dougherty's Industrial Works had 170 men working on government contracts. The war's demands also provided work for 1,700 Navy Yard laborers, and 4,000 men and women turned to the production of military clothing. The city's saddlers and harnessers soon discovered that their biggest problem was finding enough labor to meet their needs.[34]

When the North's economy turned around, wages rose as employers battled over a diminished labor supply. But though workers brought home more pay, they quickly discovered that what they earned bought less. Table 9.1 summarizes wartime fluctuations in the cost of living and concomitant shifts in real wage rates in manufacturing, the building trades, skilled labor, and unskilled labor. Although wages generally climbed after the first year of the war, most rates of increase did not match price inflation until the end of the conflict, and the relationship between wages and prices did not reach the prewar

---

32 Commons et al, *History of Labour in the United States*, 2:10, 13; *PL*, 13 June 1861.
33 *PL*, 3 July 1861, *Philadelphia Evening Bulletin*, 9 July 1861 (hereafter *EB*); *Journal of the Select Council* (11, 18 July 1861): 14, Appendixes 6, 12, 14. According to one diarist, "[a] great number of men being out of employment [enlisted] to get bread for their families." See Amanda Marklee diary, 23 July 1861, HSP.
34 *PL*, 2, 4, 23 September 1861.

Table 9.1. United States Prices and Real Wages, 1860–70

| Year | Price index | Selected Occupations (wages in 1860 dollars) | | | |
		Manufacturing	Building	Skilled	Laborers
1860	100	1.19	1.69	1.62	1.03
1861	101	1.16	1.66	1.65	1.03
1862	113	1.08	1.72	1.56	0.95
1863	139	0.94	1.89	1.43	0.86
1864	176	0.84	2.21	1.32	0.79
1865	175	0.93	2.55	1.42	0.84
1866	167	1.02	2.74	1.56	0.91
1867	157	1.10	2.94	1.63	0.96
1868	154	1.14	3.00	1.68	0.98
1869	147	1.22	3.16	1.77	1.04
1870	141	1.27	3.06	1.85	1.08

Note: Price index from Hoover data. Manufacturing and building wages from Aldrich data. Skilled wages (from 5 skilled occupations) and laborers from Weeks data. Long's wage indexes using the Aldrich and Weeks data and Hoover's price index.

Sources: Ethel D. Hoover, "Retail Prices after 1850," *Trends in the American Economy in the Nineteenth Century*, National Bureau of Economic Research, Studies in Income and Wealth, vol. 24 (Princeton, N.J., 1960), 142; Clarence D. Long, *Wages and Earnings in the United States, 1860–1890* (Princeton, N.J., 1960), 152, 154.

For original Aldrich data see Nelson W. Aldrich, "Wholesale Prices, Wages, and Transportation," *Report from the Committee on Finance* (3 March 1893), 52nd Cong., 2nd sess., Senate Report 1394.

For original Weeks data see Joseph D. Weeks, "Report on the Statistics of Wages in the Manufacturing Industries. . . ," Bureau of the Census, *Tenth Census of the United States*, vol. xx (Washington, D.C., 1880), ix–xi.

(Both reports are described by Long in *Wages and Earnings*, 6–8.)

standard until the late 1860s.[35] Over the course of the war real wages declined by roughly 20 percent.[36]

In 1880 Joseph D. Weeks of the Census Office asked selected manufacturers to report annual wages paid since 1860.[37] The returns from three Philadelphia factories (Table 9.2) provide a useful supple-

35 For further discussion of wartime wages and prices, see Clarence D. Long, *Wages and Earnings in the United States, 1860–1890* (Princeton, 1960); Ethel D. Hoover, "Retail Prices after 1850," *Trends in the American Economy in the Nineteenth Century*, National Bureau of Economic Research, Studies in Income and Wealth, vol. 24 (Princeton, 1960); Wesley Mitchell, *A History of the Greenbacks* (Chicago, 1903); Robert P. Sharkey, *Money, Class, and Party* (Baltimore, 1959), pp. 180-81; Emerson David Fite, *Social and Economic Conditions in the North During the Civil War* (1909; New York, 1963), 183–4.
36 McPherson, *Ordeal By Fire*, 205.
37 His resulting data are flawed because the samples are small and not necessarily representative and Weeks did not include a gender breakdown or the number of employees included in each table.

Table 9.2.
Selected Wage Schedules for Three Philadelphia Factories

	1860	1861	1862	1863	1864	1865	1866
Brick Factory							
Foreman	100	117	117	149	156	156	167
Burner	100	100	100	125	138	175	200
Setter	100	86	86	114	129	171	186
Stove Foundry							
Engineer	100	133	133	133	133	139	156
Finisher	100	80	101	94	207	170	188
Molder	100	93	128	71	128	218	184
Furniture Factory							
Foreman	100	100	100	125	125	125	125
Chair maker	100	100	100	117	117	117	117
Carver	100	100	100	113	113	113	113

Note: This table includes only a few representative jobs from each factory.

Source: Wesley Clair Mitchell, *History of the Greenbacks* (1903; Chicago, 1968), 520, 528, 563. Mitchell's data from Joseph D. Weeks, "Report on the Statistics of Wages in the Manufacturing Industries," Bureau of the Census, *Tenth Census of the United States* (Washington, D.C., 1880).

ment to the aggregate data in Table 9.1. In each establishment the war years are best divided into two periods: 1860 to 1862 and 1863 to 1866. Throughout the first period the brickmakers' wages stayed fairly constant, with several positions enjoying slight increases while others dropped somewhat. The pattern at a stove foundry was similar, but with a wider range. Wages at the furniture factory apparently did not fluctuate at all until after 1862. Beginning in 1863, wages at all three establishments rose, often quite dramatically. Once again, the diversity of experience – within each factory and from factory to factory – bears noting. For some, wartime wages actually rose faster than Hoover's cost of living estimates. After the economy recovered from the 1860–1 panic, Northern workers enjoyed very high employment rates, but between 1860 and 1864 most lost ground in the face of a nationwide price increase of 76 percent.

The war also left its mark on labor insofar as it changed the long-term structure of employment. Table 9.3, which details shifts in the labor force between 1860 and 1870, reveals marked alterations in the distribution of jobs. Chapters 10 and 11 will discuss the economic changes underlying these employment shifts. For the moment, a few observations will suffice. The sectors with the most rapidly growing labor forces – sugar refining, carpentry and building, umbrella manufacturing – were not engaged in war contracting.[38] The enterprises that were most clearly related to war contracting, such as boots and shoes, men's clothing, caps and hats, and saddles and harnesses, all experienced declining work forces over the war decade. The clearest war-related shifts came in the textile industry, where shortages created a permanent shift from cotton to wool manufacturing. Other categories in Table 9.3 (pages 228-9) mask smaller war-related shifts. Some railroad and machinery manufactories (included under iron products) sustained wartime growth into the postwar years, as did several of Philadelphia's leading shipbuilders. As we shall see, many of Philadelphia's manufacturing establishments adjusted their activities to meet the possibilities and constraints posed by the war. Such shifts led to short-term changes for the city's workers. But most of the long-term changes in the labor force were largely independent of the war.

Organized labor

Although the war effort involved workers in a variety of associational guises, the economic hardships posed by the conflict left them to their own devices. How did Philadelphia's wage earners respond to the war's economic fluctuations? Did they continue established, prewar modes of organization and protest? Or did unusual circumstances require new responses?

Philadelphia shoemakers in the early 1790s formed the Federal Society of Journeymen Cordwainers, one of the earliest of America's labor organizations. Soon other craft unions sprang up in major Northern cities. These early organizations sought to protect craft standards, raise wages, and improve conditions. They also served as benevolent societies, raising money for needy members. But these first craft unions crumbled during the depression following the War of 1812, and by 1820 craft unions had all but disappeared in America. Rapid economic growth and repressive measures by employers spurred northeastern craftsmen into renewed activity. This resurgence lasted until the close of the decade, when an economic downturn once again cut into labor's organizational impulse.

In the mid-1830s, after a brief flirtation with independent political activity, economically motivated unions began to dot the landscape. This response to economic growth and declining real wages produced over fifty local craft unions in Philadelphia. As the movement grew, workers in some cities formed citywide trades assemblies and several crafts established nationwide organizations. But the depression of

38 Sugar refining benefited from wartime legislation. See Chapter 10.

1837 killed off the labor movement and with it the ideal of worker solidarity. The economic growth following the mid-1840s resulted in the rise of tightly organized trade unions stressing wages, hours, and work conditions. The prosperity of the early 1850s spawned new local craft unions and several nationals. The 1854–5 recession dealt these organizations a serious blow, but when the economy revived so did most locals. Between 1850 and 1857 eleven nationals were formed;

Table 9.3. Employment Shifts Between 1860 and 1870

Type of Enterprise[a]	1860	1870	% Change
Sugar refining	168	1034	515
Carpenters and builders	878	4454	407
Umbrellas; parasols	421	1767	320
Steel[b]	562	1885	235
Sash and blind makers	262	853	226
Iron products[c]	8560	27356	220
Upholsterers[d]	300	846	182
Paints and colors; painters[e]	488	1015	108
Confectioners	308	634	106
Wood[f]	706	1301	84
Shipbuilders	1108	1849	67
Marble cutters/makers	744	1241	67
Plumbers; gas fitters	401	655	63
Glass	928	1448	56
Tin and sheet iron[g]	647	994	54
Bricks	1965	2975	51
Printers (book and job)	853	1274	49
Glue; curled hair	493	732	48
Chemicals/drugs; medicine	960	1390	45
Candles and soaps	376	529	41
Brewers[h]	596	829	39
Type founders/stereotypers	395	548	39
Furniture	1689	2298	36
Cloaks; corsets/skirts	603	819	36
Bread/biscuits	912	1238	36
Newspapers	944	1254	33
Book publishing	844	1104	31
Brushes/brooms	547	706	29
Coopers	460	586	27
Paper mills/products	973	1172	20
Leather	1326	1570	18
Bookbinding/blank books	1222	1434	17
Silverware (plated and solid)	589	634	8
Boots/shoes	8434	8317	−1
Gasworks[i]	2527	2133	−16
Men's clothing[j]	14387	11654	−19
Caps/hats[k]	1377	1062	−23
Carriages	1038	751	−28
Saddle and harness makers	718	513	−29
Millinery and straw goods	1138	761	−33
Watchmakers/jewelers	1391	817	−41
Wagonmakers; wheelwrights	875	510	−42
Shirts; collars	3290	850	−74
Total	67403	95792	42

(Table 9.3 - continued)

Textiles	1860	1870	% Change
Cotton	5118	3636	−29
Cotton-wool	3967	5731	44
Wool	1345	2658	98
Silk	1034	1276	23
Dyeing, finishing	1253	660	−47
Spinning	728	2293	215
Hosiery, knit goods	2412	5127	113
Carpet	2382	4713	98
Others	282	292	4
Textile total	18521	26386	42

[a]The first part of this table was compiled from Blodget's summaries of the census returns. "Segars" are omitted because Blodget listed fewer workers than establishments in 1870. "Canned Fruit" was left off because no category existed on the 1860 list. The table lists workers in all industries with over 500 employees in either year and all textile workers.
[b]Includes steel saws, cutlery.
[c]Includes all iron railroad manufacturing, machinery, stoves, blacksmiths, etc.
[d]Includes mattresses, bedding.
[e]1860 does not include most housepainters; 1870 does.
[f]Includes wood turners, planing and dressing mills, sawed lumber, willowware, etc.
[g]Includes roofs and sheet iron stoves.
[h]Includes beer and ale, cordials and bitters, malt.
[i]Includes gas fixtures, meters, tubes, chandeliers, lamps.
[j]Includes neckties.
[k]Only 1860 includes fur, wool, and silk hats.

Sources: Lorin Blodget, Manufactures of Philadelphia, Census of 1860 (Philadelphia, 1861); Blodget, The Industries of Philadelphia as Shown by the Manufacturing Census of 1870 (Philadelphia, 1877); Philip Scranton, Proprietary Capitalism: The Textile Manufacture at Philadelphia, 1800–1885 (New York, 1983), 304.

only three – the typographers, hat finishers, and stonecutters – survived the Panic of 1857. Although the nation's trade unions regained some of their lost ground in the final years of the decade, many were too weak to survive the secession crisis.[39]

Philadelphia's workers generally followed this national pattern. In the late 1820s the city's Mechanics' Union of Trade Associations became the nation's first citywide labor organization. In the 1830s Philadelphia was the home of numerous journeymen associations

39 This brief summary is taken from Melvyn Dubofsky, "Labor Organizations," in Encyclopedia of American Economic History, ed. Glenn Porter, (New York, 1980), 524–30; Foner, History of the Labor Movement, 1:65–214; Norman Ware, The Industrial Worker (1924; Chicago, 1964), 227–30; Joseph G. Rayback, A History of American Labor (New York, 1959), 104–7; and Foster Rhea Dulles, Labor in America, 3rd ed. (New York, 1966), 88.

and several short-lived workingmen's cooperatives. The Panic of 1837 took the wind from their sails, but when the economy improved Philadelphia's cooperatives and unions returned to activity. Between 1839 and 1857 numerous local organizations struck for higher wages.[40] The resurgent economy also brought renewed efforts at citywide organizing, and tentative communication with unions in other cities.[41] Philadelphia's unions stumbled badly following the mid-1850s. Between 1850 and 1856, thirty-eight local craft unions met in Philadelphia. In 1857 only twelve of these held their annual meetings. This figure rose to twenty-six by 1859, but plummeted to eleven in 1861.[42] Nationally, Philadelphia consistently stood as one of the nation's strongest union centers. In 1848 the city hosted the fourth annual Industrial Congress of Workingmen. During the 1850s six national unions had locals in Philadelphia. By 1861 several Philadelphians – most notably William Sylvis of the molders and Jonathan Fincher of the machinists and blacksmiths – had established themselves as prominent labor leaders.[43]

As the Civil War approached, organized labor in Philadelphia had a settled pattern. In prosperous times the city's skilled workers joined in craft unions, cooperative societies, and citywide assemblies. When the economy declined – as it did in 1837, 1857, and late 1860 – these collective efforts collapsed under the weight of unemployment and economic insecurity. At each stage in the national economic cycle, Philadelphia's workers played a central role in producing spokesmen, launching national unions, and hosting nationwide meetings.

Standard American labor histories agree that organized labor during the Civil War followed the economic tides.[44] As the workers had feared, the outbreak of hostilities paralyzed the economy and put thousands out of work. This decline crippled organized labor in the North. When the economy recovered, workers enjoyed high employment but suffered under rising prices. After mid-1862, economically motivated local trade unions reappeared as workers sought to use

40 In the 1840s these efforts resulted in frequent violent outbreaks. See Elizabeth Geffen, "Violence in Philadelphia in the 1840s and 1850s," *Pennsylvania Magazine of History and Biography* 36 (October 1969): 381–410.
41 Richard Alan McLeod, "The Philadelphia Artisan, 1828–1850" (Ph. D. diss., University of Missouri-Columbia, 1971), 129–82.
42 Edgar Barclay Cale, "The Organization of Labor in Philadelphia, 1850–1870" (Ph. D. University of Pennsylvania, 1940). Russell Weigley says there were forty-one unions in Philadelphia in 1854. See R. Weigley, "The Border City in Civil War, 1854–1865," in *Philadelphia: A 300-Year History*, ed. Weigley (New York, 1982), 338.
43 Cale, "The Organization of Labor in Philadelphia," 94–103.
44 This account is taken from Commons et al, *History of Labour in the United States*, 2:13–25; Foner, *History of the Labor Movement*, 1:338–46; Montgomery, *Beyond Equality*, 96–7, 160–2, and *passim*.

their improved bargaining position to address their new grievances.[45] In the year from December 1863 to December 1864 the number of locals listed in *Fincher's* directory jumped from 79 to 270. Other familiar signs of labor's resurgence followed. By the close of 1863 Northern workers in most major cities had held trades assemblies. New cooperative stores soon formed. And individual trades began to reestablish their national structures. John B. Andrews found that, given the spurt of organizing, the "number of [wartime] strikes was comparatively small," with 38 reported in 1863, 108 in 1864, and 85 in 1865.[46] Still, these figures reflected a rise in activity from the late 1850s.

The number and strength of Northern labor unions fluctuated substantially during the Civil War. But these shifts suggest strong continuities with the past. Changes in real wages and employment rates dictated labor's organizational successes in the 1860s as they had through the first half of the century. With these broad patterns in mind, we will consider Philadelphia's workers in three categories: highly organized craftsmen, private sector workers who organized during the war, and government contract workers.

The National Typographical Union (NTU), composed of journeymen printers, was one of the most powerful of Philadelphia's craft organizations. By 1861 the NTU had long served as a model for the nation's workingmen. In December 1850 representatives from several major cities, including Philadelphia, congregated in New York for the first "National Convention of Journeyman Printers." Their goals were to regulate wage scales "so as not to conflict with each other," to distribute lists of "rats" so that a blacklisted member could not find work in a new city, to limit apprentices, and to raise strike funds. Through the tumultuous fifties the printers continued to convene annually, with Philadelphia hosting their 1856 meeting.[47]

In January 1862 the minutes of the NTU's Philadelphia local #2 (NTU #2) listed a total of 641 members, including 16 serving in the army. Two hundred and seventy-eight (44 percent) of the nonmilitary members were in "good standing," with all dues paid. During the next three months, thirty-five new men joined the union, fifty more enlisted, and the proportion of nonmilitary members in good standing rose to 55 percent. Between April 1862 and January 1864 the union's total membership increased from 676 to 753, and the number in good standing reached 60 percent (of nonmilitary members). These

---

45 Note that the war boom (and inflation) directed labor's attention away from employment and hours issues and toward wages alone.
46 Commons et al, *History of Labour in the United States*, 2:19, 23.
47 Foner, *History of the Labor Movement*, 1:235; *FTR*, 30 April 1864.

figures suggest that as the economy improved, more NTU members became financially secure.

By January 1865 the NTU's membership had risen to 837; the share in good standing had increased from 60 to 69 percent. The membership figure included seventy-six men in uniform, many of whom would shortly return to the local labor force. By the end of October 1865 the union had absorbed these veterans and still increased its total membership by almost fifty men. The printers managed to maintain their strength through both the secession crisis and the postwar economic decline.[48]

Following the firing on Fort Sumter, Morton McMichael, the owner of Philadelphia's *North American & U. S. Gazette*, wrote to NTU # 2 seeking a temporary wage abatement. The union's response revealed the strength of this body of skilled workers. The printers referred McMichael's request to a subcommittee, which quizzed the publisher about the lucrative government advertisements that his paper ran. McMichael responded that his subscribers had fallen behind in their payments, and that the paper would fold if his printers did not join the salaried workers in accepting a pay cut. The committee recommended accepting the abatement, but the union voted it down by an overwhelming 135 to 16.[49]

On February 25, 1863, the printers met to discuss the need for increased pay rates for "book composition" and "job work." They appointed a fifteen-man committee that put together a proposal and mailed a copy to each employer, requesting a meeting to discuss their demands. On March 26 the employers turned out in force to object to the newly published pay scale. The committee listened to their arguments, and then drew up a new scale that the union passed a few days later. This episode demonstrates the printers' continued ability to initiate pay-scale negotiations and to adjust their demands in very "amicable" discussions with the employers.[50] Nine months later the union appointed a committee to revise the "book and job scale of prices." This time the employers labeled the new scale "inexpedient and inadmissible." Rather than responding harshly, the printers' committee agreed to lower their demands. Once again, the committee seemed proud to report "most amicable and pleasant" final negotiations with the employers.[51]

The well-organized printers successfully kept their wages up during the wartime inflation. But in the final year of the war they

48 NTU, *passim*.
49 NTU, 11, 18 May 1861.
50 NTU, 25 February, 14, 28 March 1863.
51 NTU, 12 December 1863; 9, 23 January, 13 February, 5, 13 March 1864; FTR, 5 March 1864.

entered into tough negotiations with the city's newspaper publishers. In the spring of 1864 the union passed a new scale of prices for newspaper composition. The issue went unresolved until a heated meeting in early September, at which several representatives of the major local newspapers claimed that they could not afford any pay raises. The committee reported back to the union that the papers did appear to be in trouble, but a small increase was still in order. The printers voted to postpone the issue in September and again in October, and then tabled the motion in their December meeting.[52]

In addition to its regular negotiations with Philadelphia's employing printers and newspaper publishers, NTU #2 regularly aided workers in battles against individual employers.[53] On December 19, 1863, the union met to discuss the volatile situation at the office of the Philadelphia *Age*. The employees had learned that the owners had been trying to replace their striking compositors with workers from New York City. The union voted to support the *Age* workers in a complete shutdown of the strike-breaking newspaper. The following week, union member James Devine formally charged John R. Ecke and another *Age* employee with "ratting" (strike-breaking), and the union named a committee to investigate. Then, on the twenty-third, policemen arrested two union members (including Devine) for assaulting Ecke. On the twenty-sixth the union formally expelled the two accused "rats" and recorded the names of nineteen men who were currently working at the offending newspaper.[54]

How did the Civil War affect NTU #2? Repeatedly, the union followed its established procedures during the crisis. When they deemed their wages unsatisfactory, they published new scales. Even when the publishers felt that the NTU's demands were unreasonable, they recognized the need to negotiate. This pattern of conflict and resolution seemed no different from earlier decades. NTU #2 also maintained its other traditional functions: It communicated with other printers' unions, sent representatives to national gatherings, and oversaw the movements of its local members.

The NTU local was composed of skilled workers who enjoyed a particularly strong organization. Most Philadelphia unions followed the national pattern and folded during the secession crisis. Their members remained disorganized until a booming economy created a large demand for labor and rapidly increasing prices, factors that provided the opportunity and impetus for renewed labor organiza-

52 NTU, 13 March, 23 April, 14 May, 10 September, 10 October, 10 December 1864.
53 See, for instance, the running dispute versus the *Daily News* over back pay, NTU, November 1861 through June 1863.
54 NTU, 19, 26 December 1863; *PL*, 24 December 1863.

tion. This resurgence helped give birth to *Fincher's Trades' Review*, which in turn spurred still greater organizational activity. By 1863 most Philadelphia workers were losing ground to rising prices. In its June 1863 inaugural issue *Fincher's* noted the frequent reports of labor shortages and increased wages, but added: "we regret to say that these flattering prospects are sadly neutralized by the unprecedented high price of all the necessaries of life." In the following months the labor newspaper continually stressed the need for wage increases in proportion to inflation. Workers must act, Fincher argued, before "the golden opportunity has slipped beyond our grasp."[55]

In April 1863 Philadelphia's tailors and shoemakers met to seek increased wages. That winter dozens of journeyman groups followed their lead. In early November 1863 the coppersmiths sent a representative from each shop to a conference to discuss a "protective society" to adjust wages to the cost of living. The following week the makers of ladies' shoes organized to seek a 12 percent wage increase; earthenware makers asked for a 20 percent raise. Later that month the city's machinists formed a committee to demand better wages. Soon *Fincher's* was full of notices announcing new unions. On November 23 local house painters won a $2 per day pay increase. In December a Germantown stockingmaker called on his fellow laborers to join together to seek more pay; three months later a second letter to *Fincher's* reported that the stockingers had won their raise and that Germantown's masons and clerks were taking similar steps. In the spring of 1864 the paper announced organizational meetings by paperhangers, coachmakers, brushmakers, harness makers, and tin and sheet-iron workers.[56]

On some occasions Fincher nudged recalcitrant Philadelphia workers into activity. A stirring editorial in December 1863 appealed to the glassblowers' pride by noting that in the previous decade they had been one of Philadelphia's strongest trade unions and "among the last to surrender." Three months later, Fincher was pleased to note the official formation of "Hollow-ware Glass-blower League of Rights, No. 1 of Philadelphia." In February 1864 he wrote that the city's bricklayers, who could work for only five months each year, should join and demand a pay raise to cover their idle time. Within a month this group had formed a permanent organization.[57]

Philadelphia's reemerging labor structure led many unions to reestablish communications with workers in other cities. In late

55 FTR, 6 June, 4, 18 July 1863, and *passim*. Emerson David Fite, *Social and Industrial Conditions in the North During the Civil War* (1909; New York, 1963), 184.
56 *PL*, 3, 9 April, 9 September, 13, 21 November 1863; *FTR*, 28 November, 19 December 1863; 12 March 1864, and *passim*.
57 *FTR*, 19 December 1863; 6, 20 February, 25 March, 30 April 1864.

November 1863 300 workingmen met at the National Guard Hall to collect money to send to New York's striking machinists. The curriers gathered in February 1864 to support a strike in Salem and South Danvers; in June the printers sent a contribution to their striking brothers in Rochester.[58] When the collarmakers requested a 30 percent raise, their employers were willing to consent only if employers in other cities did the same. The local union called on its counterparts to organize and seek similar adjustments. By late 1864 more and more Philadelphia unions affiliated with national groups.[59]

The procession of labor organizations that followed the improving wartime economy included tentative steps toward citywide collaboration. On October 27, 1863, representatives from several Philadelphia trades gathered to hear Fincher argue for collective action. A month later they reconvened to form a citywide Trades Assembly. This body began with a wave of enthusiasm and met every month for the next year. But in November 1864 Fincher still bemoaned the widespread apathy toward the workers' central organization.[60]

As the war progressed, prices rose, workers reorganized, and strikes became commonplace in Philadelphia.[61] In June 1862 the city's house painters won a wage increase, and in the following March Philadelphia's carpenters and painters gained a similar victory after a short strike.[62] Soon such job actions spread out of the building trades. In April 1863 the *Public Ledger* reported that the local journeyman bootmakers had struck for a 7 percent pay raise despite a 5 percent increase earlier in the year. Two months later, policemen arrested striking Arch Street Railway workers for obstructing the trains. As the year closed, several coal workers found themselves in court when they walked off their jobs and "threatened personal violence" against anyone who took their place.[63]

With the exception of a "riotous" strike by the Schuylkill ice gatherers, 1864 began on a calm note.[64] In mid-January the molders, who had been out for nearly a year, were the only labor group on

58 *PL*, 28 November 1863; *FTR*, 5 December 1863; 20 February 1864; NTU, 11 June 1864.
59 *FTR*, 5 March, 8 August, 10 September 1864; *PL*, 21, 30 November 1863; 30 August, 8 September 1864.
60 *FTR*, 7 November 1863; 26 November 1864, and *passim; E. B.* 28 October 1863; *PL*, 23, 25 November 1863.
61 Strikes did not completely stop during the crisis. In March 1861 150 workers on the Callowhill Street Railroad struck for higher wages. See *PL*, 7 March 1861.
62 Cale, "The Organization of Labor," 50–9; Secretary of Internal Affairs of the Commonwealth of Pennsylvania, *Annual Report, Part 3, Industrial Statistics*, Vol. 9 (Harrisburg, 1880–1).
63 *PL*, 9 April, 9 June 1863; *FTR*, 19 December 1863. The Arch Street Railway workers struck twice in June 1863. See *PL*, 4 June 1863.
64 *FTR*, 23 January 1864; *PL*, 3 January 1864.

strike.[65] But soon this lull gave way to a new wave of strikes. Toward the end of April, *Fincher's* reported that local shoemakers had become part of the almost daily labor activity.[66] That summer, Philadelphia's Reading Railroad operatives struck for ten days, forcing the War Department to seize the strategically necessary line.[67] In August 1864 a Philadelphia daily noted that "'Strikes' are again becoming numerous."[68]

As the war drew to a close, the city's employers, faced with an economic slump, sought to regain what ground they had given up in previous years. With the threat of wage reductions in the air, *Fincher's* repeatedly warned of dark days ahead. In November 1864 the paper published a letter from an Indianapolis worker announcing that employers in that city already had formed an "Employers' Protective Association" to push wages down.[69] A month later, Fincher addressed a lengthy editorial to the recent "Reduction of Wages." Eighteen months before, when labor was scarce and demand high, the newspaper had called on workers to strike while they could. By the close of 1864 business had fallen off, and Philadelphia had a growing labor surplus.[70] Fincher surveyed this changed landscape, concluding that workers had no choice but to accept the wage cuts. He acknowledged that "having created extensive combinations for the purpose of protection and defense, it goes against the grain to tamely yield." But given the state of the economy, labor had little chance of winning and could easily lose all they had fought for. His advice was to "accept all reductions of wages that cannot be avoided under protest, and prepare to enforce the penalty of retaliation at the first and every opportunity." Rather than battle before they were ready, they should give in to a superior force, and so live to fight another day.[71]

In an analysis of nineteenth-century American strikes, David Montgomery concludes that between the 1860s and the 1890s laborers

65 *Philadelphia Press*, quoted in FTR, 16 January 1864.
66 FTR, 30 April 1864.
67 John L. Blackman, Jr., "The Seizure of the Reading Railroad in 1864," *Pennsylvania Magazine of History and Biography* (January 1987), 49–60.
68 Secretary of Internal Affairs, *Annual Report; FTR*, 6 August 1864 (the labor paper did not identify the daily it quoted). This midwar increase in local strikes also followed the national pattern. In February 1863 *Scientific American* reported that "strikes are constantly occurring among our workingmen." And that November the same journal noted a "universal disturbance in and unsettled condition of all classes of laborers and mechanics." See *Scientific American* 8 (21 February 1863): 121; 22 (28 November 1863): 341. See also Foner, *History of the Labor Movement*, 1:327–9.
69 FTR, 19 November 1864.
70 For descriptions of veterans seeking work, see PL, 21 April 1863; Nicholas B. Wainwright, ed., *A Philadelphia Perspective: The Diary of Sidney George Fisher* (Philadelphia, 1967), 491, entry of 6 April 1865.
71 FTR, 17 December 1864.

were "'learning the rules of the game'" as they became "familiar with the exigencies of industrial capitalism."[72] During the war years, Philadelphia's unions improved their techniques; but the city's capitalists also became more adept at defending their interests.[73] When the Spruce and Pine Street Railroad workers asked for a raise in late 1863, the owners offered a meager fifteen cents per day, meticulously reviewed the daily receipts, and fired workers for the slightest discrepancy. After ice gatherers walked out, their employers called in the local police to break up the strikers' meetings. In April 1864, when coopers struck for their first raise in five years, one master had a journeyman arrested merely for telling an apprentice that the shop's workers might go out.[74]

Two particularly prominent wartime labor disputes, involving the molders in 1863 and the machinists and blacksmiths in 1864, demonstrate the strength of Philadelphia's employers and their ability to combat ill-prepared union initiatives. The Philadelphia Molders' Union was formed in 1855. Four years later, delegates from various parts of the country answered William Sylvis's call and congregated in Philadelphia for the molders' first national convention. In January 1860 they reconvened in Albany and officially established the national union, with Sylvis as the first national secretary. By that time the molders enjoyed a strong reputation, with several strike victories to their credit. But these early successes led them into a series of disastrous battles against belligerent founders in 1860 and 1861. In a few months they went from one of the strongest nationals to virtual obscurity, too weak to hold their 1862 meeting.[75] During the first years of the war, the Philadelphia union kept in contact with the surviving molders' locals, but the national organization ceased to function. In early 1863 Sylvis called for a new national convention in Pittsburgh. This sparsely attended meeting set the union on the road to national reorganization. Sylvis toured the country throughout the year, stirring up molders' locals, and almost singlehandedly resurrecting the national body.[76]

While the National Molders' Union slowly reawakened, Philadelphia molders pursued their own goals. In the fall of 1862 they appointed a committee to discuss wage advances with the owners.

---

72 David Montgomery, "Strikes in Nineteenth-Century America," *Social Science History* (Winter 1980): 89.
73 For discussions of the nationwide "employer backlash" see Foner, *History of the Labor Movement*, 1:352–5; Montgomery, *Beyond Equality*, 100–1.
74 *FTR*, 12 December 1863; 23 January, 23, 30 April 1864.
75 For a brief history of the molders before the war see Grossman, *William Sylvis*, 23–44; Sylvis, *William H. Sylvis*.
76 Grossman, *William Sylvis*, 55–63.

During the winter, this body repeatedly met with a seemingly receptive employer group, and after lengthy negotiations presented a revised pay scale. Their proposal included so many compromises that an optimistic Sylvis departed for his national tour before hearing the owners' response. With the workers' leader out of Philadelphia, the founders issued a new demand: that all rules regulating apprentices be repealed. In response, 218 men from four of Philadelphia's foundries went on strike. The molders' walkout was the culmination of a masterful strategy by the founders to break the resurgent union. By stalling the negotiations until February, the founders had been able to build up a large surplus, while leaving their striking workers unemployed in midwinter. Moreover, they managed to incite the molders into a hasty strike that Sylvis might have been able to avert.[77]

When the molders walked out, four major employing founders drew up a secret agreement, with each employer depositing a large sum to be forfeited if he yielded separately. Then they drafted a circular to the nation's founders requesting that no other employers hire Philadelphia's striking molders. In an effort to man their depleted establishments, the founders sent agents nationwide in search of workers. When Sylvis visited Stewart & Peterson's foundry to explain the dispute to several newly arrived scabs, the owners had him arrested. Philadelphia's founders became so renowned among employers for their union-busting that in June 1863 a committee of Cincinnati founders visited to see how their Philadelphia colleagues had managed, in the words of the *North American*, to "succeed in gaining liberty to manage their own property in their own way."

The molders failed to defeat the founders, but the strike did have its positive elements. By the end of May other locals had contributed over $4,500 to the strike fund, with contributions arriving from as far away as Canada, Ohio, and Kentucky. In a letter marking the first anniversary of the strike, Sylvis held that the balance sheet stood in the workers' favor. The molders, he argued, had succeeded in maintaining their dignity and pride in the face of hardship, with only 23 of the original 218 strikers "willing to return as voluntary slaves to the masters who cast them off." Although the foundries had remained open, Sylvis claimed that their business had dropped substantially in both quantity and quality, and that their preeminent national position had been lost.[78]

77 Sylvis later claimed that the apprentice issue was not really important to the founders and was only introduced to kill the proposed wage increase.
78 In one instance, five of eight men brought in as scabs refused to work when they learned of the strike. The Iron Molders International Union paid for their transportion home. (Some Philadelphia papers claimed that the strikers regularly threatened potential scabs with bodily harm).

In the end the molders' strike defeated both parties. By 1868 the Philadelphia local was a mere skeleton. But although the owners succeeded in quashing the union, Philadelphia never regained its place as the nation's stove foundry center. The molders' struggle revealed the limits of mid-nineteenth-century unionism, as well as the growing strength of the national organization.[79] It demonstrated that both sides – employees and labor – had evolved to a point of strength, but had not developed the mechanisms for negotiation enjoyed by the printers and publishers. Although the war created the economic context for the molders' actions, it had no clear impact on the pattern of negotiations.

About a year after the molders went on strike, another once-strong union – the Machinists and Blacksmiths – met to try to improve their declining financial position. In response to the "fluctuations of the times," Jonathan Fincher's local appointed a committee in July 1864 "to secure prompt and proper relief."[80] This "committee of 15" sent a message to employers requesting a meeting to discuss wage adjustments, and a second circular to their fellow mechanics explaining the union's goals. To the workers' dismay, this time-honored approach failed. Rather than accepting or rejecting the proposed meetings, most of Philadelphia's prominent factory owners simply ignored the union's request.[81]

With their planned "committee of conference" in danger of collapse, the mechanics assigned three representatives to visit the nonresponding employers in the hope that a personal appeal might turn the tide. At the elegant offices of Morris, Tasker and Company the three intrepid delegates met with a hostile reception from Charles Wheeler, the owner, who assured them that the firm's employees were already making more than they ever had before. Next they visited Merrick and Sons, proprietors of the Southwark Foundry, where the delegates spoke to a family member who assured them that "we can manage our own business within our walls, and will have no interference." At Baldwin Locomotive, the scene of several earlier labor disputes, M. W. Baird asked that the delegates return to their brothers and "express my contempt for the whole affair and all engaged in it." Everywhere they went, the labor spokesmen received similar responses. After visiting ten of the city's largest establishments over the course of two grueling, humiliating days, the

---

79 This summary of the molders' strike was taken from Grossman, *William Sylvis*, 64–7; Sylvis, *William H. Sylvis*, 51–5; *FTR*, 6, 13, 20, 27 June, 17 October 1863; 20 February 1864.
80 *PL*, 21 November 1863; *FTR*, 30 July 1864.
81 The machinists and blacksmiths received less than a dozen responses (all positive) to their two letters.

committee retired "without receiving a favorable verbal response from even one alone."[82]

After hearing the delegates' report, the machinists and black-smiths named a committee to consider their next step. That body concluded that the real fault lay in "the indifference of those most interested, the journeymen," and that the union needed an improved organizational structure and a better-informed rank and file. Whereas the committee chided its fellow mechanics, Fincher assaulted the uncooperative employers as unfair and hypocritical. When the city needed defending, he pointed out, the employers were more than happy to see their employees acting as a single body; but when the workers sought increased wages, the owners insisted on acting individually. Fincher and the committee agreed that if Philadelphia's machinists and blacksmiths were to wield power, they must have the numbers and the organization to back up their demands.[83]

The wartime efforts of the printers, molders, and machinists and blacksmiths were similar to those of the Philadelphia labor movement during the prewar years. Each group responded to economic fluctuations as they did in peacetime: by organizing and publishing revised pay scales. The printers were strong enough to press their cause against the employing publishers, but the less skilled and more numerous molders and machinists and blacksmiths had little chance against the powerful factory owners. To say that there was no dramatic deviation from the recent past is not to suggest that Philadelphia's labor history was stagnant, or that there was no long-term evolution. Men like Fincher and Sylvis were developing skills that would have significant consequences for the experience of organized labor in the late 1860s and 1870s. And employers were perfecting cooperative responses to these threats. For many organized Philadelphia workers, the war prompted union activity, but did not produce significant change.

Workers and war production

Philadelphians who worked in war-related production did face altered circumstances that occasionally led them to new organizational responses. Some performed totally new tasks, and others – many sewing women in particular – entered the labor force for the first time. But the most important wartime change – and the major source of labor's complaints – was the contracting system through which the

---

82 *FTR*, 30 July, 6, 13, 27 August, 3, 10, 24 September 1864; *PL*, 8, 16 August 1864; *EB*, 9 August 1864. Note that this account comes from interested parties.
83 *FTR*, 24 September 1864.

government hired some workers directly, while subcontracting other jobs to local businessmen and manufacturers.

Shortly after Fort Sumter, government workers of all stripes began complaining of irregular pay scales and declining real wages. In September 1861 a large group of knapsack strappers sought to standardize the wages paid by the city's contractors.[84] In the following month Philadelphia's German tailors attempted to establish a uniform scale for government clothing work. After failed negotiations, 1,000 tailors went out on strike and the city filled with rumors of citywide labor action.[85] In early 1862 Philadelphia's Navy Yard workers were enraged by Congress' Navy Bill, which included provisions reducing their wages. Ship carpenters, joiners, blacksmiths, and other workers in the Navy's employ struck, resolving that they would not accept a pay cut when their employers – Congress – enjoyed increased wages. They defended themselves against charges of disloyalty by insisting that they did not seek a pay raise, but merely a return to their old salary level. Within a few days the ship carpenters returned to work with increased wages, and the other Navy Yard workers soon followed.[86] In December 1863 the Arsenal's shoemakers approached Quartermaster Colonel George Crossman for a wage advance. Recognizing the danger if they struck, Crossman readily agreed. Six weeks later the shoemakers presented a memorial to the War Department asking for a 20 percent increase. Fincher defended their request on patriotic grounds, reasoning that "our gallant army" deserved the best shoes possible and the government should pay its shoemakers accordingly. Apparently this request was not met: In April 1864 several hundred boot and shoemakers refused to do any government work, claiming that wages had declined over the previous two years.[87]

Most male Philadelphians employed in war industries, like their counterparts in the private sector, used established procedures to seek wage adjustments. When the wartime inflation became too uncomfortable, they announced their grievances and suggested amended pay scales. If the government or its contractors proved

---

84 *PL*, 6, 9 September 1861. Before the war, government knapsack strappers had received $56 per 100, but by September 1861 the contractors were only offering $40 to $50 per 100.

85 But in the end, the strike broke down without substantial results. See *PL*, 23, 31 October, 5, 6, 10 November 1861; *EB*, 31 October, 6, 7 November 1861; Cale, "The Organization of Labor," 43–9.

86 *PL*, 18, 21, 22 January 1862; Cale, "The Organization of Labor," 57–8; Scharf and Westcott, *History of Philadelphia*, 1:791.

87 *PL*, 5 December 1863; *FTR*, 16 January 1864; *PL*, 12 April 1864. On April 20, 1864, the *PL* reported that 200 local shoemakers still refused to do government work. See *Pl*, 20 April 1864.

unsympathetic, the workers walked out and offered their services to private business. Navy Yard workers addressed their complaints to Congress, and arsenal shoemakers linked their interests to the soldiers' welfare; but their organizational techniques and their demands followed established patterns.[88]

The plight of Philadelphia's sewing women attracted unusual public attention, leading to distinctive, but still familiar, organizational responses. In the first days of the war the vacated Girard House Hotel and the Schuylkill Arsenal became centers of uniform production, with some of Philadelphia's most fashionable ladies joining wage-earning sewing women in making clothing for the army.[89] As the economy dipped, thousands of women flocked to the arsenal in search of jobs. When the government opened a new clothing house in late September 1861, over five thousand women rushed the building. A week later, the *Public Ledger* reported that the early morning crowds continued unabated, with the aged and infirm losing out because they could not push their way to the entrance.[90]

Government sewing women repeatedly appeared at the center of controversy during the war. Their most consistent source of discontent was the policy of contracting out work to private businessmen. In the fall of 1861 women from the arsenal met at Temperance Hall to express their anger. The president of the meeting declared:

> Our husbands, sons, brothers, and even fathers have gone to fight for the Government, and we are not willing that the Government should be used by base hearted contractors for selfish purposes, and we will not submit to the starvation prices offered by these men, while they make the Government pay them full prices, which we are deprived of.

88 Of course the government occasionally stepped in to protect the national interest. Such was the case in 1864 when federal troops temporarily replaced striking Reading Railroad workers. For further evidence of the use of federal troops to combat striking workers see Foner, *History of the Labor Movement*, 1:328–9; Blackman, "Seizure of the Reading Railroad."

89 Septima M. Collis, *A Woman's War Record, 1861–1865* (New York, 1889), 12–13; Winnifred K. MacKay, "Philadelphia During the Civil War," *Pennsylvania Magazine of History and Biography* (January 1946): 12–13; Scharf and Westcott, *History of Philadelphia*, 1:762.

90 Scharf and Westcott, *History of Philadelphia*, 1:782; *PL*, 2 October 1861. Foner estimates that the wartime industrial expansion and the concomitant removal of male workers created 100,000 new jobs for Northern women. See Philip S. Foner, *Women and the American Labor Movement*, 2 vols. (New York, 1979), 1:109. A contemporary observer estimated that the war added 300,000 women to the labor market, and a second observer reckoned that Boston alone added 25,000 new "needlewomen." See Alice Kessler-Harris, *Out To Work: A History of Wage-Earning Women in the United States* (New York, 1982), 76; John B. Andrews and W. D. P. Bliss, *History of Women in Trade Unions* (1911; reprinted. New York, 1974), 95.

The seamstresses went on to resolve that they would "cheerfully submit" to any wage reductions to support the war, but they objected to private contractors profiting at their expense.[91]

Despite these protests, the Commissary Department soon settled on a mixed production system, with private contractors supplementing the arsenal output. The sewing women found the system fraught with inequities: some enjoyed the government's relative benevolence, whereas others labored under parsimonious, and often unscrupulous, contractors. Shortly after Gettysburg, Colonel Crossman ordered the discharge of all women other than the "near relatives" of soldiers. Two hundred seamstresses met to protest the ruling, and *Fincher's* quickly came to their defense, arguing that the firing of experienced workers was bad for the army as well as against labor's interests.[92]

By bringing 900 inexperienced seamstresses into the arsenal, Crossman left an equal number of experienced workers at the mercy of Philadelphia's war contractors. In their new jobs these women made the same clothing that they had been making for years, but with pay reductions of 25 to 40 percent or more.[93] One letter to the *Press* reported that "two worthy, honest, industrious women" employed by a haversack subcontractor earned only five cents per haversack, and between them they could only make five in a fourteen-hour day. This figure was less than half the twelve and a half cents paid for each haversack at the arsenal.[94]

Despite wartime inflation, the wages of Philadelphia's sewing women – both in and out of the arsenal – declined between 1861 and 1864. Table 9.4 compares the 1861 arsenal pay scale with the salaries paid at the arsenal and by private contractors in 1864. For almost every article, the arsenal's scale decreased over the period; contract workers fared far worse.

The hundreds of underpaid or unemployed sewing women soon attracted attention from Philadelphia society. In late 1863 *Fincher's* called on the city's working women to form trade associations to better their wages, and the *Public Ledger* suggested that Philadelphia's working women should overcome their "foolish pride" and take advantage of the high paying jobs of house servant. The following

91 *PL*, 4 September 1861.
92 Kessler-Harris, *Out To Work*, 77–8; *FTR*, 8, 15 August 1863; Andrews and Bliss, *History of Women in Trade Unions*, 95.
93 *FTR*, 5 September 1863, gives several pay comparisons.
94 *FTR*, 12 December 1863 (*Fincher's* quoted an article in the *Press*). The wages in New York followed a similar pattern. See Foner, *Women and the American Labor Movement*, 1:113–14.

Table 9.4. Wages for Sewing Women, 1861 vs 1864

Item	1861: Arsenal	1864: Arsenal	1864: Contractor
Shirts	$0.17.5	$0.15	$.08
Drawers	.12.5	.10	.07–.08
Infantry pants	.42.5	.27	.17–.20
Cavalry pants	.60	.60	.28–.30
Lined blouses	.45	.40	.20
Unlined blouses	.40	.35	.15–.20
Cavalry jackets	1.02.5	1.00	.75–.80
Overalls	.25	.20	.06
Bed sacks	.20	.20	.07

Source: Fincher's Trades' Review, 1 October 1864.

spring a Philadelphia woman wrote to *Scientific American* noting the plight of working women, and offered a $50 reward for "the best paper on 'improving the condition of working women.'"[95]

By April 1864 the plight of Philadelphia's sewing women had become nearly intolerable. On April 5 one woman reported yet another reduction in the contractors' wages for sewing pants. "At the former price [of 50 cents]," she explained, "we could support ourselves, but at the last deduction [to 30 to 35 cents] it is impossible to sustain life, even if we toiled the entire twenty-four hours." In response to this worsening situation, a group of concerned citizens formed the "Working Women's Relief Association," and invited "dressmakers, milliners, Arsenal hands, and all workers on army clothing" to come forward with anonymous statements. Although approving of the association's intent, *Fincher's* rejected the secrecy of the plan, preferring an open attack on unfair employers.[96]

On April 18, 1864, the city's seamstresses gathered at Sansom Street Hall to discuss their condition. The meeting dismissed "all idea of arraying labor against capital" in favor of a more modest resolution "begging" Colonel Crossman to raise wages at the arsenal. *Fincher's* noted that the evening successfully aired the women's grievances,

95 *FTR,* 5 December 1863; *PL,* 27 November 1863; *Scientific American* 20 (14 May 1864): 310. Also see *EB,* 27 October 1863; *PL,* 11 April 1864.
96 *PL,* 5, 8 April 1864; *FTR,* 16 April 1864; Foner, *Women and the American Labor Movement,* 1:116; Andrew and Bliss, *History of Women in Trade Unions,* 95.

but disapproved of the philanthropists who orchestrated the gathering. The skeptical paper noted that when one participant argued that the limited resolution ignored the city's other working women, and insisted that the only solution lay in organization and not abject resolutions, the president of the meeting tried to "put down this speaker." *Fincher's* concluded by cautioning the seamstresses "against any further attempts to be misled."[97]

Through the spring of 1864, Philadelphia's sewing women held large meetings to publicize their plight, and *Fincher's* continued to criticize outside instigators.[98] In July the Working Women's Relief Association appointed a committee to visit Lincoln and Stanton to seek aid. The committee's petition claimed that the cost of living in Philadelphia had increased by 75 percent since the war began, while pay at the Arsenal had dropped 30 percent. This situation, they insisted, required "IMMEDIATE AID" that should come in the form of increased arsenal wages, expanded arsenal operations, and equal pay for women working for contractors. On Lincoln's request, Stanton ordered that the arsenal hire more women and raise their wages by 20 percent, but he did not address the issue of low wages paid by contractors.[99]

Although Stanton's order answered their most immediate demand, the seamstresses continued to discuss the need for a union. By early 1865 government contractors had taken an increasing share of what had once been arsenal work. In January the seamstresses held a large demonstration to protest this disheartening trend. Once again, Fincher applauded the initiative, though criticizing the meeting's lack of focus. The only answer, he contended, was for the sewing women to form a cooperative society and bid for government contracts like any other business. He warned: "You may make speeches and pass resolutions till dooms-day, but you will accomplish nothing, until you *place yourselves in competition with the contractors.*"[100]

But the women chose an entirely different approach. At a mass meeting they elected a delegation to bring their demands directly to the president. Lincoln gave the women a warm reception, and sent a message to Colonel Thomas, the acting Quartermaster: "I shall be

---

97 FTR, 23 April 1864; PL, 16, 19 April 1864. In New York the embattled working women had already accepted the aid of the city's workingmen in forming a Sewing Women's Protective and Benevolent Society. Foner, *Women and the American Labor Movement*, 1:114–16.

98 FTR, 30 April, 7, 14, 21 May 1864; PL, 27 April, 2, 4, 6 May 1864.

99 Roy P. Basler, ed., *The Collected Works of Abraham Lincoln*, 8 vols. (New Brunswick, NJ, 1953), 7:466–7; EB, 3 August 1864; PL, 22 August 1864; Foner, *Women and the American Labor Movement*, 1:116; Andrews and Bliss, *History of Women in Trade Unions*, 95.

100 PL, 13, 20 September 1864; 20, 23 January 1865; FTR, 28 January 1865.

personally obliged if you can hereafter manage the supplies of contract work for the Government made up by women so as to give them remuneratve wages for their labor."[101] The president won widespread acclaim for his prompt response. But his orders did not touch the existing contracts; they merely assured that for the remaining months of the war the arsenal would be used to full capacity.[102]

How did the Civil War affect Philadelphia's laborers? Government contracting provided some workers with jobs while others reaped the benefits of a pressing demand for work. But although the war created jobs, it did not often change the nature of work. Some establishments prospered, others floundered; however, the manufacturing structure of the city was not substantially altered.[103] Philadelphia's unions were primarily concerned with combating the effects of wartime inflation. Although the wartime economy prompted a burst in labor organizing, the resulting negotiations generally followed antebellum patterns.

Only the sewing women, with their highly visible plight and limited organizational background, sought different solutions. Whereas male laborers dealt directly with employers, these women drew the attention of benevolent-minded Philadelphians and took their resolutions directly to President Lincoln. But although this strategy rejected the advice of male labor leaders, the seamstresses' actions were in keeping with traditional practice. In 1835 several hundred Philadelphia women had formed the Female Improvement Society, "the first city federation of working women's organizations." This organization owed its existence to local publisher and philanthropist Mathew Carey, who also presided over its early meetings. One of the society's first actions was to petition the secretary of war for increased wages for uniform manufacturing.[104] In the 1830s and 1840s working women frequently petitioned state and national legislatures to intercede in their behalf. Generally such efforts proved fruitless.[105] The thousands of women who entered the labor force for the first time during the Civil War traveled similar paths. Lacking both the organizational traditions and the strong bargaining position

101 *Friends' Intelligencer* 48 (4 February 1865): 761; *PL*, 4 February 1865; James G. Randall, *Lincoln the President*, 3 vols. (New York, 1952), 3:46; Foner, *History of the Labor Movement*, 1:331, quoting *Boston Daily Evening Voice*, 28 January 1865; Andrews and Bliss, *History of Women in Trade Unions*, 95–6.
102 *PL*, 4 February 1865; *FTR*, 4, 11 February 1865. In March 1865 the sewing women of Cincinnati addressed a lengthy petition to President Lincoln requesting assistance. See Foner, *Women and the American Labor Movement*, 1:116–7; Kessler-Harris, *Out To Work*, 80–1; Andrews and Bliss, *History of Women in Trade Unions*, 96.
103 See Chapters 10 and 11.
104 Andrews and Bliss, *History of Women in Trade Unions*, 13, 39–40.
105 This technique was especially prevalent in the battle for the ten hour day. See Kessler-Harris, *Out To Work*, 77.

of their male counterparts, these women were unable to meet Fincher's prescriptions. But as in the 1830s, their plight attracted outside attention that enabled them to organize and publicize their demands. Rather than threatening strikes or forming competing cooperatives, tactics that were too ambitious for their circumstances, the sewing women chose to petition Lincoln, relying on his benevolence. In so doing, Philadelphia's female wage earners followed their own traditions.[106]

Conclusion

Philadelphia's workers responded to the decline and subsequent expansion of the wartime economy as they had to earlier economic fluctuations. Local, city, and national bodies emerged to combat declining real wages, and the city's labor leaders struggled to keep their larger agenda in the workers' consciousness. When Jonathan Fincher launched his *Trades' Review* in June 1863, he promised to use it as a tool for the "securing of permanent advantages to the laboring man."[107] Although founded in wartime, the newspaper took note of the conflict only insofar as it touched labor's interests. Fincher repeatedly urged Philadelphia's workers to take advantage of the wartime prosperity and demand wage increases. But two long-range movements – cooperative consumerism and the eight-hour workday – dominated Fincher's thoughts.

In the 1840s and 1850s American workers had periodically tried to improve their lot by forming cooperatives. With wartime inflation, consumers in several Northern cities formed cooperative Rockdale stores. One of the first appeared in Philadelphia under the direction of Thomas Phillips, a local shoemaker and ex-Chartist who opened a small Rockdale shop in December 1862.[108] Although such establishments played a minor role in wartime Philadelphia, Fincher consistently proclaimed his support for "the cooperative system in its broadest sense," encompassing both manufacturing and cooperative stores.[109]

---

106 In addition to his orders to aid the sewing women, Lincoln did occasionally intercede to aid petitioning male laborers. These petitions, which did not involve Philadelphia workers, suggest that the war did spawn some unusual measures by male workers. See Foner, *History of the Labor Movement*, 1:331–3.

107 *FTR*, 6 June 1863.

108 Edward Charles Rozwenc, *Cooperatives Come to America: The History of the Protective Union Store Movement, 1845–1867*, (1941; reprint ed., 1975), 115; Clifton K. Yearley, Jr., "Thomas Phillips, A Yorkshire Shoemaker in Philadelphia," *Pennsylvania Magazine of History and Biography* 2 (April 1955): 171–9; Joseph G. Rayback, *A History of American Labor* (New York, 1959), 97–8, 112; Foner, *History of the Labor Movement*, 1:178–83; *FTR*, 3, 24 December 1864; 1 April 1865.

109 In late October 1863 Fincher tried to help establish a citywide cooperative, and in subsequent issues he repeatedly argued for similar ventures. See *FTR*, 6 June, 3, 31 October 1863; 19 November 1864; Yearley, "Thomas Phillips," 177.

The eight-hour movement also began several decades before the Civil War. In 1836, soon after the passage of the ten-hour day, Philadelphia's *National Laborer* announced that the city's mechanics would not rest until they had won an eight-hour workday agreement. Fifteen years later the Assembly of Associated Mechanics and Workingmen formed in Philadelphia to seek an eight-hour day, and throughout the 1850s other city and national groups took up the call. But despite their early initiatives, the nationwide campaign did not begin in earnest until 1863, with Fincher among its strongest supporters.[110]

Fincher realized that as long as the nation's attention remained riveted on the battlefield, workers could not expect the immediate security of an eight-hour day. The appropriate strategy, he argued, was to demand an hours reduction that would come into effect with the war's end. He turned the proposal into an act of patriotism, designed to protect discharged soldiers from the "superabundance of labor" that would occur when they returned home.[111] At the war's close, when many veterans could not find work, Fincher "propose[d], as a Nation's gift to the workingmen in the army, AN EIGHT HOUR SYSTEM."[112]

After Appomattox, Fincher inaugurated an expanded *Trades' Review*, offering a lengthy commentary on labor's goals. He called for a "higher social position" for labor, without the historic "stigma of degradation." And he reiterated the demand for reduced hours and improved wages. These could only be met by increased labor combinations and, if necessary, new cooperative societies in which workers "would receive the full value of our labor."[113] But in just over a year the paper failed and Philadelphia's journeymen lost their most powerful organ.

How did the different parts of labor's wartime experience fit together? After a few halting efforts in early 1861, Philadelphia's workers did not assemble as a cohesive political force seeking to mold public policy in a time of crisis. On the other hand, there is little sign that patriotic laborers sought to put aside their economic demands "for the duration." Rather, the conflict that raged in the South rarely played a direct role in labor negotiations or strategy. As citizens, they took part in filling the ranks, aiding the troops, celebrating victories, and participating in the various aspects of home-front life. As wage

110 For a brief background of the eight-hour movement see Foner, *History of the Labor Movement*, 1:363–9.
111 *FTR*, 27 June, 31 October 1863.
112 *FTR*, 20 May 1865.
113 *FTR*, 3 June 1865.

earners, they organized and pursued wage adjustments much as they had done for decades. In each sense workers, like all Philadelphians, continued their peacetime roles.

But what of workers' positions vis-à-vis Philadelphia elites? Did the Civil War create or exacerbate class differences? Various issues, including pro-Southern sentiment, arbitrary arrests, contract fraud, emancipation, military policies, unruly soldiers, and – most important – conscription, divided Philadelphians during the war. But most of these were not distinctly working-class issues. Only the commutation and substitute provisions of the draft posed an unequal burden on Philadelphia's workers. The city's labor leaders supported conscription, while attacking these class-biased rules. Rank-and-file workers who did not wish to serve evaded the draft enrollers, or simply failed to appear when called. If we are to believe the widespread fears, members of Philadelphia's working class could have rioted in July 1863; only a strong military presence kept them in check. But enthusiastic recruiting minimized the weight of subsequent drafts, and public tensions never reached their earlier level.

Besides conscription, the wartime disputes cut across class lines, or involved other elements of society. Most of Philadelphia's antiwar Democrats came from the city's elite.[114] And the victims of government suppression and arbitrary arrests were often leading citizens. Even when they objected to the administration's policies, Northern workers did not turn to "copperheadism" in large numbers.[115] New York's 1863 draft rioters used the opportunity to assault that city's blacks. Philadelphia never erupted in serious racial violence during the war, and Democrats of all classes expressed hostility to emancipation and the arming of blacks.[116] Although the war years were not entirely harmonious in Philadelphia, they did not create cleavage along class lines.

Conversely, the widespread interest in the war effort might have brought the city closer together. Even when they disagreed over government policy, most Philadelphians supported the war effort. Recruiting and aid to volunteers brought citizens from all over Philadelphia together in a shared purpose.[117] The city's immigrants and blacks sought to parlay loyal military service into improved standing

114 William Dusinberre, *Civil War Issues in Philadelphia 1856–1865* (Philadelphia, 1965), 135, 156–8.
115 Montgomery, *Beyond Equality*, 101–13.
116 Dusinberre, *Civil War Issues*, 151–178.
117 Even those who opposed the war, or objected to its management, could take an interest in raising money for voluntary societies or bounty funds.

within the community.[118] But Philadelphia's workers, like blacks and women, did not substantially improve their position during the war. Employers kept the upper hand in most wage negotiations. The city's elites continued to exercise control over Philadelphia's benevolent societies and organized public rituals. In short, the war years did not recast the city's economic and social hierarchies.

We may summarize the Civil War's impact on Philadelphia's workers by returning to the first three of Arthur Marwick's four tiers. Laborers felt some of the war's destructive aspects as they faced unemployment in 1861, followed by declining real wages in subsequent years. The experiences of organized labor and the persistent class structure suggest Philadelphia's institutional and social continuities despite the war's tests. And the individual contributions of workers in the field and in benevolent organizations indicate the range of participation among Philadelphians as well as the associational networks underlying those contributions.

But the legacy of the Civil War for organized labor in Philadelphia is not easily gauged. The organizational strides that accompanied the midwar boom left labor unions stronger in 1865 than they had been before the war, and with the help of Sylvis and Fincher Philadelphia held a prominent position in the American labor movement. In 1866 Sylvis was instrumental in the formation of the National Labor Union, and three years later, shortly after Sylvis's death, the NLU held its annual meeting in Philadelphia. In late 1869 the Knights of Labor was formed in Philadelphia. But though the Knights slowly grew, workers both locally and nationally suffered through the depression of the mid-1870s, losing much that they had gained during the prosperous war years.[119] The Civil War produced neither substantial short-term adjustments in labor's strategies nor long-term shifts in its organizational successes.

118 Dennis Clark, *The Irish in Philadelphia: Ten Generations of Urban Experience* (Philadelphia, 1973) 123. Supporters of street car segregation often noted that respectable black women were unable to ride the cars to visit their soldier husbands in Camp William Penn. See Philip S. Foner, "The Battle to End Discrimination Against Negroes on Philadelphia Streetcars: (Part I) Background and Beginning of the Battle," *Pennsylvania History* 40 (October 1973): 269–73, 287.
119 Dorothy Gondos Beers, "The Centennial City, 1865–1876" in *Philadelphia*, ed. Weigley, 433–6; Dubofsky, "Labor Organizations," 530–1; Foner, *History of the Labor Movement*, 1:370–474.

10   The fortunes of war:
The Civil War and Philadelphia's manufacturing development

Historiography

From the first secessionist rumblings of 1860 until long after Lee and Grant shook hands at Appomattox, both North and South felt the economic weight of the Civil War. Some Philadelphians suffered; others prospered; most found themselves adjusting to a variety of new circumstances. These adaptations required adroitness from merchant, manufacturer, and laborer alike, as the economic pendulum swung back and forth throughout the war. This chapter will consider both the immediate and long term effects of these changes on Philadelphia's manufacturing.

Many chroniclers of the Civil War have sought to gauge its ultimate impact on the American economy. In *The Rise of American Civilization* Charles and Mary Beard contended that the fall of the Southern planters and the concomitant rise of Northern capitalists and Western farmers justified calling the war "The Second American Revolution."[1] In 1940 Louis Hacker elaborated on this theme by stressing the stimulating effects of wartime legislation.[2] The belief that the war spurred American industrial expansion prevailed until 1960 when Thomas C. Cochran surveyed the quantitative material and asked: "Did the Civil War retard industrialization?"[3] Two early responses to Cochran, by Stephen Salsbury and Pershing Vartanian, defended Beard and Hacker. Salsbury chided Cochran for an over-reliance on statistics, and Vartanian claimed that the revisionist had misread the numbers.[4] But a 1964 conference convened to discuss the

1   Charles A. and Mary R. Beard, *The Rise of American Civilization* (New York, 1927), 2: 52–121.
2   Louis M. Hacker, *The Triumph of American Capitalism* (New York, 1940), chapter 24. For a good discussion of the Beard–Hacker thesis see Stanley L. Engerman, "The Economic Impact of the Civil War," *Explorations in Entrepreneurial History* (now *Explorations in Economic History*) 3 (Spring 1966): 176–8.
3   Thomas. C. Cochran, "Did the Civil War Retard Industrialization?" *Mississippi Valley Historical Review* (now *Journal of American History*) 48 (September 1961): 197–210.
4   Stephen Salsbury, "The Effects of the Civil War on American Industrial Development" in *The Economic Impact of the American Civil War*, ed. Ralph Andreano (Cambridge, Mass., 1962), 161–8; Pershing Vartanian, "The Cochran Thesis: A Critique in Statistical Analysis," *Journal of American History* 51 (June 1964): 77–89.

degree of "economic change in the Civil War era" concluded that with the exception of commercial banking, America's economic institutions were not dramatically changed by the conflict.[5] Two years later, in perhaps the best treatment of the issue, Stanley Engerman waded through the growing body of literature and awarded a tentative victory to the anti-Beard – Hacker forces.[6]

Although these investigations helped cast light on the economic impact of the Civil War, their sweeping approach left much in the shadows. Subsequent studies have addressed several of the more specific questions raised by the debate. Claudia Goldin and Frank Lewis computed dollar estimates of the direct and indirect "costs" of the war, and concluded that the price of the conflict clearly outweighed the benefits accrued by either side.[7] Scholars of manufacturing development have found only irregular war-induced technological innovation, and only minor benefits to the iron industry afforded by the wartime demand for small arms.[8] On the financial front, the most spirited debate has centered on the causes and impact of declining wartime real wages.[9] And economist Jeffrey Williamson has argued that Civil War financing contributed to postwar growth.[10]

Although scholars have examined the economic impact of the Civil War from various perspectives, the scale of the conflict – and the influential formulations of the Beards and Cochran – seem to have directed the debate toward "macro" concerns. As a result, we know more about national patterns than regional and individual vari-

---

5 David T. Gilchrist and W. David Lewis, eds., *Economic Change in the Civil War Era* (Greenville, Del., 1965), 171–4.
6 Engerman, "The Economic Impact of the Civil War," 192. For a second strong overview of the literature see Harry N. Scheiber, "Economic Change in the Civil War Era: An Analysis of Recent Studies," *Civil War History* 11 (December 1965): 396–411.
7 Claudia Goldin and Frank Lewis, "The Economic Cost of the American Civil War," *Journal of Economic History* 35 (June 1975): 299–326.
8 Saul Engelbourg, "The Economic Impact of the Civil War on Manufacturing Enterprise," *Business History* 21 (1979): 148–62; Richard Wacht, "A Note on the Cochran Thesis and the Small Arms Industry in the Civil War," *Explorations in Entrepreneurial History* 4 (Fall 1966): 57–61.
9 Reuben Kessel and Armen Alchian, "Real Wages in the North During the Civil War: Mitchell's Data Reinterpreted" in *The Economic Impact of the Civil War*, 2nd. ed., ed. Ralph Andreano (Cambridge, Mass, 1967); Stephen DeCanio and Joel Mokyr, "Inflation and the Wage Lag During the American Civil War," *Explorations in Economic History* 14 (October 1977): 311–36.
10 Jeffrey Williamson, "Watersheds and Turning Points: Conjectures on the Long-Term Impact of Civil War Financing," *Journal of Economic History* 34 (September 1974): 636–61.

ations.[11] I propose here to reverse that emphasis and to focus on the immediate and long-term economic effects of the Civil War on Philadelphia and its citizens. This, I hope, will shed new light on the larger questions, while also enlarging our sense of what it meant to be a Philadelphian during the war.

Philadelphia's antebellum economy

By the mid-nineteenth century, Philadelphia had long enjoyed a reputation as one of the nation's leading commercial and manufacturing centers. In the decades following the 1820s the city added locomotives, railroad equipment, iron ships, and heavy machinery to its traditional industrial mix of textiles, chemicals, metals, and wood.[12] By 1860 it boasted 6,314 manufacturing establishments, including 525 in textiles, 649 in iron and steel, and 1,523 in clothing or personal wear.[13] Seventeen and a half percent of the city's laborers worked in manufacturing, a figure surpassed only by Pittsburgh, Cincinnati, Richmond, Newark, and Lowell.[14] Only New York City among American urban centers could claim a larger manufacturing product (see Table 10.1).

Philadelphia's nineteenth-century growth owed less to commerce – the city's share in national imports and exports declined steadily between 1820 and 1860 – than to an early and successful transition to manufacturing. As it lost its national position of financial and commercial preeminence, Philadelphia expanded by sending manufactured products to other northeastern cities and by developing a highly advantageous relationship with its own hinterland.[15]

Although Philadelphia was at the forefront of an industrializing America, the city's manufacturers did not march lockstep to a single

11 Exceptions of course do exist. For a regional study see Carl M. Becker's "Entrepreneurial Invention and Innovation in the Miami Valley during the Civil War Era," *Bulletin of the Cincinnati Historial Society* 22 (January 1964): 6–28. For a good description of the impact of the war on a major war industry center see Michael H. Frisch, *Town Into City: Springfield, Massachusetts, and the Meaning of Community, 1840–1880* (Cambridge, Mass., 1972). Philip Scranton's work on Philadelphia textiles (discussed later in this chapter) includes the best detailed analysis of the war's impact on a particular industry in a single city.
12 For two excellent descriptions of Philadelphia's antebellum economy see Thomas C. Cochran, "Philadelphia: The American Industrial Center, 1750–1850," *Pennsylvania Magazine of History and Biography* (July 1982): 323–40; and Diane Lindstrom, *Economic Development in the Philadelphia Region, 1810–1850* (New York, 1978).
13 Lorin Blodget, *Manufacturers of Philadelphia, Census of 1860* (Philadelphia, 1861).
14 Allan Pred, *Urban Growth and City-Systems in the United States, 1840–1860* (Cambridge, Mass., 1980), 89.
15 Pred, *Urban Growth and City-Systems*, 84–97; Lindstrom, *Economic Development in the Philadelphia Region*, 8–18, 31, 38.

Table 10.1. Manufacturing Output in Major U.S. Cities, 1860

City	Population	Value of Product
New York	813,669	$159,107,369
Philadelphia	565,529	135,979,777
Cincinnati	161,044	46,436,638
Boston	177,840	36,119,018
Brooklyn	266,661	34,241,520
Newark	71,941	22,647,496
St. Louis	160,773	21,772,323
Baltimore	212,418	21,083,517

Source: U. S. Bureau of the Census, "Statistics of the United States," *Eighth Census of the United States* (Washington, D.C., 1866).

tune of industrial expansion. A vast assortment of manufacturing enterprises coexisted in Philadelphia in 1860, representing diverse sizes, employee organizations, and power sources.[16] While the machine works of Alfred Jenks and Sons and M. W. Baldwin and Co.'s Locomotive works employed the latest industrial technology, 229 cigar-making establishments – with an average of less than six workers each – carried on traditional hand-rolling.[17] The textile industry alone included the entire spectrum of Philadelphia's manufacturing activity, producing carpets, hosiery, fancy knits, silk, and all classes of cotton, wool, and mixed fiber fabrics in a complex array of interdependent manufacturing formats scattered throughout the city.[18] By 1861 Philadelphia was home to an extremely diverse array of shops and manufactories. This diversity made the City of Brotherly Love particularly well prepared to adjust to rapidly shifting wartime demands.

Manufacturing change over the war decade

The 1860 Census of Manufacturing provides a good portrait of Philadelphia's manufacturing on the eve of the Civil War; the 1870

16 Bruce Laurie and Mark Schmitz, "Manufacture and Productivity: The Making of an Industrial Base, Philadelphia, 1850–1880," in *Philadelphia*, ed. Theodore Hershberg, (New York, 1981), 49. In 1860 forty-two different branches of Philadelphia manufacturing produced over $1 million each in output. See Pred, *Urban Growth and City-Systems*, 89.

17 J. Leander Bishop, *A History of American Manufacturers from 1608–1860*, 2 vols. (Philadelphia, 1864), 2: 534–42; Sam Bass Warner, Jr., *The Private City, Philadelphia in Three Periods of Its Growth*, 2nd ed. (Philadelphia, 1987), 71; Blodget, *Manufactures of Philadelphia, Census of 1860*.

18 Philip Scranton, *Proprietary Capitalism: The Textile Manufacture at Philadelphia, 1800–1885* (Philadelphia, 1983), 268–71. Also see P. Scranton, "Milling About, Family Firms and Urban Manufacturing in Textile Philadelphia, 1840–1865," *Journal of Urban History* 10 (May 1984); 259–94.

Census of Manufacturing describes manufacturing output at the close of the war decade. Taken together, the two censuses offer an overview of the relationship between the city's manufacturing sector and the war. But the comparison is flawed in that the 1870 data describe Philadelphia after five years of postwar development. Edwin T. Freedley's estimates of manufacturing output in 1866 lessen the problem by portraying Philadelphia's manufacturing shortly after the war. These three sources provide a general view of the changing shape of Philadelphia's manufacturing during the war.[19]

Between 1860 and 1870 the value of Philadelphia's manufacturing output increased from $141 million to $338 million, for a total increase of 140 percent. Nearly half of this expanded value reflects the inflation of the 1860s, rather than actual increased production. Ethel Hoover's index of wholesale prices for Philadelphia shows an increase of 41.0 percent over the decade.[20] Thus the actual increase in manufacturing output between the census years was closer to 70 percent. Manufacturing value-added over the same period increased 52.9 percent, after adjustment for inflation. Much of this rise was due to a 40 percent expansion in Philadelphia's manufacturing work force: the city's value-added per worker rose only 9.2 percent over the war decade.

The available evidence suggests that in comparison with the rest of the nation, Philadelphia's economy performed fairly well. America's manufacturing value-added grew 113 percent between 1839 and 1859, but only 26 percent during the war decade.[21] By this standard, Philadelphia's 52.9 percent growth between 1860 and 1870 seems quite impressive. Moreover, despite increased capital per worker, the nation's value-added per manufacturing worker actually declined 13

19 Blodget, *Manufactures of Philadelphia, Census of 1860*; Blodget, *The Industries of Philadelphia, as shown by the Manufacturing Census of 1870* (Philadelphia, 1877); Edwin T. Freedley, *Philadelphia and its Manufactures* (Philadelphia, 1867), 580–4. Blodget's tables are simplified summaries of the Censuses of Manufacturing, presenting the results in over 400 categories. Freedley, a prominent Philadelphian and an historian of American manufacturing, divided Philadelphia's total output for 1860 and 1866 into roughly 140 manufacturing categories. He based his 1866 estimates on personal visits and information from manufacturers, informed observers, and tax returns. For a biography of Freedley see *The National Cyclopedia of American Biography* (New York, 1900), 10:124. Of course I am not suggesting that Freedley's data are as reliable as those of the United States Census. But his figures do provide useful supplementary data.

20 Quoted in Andreano, ed., *The Economic Impact of the American Civil War*, first edition, 178. Because Hoover's data are for the calendar year, whereas the census years begin on June 1, I have adjusted Hoover's figures by giving the "9" years a weight of 7 and the "0" years a weight of 5 and then dividing by 12.

21 Robert E. Gallman, "Commodity Output 1839–99," in *Trends in the American Economy in the 19th Century*, vol. 24, Series on Income and Wealth, National Bureau of Economic Research (Princeton, 1960), Table 3, 24.

percent in the decade following 1860.[22] These differences, however, are largely a result of Philadelphia's relatively low inflation rate. Although local wholesale prices rose 41 percent over the war decade, national prices jumped 59.6 percent.[23] If we deflate the Philadelphia data by the national price index much, but not all, of the difference disappears.[24]

The growth rate between 1860 and 1870 suggests that the war did not greatly harm Philadelphia's economy; however, the figures are not entirely satisfactory because they include five postwar years – years that Edwin Frickey's index of national manufacturing suggest were particularly prosperous ones.[25] Freedley's figures for Philadelphia show a rise in total output from $135 million in 1860 to $225 million in 1866.[26] This increase, however, was entirely a product of the war's inflation. If we deflate the figure by using Hoover's Philadelphia wholesale price index for 1866, we are left with a net *decline* of 15 percent in total output from 1860 to 1866.[27] If Freedley's figures are correct, the entire 1860 to 1870 expansion in manufacturing output occurred in a few vigorous postwar years.

There are no national middecade figures to set against Freedley's data, but the 1865 state censuses of manufacturing from New York and Massachusetts indicate that the direction of his figures is correct. Massachusetts' manufacturing value-added dropped from $127 million (in 1879 prices) in 1860, to $98 million in 1865, before climbing to $145 million in 1870. New York's experience was even more volatile. The census of 1860 shows a manufacturing value-added of $173 million (again, in 1879 prices); by 1865 that figure had plummeted to $72 million, and in 1870 it had risen to $221 million.[28] Freedley's data suggest that over the war Philadelphia fared better than either New York or Massachusetts.[29]

22 Engerman, "Economic Impact of the Civil War," 179.
23 This is taken from Gallman's price index. The weighted Hoover national index shows a similar increase of 59.4 percent between the census years.
24 But to the extent that Hoover's Philadelphia index accurately reflects the prices paid for locally manufactured goods, the statement that the city's manufacturing sector fared particularly well is accurate.
25 Edwin Frickey, *Production in the United States, 1860–1914* (Cambridge, Mass., 1947).
26 Freedley's figures for 1860 are slightly different from Blodget's, presumably because he employed somewhat different standards of inclusion. In the following discussions I have always compared Freedley's 1866 estimates with his own figures for 1860, thus assuring the most suitable point of comparison.
27 In this calculation I have treated Freedley's estimates as figures for the calendar year.
28 Engerman, "The Economic Impact of the Civil War," 181. The differences between the New York and Massachusetts patterns are largely owing to New York's rapid labor force fluctuations.
29 Of course the Philadelphia data described 1866 rather than 1865.

Sectoral shifts

Both Freedley's 1866 estimates and Blodget's surveys of the 1860 and 1870 censuses summarize Philadelphia's total output by type of manufacturing. Tables 10.2 and 10.3 describe the increases in total output in the city's major sectors.[30] Most of the most successful sectors, including cordage and ropes, photographs and materials, carpets, and china and earthenware, had no apparent relationship to the war. Some successful sectors might have enjoyed indirect boosts from the war. The growth of fertilizer production might reflect demands rising out of a wartime decline in available labor. But as Engerman has pointed out, the North's agricultural expansion owed more to foreign demand than domestic developments.[31] The rapid expansion in sugar refining, aided by protective tariffs and reliance on foreign raw sugar to replace Southern supplies, seems to have been at least partly attributable to the war.[32] And the building industry probably owed some of its growth to the booming wartime economy and declining real wages.[33] Freedley's extremely high "tobacco and snuff" figure poses an interpretative dilemma, particularly since the Census of 1870 lists the same two categories with a combined output of only about $280,000.[34] Much of this apparent middecade leap in tobacco manufacturing probably reflects different standards of enumeration, but the city's tobacco traders did enjoy a "catch-up" boom in the immediate postwar years. The Board of Trade's annual reports list a total of over 1.16 million pounds of tobacco and snuff subject to tax in the year ending June 1864; in 1866 this figure swelled to 2.1 million pounds.[35]

But with some possible exceptions, Tables 10.2 and 10.3 offer little evidence of war-induced growth among the most successful manufacturing sectors. What then became of those enterprises that "should" have done best during the war years? Philadelphia's manufacturers furnished the army with nearly everything it could use. But though individual entrepreneurs certainly profited from these endeavors, war contracting does not seem to have boosted specific

30 In each of these tables I have grouped similar types of manufacturing and excluded small items ($500,000 or less) in the interest of clarity. Although general comparisons between the two tables are certainly possible, they do not represent identical groupings. Note that the values of output are in current dollars.
31 Engerman, "The Economic Impact of the Civil War," 186.
32 Emerson David Fite, *Social and Industrial Conditions in the North During the Civil War* (1909; reprint ed., New York, 1963), 4, 80–1.
33 See Chapter 11.
34 This subcategory does not appear in Tables 10.3 and 10.5 because it is too small.
35 Philadelphia Board of Trade, *32nd Annual Report* (Philadelphia, 1865), 109; *34th Annual Report* (Philadelphia, 1867), 89–92.

Table 10.2. Type of Manufacturing in Philadelphia (Freedley Data): Change in Total Output, 1860–66 (in thousands of $s)

Type of Manufacturing	1860	1866	Percentage Shift[a]
Tobacco and snuff	72	1,500	1980.4
Fertilizers	184	2,000	985.2
Cordage and ropes	238	2,000	740.9
Photos and materials	180	1,000	454.9
Iron products[b]	2,892	13,123	353.8
Saws	271	950	251.1
Carpets: ingrain, rag and hemp	2,686	9,300	246.3
Sugar refining	6,357	21,000	230.4
Glue, sandpaper, hair	540	1,750	224.2
Liquors (several)	3,406	8,254	142.3
Paper products[c]	784	1,800	129.7
Machinery	3,119	6,500	108.4
Tin, copper, sheet iron	610	1,250	105.1
Cigars	1,243	2,500	101.1
Paper, printings, etc.	692	1,216	75.7
Bread, ship bread and crackers	2,000	3,500	75.0
Oils: linseed etc.	1,450	2,500	72.4
Clothing: men and boys	11,319	18,994	67.8
Carriages, children's carriages	1,076	1,766	64.2
Woolen goods	4,390	7,179	63.5
Furniture and upholstery	1,839	3,000	63.1
Type and stereotype	397	600	51.1
Hardware, except saws	486	725	49.3
Paints (includes white lead)	1,857	2,750	48.1
Cotton twine, yarn, etc.	1,039	1,500	44.4
Blank books and bookbinding	978	1,400	43.2
Stoves and heating appliances	1,793	2,500	39.5
Ink, lampblack, blacking	434	600	38.1
Chemicals, drugs, medicines	3,536	4,835	36.7
Perfumery and fancy soap	646	850	31.6
Confectionery	766	1,000	30.5
Clothing: ladies'[d]	695	900	29.4
Glass, fruit jars	1,159	1,500	29.4
Fringe, tassels	1,170	1,500	28.2
Marble and stone	983	1,250	27.2
Brick[e]	1,306	1,650	26.4
Jewelry, gold pens[f]	2,138	2,680	25.4
Hosiery, shirts, drawers	2,004	2,500	24.8
Umbrellas and materials	1,203	1,500	24.7
Varnishes	403	500	24.1
Cotton and mixed goods	6,172	7,427	20.3
Cars, car wheels and springs	1,125	1,350	20.0
Printing, etc.	5,040	6,000	19.1
Carpentering	1,267	1,500	18.4
Looking glasses, frames	646	750	16.1

branches of industry.[36] For example, Freedley's figures show that the 1860 to 1866 growth in value of output in men's clothing was no more than the expansion of citywide manufacturing. The growth in hosiery, shirts, and drawers; railroad cars, car wheels, and springs;

36 For a fuller discussion of war contracting, see Chapter 11.

(Table 10.2 - continued)

Lumber: planed and sawed	522	600	15.0
Brushes and brooms	528	600	13.6
Gas fixtures, etc.g	3,779	4,142	9.6
Wagons and carts	917	1,000	9.1
Dyeing, etc.	554	600	8.4
Hats, caps and cap fonts	1,393	1,500	7.7
Silver ware and plated ware	1,022	1,100	7.6
Saddlery and harness	929	1,000	7.6
Locomotive engines	1,420	1,500	5.6
Soap and candles	2,031	2,108	3.8
Plumbing and gas fitting	588	600	2.0
Provisions, etc.	4,410	4,500	2.0
Millinery, straw goods	946	950	0.4
Silks (several)	598	600	0.3
Flour and meal	2,997	3,000	0.1
Lead (several)	550	550	0.0
Coffee and spices	1,128	1,123	−0.5
Leather (several)	3,730	3,689	−1.1
Calico printing	2,557	2,500	−2.2
Firearms and ammunition	378	350	−7.3
Boots and shoes	5,475	4,237	−22.6
Alcohol and camphene	735	550	−25.1
Total	119,778	195,648	63.3
Freedley's totalh	135,980	225,139	65.6

aPercentage shifts are based on unrounded data.
bIncludes bar iron and iron used in railroad construction.
cIncludes paper boxes, bags, envelopes, and hangings.
dIncludes hoop skirts.
eIncludes fire bricks.
fIncludes gold and silver assay, gold foil.
gIncludes gas, gas meters, lamps.
hFreedley's table includes $7,700,000 in "miscellaneous articles" for 1860 and $12,600,000 in "miscellaneous" in his 1866 estimates. Sectors with $500,000 or less in output (except firearms and ammunition) are excluded.

Note: Many of the categories in this table combine several types of manufacturing from Freedley's table.

Source: Edwin T. Freedley, Philadelphia and Its Manufactures (Philadelphia, 1867), 581–84.

wagons and carts; hats and caps; saddlery and harness; and locomotive engines – all sectors involved in government contracting – fell below the citywide growth rate for the same period. Table 10.3 reveals similar patterns over the war decade: Wagons and parts and shipbuilding expanded at roughly the same pace as all manufacturing; boots and shoes, mens' clothing, carriages and coaches, hats and caps, and saddles and harnesses all grew more slowly than total manufacturing.[37] The value of arms and ammunition output fell below its prewar level in both 1866 and 1870. This evidence suggests

37 Again, the apparent growth reflects an inflated currency.

Table 10.3. Type of Manufacturing in Philadelphia (census data): Change in Total Output, 1860–70 (in thousands of $s)

Type of Manufacturing	1860	1870	Percentage Shift[a]
Pickles, preserved fruit	22	579	2525.1
Carpenters and builders	1,257	17,881	1322.6
China and earthenware	117	978	735.6
Fertilizer	207	1,464	605.5
Glue, curled hair, etc.	560	3,850	587.5
Sashes and blinds	331	1,911	477.6
Distillers and rectifiers	1,499	6,160	310.9
Sugar refining	6,357	25,863	306.9
Chemicals, medicine	3,191	12,933	305.3
Upholstery, bedding	422	1,675	297.3
Cordage	253	970	283.5
Confectioners	551	1,972	257.8
Lumber: planed and sawed	994	3,324	234.5
Paint and painters[b]	1,493	4,195	180.9
Plumbers and gas fitters	556	1,550	178.7
Iron and steel products[c]	14,775	42,711	189.1
Marble cutters	1,019	2,663	161.3
Oils and petroleum	1,540	3,874	151.6
Paper products	1,465	3,671	150.6
Textiles (all)[d]	23,562	71,233	202.3
Newspapers	1,741	4,297	146.8
Cabinets, furniture[e]	1,858	4,579	146.4
Wagons and parts	1,162	2,809	141.8
Breweries[f]	2,223	5,211	134.4
Ink and blacking	353	825	133.5
Bricks	1,290	2,983	131.2
Shipbuilding (all kinds)[g]	1,435	3,301	130.0
Fur manufacturing	372	842	126.5
Coopers	484	1,068	120.7
Umbrellas	1,207	2,525	109.2
Boots and shoes	5,330	10,856	103.7
Gold, jewelry, watches[h]	3,061	6,051	97.7
Type founders, stereotypers	421	815	93.7
Brooms and brushes	548	1,049	91.4
Brass founders	572	1,083	89.4
Bookbinders	978	1,820	86.1
Publishers	2,260	4,193	85.5
Engravers	328	568	73.1
Bread, crackers	2,215	3,712	67.6
Lithography	376	628	67.1
Cigars	1,228	2,042	66.3
Flour mills	3,098	4,921	58.8
Leather	4,023	6,254	55.5
Ladies' cloaks, skirts, etc.[i]	719	1,094	52.1
Printers: job and card	1,435	2,176	51.6

that if government contracting sectors enjoyed wartime growth, they could not parlay their successes into peacetime expansion.

Tables 10.2 and 10.3 indicate that the fastest growing wartime industries were largely unrelated to the war. Tables 10.4 and 10.5 approach the problem from a somewhat different direction by arrang-

(Table 10.3 - continued)

Dental products[j]	523	780	49.2
Gilt frames, mirrors	630	902	43.1
Men's clothing, neckties	9,984	13,922	39.4
Cured meats	4,576	6,253	36.7
Glass, windows, bottles	1,245	1,661	33.4
Perfumery and fancy soaps	713	880	23.4
Musical instruments	476	586	23.1
Carriages and coaches	1,051	1,290	22.7
Hats and caps, boys/men	1,437	1,720	19.7
Candles and soap	2,077	2,394	15.3
Saddles and harnesses	960	1,078	12.3
Gas works etc.[k]	4,419	4,737	7.2
Shirts, collars	1,335	1,230	−7.9
Silverware and plated ware	1,000	774	−22.6
Guns and ammunition	387	244	−36.8
Total	129,701	323,610	149.5
All manufacturing[l]	141,049	338,168	139.8

[a]Percentage shifts are taken from the unrounded figures. Sectors with $500,000 or less in total output (except guns and ammunition) are excluded.
[b]In 1860 this category did not include all housepainters.
[c]Includes all iron, steel, and tin products as well as machinery. See the text for a more detailed discussion.
[d]Includes a wide range of textile products and textile dyeing. See the text for a more detailed discussion.
[e]Includes billiard tables.
[f]Includes malt but not cordials, bitters, or liquors.
[g]Includes spar makers and related professions.
[h]Includes gold and silver assayers.
[i]Includes corsets and bonnet frames.
[j]Includes artificial teeth and surgical instruments.
[k]Includes gas, gas meters, gas fixtures, gas pipes.
[l]Includes sectors with less than $500,000 in total output.

Source: Lorin Blodget, Manufactures of Philadelphia, Census of 1860 (Philadelphia, 1861); Blodget, Manufactures of the City of Philadelphia, Census of 1870 (Philadelphia, 1877).

ing the leading branches of manufacturing in order of their share of the 1860 total output. Freedley's estimates (Table 10.4) suggest a reshuffling among the city's leading manufacturing branches. Sugar refining, for instance, doubled its share in total output, moving past men's clothing into first position. The next largest percentage gains went to iron products and carpet manufacturing. The biggest losers among Philadelphia's major manufacturing products were boots and shoes, provisions, cotton and mixed goods, leather, and printing. Some of these losses were war related. When the war began, many Northern boot and shoe manufacturers replaced a lost market in slave shoes with a new military market.[38] In 1866 they were suddenly

38 Engerman, "Economic Impact of the Civil War," 185.

Table 10.4. Type of Manufacturing (Freedley data): Share of Total Output in 1860 and 1866 (in thousands of $s)

Type of Manufacturing	1860 Output	Percentage Share	1866 Output	Percentage Share	Shift in Percentage Share
Clothing: men and boys	11,319	8.3	18,994	8.4	0.1
Sugar refining	6,357	4.7	21,000	9.3	4.7
Cotton and mixed goods	6,172	4.5	7,427	3.3	-1.2
Boots and shoes	5,475	4.0	4,237	1.9	-2.1
Printing, etc.	5,040	3.7	6,000	2.7	-1.0
Provisions, etc.	4,410	3.2	4,500	2.0	-1.2
Woolen goods	4,390	3.2	7,179	3.2	0.0
Gas fixtures, etc.	3,779	2.8	4,142	1.8	-0.9
Leather (several)	3,730	2.7	3,689	1.6	-1.1
Chemicals	3,536	2.6	4,835	2.1	-0.5
Liquors (several)	3,406	2.5	8,254	3.7	1.2
Machinery, tools, etc.	3,119	2.3	6,500	2.9	0.6
Flour and meal	2,997	2.2	3,000	1.3	-0.9
Iron products	2,892	2.1	13,123	5.8	3.7
Carpets, ingrain	2,686	2.0	9,300	4.1	2.2
Calico printing	2,557	1.9	2,500	1.1	-0.8
Jewelry, gold pens	2,138	1.6	2,680	1.2	-0.4
Soap and candles	2,031	1.5	2,108	0.9	-0.6
Hosiery, shirts, drawers	2,004	1.5	2,500	1.1	-0.4
Bread and crackers	2,000	1.5	3,500	1.6	0.1
Paints, except white lead	1,857	1.4	2,750	1.2	-0.1
Furniture and upholstery	1,839	1.4	3,000	1.3	0.0
Stoves, etc.	1,793	1.3	2,500	1.1	-0.2
Oils: linseed, etc.	1,450	1.1	2,500	1.1	0.0
Locomotive engines	1,420	1.0	1,500	0.7	-0.4
Hats	1,393	1.0	1,500	0.7	-0.4
Cigars	1,243	0.9	2,500	1.1	0.2
Total	91,030	66.9	151,720	67.4	
Freedley's total	135,980	100.0	225,139	100.0	

Note: This table only includes categories with over 1 percent of the total output in either year. Enterprises are ranked by share of 1860 output. See notes in Table 10.2.
Source: Edwin T. Freedley, *Philadelphia and Its Manufactures* (Philadelphia, 1867), 581–84.

without both of these large markets. Perhaps the leather industry shared indirectly in the shoe industry's misfortunes. And cotton manufacturing declined dramatically after Southern cotton supplies dried up.

The 1870 figures, summarized in Table 10.5, generally reinforce Freedley's data. Sugar refining grew in the last half of the decade, but at a much slower rate, whereas textiles and iron manufacturing continued to dominate Philadelphia's industrial development. Some discrepancies do suggest either different categorizations or fundamental post-1866 shifts. Freedley showed a decline in the share of chemical and medicine output between 1860 and 1866, but by 1870 this important branch of Philadelphia manufacturing had increased its total share from 2.26 percent to 3.82 percent. And if Freedley's data are to be believed, Philadelphia's boot and shoemakers made an extremely

Table 10.5. Type of Manufacturing (census data): Share of Total Output in 1860 and 1870 (in thousands of $s)

Type of Manufacturing	1860 Output	Percentage Share	1866 Output	Percentage Share	Shift in Percentage Share
Textiles (all)	23,562	16.7	71,233	21.1	4.4
Iron and steel products	14,775	10.5	42,711	12.6	2.2
Men's clothing	9,984	7.1	13,922	4.1	−3.0
Sugar refining	6,357	4.5	25,863	7.6	3.1
Boots and shoes	5,330	3.8	10,856	3.2	−0.6
Cured meats	4,576	3.2	6,253	1.8	−1.4
Gas works, etc.	4,419	3.1	4,737	1.4	−1.7
Leather	4,023	2.9	6,254	1.8	−1.0
Chemicals, medicine	3,191	2.3	12,933	3.8	1.6
Flour mills	3,098	2.2	4,921	1.5	−0.7
Gold, jewelry, watches	3,061	2.2	6,051	1.8	−0.4
Publishers	2,260	1.6	4,193	1.2	−0.4
Breweries	2,223	1.6	5,211	1.5	0.0
Bread, crackers	2,215	1.6	3,712	1.1	−0.5
Candles and soap	2,077	1.5	2,394	0.7	−0.8
Cabinets, furniture	1,858	1.3	4,579	1.4	0.0
Newspapers	1,741	1.2	4,297	1.3	0.0
Oils and petroleum	1,540	1.1	3,874	1.1	0.1
Distillers and rectifiers	1,499	1.1	6,160	1.8	0.8
Paint and painters	1,493	1.1	4,195	1.2	0.2
Paper products	1,465	1.0	3,671	1.1	0.0
Hats and caps, boys/men	1,437	1.0	1,720	0.5	−0.5
Shipbuilding (all kinds)	1,435	1.0	3,301	1.0	0.0
Printers: job and card	1,435	1.0	2,176	0.6	−0.4
Carpenters and builders	1,257	0.9	17,881	5.3	4.4
Glue, curled hair, etc.	560	0.4	3,850	1.1	0.7
Total	106,872	75.8	276,949	81.9	
All manufacturing	141,049	100.0	338,168	100.0	

Note: This table only includes categories with over 1 percent of the total output in either year. See notes to Table 10.3.
Source: Lorin Blodget, Manufactures of Philadelphia, Census of 1860 (Philadelphia, 1861); Blodget, Manufactures of the City of Philadelphia, Census of 1870 (Philadelphia, 1877).

strong recovery between 1866 and 1870. (This perhaps indicates that renewed access to the Southern market for cheap shoes more than offset the loss of military contracts.) Conversely, his estimates show men's clothing manufacturers maintaining a consistent share in the city's total output through 1866, but the census data suggest that that share had declined substantially by 1870.

The two largest manufacturing categories in Table 10.5 – textiles and iron and steel – include a wide array of different enterprises, leaving room for the possibility that the war affected certain sub-categories while leaving the aggregate patterns relatively undisturbed. This certainly was the case in textiles. By adjusting to lost Southern cotton supplies and the concomitant rise in demand for woolen goods, most Philadelphia textile manufacturers survived the war decade in a substantially altered but extremely prosperous fashion. The 1860 census shows seventy-two firms engaged in cotton manufacturing and only nineteen producing woolen products; ten years later, thirty firms remained in cotton and thirty-four produced wool. In his study of Philadelphia textiles, Philip Scranton found that the city's wartime manufacturers profited from government contracting, tariff protection, and their own flexibility. These factors led to a 142 percent (adjusted for inflation) increase in textile capital in the 1860s as compared to a 96 percent rise in capital over the previous decade.[39]

The evidence for substantial war-related growth by Philadelphia's iron and steel manufactories is less clear. As we shall see, Baldwin Locomotives enjoyed a prosperous wartime relationship with the government. But though the expansion in locomotive production during the 1860s was rapid, its growth rate only matched that of iron and steel as a whole. Iron shipbuilding also received a substantial wartime boost, as Cramp Shipyards drew citywide attention by constructing the hull of the New Ironsides and several other naval ironclads. But the combined output of all forms of shipbuilding grew more slowly over the decade than the rest of Philadelphia's manufacturing. The census returns also indicate that the city's numerous machine shops expanded quite rapidly over the war decade.[40] These certainly felt the indirect benefits of the war as woolen manufacturers, shipbuilders, and various war contractors demanded their services.[41] The spurt in the building trades' share of total output, and the concomitant growth in the production of lumber (Table 10.3), partially reflects Philadelphia's wartime building boom.[42] This expansion was not directly linked to the war (except to the extent that the city saw substantial government hospital construction during the war years), but certainly owed much to the war-induced prosperity and perhaps to declining real wages.

Conclusion

When the Civil War began, Philadelphia stood as one of America's major manufacturing centers. Ten years later, after enjoying a relatively profitable decade, the city retained its national position. Its size and diverse industrial base helped guarantee that the war would

39 Scranton, *Proprietary Capitalism*, 304, 309. See Chapter 11 for a detailed discussion of Scranton's findings for the war years.
40 Censuses of 1860 and 1870. Different categorizing makes it impossible to give completely comparable figures, but various forms of machinery roughly tripled in unadjusted value.
41 Frank H. Taylor, *Philadelphia in the Civil War* (Philadelphia, 1913), 14.
42 See the discussion of wartime building rates in Chapter 11.

not abruptly reshape its economy. The shifts in Philadelphia's manufacturing structure over the war decade were generally consistent with long-established patterns of development within the industrial sector. In her analysis of Philadelphia's prewar manufacturing development, Diane Lindstrom found that between 1810 and 1840 textile manufacturing had the largest increase in share of total value-added; machinery and drugs and medicines ranked second and third.[43] Each of these sectors continued its pattern of growth during the war decade. The advent of war disrupted these developments, but did not drastically alter the familiar pattern of change.

Philadelphia's manufacturing data, then, concur with views of those scholars who downplay the Civil War's long-term impact on Northern manufacturing. But other economic questions remain. What were the war's short-term effects on the economic life of the city? How did the war-related shifts mold the lives of individual Philadelphians? Did the demand for military goods, for instance, centralize economic power in fewer hands while leaving citywide manufacturing output relatively undisturbed? The following chapters examine how the wartime economy shifted from year to year and its impact on Philadelphia's entrepreneurs.

43 Lindstrom, *Economic Development in the Philadelphia Region*, 43.

11 *The economic life of wartime Philadelphia*

The secession crisis

A complete treatment of the economic impact of the Civil War must consider both the conflict's role in shaping long-term economic trends and its effect on the daily life of businessmen and wage earners. Thus far we have argued that in Philadelphia, as in most of the North, the war did not dramatically alter the existing structure of manufacturing. Our next task is to consider the war's economic ebbs and flows, and to ask how the city responded to these new trials and opportunities.

In late 1860 the North's economy had only barely recovered from the disasters of the 1857 panic and ensuing depression when it faced the rising uncertainty of worsening sectional schisms. The Southern drain of specie after Lincoln's election caused a brief money panic, forcing many Northern banks into temporary suspension.[1] Throughout the winter of 1860–1 the economy wallowed in the economic doldrums. Credit tightened; manufacturers cut back on production, putting laborers out of work as the winter frosts arrived; retailers, their shelves already emptied of fall stock, opted against purchasing new goods; consumers adopted new habits of frugality.[2] Businesses seeking to meet spring payments often found collection from their debtors nearly impossible. R. G. Dun and Company reported 859 business failures in January 1861, 404 more than in the previous January, and 34 more than in January 1858.[3]

In February New York's *Merchants' Magazine and Commercial Register* assured its readers that "no one need doubt the honor of the Southern merchant . . . his indebtedness will be faithfully discharged

1 *Merchants' Magazine and Commercial Review* (New York) 44 (January 1861):75–6 (hereafter *MM*); Charles Franklin Dunbar, "The Crisis of 1860," *Economic Essays* (New York, 1904), 302; Victor S. Clark, *History of Manufacturing in the United States* 3 vols. (New York, 1949), 2:8; Nicholas B. Wainwright, *History of the Philadelphia National Bank: A Century and a Half of Philadelphia Banking, 1803–1953* (Philadelphia, 1953), 115.
2 For good descriptions of the economic crisis, see Dunbar, "The Crisis of 1860"; Clark, *History of Manufacturing in the United States*, 2: chapter 2; Emerson David Fite, *Social and Industrial Conditions in the North During the Civil War* (1909; reprint, ed., New York, 1963), *passim*; and the "Commercial Chronicle and Review" column in the *Merchants' Magazine*.
3 *MM* 46 (March 1861): 316–7.

as promptly as events permit."[4] The folly of this optimism soon became apparent, as Southern debtors defaulted and trade with the new Confederacy came to a standstill. R. G. Dun's annual circular of 1862 estimated that unpaid Southern liabilities owed Northern businesses ran to nearly $300 million.[5] Northern capitalists, large and small, found themselves paying the price for the sudden cessation of the profitable relationship that they had developed with the noncommercial South. By the close of 1861 an estimated 5,935 of 172,237 Northern businesses had failed, with total liabilities of nearly $180 million.[6]

Shortly after Independence Day 1861, a national journal addressed the problem of "The War and Business," concluding that "it is not the existence of a war that paralyzes trade and commerce, so much as the uncertainty."[7] But just as the government slowly learned the art of waging war, so did Northern businessmen gradually absorb the lessons they needed to profit in the suddenly changed circumstances. Often the needs of the former furthered the interests of the latter.

The national call to arms following the firing on Fort Sumter produced a flurry of activity as state military organizations competed for an inadequate supply of arms and uniforms. The winter gloom gave way to a frenzied spring and summer, during which hundreds of entrepreneurs sought to turn this new demand to their advantage.[8] Through 1861 and early 1862 the government's demand for military goods kept Northern business afloat.[9]

At the war's outset the government's financial structure, like its military organization, was inadequate to deal with the crisis at hand.[10] Faced with mounting mobilization costs, Treasury Secretary Salmon P. Chase, with the aid of Philadelphian Jay Cooke, turned to eastern bankers to underwrite massive loans. But as 1861 came to a

4 *MM* 44 (February 1861): 203.
5 *MM* 46 (March 1862): 317.
6 In 1857 only 4,257 Northern establishments had gone under, but their total liabilities exceeded the 1861 figure by nearly $90 million. R. G. Dun and Company attributed this difference to the disproportionate number of large importing and commission houses that failed in 1857 and to the timing of the 1860–1 crisis, which hit after the fall trading season had passed. See *New York Times*, 1 January 1862 (hereafter *NYT*).
7 *Scientific American* 5 (4 July 1861): 3 (hereafter *SciAm*).
8 Glenn Porter and Harold Livesay, *Merchants and Manufacturers: Studies in the Changing Structure of Nineteenth-Century Marketing* (Baltimore, 1971), 120–1; Clark, *History of Manufacturing in the United States*, 2:9; Fite, *Social and Industrial Conditions*, 96; *MM* 45 (July, October 1861): 105, 434.
9 *MM* 45 (July 1861): 105; *MM* 46 (March 1862): 308.
10 See Allan Nevins, "A Major Result of the Civil War," *Civil War History* 5 (September 1959): 237–50; Bray Hammond, "The North's Empty Purse, 1861–1862," *American Historical Review* 67 (October 1961): 1–20; B. Hammond, *Sovereignty and an Empty Purse: Banks and Politics in the Civil War* (Princeton, 1970).

close, the drain of specie forced both the government and private bankers to suspend specie payments, throwing the economy into a new crisis. Congress responded with the Legal Tender Act of February 1862, which authorized the printing of paper money (greenbacks) not backed by gold or silver. With the price of gold no longer pegged to the dollar, and with the money supply booming, inflation raged.[11]

The new monetary structure helped assure large profits for Northern businessmen. As prices rose, retailers found that their stocks on hand grew in value while their debts remained constant, thus allowing them to escape the cycle of long-term credit that had long encumbered commercial relationships. Manufacturers shared in this debtor paradise, reaping the benefits of a wartime "wage lag" that pushed the brunt of the inflationary burden onto Northern laborers.[12] Within a year after Fort Sumter, the initial panic had given way to a war boom. In 1862 only 1,652 Northern businesses failed, a decline of almost 4,300 from the previous year and more than 1,000 fewer than in any year since the Panic of 1857. Cautious investment, easy money, and general wartime prosperity left the North with a total of only 1,545 failures in the three years from 1863 to 1865.[13]

Philadelphians in crisis

As a leading commercial and manufacturing center, Philadelphia shared in the losses stemming from severed Southern ties and the general economic uncertainty of 1860 and early 1861. Three weeks after Lincoln's election the *Public Ledger* optimistically reported that the city's manufacturers seemed undisturbed by the state of affairs; but a few days later Philadelphia's cotton manufacturers met and recommended that cotton and woolen mills run at half time and that long-term credit in dry goods transactions be curtailed.[14] As the crisis progressed, Philadelphia's merchants – with over $24 million in uncollectible Southern debts – suffered severe losses. One hundred and forty-four of 8,261 Philadelphia businesses failed in 1860.[15] In 1861

---

11 Hammond, *Sovereignty and an Empty Purse*, chapters 4–8. For an excellent monthly account of the business fluctuations see the *Merchants' Magazine*. For Jay Cooke's wartime activities see Ellis Paxson Oberholtzer, *Jay Cooke: Financier of the Civil War* 3 vols. (Philadelphia, 1907), 1: chapters 4–12; and Henretta M. Larson, *Jay Cooke, Private Banker* (Cambridge, Mass., 1936).

12 Fite, *Social and Industrial Conditions*, 106; Porter & Livesay, *Merchants and Manufacturers*, 118–9; Stephen DeCanio and Joel Mokyr, "Inflation and the Wage Lag During the American Civil War," *Explorations in Economic History* 14 (October 1977): 311–36.

13 *NYT*, 18 January 1867.

14 *Philadelphia Public Ledger*, 27, 29 November, 3 December 1860 (hereafter *PL*); J. Thomas Scharf and Thompson Westcott, *History of Philadelphia*, 3 vols. (Philadelphia, 1884) 1:378.

15 The 144 failures in 1860, 39 more than in the previous year, included the early effects of the 1860–1 panic.

389 local businesses failed, with over $21 million in liabilities. With less than 5.1 percent of Northern enterprises in 1861, Philadelphia accounted for 6.6 percent of the North's business failures and 11.9 percent of the lost liabilities.[16]

Although Philadelphians suffered through the 1860–1 business stagnation, glimmers of optimism began piercing the gloom even as the national economy reached its nadir. Some Germantown woolen manufacturers ignored their associates' suggestions and kept their factories running through the winter; in late January several Manayunk manufactories ended their emergency cutbacks and returned to full-time operation.[17] On March 27 the *Germantown Telegraph* reported: "Although the manufacturing establishments in the rural portions of the city are not all running full time, many of them are, and others are making arrangements to do so." A few days later the *Christian Recorder* announced that "[b]usiness is preceptibly reviving in the city." Building contractor William Eyre surveyed the economic horizon in May 1861, and concluded that although business was generally "very flat indeed," he was "pretty well employed" in several projects.[18]

Philadelphia financiers responded to the crisis with caution.[19] Local banks, finding few takers for their funds, turned to investments in railroad and canal stocks and government securities.[20] In May the financial instability caught up with Sidney George Fisher's millionaire brother Henry, forcing him into a temporary suspension. At first it appeared that the diarist also faced economic discomfort, for Henry's account books included $20,000 in loans to his gentleman brother. Although both brothers successfully weathered the storm, Fisher wrote ruefully of acquaintances up and down Market Street unable to meet their obligations after Southern business associates defaulted on their debts.[21]

After the war's first year, Philadelphians' business prospects improved dramatically. In many cases the war enthusiasm provided a

16 *NYT*, 1 January 1862; *American Annual Cyclopedia and Register of Important Events of the Year 1861* (New York, 1872), 312.
17 *Germantown Telegraph*, 27 March 1861 (hereafter *GT*); *Christian Recorder*, 26 January 1861 (hereafter *CR*).
18 *GT*, 27 March 1861; *CR*, 30 March 1861; William Eyre diary, 5 May 1861, Film MS-E, Swarthmore College Library, Swarthmore, PA.
19 See for instance, *Evening Bulletin*, 5, 17, 29 April, 11 May 1861 (hereafter *EB*).
20 Wainwright, *History of the Philadelphia National Bank*, 116.
21 Nicholas B. Wainwright, *A Philadelphia Perspective: The Diary of Sidney George Fisher* (Philadelphia, 1967), 388–90, entries of 7, 11, 19 May 1861. For further diary evidence of the economic gloom during the first half of 1861 see James Tyndale Mitchell diary, 17 January 1861, privately owned; Katherine Brinley Wharton diary, 12 February 1861, Historical Society of Pennsylvania, Philadelphia (hereafter HSP); Lewis R. Ashhurst diary, 23 January, 28 March, 22 April, 10 June, 11 July 1861, HSP.

stimulus to business recovery. Booksellers hawked manuals of tactics and infantry drills. Clothiers advertised military-style hats, neckties, and collars. And storefronts of all kinds featured colored bunting and pictures of Union heroes.[22] Some manufacturers found harried quartermasters to be even more profitable customers than patriotic citizens. By July 1861 many enterprising businessmen had secured government contracts to supply the army with arms, uniforms, and supplies. Thomas Potter, a local manufacturer, won a contract to produce 50,000 knapsacks, and promptly put 2,400 men and women to work. Two local wagon builders, employing 600 workers, stayed open day and night filling the army's demand. In southern Philadelphia, where cotton and woolen mills had been closed since the first signs of war, two manufactories reopened to do government work.[23]

In early September the *Public Ledger* surveyed the manufacturing terrain and found ample cause for optimism. Two local shipyards were busy putting the final touches on government gunboats, and I. P. Morris and Company provided the machinery for both vessels. What was more important, the *Ledger* reported that most of Morris and Company's three to four hundred employees were actively filling private contracts, as were the laborers at several other machine shops and rolling mills. Elsewhere in the city, dozens of contractors employed over four thousand workers in filling clothing contracts, local saddlers had more work than they could handle, and wagon manufacturer Henry Simons added ambulances and artillery to his already lucrative line of military wagons.[24] In many cases resourceful manufacturers retooled to meet the new war demands. Thus the North, Chase, and North founders turned over their entire establishment to the production of shot and shell; Sheble and Fisher's pitchfork and rake factory began making swords and bayonets; and Van Dyke and Company's chandelier works turned out a thousand pairs of cavalry spurs each day.[25]

In his February 1862 annual report to the Board of Trade, Lorin Blodget acknowledged that the war had "disturbed and deranged" business in Philadelphia. But he found it "remarkable that the trade and manufactures of this city could exhibit such elasticity as they have done." Most manufacturers and workers were fully occupied.

---

22 Such ads appeared in all the major newspapers, especially in the first year of the war. For a particularly good description, see *PL*, 13 June 1861.
23 *PL*, 10, 20, 19, 24 July 1861.
24 *PL*, 2 September 1861.
25 *PL*, 23 September 1861. For further comments on local manufacturing developments see *GT*, 4 September 1861; *EB* 4 September 1861; *SciAm* 21 September, 5, 12 October 1861; *GT*, 30 October 1861. Also see Chapter 12.

And those who could not carry on their usual business had found "some associated branch . . . to give them full and remunerative employment." Despite these adjustments, Blodget estimated that manufacturing output for the year ending in June 1862 would be 10 to 15 percent less than the preceding year.[26] In June 1863 a reporter from the *Scientific American* who visited Sellers's manufactory found "they never were more busily employed in the manufacture of lathes, planers, and all the various machines that are employed for making the parts of engines." This, the journal concluded, suggested the far-ranging impact of the recent prosperity.[27] And when Sidney George Fisher strolled through Philadelphia in late 1862, he noted: "Tokens of redundant & rapid prosperity are visible everywhere," with only an occasional soldier as evidence that "the country is in the midst of a gigantic war."[28] After the war's first year, Philadelphia, like the rest of the North, enjoyed the fruits of war-induced prosperity.

Philadelphia's wartime economy

Few businesses failed in Philadelphia after the war's first year. Whereas 389 local firms, with liabilities of over $21 million, went out of business in 1861, only 60 Philadelphia companies, with liabilities of $1.3 million, failed in 1862.[29] Several quantitative indexes enhance our understanding of economic life in Philadelphia during the prosperous midwar years.

We have already seen that the wartime inflation led Philadelphia's workers to a new round of organizing and strikes for improved wages. How did it affect those who could not find work? One measure of an economy's success is its poverty level. The annual population of Philadelphia's almshouse, as reported by the Guardians of the Poor, provides a rough indicator of fluctuations in the number of the city's indigents.[30] These figures, presented in Table 11.1, show a marked jump in the almshouse population in the first year of the war, followed by several years at roughly prewar levels. It was not until the war ended, and the economy dipped, that almhouse

26 Lorin Blodget, *Twenty-Ninth Annual Report of the Philadelphia Board of Trade* (Philadelphia, 1862), 5–6, 90.
27 *SciAm*, 14 June 1863.
28 Wainwright, *A Philadelphia Perspective*, 442, entry of 26 November 1862.
29 *NYT*, 1 January 1863. In 1863 the liabilities of failed businesses dropped further still, to $442,000. Chapter 12 will examine the patterns of business failure more fully.
30 *Statement of the Accounts of the Guardians of the Poor of the Philadelphia Almshouse* (Philadelphia, 1859, 1860, 1861); *Annual Statement of the Guardians for the Relief and Employment of the Poor of the City of Philadelphia* (Philadelphia, 1862 through 1869).

Table 11.1. Philadelphia's Monthly Almshouse Population, 1858–67

	1858	1859	1860	1861	1862	1863	1864	1865	1866	1867
January	2,908	3,032	2,990	3,184	2,808	2,680	2,614	2,930	3,392	3,418
February	3,128	3,039	2,995	3,209	2,868	2,724	2,660	3,002	3,552	3,555
March	2,944	2,700	2,732	2,945	2,840	2,712	2,543	2,802	3,429	3,426
April	2,477	2,436	2,354	2,717	2,619	2,551	2,441	2,618	3,068	3,286
May	2,268	2,251	2,287	2,700	2,482	2,436	2,298	2,541	2,974	2,892
June	2,260	2,248	2,187	2,689	2,434	2,346	2,224	2,482	2,877	2,807
July	2,275	2,284	2,223	2,704	2,402	2,307	2,263	2,502	2,834	2,786
August	2,316	2,326	2,261	2,712	2,379	2,307	2,300	2,563	2,766	2,823
September	2,268	2,373	2,276	2,648	2,347	2,345	2,377	2,658	2,822	2,859
October	2,355	2,468	2,355	2,637	2,354	2,415	2,480	2,691	2,905	2,859
November	2,616	2,619	2,458	2,665	2,456	2,510	2,551	2,866	3,016	3,052
December	2,840	2,767	2,787	2,739	2,599	2,576	2,719	3,077	3,266	3,218
Total	30,655	30,543	29,905	33,549	30,588	29,909	29,470	32,732	36,901	36,981

Note: The annual totals given for 1858 and 1860 were 30,727 and 29,895. These figures differ slightly from the sums of the monthly figures.

Sources: Statement of the Accounts of the Guardians of the Poor of the Philadelphia Almshouse (Philadelphia, 1859, 1860, 1861); *Annual Statement of the Guardians for the Relief and Employment of the Poor of the City of Philadelphia* (Philadelphia, 1862–69).

Table 11.2. Hoover's Wholesale Price Index,
1855–70 (1850–59 = 100)

	United States	New York	Philadelphia
1855	109.6	112.9	110.4
1856	109.5	107.7	110.2
1857	118.5	113.9	112.2
1858	98.2	95.4	99.7
1859	101.3	97.5	99.4
1860	99.6	95.4	98.7
1861	102.9	91.3	98.1
1862	119.5	106.7	131.9
1863	152.3	136.5	190.6
1864	220.9	198.0	288.4
1865	210.9	189.8	223.0
1866	197.4	178.5	193.2
1867	182.7	166.2	176.0
1868	177.3	162.1	170.4
1869	168.4	154.9	156.1
1870	149.1	138.5	134.7

Source:
Ralph Andreano, ed., *The Economic Impact of the American Civil War* (Cambridge,
Mass., 1862), 178. (Citing Ethel Hoover, *Historical and Comparative Rates of Production, Productivity, and Prices.*)

figures rose again.[31] This evidence suggests that the war did not add
to the number of Philadelphians at the bottom of the economic
spectrum.[32] Declining real wages diminished workers' standard of
living, but high employment, military bounties, and aid to families of
volunteers apparently combined to keep the numbers of dependent
poor down.[33]

Rapid, unpredictable inflation also left its mark on local businessmen and investors of all types. Available price indexes differ some-

31 The annual reports of the Guardians of the Poor give no indication that the policy
toward housing the poor changed during the war years.
32 In her study of Philadelphia's "wandering poor," Priscilla Ferguson Clement
found a decline in "vagrants per thousand in Philadelphia prison" from the
beginning of the war until 1864, and then a slight rise until the war's end. The total
did not reach prewar levels until the early 1870s. Clement noted that many male
"tramps" joined the army and that therefore during the war years, women made
up over half the imprisoned vagrants. See P. Clement, "The Transformation of the
Wandering Poor in Nineteenth-Century Philadelphia," in *Walking To Work, Tramps
in America, 1790–1935*, ed. Eric H. Monkkonen (Lincoln, Neb., 1984), 61, 65, 67.
33 Of course such war-related economic forces created shifts in the composition of
Philadelphia's needy population. See Chapter 5.

what, but all agree that after the war's first year prices jumped dramatically and continued to rise through 1864. Ethel Hoover's consumer and wholesale price index (Table 11.2) suggests that Philadelphia's wholesale prices rose faster than the national average and consistently ran far above the New York mark.[34] Although the years following the panic were, in Emerson Fite's words, "a distinctly money making age,"[35] even successful businessmen suffered through the uncertainty of prices subject to the whims of gold speculation and tariff legislation. Wealthy drug merchant George W. Fahnestock en-° gaged in "long discussions over the financial aspect of the times" in early 1863. "Stocks of all descriptions," he wrote, "are going up daily and gambling seems the order of the day."[36] In June 1863 building contractor William Eyre surveyed the local economy:

> . . . the prices of almost all kinds of food & clothing as also fuel
> have advanced very much, no doubt owing to the increased de-
> mand made by the war, together with the withdrawal of labor
> forces from the producing channells [sic] and the great inflation of
> our currency by the paper issues of the Government.[37]

The following July wealthy Philadelphia manufacturer Joseph Harrison reported to a friend in England that "[t]hings are pretty gloomy here in many ways. All is distress as to the value of anything."[38]

How did Philadelphia's business community respond to this distress? Building construction is a particularly useful index of local optimism and prosperity. The best available national estimates indicate that general residential housing construction dropped at the beginning of the war and stayed below 1860 levels until 1866.[39] In Philadelphia construction of all types of buildings also dropped precipitously from 1860 to 1861 (see Table 11.3), but in the City of Brotherly Love the building industry enjoyed a dramatic recovery the following year. Annual building construction peaked in 1863 – with

34 Ralph Andreano, ed., *The Economic Impact of the American Civil War* (Cambridge, Mass., 1962), 178, 181. I have used Hoover's index because she included estimates for Philadelphia. For other data on wartime prices see George F. Warren and Frank A. Pearson, *Prices* (New York, 1933), 12; Wesley Clair Mitchell, *A History of the Greenbacks* (Chicago, 1903) 429–69; United States Department of Commerce, Bureau of the Census, *Historical Statistics of the United States, 1789–1945: A Supplement to the Statistical Abstract of the United States* (Washington, D.C., 1949), 231. This last source includes the Snyder–Tucker General Price Index as well as the Warren–Pearson Indexes.
35 Fite, *Social and Industrial Conditions*, 105.
36 George W. Fahnestock diary, 9, 16 January 1863, HSP.
37 Eyre diary, 15 June 1863.
38 Harrison to Thomas L. Luders, Joseph Harrison Letterbook, 1 July 1864, HSP. Also see Jacob Elfreth, Sr., diary, 29 June 1864; Haverford College Library, Haverford, Pa.; Jacob Elfreth, Jr., diary, July (several), Haverford College Library.
39 Manuel Gottleib, *Estimates of Residential Building, United States, 1840–1939* (Washington, D.C., 1964) 61, 70.

Table 11.3. Buildings Erected in Philadelphia, 1855–68

	Dwellings	Stores	Factories	Foundries	Other	Total	Additions/ Alterations[a]
1855	914	32	17	—	166	1129	254
1856	1633	118	29	4	242	2026	610
1857	1305	91	22	5	234	1657	550
1858	1347	80	30	1	213	1671	498
1859	1657	55	47	5	291	2055	570
1860	2148	43	31	1	249	2472	588
1861	1535	18	9	—	111	1673	204
1862	2154	43	37	3	173	2410	194
1863	2465	34	57	6	233	2795	265
1864	1166	33	62	11	318	1590	536
1865	1413	48	94	2	466	2023	743
1866	1913	91	88	9	470	2571	739
1867	2974	99	54	—	—	3127	—
1868	4109	111	34	6	296	4556	—

[a]Additions/alterations figures only available through 1866.

Note: The 1867 data do not include figures for "Foundries" or "Other."

Source: Philadelphia Board of Trade, Thirty-fourth Annual Report (Philadelphia, 1867); Thirty-sixth Annual Report (Philadelphia, 1869).

300 more establishments erected in that year than in 1860 – and then fell by 1,200 new buildings in 1864, the year in which the local price index climbed to its zenith.[40] Table 11.3 indicates that Philadelphia's manufacturers continued to expand despite the rising costs of construction. In the turbulent year after Lincoln's election only nine new factories and no new foundries went up in the city. But in 1862 Philadelphians erected 40 new factories and foundries, and in the next three years 232 more sprang up, dramatically eclipsing the 1855 to 1860 mark.[41] Much of this construction was probably in response to military needs. For instance, Alfred Jenks and Sons, manufacturers of cotton and wool machinery, switched to the rifle business in 1862 and erected a 920-foot arsenal.[42] M. W. Baldwin and Company's Locomotive Works, which profited heavily during the war, built a new foundry, erecting shop, and smith shop in the course of the conflict.[43]

Many manufacturers built new establishments during the war years; however, retailers acted far more cautiously. Only 176 new

40 For a discussion of the 1863 building boom see PL, 30 November 1863. Also see Dennis Clark, The Irish in Philadelphia: Ten Generations of Urban Experience (Philadelphia, 1973), 51.
41 Note that the steady increase in new factory construction persisted through 1864, when the construction of dwellings dropped by over 50 percent.
42 J. Leander Bishop, A History of American Manufactures from 1608 to 1860 (Philadelphia, 1864), 540; SciAm, 6 September 1862.
43 Bishop, History of American Manufactures, 542.

stores were built in the city between 1861 and 1865, compared to 387 in the five prewar years. The 1860–1 panic weeded out weak establishments: By 1864 there were fewer companies in Philadelphia than there had been in 1861.[44] Although some war profiteers lived in the lap of luxury, many citizens reduced their expenditures in the face of high prices, political uncertainty, and new tax laws.[45] In October 1863 the Merchants' Magazine reported that Philadelphia's 8,261 stores had allowed their stocks to decline from a prewar value of $67.51 million down to only $45 million. In so doing, they greatly increased their profit margins by selling off old stock at new prices. Seventeen months later, the widespread rumors of peace (and price declines) led the Merchants' Magazine to advise retailers "to keep a small stock of goods on hand, so as to be able to purchase when prices are low."[46] These cautious strategies militated against new construction.

Philadelphia's building rates describe how individuals and firms balanced the desire for expansion against rising costs of materials, whereas its import and export statistics (see Table 11.4) reveal the war's impact on local trade, another useful index of the city's economic vitality.[47] The value of Philadelphia's imports – hampered by wartime protective tariffs – declined sharply in absolute terms and also fell as a percentage of national imports. Rising prices helped raise the value of Philadelphia's wartime exports well above the antebellum figures, and the blockade of Southern ports contributed to the city's increased share of national exports. Between 1865 and 1866 Philadelphia lost ground to national increases in the value of exports and imports, but by 1875 the city's share of foreign trade – both imports and exports – had risen above the 1860 levels. By the middle of the century Philadelphia could no longer rival New York for commercial dominance; however, the Civil War does not seem to have substantially altered its position as a shipping center.

Philadelphia's position as a major financial center was perhaps strengthened by the Civil War. The wartime experience of its banks reflects the flexibility and resiliency that marked much of the city's economic life throughout the conflict. On the eve of the war, Philadelphia ranked third behind New York and Boston with twenty commercial banks, fifteen with assets over $1 million.[48] On Novem-

---

44 Fite, Social and Industrial Conditions, 107. Of course retailers did not account for this entire decline.
45 See GT, 30 April 1862.
46 MM 49 (October 1863): 296–9; MM 52 (March 1865): 206.
47 Of course these figures also reflect the economic fluctuations in Philadelphia's hinterlands.
48 Keith Edward Wagner, "Economic Development in Pennsylvania During the Civil War, 1860–1865" (Ph.D. diss., Ohio State University, 1969), 225.

Table 11.4. Philadelphia's Foreign Trade (millions of $)

Year	Philadelphia Imports	Philadelphia Exports	United States Imports	United States Exports	Percentage of U.S. Imports	Percentage of U.S. Exports
1850	12.1	4.5	178.0	152.0	6.8	3.0
1855	15.3	6.3	261.0	275.0	5.9	2.3
1856	16.6	7.1	315.0	327.0	5.3	2.2
1857	17.9	7.1	361.0	363.0	5.0	2.0
1858	12.9	6.0	283.0	325.0	4.6	1.8
1859	15.6	5.3	339.0	357.0	4.6	1.5
1860	14.5	7.8	362.0	400.0	4.0	2.0
1861	8.1	10.3	336.0	249.0	2.4	4.1
1862	8.3	11.5	206.0	230.0	4.0	5.0
1863	6.3	10.6	253.0	332.0	2.5	3.2
1864	9.1	13.7	330.0	340.0	2.8	4.0
1865	5.6	12.6	249.0	356.0	2.2	3.5
1866	7.3	17.9	446.0	565.0	1.6	3.2
1867	14.1	14.4	418.0	461.0	3.4	3.1
1868	14.2	15.7	372.0	477.0	3.8	3.3
1869	16.4	15.9	437.0	439.0	3.8	3.6
1875	24.0	31.8	554.0	666.0	4.33	4.77

Sources: Commercial Exchange of Philadelphia, Sixteenth Annual Report (Philadelphia, 1870), 18; J. Thomas Scharf and Thompson Westcott, History of Philadelphia, 3 vols. (Philadelphia, 1884), 3:2222 (1875 data for Philadelphia); Bureau of the Census, Historical Statistics of the United States, 1789–1945 (Washington, D.C., 1949), 217.

ber 22, 1860, the city's bankers met to discuss the crippling drain of specie to the South and voted to suspend specie payments. This decision proved premature, and soon Philadelphia's leading banks lifted their suspension. In the business crisis following the firing on Fort Sumter, local banks suffered and dividends dropped dramatically, but none failed in the year beginning December 1, 1860.[49] At first the major banks found few borrowers, and turned to railroad stocks as an outlet for excess capital. But in May 1861 the Pennsylvania legislature issued a $3 million 6 percent bond that the state's bankers – with cajoling from Jay Cooke – quickly oversubscribed.[50] That summer banks in Philadelphia, New York, and Boston lent the U. S. government $50 million in specie in exchange for 7.3 percent Treasury notes to be sold to the public. By the end of 1861 the banks had taken on two more loans, and public confidence in the government's ability to finance the war had slipped, resulting in a run on specie. On

49 Wainwright, History of the Philadelphia National Bank, 115–17; Wagner, "Economic Development in Pennsylvania," 228. Several of the city's less stable savings societies failed during the crisis.
50 Ellis Paxson Oberholzer, Philadelphia: A History of the City and Its People, 4 vols. (Philadelphia, 1912), 2:106–10.

December 30 New York's banks again suspended payments, and the Philadelphia banks followed suit the next day.[51]

Congress responded to this fiscal nightmare with the Legal Tender Act of February 1862, which created new government notes – greenbacks – backed by bonds rather than specie. This move aided bankers by easing credit and expanding the paper in circulation. But, as creditors, the bankers were harmed by the subsequent inflation and uncertainty. Between 1862 and 1864 although most of the state's banks paid dividends to their shareholders, the banks' investors lost ground to inflation.[52] In February 1863 Congress passed the National Banking Act, creating a national banking system. By becoming national banks, Philadelphia's old state banks escaped state taxes and enjoyed a windfall profit by liquidating their specie reserves, which they no longer had to hold as security.[53] In 1864 the Philadelphia National Bank paid dividends of 13 percent, the third highest figure in its history. The following January, after selling its gold at an enormous premium, the bank paid an extra dividend of 25 percent and a total dividend for the year of 40 percent.[54]

After the war's first year, private banking houses – with Philadelphia's Jay Cooke and Company and Drexel and Company playing key roles – supplanted the established banks as major federal financiers. But the national banks continued to purchase city and state loans and to donate funds for patriotic purposes. In April 1861 the Philadelphia National Bank contributed $9,000 to Philadelphia's Committee of Public Safety to help defend the city. In July 1862 it gave $5,000 to the local bounty fund. When Lee invaded Pennsylvania in 1863, the bank lent the state $72,000 to help finance the militia buildup. In later years the bank repeatedly stepped forward with large loans to volunteer bounty funds.[55] The Philadelphia National Bank and the city's other leading banks consistently chose to invest in the defense of the city, the state, and the nation. In so doing, they protected their own future and – because these contributions were always well publicized – earned public good will.[56]

The shift from long-term credit financing to cash transactions and

51 Wainwright, History of the Philadelphia National Bank, 117.
52 Wagner, "Economic Development in Pennsylvania," 247–8.
53 Wainwright, History of the Philadelphia National Bank, 120–1. Between November 10 and December 12, 1864, the specie in Philadelphia banks plummeted from $3,940,341 to $1,983,502. See Wagner, "Economic Development in Pennsylvania," 251.
54 Wainwright, History of the Philadelphia National Bank, 122–3.
55 Wainwright, History of the Philadelphia National Bank, 116–23.
56 For a good description of the importance of both of these goals in motivating bankers see Oberholzer, Jay Cooke, 1:107–10.

short-term loans certainly hurt Philadelphia's creditors.[57] But the banks turned their excess capital into profits through stock speculation, and reaped the benefits of their entrance into the new national banking system. More than almost any aspect of the economy, the war left banking substantially altered.[58] But Philadelphia's financial sector maintained its prominent national position.

Pennsylvania's railroads, like those elsewhere in the North, enjoyed enormous profits during the war years. The 1860–1 recession and the subsequent decline in demand for coal hurt the state's lines, but the war brought a sudden demand from the military, and railroad earnings in 1861 exceeded those of 1860. Between 1862 and 1865 rising military use of private lines combined with the strong performances of agriculture and mining to assure the state and national railroads a series of banner years.[59] Two Philadelphia-based lines – the Pennsylvania Railroad and the Philadelphia–Wilmington–Baltimore Railroad – proved particularly vital to the North's military effort, and benefited accordingly.[60] From 1860 to 1865 the volume of goods, both private and military, carried by the Pennsylvania Railroad doubled from 1.3 to 2.8 million tons.[61]

In the nation as a whole, labor shortages and expensive materials impeded new railroad construction. Between December 1860 and December 1865 the track in use nationwide increased only 4,450 miles (from 30,626 to 35,085), as opposed to a jump of 12,252 miles during the previous five years.[62] But in Pennsylvania the wartime profits were accompanied by widespread construction. At the close of 1860 there were 2,598 miles of track statewide. Five years later that figure had risen to 3,728 miles. A state with under 12 percent of the national railroad track mileage in 1860 was responsible for over 25 percent of its wartime growth.[63]

Philadelphia's railroad companies brought profits to their shareholders and underwent capital expansion during the war. The

---

57 Wesley Mitchell went so far as to say that the inflation following the issuance of the greenbacks actually hurt those who lent capital more than wage earners. See W. Mitchell, *History of the Greenbacks*, 368.

58 See David T. Gilchrist and W. David Lewis, eds., *Economic Change in the Civil War Era* (Greenville, Del., 1965), 23–40, 172.

59 Fite, *Social and Industrial Conditions*, 42–5.

60 Wagner, "Economic Development in Pennsylvania," 260–3. For a good description of the military service of Philadelphia's railroads see Frank H. Taylor, *Philadelphia in the Civil War* (Philadelphia, 1913), 44–7.

61 Wagner, "Economic Development in Pennsylvania," 255–95; Fite, *Social and Industrial Conditions*, 44.

62 Andreano, ed., *Economic Impact of the American Civil War*, 189.

63 This expansion was largely due to rising demand for coal. See Wagner, "Economic Development in Pennsylvania," 275–9.

Philadelphia–Wilmington–Baltimore line paid dividends of 6.5 percent in 1860 and 1861, 9 percent in 1862, and 10 percent in the following three years. Between 1862 and 1865 the company also purchased 15 new locomotives and 322 new cars. Philadelphia's Pennsylvania Railroad, the state's largest line, paid dividends of 6 percent in 1861, 8 percent in 1862, 9 percent in 1863, and 10 percent in both 1864 and 1865. These profits, too, came after the company committed large amounts of capital to wartime expansion.[64] This strong wartime record led one historian of Pennsylvania's wartime economy to conclude that "without exception the major railroad companies of the state were much better off financially in 1865 than they had been in 1860."[65]

The railroad companies' prosperity soon spilled over into local industry. When the war began, the owners of Baldwin Locomotive Works, one of the city's largest manufactories, faced so sharp a decline in demand that they contemplated switching to shot and shell production. But after a difficult 1861 in which it built only forty locomotives, the Philadelphia factory began receiving a flow of orders from the city's prosperous railroad companies. In late 1864 R. G. Dun's reporter wrote that the company was clearing $10,000 a week. In 1862 Baldwin Locomotives built 75 locomotives; in 1863, 96; in 1864, 130; and 1865, 115.[66]

The R. G. Dun reports on Richard Norris & Son, another Philadelphia locomotive manufacturer, tell a similar story. In 1861 the owners of this large business cut back their operations, but apparently without "asking any favors" of their creditors. By the following year they had successfully worked their way through the hard times, and in 1864 R. G. Dun reported: "Dg an immense Govt & regular bus & have been making money rapidly." But whereas Baldwin extended its wartime successes into the decades to come, Norris and Son ran into serious trouble during the postwar depression, closed temporarily, and then folded.[67]

Confederate maritime raiders destroyed 110,000 tons of Northern shipping during the war, forcing many shippers to sell their vessels to

64 Wagner, "Economic Development in Pennsylvania," 291–3. Of course these dividends did not match the wartime inflation rate. The key point is that the railroad companies expanded substantially while still paying out dividends.
65 Wagner, "Economic Development in Pennsylvania," 294.
66 Although military needs aided the company, government contracting does not fully explain the dramatic wartime rise in production: Between May of 1862 and June 1864 Baldwin built thirty-three engines for the military lines. See *History of the Baldwin Locomotive Works* (Philadelphia, 1897), 56–7; Pennsylvania, vol. 136:557, R. G. Dun & Co. Collection, Baker Library, Harvard University Graduate School of Business (hereafter *RGD*). See the Appendix for a discussion of these reports.
67 *RGD* 138:87.

foreigners who could sail under neutral flags.[68] The value of exports leaving Philadelphia in American vessels dropped from $8.8 million in 1862 to $3.4 million in 1864; exports in foreign vessels increased from $2.7 million in 1862 to $10.2 million in 1864.[69] Foreign ships also carried the larger share of imports into Philadelphia in 1864 and 1865, a marked contrast with 1860 when American vessels carried over 80 percent of that traffic. In the years immediately following the war, shipping on American vessels expanded, but trade on foreign carriers did not decline to prewar levels.[70]

Despite the wartime drop of foreign trade on American ships, Philadelphia's shipyards, both public and private, kept up a frenetic pace. The push to build new naval ships and refit old vessels kept the Navy Yard continually "thronged with workmen." On August 24, 1861, the Navy launched the 1,200-ton ship of war *Tuscarora*, built in Philadelphia in only fifty-eight days.[71] Of fifty-two naval ironclads built in 1861, five were constructed at Philadelphia's Navy Yard and four more came out of private shipyards in the city.[72] On May 10, 1862, an enormous crowd turned out in Kensington to witness the official launching of the ironclad *New Ironsides*. This vessel represented a $780,000 government contract for Philadelphia industry – the hull was built at Cramp and Sons' shipyards and the machinery at Merrick and Sons – and its launching stimulated feelings of civic pride in a citizenry that had suffered through a discouraging year of warfare.[73] By the war's close Philadelphia had built nineteen ships of war for the Union, with much of the work accomplished by private local companies.[74]

---

68 Edward C. Kirkland, *Industry Comes of Age* (1961; paperback ed., Chicago, 1967), 296.
69 These increases were faster than the inflation rate.
70 Commercial Exchange of Philadelphia, *Sixteenth Annual Report* (Philadelphia, 1870), 18. The share of American imports and exports carried on American ships declined from about 70 percent in the 1850s to 15 percent in 1897. Thus the Civil War probably accelerated the decline in America's merchant marine, but certainly did not create it. See Kirkland, *Industry Comes of Age*, 296–301.
71 *SciAm*, 5 October 1861; Taylor, *Philadelphia in the Civil War*, 201.
72 *American Annual Cyclopedia, 1861*, 503. These figures include vessels in production at the close of 1861.
73 *SciAm*, 14 December 1861; *American Annual Cyclopedia, 1861*, 503; *GT*, 7, 15 May 1862; Scharf and Westcott, *History of Philadelphia*, 1:797.
74 Taylor, *Philadelphia in the Civil War*, 203. Philadelphia's shipbuilders and machine shops also remained active in nonmilitary construction. In 1860 William H. Cramp recognized the changes in the industry and switched his thirty-year-old business from wooden to iron craft. Government contracts helped smooth this transition, but Cramp and Sons continued working for the private sector as well. Immediately after the war, Cramp and Sons won a major contract with the American Steamship Company. See *SciAm*, 11 July 1863; Scharf and Westcott, *History of Philadelphia*, 3:2239, 2338–9.

Many of Philadelphia's largest commercial and manufacturing concerns prospered by adjusting to the changed circumstances of a wartime economy, but none matched the chameleon-like textile manufacturers in adapting to new demands. Two interrelated factors molded the wartime experiences of Philadelphia's textile manufacturers: the abrupt end of cotton imports from the South, and the sudden demand for uniforms, blankets, tents, and related military supplies. As we have seen, the pronounced wartime shift from cotton to wool manufacturing left this sector of the city's economy permanently altered. Shortly before the war, Congress passed the Morrill tariff, which protected American woolens from British competition. During the conflict, with cotton scarce, the domestic, nonmilitary consumption of wool ran to 138 million pounds annually, as compared to 85 million pounds per year before the war. Fite estimates that 75 million pounds of wool a year went into military production.

Philip Scranton has compared the adaptive qualities of Philadelphia's and Lowell, Massachusetts' textile manufacturing. Antebellum Lowell was dominated by ten large textile corporations devoted to the manufacture of staple cotton goods. Philadelphia, with a work force of comparable size, had 300 separate textile firms producing all manner of goods in a wide array of settings. Whereas elite corporate boards oversaw the Lowell companies, single proprietors or small partnerships ran the smaller Philadelphia firms. The Philadelphia system, although seemingly on a lower rung of the corporate evolutionary ladder, proved to be much more adept at meeting the wartime challenge. As Scranton observes: "the characteristic flexibility of Philadelphia's format (and the high skill levels of its work force that bred that capacity) brought a war textile boom to the city at the time the Lowell mills were either silent or floundering."[75]

Many of Philadelphia's textile mill owners turned to war contracting; however, some local clothiers sought to profit indirectly from the war. Charles Stokes ran advertisements asking: "What is the use of a great *seat of war* for a *standing army*?" He went on to promise that his establishment made *"breeches . . . to cover the rear."*[76] Some stores turned over part of their floor space to fancy uniforms and accoutrements. Stokes published notices explaining how soldiers

75   Philip Scranton, "Milling About, Family Firms and Urban Manufacturing in Textile Philadelphia, 1840–1865," *Journal of Urban History* 10 (May 1984): 279. This article offers an excellent summary of his argument, but also see Philip Scranton, *Proprietary Capitalism: The Textile Manufacture at Philadelphia, 1800–1885* (Philadelphia, 1983), 272–313.
76   *EB*, 9 July 1861.

could measure themselves to ensure a perfect fit.[77] William H. Horstmann and Sons, the city's largest prewar dealer in military regalia,
had a particularly active trade among Philadelphia's officers.[78] Other
clothiers expanded their trade in mourning wear in response to the
wartime demand.[79] Philadelphia's textile and clothing manufacturers, like its other industrial branches, profited from the war by adjusting familiar practices to meet new needs.[80]

Government contracting

Government contracting is a major connecting thread in the story of
the Civil War's impact on the Philadelphia economy. We have seen
that the demand for military goods helped to reinvigorate a stagnant
economy in 1861, and to drive that economy through several prosperous midwar years. Philadelphia's shifting textile production owed
much to the army's varied demand. Our examination of specific
industries yielded repeated evidence of profitable dealings with the
army. Some establishments, like Merrick and Sons and Baldwin
Locomotives, found their traditional services in particularly high demand. Others, such as Jenks and Sons' machine shop, enhanced their
profits by adjusting their operations.

　　Now that we have examined the shadows on the cave wall, it is
time to directly confront the contracting system. How important was
government contracting to Philadelphia's wartime economy? How
was the system organized? Who profited and who suffered? We will
begin with an analysis of the scale of government contracting. This
will be followed by a description of the evolution of the contracting
system. And we will conclude with a brief examination of one contractor's often rocky relationship with the government.

　　Although there has been ample discussion of the effect of government contracting on the Northern economy, precise data on the
magnitude of contracting are elusive. One scholar has calculated that
"army contractors handled at least a billion dollars of government
money during the war, and . . . by conservative estimate, retained a

77　Perhaps preying on the fears of anxious kinfolk, Stokes's notices also hawked
　　bulletproof vests alongside military finery. For examples of war-related clothing
　　advertisements see the almost daily notices for Tower Hall, Brown Stone Clothiers,
　　and Charles Stokes in the *Evening Bulletin* and the *Public Ledger*.
78　Bishop, *History of American Manufactures*, 552–3; *RGD*, 137:404.
79　For an example of a large mourning store ad see *EB*, 10 July 1861. For a description
　　of the wartime profits earned by William Simpson, a major mourning goods
　　manufacturer, see Scranton, *Proprietary Capitalism*, 285.
80　For a discussion of the range of war contracting and its impact on individual
　　entrepreneurs, see Chapter 12.

Table 11.5. Purchases at the U.S. Military Depots, Selected Items (figures in thousands)

Articles	Philadelphia	Total[a]	Philadelphia's % of Total
Drawers	4,697	10,738	43.7
Shirts	4,350	11,092	39.2
Greatcoats	1,500	3,827	39.2
Blankets	2,880	7,803	36.9
Boots	909	2,542	35.8
Stockings	7,902	20,320	38.9
Hats, caps, forage caps	2,872	7,130	40.3
Knapsacks	1,209	3,588	33.7
Haversacks	1,714	4,565	37.5
Canteens	1,980	5,200	38.1
Tents (several types)	1,204	2,589	46.5
Axes, spades, shovels, etc.	665	1,630	40.8
Mess pans	447	1,026	43.6
Material (thousands of yards)			
Woolen cloths and kerseys	15,733	20,908	75.2
Cotton duck	438	5,402	8.1
Flannels	11,246	19,611	57.3
Muslin twills and corset jeans	4,663	5,860	79.6
Worsted lace	6,817	8,185	83.3
Tent buttons (in thousands)	2,442	4,345	56.2

[a]"Total" consists of purchases at the New York, Philadelphia, and Cincinnati depots after May 1861.
Source: Official Records, ser. III, vol. 5, 283–86.

half of it."[81] As a major manufacturing center at the hub of several key rail lines, Philadelphia certainly shared in the war contracting bonanza. After the war, the quartermaster general submitted summaries of purchases made at the supply depots in Philadelphia, Cincinnati, and New York (Table 11.5) suggesting that a substantial share of raw materials and completed articles passed through Philadelphia. But several obstacles stand between these numbers and an accurate estimate of Philadelphia's contracting profits. As Table 11.6 indicates, the Quartermaster's Department paid a wide range of prices for goods, making it impossible to translate sales figures into dollar returns. More important, Philadelphians did not win every contract signed at the local depot.[82] Major national manufacturers often sought lucrative contracts in distant cities through the aid of industrious agents. And successful bidders frequently subcontracted

81 Fred A. Shannon, The Organization and Administration of the Union Army, 1861–1865, 2 vols. (Cleveland, 1928), 1:71. Almost certainly this estimate is low, because it excludes contracts made by privately outfitted regiments as well as any uncompensated state military expenses.

82 Of 165 contracts (every tenth signed) listed in the Philadelphia depot's "Register of Contracts Relating to the Supplying of Clothing and Equipage," (August 15, 1862 to March 14, 1865) 128, or 78 percent, were received by Philadelphia companies. See #2227, Record Group 92, National Archives, Philadelphia Branch (hereafter #2227, RG 92, NA, Philadelphia Branch).

Table 11.6. Prices Paid by the Quartermaster's Department for Clothing and Equipage, Selected Items

Article	Lowest Price	Highest Price
Uniform hats	$ 1.62	$ 2.19
Forage caps	0.35	1.04
Uniform coats	4.08	14.67
Caduceus	0.35	0.80
Trousers, footmen's	2.05	5.40
Shirts		
Flannel	0.45	3.01
Knit	0.69	2.34
Drawers		
Flannel	0.37	1.90
Knit	0.72	1.78
Stockings	0.23	0.53
Boots		
Sewed	3.00	4.83
Pegged	1.45	4.08
Greatcoats		
Footmen's	6.50	13.17
Horsemen's	7.74	16.11
Blankets		
Woolen	2.19	7.75
Rubber	2.00	5.00
Hospital tents / flies	56.40	227.60
Wall tents / flies	23.50	55.00
Common tents	9.87	25.00

Note: All figures rounded to nearest cent.

Source: Official Records, ser. III, vol. 5, 286.

their work out to firms in other cities. Thus a Philadelphian's name on a contract did not guarantee that the work was done locally.[83]

In his study of the Philadelphia textile industry, Philip Scranton sought to determine the impact of government contracting on Philadelphia firms, but he often found his way blocked by a web of untraceable middlemen. Scranton's analysis of hosiery contracts turned up fifteen Philadelphia firms, contracting in their own names, that delivered 2.25 million pairs of woolen stockings (valued at $765,000) of a total of 15.5 million sold to the army.[84] To this figure Scranton added an estimated two to three million pairs furnished by local subcontractors. Overall, thirty Philadelphia textile firms earned $12 million in *direct* government contracts, or almost five times as

83 For a good description of the interpretative problems posed by the contract records see Scranton, *Proprietary Capitalism*, 282. The government paid dearly for the services of energetic middlemen who took a healthy profit for bringing suppliers and government buyers together. See James A. Huston, *The Sinews of War: Army Logistics, 1775–1953*, (Washington, D.C., 1966), 180.
84 This figure included contracts in Cincinnati and New York.

much as the total value of the local woolens and woolen hosiery output recorded in the 1860 census. These findings led Scranton to the cautious conclusion that "war demand sustained the factory manufacture of textiles in Philadelphia and allowed a sizeable group of firms to expand their facilities, some dramatically."[85]

The problems inherent in an analysis of the magnitude of government contracting underscore the complexity of the Union army's supply system. The outbreak of the war caught the North totally unprepared to feed and outfit a major army. In a few months Quartermaster General Meigs oversaw the development of a massive organization capable of supplying the largest military body ever assembled. Allan Nevins wrote that "one of the most important effects [of the war] was an irresistible impetus toward greater and greater organization." This impetus, he argued, came largely as a result of Meigs's efforts.[86] This raises the possibility that the true "impact" of contracting on Philadelphia is to be found less in quantitative indexes than in institutional evolution. How did the maturing government contracting system fit into Philadelphia's existing institutional structure?

Before the war, all the uniforms for the nation's 16,000-strong regular army came from Philadelphia's Schuylkill Arsenal. The pressing demands of the 1861 crisis quickly exhausted this single depot's meager stores, and numerous obstacles, including a paucity of military-quality material and an absence of qualified government agents, impeded the early efforts to meet the need. In those first few weeks necessity produced a patchwork system that managed to keep the army clothed through the 1861–2 winter. Most troops enlisted through state regiments and the understaffed Quartermaster's Department generally relied on individual states to outfit their own men. This led to a chaotic scramble for uniforms and supplies. In towns across the North, women met to sew stockings and uniforms for the volunteers. Wise merchants imported necessary materials, and competing state and regimental quartermasters frantically bid up the prices. As sturdy material became unavailable, manufacturers made do with ordinary cloths or cheap "shoddy," which soon failed to withstand the test of long marches.[87]

In Philadelphia this larger drama played itself out in miniature

---

85 Scranton, *Proprietary Capitalism*, 286–8.
86 Nevins, "A Major Result of the Civil War,".240. This organizational theme is also central to Nevins's *The War for the Union*, 4 vols. (New York, 1959–1971).
87 *Official Records*, ser. III, vol. 2:802–3 (hereafter *OR* III, 2:802–3); Russell F. Weigley, *Quartermaster General of the Union Army: A Biography of Montgomery C. Meigs* (New York, 1959), 183; Scranton, *Proprietary Capitalism*, 280; Shannon, *Organization and Administration*, 1:53.

through the first year of the war. On April 18, 1861, soon after 500 Pennsylvania Volunteers left for the nation's capital, R. C. Hale, the quartermaster general of the state militia, set off for Philadelphia to gather uniforms. Finding the supply at the U. S. Arsenal already depleted, Hale established an emergency clothing depot in the vacant Girard House Hotel. Hundreds of working-class women sewed side by side with ladies from Philadelphia's upper crust to produce over 10,000 uniforms in less than ten weeks. Supplementing this activity, Hale began to purchase uniforms from local contractors. Initially, he merely solicited bids from prominent clothing firms, but later he took to publicly advertising for proposals. Once the hysteria subsided, Pennsylvania settled into a multitiered supply system with Philadelphia's activities at its core. Sewing women worked at the Schuylkill Arsenal and the Girard House; others took materials home to sew; contractors sold cloth and finished products to the quartermaster; dozens of sewing circles throughout the city and the state knitted stockings for the volunteers.[88]

This system kept the army supplied through the war's first winter, but not without criticisms from many quarters. The loudest complaints were of uniforms and equipment falling apart under hard use. Others pointed to dishonest government agents and unscrupulous war profiteers.[89] The cries of fraud generated a series of government investigations. In June 1861 Pennsylvania's Governor Andrew G. Curtin named a five-man committee to inquire into "alleged army frauds" within the state. After nine weeks of interviews the commission blamed the inadequacy of the Girard House uniforms on poor material rather than on faulty workmanship or improper inspection. Although the commission turned up no clear fraud, it found ample evidence of poor judgment and unpatriotic profiteering.[90] In January 1862 the state House of Representatives named its own five-man committee to investigate contracting. Testimony revealed that at least one state agent had taken kickbacks and DuHadaway and Dodson, a Philadelphia firm, had used the services of Joshua Kames, a friend of the governor, to help them gain a major blanket contract.[91] The

88 "Quartermaster General's Report," *Pennsylvania Executive Documents, 1861* (Harrisburg, 1862) 1:9; Scharf and Westcott, *History of Philadelphia*, 1:760; Oberholtzer, *Philadelphia*, 2:361; Winnifred K. MacKay, "Philadelphia During the Civil War, 1861–1865," *Pennsylvania Magazine of History and Biography* (January 1946): 12–13; Huston, *The Sinews of War*, 184.
89 Shannon, *Organization of the Union Army*, 1:72–3. Philadelphia's newspapers often contained harsh attacks on war contractors and fraudulent officials. See *Philadelphia Inquirer*, 15, 21 May 1861; *PL*, 27 May 1861; *CR*, 1 June 1861. See also *Report of the Commission Appointed to the Governor of Pennsylvania to Investigate Alleged Army Frauds, August, 1861* (Harrisburg, 1861), 42–3.
90 *Report of the Commission, passim.*
91 "Legislative Document No. 80," *Pennsylvania Legislative Documents, 1862* (Harrisburg, 1863), 1272–315.

various investigations left little doubt that the state's interests had been injured by irregular practices that often put money in the hands of well-connected middlemen. At the national level, the growing concern over fraudulent contracting led to an investigation under New York Congressman Charles H. Van Wyck. The Van Wyck Committee's 2,000 page report described wide-ranging corruption, largely centered in Fremont's Department of the West.[92]

Despite the misdeeds unearthed by these investigations, the Quartermaster's Department successfully weathered 1861. The new year brought several adjustments that improved the efficiency of both the state and the national supply systems. In January President Lincoln sent Secretary of War Simon Cameron overseas as minister to Russia and replaced that inept cabinet member with the tough-minded Edwin M. Stanton.[93] Stanton immediately arranged for the review of all firms holding War Department contracts. And Congress passed legislation requiring open bidding for government contracts.[94]

At the close of 1861 state Quartermaster General Hale observed that "the rebellion found us unprepared to carry on a war of the magnitude it has assumed," but "we have passed through the period of trial." On March 31, 1862, he turned over Pennsylvania's military inventory to Meigs. This completed the evolution from a highly localized supply system to a centrally controlled structure under the federal quartermaster general. From that point on, the U. S. Quartermaster's Department oversaw all government contracts, and issued uniforms and equipment to the Pennsylvania troops. When the Pennsylvania Volunteers answered Lincoln's calls, Hale sent an emissary to Colonel G. H. Crossman, the Union's deputy quartermaster general stationed at the Philadelphia depot. This system proved extremely efficient in outfitting new volunteers, but in February 1862 a joint resolution of the Pennsylvania General Assembly instructed the state quartermaster general to make the necessary contracts to clothe the state's sick and wounded volunteers. And when Curtin called for emergency troops to repulse Lee's 1862 invasion, Hale's department had to scour Philadelphia for supplementary

92 "Government Contracts," *House Reports*, 37th Cong., 2nd sess., vol. 2 (Washington, 1863); Shannon, *Organization of the Union Army*, 1:58–65; Weigley, *Quartermaster General of the Union Army*, 195–7.

93 Weigley, *Quartermaster General of the Union Army*, 212. For an excellent treatment of Stanton's career see Benjamin P. Thomas and Harold M. Hyman, *Stanton: The Life and Times of Lincoln's Secretary of War* (New York, 1962). For an energetic defense of Cameron see Brooks M. Kelley, "Fossildom, Old Fogeyism, and Red Tape," *Pennsylvania Magazine of History and Biography* 40 (January 1966): 93–114.

94 Thomas and Hyman, *Stanton*, 156. For a good description of the organization of the quartermaster general's office under Stanton see Weigley, *Quartermaster General of the Union Army*, 215–36.

supplies. Thus even after Meigs took over the reins, the state continued to play a role in supplying clothes for volunteers.[95]

If the military supply system during the war's first year earned mixed reviews, the quartermaster general's activities for the rest of the conflict met with widespread approval. By mid-1862 Stanton and Meigs had produced the best-equipped army in history.[96] With his depots already well stocked, Meigs continued to advertise for new contractors so that each of the three major depots could outfit 100,000 new recruits at short notice as well as keep up with the ordinary needs of 200,000 men already in the field.[97] But these successes did not signal an end to corruption. In late 1863 one of Assistant Secretary of War Charles A. Dana's men helped to arrest several Philadelphia businessmen involved in a fraudulent grain deal.[98] That same year Philadelphian John Dubree, a "late measurer of leather at the Arsenal," was found guilty of cutting leather below specifications.[99] In 1865 Meigs sent Colonel George Rutherford to Philadelphia to investigate rumors of faulty kersey coming out of the depot. Rutherford discovered that the "official" standard in Philadelphia was below the government's printed specifications. And none of the kersey that he inspected met even the lowered Philadelphia guidelines. These "shoddy" materials came from four contracts, all involving Philadelphia merchant houses.[100]

Four years of public anger over shoddy materials and war profiteers culminated in the 1865 court-martial of tent contractor William B. Cozens. The R. G. Dun records show that in January 1859 Cozens and a Mr. Altemus formed a small firm, valued at about $6,000, trading in dry goods on commission. The partnership enjoyed a good trade until the war, after which their business took off with the aid of government contracts. In mid-1864 Altemus retired a rich man, and Cozens continued at the head of a wealthy firm. In October R. G. Dun's agent reported: "C. is a large Govt contractor & has been arrested in connection with an Inspector at the US Arsenal here, under a general charge of fraud." With Cozens's fate uncertain, the

---

95 "Report of the Quartermaster General," *Pennsylvania Executive Document, 1862* (Harrisburg, 1863), 3–8.
96 James M. McPherson, *Ordeal By Fire: The Civil War and Reconstruction* (New York, 1982), 167; Huston, *The Sinews of War*, 186–7.
97 OR III, 2:371–3, 732–3; Weigley, *Quartermaster General of the Union Army*, 251–3.
98 Charles A. Dana, *Recollections of the Civil War*, (1898; New York, 1963), 150–2; Shannon, *Organization of the Union Army*, 1:74–5.
99 *PL*, 18 September through 10 October 1863.
100 Scranton, *Proprietary Capitalism*, 290–1. Several contractors and inspectors remained under investigation in 1865. See Shannon, *Organization of the Union Army*, 1:103.

firm could not survive, and in March 1866 R. G. Dun reported that Cozens and Company had gone out of business.[101]

Cozens's fall began with his arrest on September 15, 1864. After his release, Cozens found that the government had stopped payments on his outstanding vouchers. Five months later a court-martial convened to try Cozens on twenty-four counts of fraud, involving nineteen army contracts.[102] The prosecution charged that Cozens repeatedly sold faulty tents to the government and that he bribed the arsenal's tent inspector to accept them. The trial, which dragged on into June, attracted considerable public attention.[103] Cozens claimed that his wartime successes stemmed from a combination of good luck and successful gambles. At the outset of the war his business had a large stock of cotton duck on hand, and thus he was able to provide the quartermaster with desperately needed tents. He then took the profits from these contracts and ordered large quantities of duck. Thus in ensuing years Cozens was able to sell tents at inflated prices with materials bought in the 1861 market. Throughout the lengthy trial Cozens insisted that he knew nothing about tent-making, therefore relying on a local manufacturer. Although he admitted that his tents did not meet the written government specifications, Cozens explained that no tents sold in Philadelphia did so because Inspector William Neal always requested smaller tents on the assumption that they were just as good and less expensive.

Although Cozens produced a long list of Philadelphia luminaries attesting to his good character and honesty, the military court found the contractor guilty of fraud. In December 1865, sixty-eight of Cozens's defenders, including Jay Cooke, Jonathan Wanamaker, J. B. Lippincott & Company, George W. Childs, and Caleb Cope, petitioned President Johnson to disallow the decision. The case dragged on until September 1867 when Johnson finally reversed the court's findings. Finally, four years after the war's conclusion, Cozens received a payment of $14,000 as reimbursement for his losses.[104]

What conclusions can we draw about government contracting in

---

101 *RGD* 137:714.
102 Cozens complained bitterly that the secretary of war had no constitutional right to order the court-martial of private citizens.
103 The *Public Ledger* frequently ran lengthy summaries of the day's proceedings and even noted when the court adjourned without hearing testimony.
104 This discussion has been largely taken from the William B. N. Cozens Papers at the Historical Society of Pennsylvania. This file includes about a hundred documents concerning the trial and subsequent pleas for redress. The case is well summarized in *Argument of F. Carroll Brewster, Esq., on behalf of William B. N. Cozens, delivered at Philadelphia, June 12th, 1865* . . . (Philadelphia, 1865). A copy of this printed document is in Folder #1 of the Cozens Papers. For detailed coverage of the trial see the *Public Ledger*, 14 February 1865 through 29 June 1865.

Philadelphia? Clearly, certain local businessmen profited enormously from the war. The Union army poured millions of dollars into outfitting its troops, and Philadelphia's manufacturers managed to garner more than their share of the rewards. But this is far from the whole story. It is evident that the system of supplying the army evolved from a largely local operation to one guided by Washington. The Quartermaster's Department, like the Sanitary Commission and the army itself, turned Philadelphia into a cog in a much larger machine. In that sense, as Nevins noted, the war was truly a centralizing event.

But though the structure of wartime supply took a centralized form, Philadelphia and its citizens did not passively slip into a federally dictated role. Individuals and small voluntary groups continued to send packages to the front. The government's two-tiered contracting system allowed much work to remain under private direction.[105] And even after the Quartermaster's Department took over normal activities, state officers stepped in to supervise emergency contracting. Moreover, although the federal supply system certainly made its presence felt, local businessmen persisted in putting their mark on the contracting process. The Cozens case and the earlier fraud investigations are evidence of this persistent "customizing". Beneath Meigs's national organization, individual Philadelphia contractors relied on personal contacts and occasional kickbacks to secure government business. And government inspectors amended the quartermaster's official specifications to meet local circumstances.

And if the centralized system maintained many local characteristics, it also appears that the contracting process did not accelerate economic centralization in Philadelphia. Surveys of the "abstracts of contracts" signed in the city reveal a widespread participation in the contracting process. The roughly 1,500 "clothing and equipage" contracts registered between August 1862 and March 1865 were generally for very small amounts; frequently several companies contracted for the same item on the same day.[106] One hundred and one different companies signed the 278 agreements recorded in a separate volume of equipment contracts; of these, 75 signed only 1 or 2 contracts.[107] Thus although the contracting system was centralized, the federal agents seem to have divided the spoils among many Philadelphia companies rather than granting any special advantages to a few leading firms.[108]

---

105 As we have seen, this private contracting was a source of controversy among Philadelphia's sewing women who preferred the higher wages they received for arsenal work. See Chapter 9.
106 "Register of Contracts Relating to the Supplying of Clothing and Equipage."
107 "Abstracts of Contracts, 1862–1864," #2226, RG 92, NA, Philadelphia Branch.
108 This conclusion is reinforced by the findings in the next chapter.

Economic change and individual experiences: Two case histories

Philadelphia's wartime economic experience is best characterized by a period of panic and dislocation followed by a successful adjustment to the war's demands and opportunities. Workers faced initial unemployment and then widespread demand for their services; private firms failed or cut back their activities during the crisis but soon business boomed; and efforts to outfit the army began with a period of chaotic experimentation before settling into a workable system that – in fact, if not by design – accommodated individual and local interests as well as the Union's military agenda.

This general pattern of confusion and experimentation followed by adjustment, organization, and improved efficiency unfolded at different paces in each aspect of Philadelphia's economic world, much as it did in other areas of wartime life – recruitment, benevolence, civic ritual. The next chapter will examine how individual economic experiences differed beneath this template. But before so doing, let us consider the personal histories of two Philadelphians. Each man, the first in a diary and the second in business correspondence, left a detailed record of how the war's economic ebbs and flows interacted with private concerns to mold his wartime experiences.

The war's economic fluctuations combined with entirely personal twists of fate to send Washington Penrose, a Philadelphia patternmaker in his early fifties, on a financial roller-coaster ride. McElroy's annual city directories from 1860 through 1867 list Penrose as a "patternmaker" living at 1541 North Eleventh Street. But this record of residential stability masks a business career (described rather impressionistically in Penrose's personal diary), that proceeded by fits and starts before achieving substantial success near the war's close.[109]

Although the economy struggled in the tumultuous months following Lincoln's inauguration, Penrose repeatedly reported that he had "plenty of work." This prosperous pattern continued until May 1861 when his orders dried up. On May 18 he wrote: "Every kind of business except war appears at a stand still."[110] But by late July the business recovery had reached down to Penrose's level, and until the end of November he limped along, working part of each week though never securing steady employment.

In December Penrose's weekly entries once again reported "not much offering."[111] This discouraging situation led the patternmaker into an ill-fated business venture with one-time carpenter John

109   Washington Penrose diary, HSP, *passim.*
110   Penrose diary, 2 March through 4 May, 11, 18 May 1861.
111   Penrose diary, 7, 14, 21, 28 December 1861.

Tibbens.[112] On January 1, 1862, these two small businessmen rented a pair of rooms on Germantown Avenue and launched the firm of Tibbens, Penrose, & Company, lamp manufacturers. For two months Penrose split his time between lamp manufacturing and a resurgent patternmaking trade. Then in late February he ended the partnership, explaining that it required too much capital.[113] Two weeks later, flush with the success of this short-lived excursion into private enterprise, Penrose decided to expand his operations. He purchased new woodworking machinery, rented space in a Fifteenth Street building, and from March until July 1862 worked at both patternmaking and furniture manufacturing.[114] This new business apparently prospered, for Penrose devoted an increasing share of his workweek to the Fifteenth Street shop and by mid-July had several hands working under him.[115]

Until the summer of 1862, then, Penrose's economic experience mirrored the city's larger patterns. He shared in the general business depression of 1860–1; later that year he slowly returned to full-time employment; in early 1862 he opened a new and successful business. But on August 16, 1862, Penrose's personal experience departed from the national norm when a wood chip flew from his still-new lathe and cut him over the left eye. This accident kept the patternmaker from his work, starting him on a rapid decline. In October he sold his interest in the Fifteenth Street shop. That winter, as failing vision and frequent headaches kept him from work, Penrose sold off his machinery and his watch, and finally took to peddling eggs and renting out a room.[116]

In February 1863 the disabled patternmaker, still blind in one eye, returned to irregular pattern work.[117] A year later, Penrose bought a wood bench, brought his tools home, and went back into the pattern business for himself.[118] This time his progress was swift and uninterrupted. In March he added a new lathe. A month later, he rented a pattern shop and moved his business out of his home. The next week Penrose hired an assistant, and on April 23, 1864, he

---

112 Tibbens's earlier trade is taken from McElroy's Philadelphia City Directory, 1860 (Philadelphia, 1860).
113 Penrose diary, 25 February 1861.
114 Penrose diary, 7, 10 March 1862, and passim.
115 On July 12, 1862, Penrose wrote: "Business dull we let all our hands go." This entry suggests that he had a small work force by then.
116 Penrose account book.
117 For the next year Penrose included regular reports of his workweek among his sparse diary entries. These entries only refer to "pattern work" but it appears that he was hiring himself out on a contract basis in other persons' shops.
118 Penrose diary, 15 February 1864.

proudly recorded that "work is very abundant." In early August, after several prosperous months, Penrose found that he and his helper had "more work than we can do" and hired a second patternmaker.[119] By the end of the war, Penrose's hired men were regularly putting in over 110 hours a week between them, and his son Nathan often worked a few days a week in the shop. Although his infirmities restricted him to only a few hours of work a day, Penrose was a far more prosperous man at the end of the war than he had been in 1860.

George F. Lee began his business career in his father's bricklaying company and by 1844 he headed a national gasworks construction concern with branches in St. Louis, New York, and Chicago. In 1861 he lived comfortably off his various investments, many of which were in Chicago real estate and loans. Lee's first response to the secession crisis was strongly Democratic and distinctly pro-Southern. On March 12, 1861, the Philadelphia capitalist wrote that "the Irrepressible conflict has been fought & the South & Justice is victorious."[120] But after the firing on Fort Sumter, Lee swallowed his dislike for the Republicans, reporting to his close Chicago friend, Judge Mark Skinner, that "we have noisy times in these parts [but there is] only one party now."[121] By May he had "accepted as high private in our hom[e] guard & been made treasurer of our department."[122] Soon Lee wrote that he was investing $20,000 in "*Uncle Sam* . . . although he don't pay so large interest" because "I have great faith in his ["Sam's"] honesty and ability to pay" and also because "as a lover of our Union . . . I feel a moral claim on me in the matter."[123]

Whereas Lee the patriot rallied to the cause, Lee the investor faced mounting problems from his stable of worried debtors. In February 1861 James R. Burtis, one of Lee's Chicago tenants, sent a pleading letter complaining of hard times and asking for a reduced mortgage. Lee refused the reduction, but offered a small annual salary in payment for Burtis's occasional services as his Chicago agent.[124] The following month Lee granted W. B. Keen, a Chicago book dealer, a reduced rent because of the national crisis.[125]

Lee's 1861 correspondence was filled with similar pleas from

---

119 Penrose diary, 6, 18 August 1864.
120 Lee to W. B. Keen, George F. Lee Papers, 12 March 1861, HSP. All subsequent notes are from this collection.
121 Lee to Mark Skinner, 18 April 1861.
122 Lee to James R. Burtis, 18 May 1861. Lee clearly took this position quite seriously, for his Thirteenth Ward Home Guard account book lists his own donation of $1,000 as the first and largest given to the organization.
123 Lee to Skinner, 17 May 1861.
124 Burtis to Lee, 21 February 1861; Lee to Burtis, 25 February 1861.
125 Keen to Lee, 1, 7, 8 March 1861; Lee to Keen, 12 March 1861.

other debtors. In May he consented to J. B. Rice's request to delay his payments until the exchange rate improved.[126] That winter Rice wrote that "the present war . . . has lessened values in property," and asked for a reduction in his mortgage. Lee promised to consider the request, but pointed out that he, too, was suffering.[127] In May 1861 G. M. Van Ordel, another Chicagoan, sent Lee a letter he had received from a local ironworks that argued that "big losses at the South and So.West" left them "all used up" and unable to pay their debts. Van Ordel passed this note on to Lee to explain his inability to meet his loan payments.[128] Lee sent nearly identical notes to two especially slow debtors in September, saying that he disliked being "hard with any one [in] these times" but had to insist that they at least pay the interest due on their loans.[129]

By the end of 1861 Lee had granted most of his tenants and debtors some sort of leniency. The following year began as its predecessor ended, with Lee firing off numerous reminders of interest due. On January 22 he threatened to sue Charles B. Brown for nonpayment.[130] But soon his correspondence revealed signs of an improving economy. In February Keen, who in 1861 had begged for a rent decrease, inquired about renewing his lease.[131] Lee responded by offering his tenant a $115 per month rent for one year or $220 per month for two years. Keen's acceptance of the longer lease reflected his belief that the crisis would soon end and rents would rise.[132] By the summer of 1862 Keen was doing so well that he wrote asking to borrow $5,000 to build a new dwelling.[133] Van Ordel's own debtors must have been paying more promptly, for his checks began arriving on time, and in September he paid off his loan.[134] Even the hapless Burtis sent in his August payment only one month late.[135]

In February 1862 Lee told Skinner that he sought no further loan opportunities, preferring to follow his patriotic urges and invest in

126 J. B. Rice to Lee, 16, 22 May 1861, Lee to Rice, 20 May 1861.
127 Rice to Lee, 7 November 1861; Lee to Rice, 11 November 1861. Lee apparently granted Rice's request, but in a later letter to Skinner he noted his annoyance because Rice had previously profited at Lee's expense when Chicago prices had risen after a contract had been signed. See Lee to Skinner, 16 November 1861.
128 G. M. Van Ordel to Lee, 27 May 1861.
129 Lee to J. Greenbaum, Esq., and Lee to Charles B. Brown, 1 September, 1861.
130 Lee to Brown, 22 January 1862. Lee had never before sued a debtor for nonpayment. Brown responded with his interest payment and a plea for understanding because of his youth and good character. See Brown to Lee, 31 January 1862.
131 Keen to Lee, 12 February 1862.
132 Lee to Burtis, 4, 14 April 1862.
133 Keen to Lee, 30 July 1862. In a reply of 9 August 1862, Lee refused this request.
134 Van Ordel to Lee, 26 May, 20 September 1862.
135 Burtis to Lee, 14 September 1861. See also Lee to Greenbaum, 28 July 1862; Greenbaum to Lee, 24 September 1862.

government loans.[136] He later proudly explained that he had bought U. S. notes "the *1st day the Books were opened*," thus assuring that "my boy would have tangible evidence of *my faith*."[137] A similar civic-mindedness led him to become involved in various public matters, such as aid for foundlings and deserted children.[138]

Some of the men who owed Lee money responded to the rising financial tide by becoming more prompt in their payments. Others, however, sought to turn the economic improvement to their own advantage. In late September 1862 Rice, who had spent much of 1861 asking for extensions and reductions, requested a larger second loan at an interest rate reduced from 10 percent to 8 percent. When Lee offered a compromise at 9 percent, Rice paid off his original loan ahead of schedule, assuming that he could get money at 8 percent elsewhere.[139] Similarly, Brown paid off his entire $5,000 mortgage ahead of time, choosing to seek an 8 percent loan in Chicago rather than stay with Lee and provide additional security for an extended loan.[140]

Although these early payments reduced Lee's financial activities, Keen and the government continued to be sources of trouble for the Philadelphia capitalist. When Keen refused to pay his rent in coin, Lee instructed Burtis to accept the controversial greenbacks in payment but to use the "identical papers" to pay the Illinois property tax. As a diehard Democrat, Lee hated "the despotic act" that brought the greenbacks into existence, declaring that "I am willing to & do maintain the credit of the Govt by investing all I have in its legal constitutional bonds; but will not if I can help it, sanction the unconstitutional acts of the administration."[141]

The problems of a creditor in inflationary times continued to plague Lee in early 1863. As the year began, he wrote to Burtis that he was "deep into U. S. loans & will lose heavily" but, he added, "I

136 Lee to Skinner, 17 February 1862. Lee regularly equated investment in government bonds with patriotism. See Lee to Skinner, 28 March 1862.
137 Lee to Skinner, 28 March 1862.
138 Although his forays into public service were not necessarily war related, Lee explicitly explained his actions as an effort to fill in for benevolent citizens who had joined the army. See Lee to Skinner, 18 May 1862.
139 Rice to Lee, 30 September, 9 October, 5 November; Lee to Rice, 2, 13 October 1862. The fact that interest rates were continually below inflation rates seems to suggest that capitalists misjudged the duration of the wartime inflation.
140 Lee to Brown, 1 October 1862; Brown to Lee, 24 October 1862; Skinner to Lee, 5 November 1862.
141 Lee to Burtis, 20 November 1862. Lee had hoped to force Illinois into a lawsuit over his right to use the greenbacks to pay his state property taxes, but in the ensuing correspondence Burtis proved too slow-witted to understand Lee's plan. Eventually, after learning that Illinois had won a similar case, Lee instructed Burtis to buy gold with Keen's greenbacks and pay the tax in coin. See several letters to and from Burtis in November and December 1862.

would give all I have to save my government."[142] Yet he was not quite so ready to absorb losses to support his lessees. When Keen wrote asking for $50 to paint the front of his store, Lee objected, arguing that "he is making money *very fast* & I am loosing it *very fast*."[143] And when the attorney of another Chicago debtor inquired about extend¬ ing his client's loan at a reduced rate, Lee became furious. Although he was unwilling to offer a short-term reduced loan, Lee did offer a three-year extension at 9 percent (as opposed to the existing 10 percent), or ten years at 8 percent.[144] This offer reflected Lee's belief that the upcoming years would be grim for creditors.

Clearly, Lee was made uncomfortable by the shifting financial winds. In mid-1863 he complained to Judge Skinner that national developments seemed to be making others rich while leaving him poorer. Later that year he bitterly wrote to his old friend that "we have fallen upon evil times," with the "professed Christians" of Chicago's North Presbyterian Church repudiating their debt to him, and Keen getting rich.[145] But by 1864 his business dealings returned to an even keel. Keen accepted a rent increase; Burtis sold his house and got out of debt after long months of struggle; and the Chicago church settled its debt.[146] By year's end, Lee had the bulk of his capital in government loans; he no longer needed to spend his time haranguing slow debtors.[147]

How do these two vignettes contribute to our understanding of the economic life of Civil War Philadelphia? On one level they illus- trate the impact of the wartime economic fluctuations on individual experience. When the economy declined in 1861, Penrose complained of "dull" business and Lee received pleas rather than checks from his debtors. When business improved, Penrose pursued various en- deavors and Lee's correspondents suddenly wished to renegotiate their loans or settle up ahead of schedule. Penrose's skills and Lee's money changed in value with the shifting economic tides.

In this sense these stories are "typical" of the larger patterns. But each says more about the importance of individual experience as a filter through which all economic variables must pass. Penrose re- peatedly sought to use his artisan skills as a springboard for his

142 Lee to Burtis, 15 January 1863.
143 Lee to Burtis, 12 March 1863.
144 Luther Rossiter to Lee, 9 March, 7, 21 April 1863; Lee to Rossiter, 11, 18 April 1863.
145 Lee to Skinner, 18 November 1863.
146 Burtis to Lee, 21 January, 22 February, 15 April 1864; Lee to sister Mary, 14 November 1864.
147 The Lee Papers include far fewer business letters in 1864 than in 1863, and fewer still in 1865. Both the volume and content of this correspondence suggests that the capitalist had fewer creditors as the war neared an end, and those he did have apparently paid their installments without prompting.

business aspirations. The war provided a context, but his own ambitions and a freak accident were more important than external developments in dictating his fate. In Lee's case personality often pulled against the logic of years in business. In his dealings with his debtors Lee pressed for prompt payment, but continually accepted delays that went against his own interests. When the worm turned, and money was no longer scarce, Lee's debtors repaid his loyalty by paying up ahead of time and finding cheaper money elsewhere, thus robbing him of his anticipated interest. Similarly, in buying government bonds Lee regularly claimed that he was letting his heart overrule his pocketbook by accepting lower returns than he could find in the private market.

Lee's letters also illustrate how the government's war finance measures helped limit private capital formation, and therefore temporarily stunted economic growth. At the macro level the argument, as advanced by Jeffrey Williamson and greatly simplified here, runs as follows. Despite much talk of taxes and tariffs, the government paid for the war largely through the sale of interest-bearing loans. These loans competed with private enterprise for investment dollars, and their success was at the expense of capital formation.[148]

Although Lee's debtors repeatedly forced the issue by retiring their loans ahead of schedule, the capitalist actively chose to put all of his excess funds in government bonds rather than reinvesting in private enterprise. On several occasions he explicitly refused requests for loans, and often told Judge Skinner that he had no interest in finding new uses for his money. If we are to believe Lee, this process was not merely an instance of attractive government investments "crowding out" private sector loans. On the contrary, he consistently claimed that by investing in his government he was accepting a financial loss in the name of patriotism.[149]

Lee and Penrose, like William Cozens, responded to the war's financial challenges and opportunities in distinct ways. The war changed each man's economic well-being, but their different economic experiences were as much a product of their peacetime situations and personal traits as they were a function of government measures. Philadelphia's entrepreneurs followed disparate paths during the war years. The following chapter will explore the varieties of experience within the city's business community.

148 See Jeffrey Williamson, "Watersheds and Turning Points: Conjectures on the Long-Term Impact of Civil War Financing," *Journal of Economic History* 34 (September 1974): 644–8.
149 Williamson notes that "appeals to patriotism" might have helped shift the balance toward government investment, but he adds that he knows of little evidence to support this conjecture. See "Watersheds and Turning Points," 646, fn. 18.

12 Winners and losers: The R.G. Dun credit reports

R. G. Dun and Company

The preceding chapters have examined the Civil War's effect on Philadelphia's economy from several perspectives. The data tell a varied story, but they converge at key points. Every economic sector shared in the 1861 decline and subsequent recovery. All felt the impact of lost government contracts and declining gold prices following the end of hostilities. And the evidence suggests that the war's impact was broad rather than deep: It touched on every aspect of the city's economic life, but did not dramatically alter most of it.

The next step is to explore more fully this breadth of experience. How did small entrepreneurs, like Washington Penrose, muddle their way through the war years? What became of business concerns that lacked the size and strategic position of Baldwin Locomotives or Merrick and Sons? The credit reports of R. G. Dun and Company give us a unique compromise between detailed manuscript sources and broad quantitative data. In 1841 New York wholesaler Lewis Tappan established the Mercantile Agency to gather credit information for sale to subscribers. Tappan collected his information from correspondents – mostly lawyers – who were well acquainted with local businesses. In 1859 R. G. Dun assumed ownership of the rapidly expanding Mercantile Agency.[1] R. G. Dun's correspondents typically filed semiannual reports on local businesses. Any business that had applied for credit or appeared likely to seek loans was liable to fall under R. G. Dun's net.[2] A complete report of a business included the names of all partners, an estimate of the establishment's net worth, any unusual activities that might affect its credit, a comment on the

---

1 Sydney Ratner, James H. Soltow, Richard Sylla, *The Evolution of the American Economy* (New York, 1979), 230. Also see James. D. Norris, *R. G. Dun & Co, 1841–1900: The Development of Credit-Reporting in the Nineteenth-Century* (Westport, Conn., 1978); Stephen G. Mostov, "Dun and Bradstreet Reports as a Source of Jewish Economic History: Cincinnati, 1840–1875," *American Jewish History* 72 (March 1983): 333–9. The Philadelphia branch of the Mercantile Agency opened in 1845.

2 It is very difficult to gauge the completeness of the R. G. Dun reports. One study of Cincinnati Jews found that 77 percent of the wholesalers in the 1860 census appeared in the R. G. Dun records, and the reports included roughly one-half of the retailers and one-fourth of all clerks and peddlers. See Mostov, "Dun and Bradstreet Reports," 337.

character of the owner, and a credit rating – usually "poor," "good," "very good," or "excellent." In practice, however, the entries varied tremendously. In some cases the reporter submitted complete updates every six months, while in other instances the entries came years apart. Often R. G. Dun's correspondents were content with very brief comments or merely recorded "no change." But sometimes their reports included colorful character critiques or unusual detail.

Patterns of failure in Philadelphia

The R. G. Dun reports for Philadelphia County are a particularly useful source for this study because they provide annual data on a large number of Philadelphia businesses, thus allowing for certain quantitative manipulations, and because they include details on the wartime experiences of numerous small enterprises. I have tried to tap these qualities by two "samplings" of the ledgers. In the first I surveyed every twentieth page, recording data on all businesses that were established after 1855 or were in operation during the war years. This procedure yielded 491 cases.[3] In addition I went through every page of the ledgers, recording complete information on all enterprises that had prewar ties with the South or wartime government contacts – two obvious categories that would have felt the impact of the war.[4]

The most broadly useful quantitative evidence from the R. G. Dun sample deals with the survival of businesses. What sorts of firms went out of business? When did they shut their doors? Table 12.1 summarizes the patterns of failure among the sampled wartime businesses. Of 340 firms on which complete data were taken (column 1), 79 (23.2 percent) went out of business before 1866. If we add the estimates from the 134 partial cases, this figure rises to 134 of 452 enterprises (29.6 percent).[5] The data are less sensitive to annual fluctuations, but the evidence reinforces the earlier conclusion that business struggled during the war's first year. Table 12.1 also makes clear the shock following the war's conclusion. Of 349 companies in

3 For a complete description of the reports and of this sampling technique see the Appendix.
4 I call this a "sample" even though I attempted to take down every case that fit these criteria, because the ledgers are extremely difficult to read and even more difficult to scan. Consequently, although I am sure that my record is not complete, I am also confident that my omissions were "random." Of course mention of ties with the South or with the government were subject to the whim of the correspondent. These certainly did not include every such firm.
5 See Appendix. The "estimated" cases failed more frequently because the firms with incomplete information were generally smaller. This phenomenon is discussed below.

Table 12.1. The R. G. Dun Sample: All Firms, Final Year in Business

	Complete Cases	Estimated Cases	Total[a]
1861	15	10	25
1862	15	27	42
1863	8	12	20
1864	13	3	16
1865	28	3	31
1866	19	4	23
1867	10	8	18
1868	12	27	39
1869	5	6	11
1870+	215	12	227
Total	340	112	452
Out of business 1861–65	79	55	134
% out of business	23.2	49.1	29.6

[a]These figures only include those cases with complete or estimated data. They do not include businesses formed after 1855 which folded before 1861. See the text and Appendix for definitions of terms.

Source: R. G. Dun & Co. Collection, Baker Library, Harvard University Graduate School of Business.

existence at the start of 1865, an estimated 31 (8.9 percent) went out of business in that year.[6]

R. G. Dun's reporters occasionally noted unusual changes in the fortunes of a business. Table 12.2 casts light on the wartime ebb and flow by summarizing the R. G. Dun commentaries in three categories: rises in business, declines in business, and serious trouble. It provides further evidence that wartime business suffered through an initial year of hardship, followed by several years of recovery, and then a second decline near the end of the conflict. Table 12.2 also suggests how varied the experiences of firms could be. In 1862 42 of 342 (12.3 percent) companies went out of business, 14 (4.1 percent) were in serious trouble, another 13 (3.8 percent) experienced difficulties; but 11 other firms (3.2 percent) had already begun to recover.

The R. G. Dun material also allows us to consider the experiences of different types of firms. This study isolates three variables – age, size and type of enterprise – and considers the relationship of each to success and failure. Table 12.3 compares the pattern of failure for

6 These annual fluctuations are potentially biased by a shifting "population at risk." But the totals in Table 12.2 suggest that these shifts are not great.

Table 12.2. The R. G. Dun Sample: Evidence of Annual Fluctuations, 1855–69

	1855	1856	1857	1858	1859	1860	1861	1862	1863	1864	1865	1866	1867	1868	1869
Total[a]	218	248	265	300	338	364	341	342	339	336	321	293	253	224	217
Rose[b]	0	0	0	0	3	0	4	11	10	8	3	0	3	1	0
Declined[c]	0	2	2	3	4	4	9	13	2	10	4	3	7	3	2
Trouble[d]	2	2	9	10	4	8	21	14	2	9	4	1	4	4	3
Out of business[e]	0	1	2	9	4	5	25	42	20	16	31	23	18	39	11
Unknown[e]	72	64	64	57	43	36	56	53	59	17	16	24	53	69	66
% Rose	0.0	0.0	0.0	0.0	0.9	0.0	1.2	3.2	2.9	2.4	0.9	0.0	1.2	0.4	0.0
% Declined	0.0	0.8	0.8	1.0	1.2	1.1	2.6	3.8	0.6	3.0	1.2	1.0	2.8	1.3	0.9
% Trouble	0.9	0.8	3.4	3.3	1.2	2.2	6.2	4.1	0.6	2.7	1.2	0.3	1.6	1.8	1.4
% Out of business	0.0	0.4	0.8	3.0	1.2	1.4	7.3	12.3	5.9	4.8	9.7	7.8	7.1	17.4	5.1

[a]Total: all businesses definitely in existence.
[b]Rose. Declined: entries noting unusually good or bad years.
[c]Trouble: entries noting serious trouble (e.g., suspension).
[d]Out of business: complete and estimated cases from Table 12.1.
[e]Unknown: cases where the business was not clearly in or out of operation. They are not included in totals, but are added here to show margin for error in percentage calculations. Percentages do not include unknowns.

Note: The data from 1855–60 are given to show the prewar fluctuation. These figures are not comparable to later data because they do not include companies formed before 1856 that failed before 1861.

Source: R. G. Dun & Co. Collection, Baker Library, Harvard University Graduate School of Business.

Table 12.3. The R. G. Dun Sample: Final Year in Business x Year Established

	Pre-1851			1851–55			1856–60			1861–65			All complete cases
	I[a]	II[b]	III[c]	I	II	III	I	II	III	I	II	III	
1856	—	—	—	—	—	—	1	0	1	—	—	—	—
1857	—	—	—	—	—	—	0	2	2	—	—	—	—
1858	—	—	—	—	—	—	8	1	9	—	—	—	—
1859	—	—	—	—	—	—	4	0	4	—	—	—	—
1860	—	—	—	—	—	—	4	1	5	—	—	—	—
1861	3	2	5	3	3	6	9	4	13	0	0	0	15
1862	2	3	5	2	4	6	8	15	23	1	0	1	15
1863	2	3	5	0	3	3	3	4	7	2	1	3	8
1864	3	0	3	1	0	1	3	1	4	6	0	6	13
1865	5	1	6	3	1	4	8	0	8	5	1	6	28
1866	1	0	1	2	2	4	4	1	5	6	1	7	19
1867	1	3	4	1	1	2	2	2	4	3	1	4	10
1868	2	2	4	2	8	10	2	6	8	5	5	10	12
1869	0	0	0	1	0	1	1	2	3	3	2	5	5
1870+	54	2	56	40	3	43	39	0	39	27	2	29	215
Total	73	16	89	55	25	80	96	39	135	58	13	71	340
Failed 1861–65	15	9	24	9	11	20	31	24	55	14	2	16	79
% Failed 1861–65[d]			27.0			25.0			48.2			22.5	23.2
% Survived to 1870			62.9			53.8			34.2			40.8	63.2
% Failed in first 5 years									15.6			22.5	

[a] I: complete data.
[b] II: estimated data.
[c] III: I plus II.
[d] % Failed 1861–65 only includes businesses in existence in 1861.

Note: For discussion of sources and methods see Appendix.

Source: R. G. Dun & Co. Collection, Baker Library, Harvard University Graduate School of Business.

businesses of varying ages. The results clearly demonstrate the relative stability of older establishments. Of 89 businesses that were at least a decade old before the war, 56 (62.9 percent) survived until the end of the 1860s and only 24 (27 percent) went out of business before 1866. These older firms showed little annual fluctuation in their pattern of failures during the war years. In contrast, nearly half (55 of 114) of the businesses formed within five years of the war and surviving until 1861, went under during the conflict; only 39 (34.2 percent) remained intact until the end of the decade. This group was particularly susceptible to the 1861 crisis, with 36 failing in 1861 or 1862. Those firms that were formed during the war years – largely after the secessionist crisis – fared better than the slightly older companies that battled the 1860–1 panic, but they suffered severely during the postwar depression. Only 16 of 71 (22.5 percent) firms founded between 1861 and 1865 failed during the war, whereas 26 of 55 (47.3 percent) of those establishments that survived through 1865 went under by 1870.

Table 12.3 also suggests that companies formed during the war had more difficulty in their early years than the companies launched in the five prewar years. Whereas 22.5 percent of the companies formed between 1861 and 1865 did not survive until 1866, only 15.6 percent of the companies founded between 1856 and 1860 folded before 1861. This difference would certainly have been greater save for the fact that most of the 1861–5 firms came into existence after the 1861 panic, whereas many in the 1856–60 cohort had to struggle through the crisis of 1857.[7]

If long-established firms tended to fare best during the secession crisis, wealth proved an even stronger guarantor against wartime failure. Table 12.4 analyzes the importance of net worth in assuring business survival. Among the largest companies, only 4 of 43 (9.3 percent) closed down during the war, and 35 (81.4 percent) survived until 1870. At the other end of the scale, over one-fourth of the firms known to be worth under $15,000 failed during the war, and only 57.5 percent survived until 1870.[8] Of course these figures do not demonstrate that larger companies actually did better than smaller companies during the war. Rather, they show that companies with substantial capital were best equipped to weather the early storm, whereas the owners of small establishments often went out of business because they could not meet their short-term obligations.

7 That is, even if the two panics had been of identical severity, their relative timing would have affected the two cohorts differently.
8 Most of the companies of "unknown" size, which folded in especially large numbers during the war, were probably quite small.

Table 12.4. The R. G. Dun Sample:
Final Year in Business x Estimated Worth

	I[a]	II[b]	III[c]	IV[d]	V[e]	Unknown	Total
1861	1	1	1	3	6	3	15
1862	0	1	1	1	11	1	15
1863	1	0	0	2	3	2	8
1864	0	1	2	1	6	3	13
1865	2	0	3	2	18	3	28
1866	3	0	1	4	11	0	19
1867	1	3	1	0	5	0	10
1868	0	0	1	1	9	1	12
1869	0	0	3	0	2	0	5
1870+	35	24	32	24	96	4	215
Total	43	30	45	38	167	17	340
Unknown	6	2	5	23	90	7	133
% Failed 1861–65	9	10	16	24	26	71	23
% Survived to 1870	81	80	71	63	57	24	63

[a]I: over $99,999
[b]II: $50,000–99,999
[c]III: $25,000–49,999
[d]IV: $15,000–24,000
[e]V: under $15,000

Note: The table includes only complete cases. The percentages do not include cases with unknown final years. A disproportionate number of these unknowns were smaller businesses. See the text and Appendix for a discussion of sources and methods.

Source: R. G. Dun & Co. Collection, Baker Library, Harvard University Graduate School of Business.

The findings in Tables 12.3 and 12.4 raise the possibility that they are identifying the same trend: that the oldest companies were also the largest. Table 12.5 attempts to weigh the relative importance of age and size by comparing, by "age cohort," the wartime experiences of large and small firms. The data from the smallest companies (category I in Table 12.4) yield no clear pattern. Six of 15 (40 percent) "old" small firms failed to survive to 1866,[9] whereas only 10.3 percent of the companies founded between 1851 and 1855 went out of business during the war. Those small companies founded in the five prewar years suffered particular hardships, with only 42.6 percent surviving until 1870.

The largest companies in Table 12.5 (categories IV and V in Table

9 These fifteen pre-1851 small firms make up about one-fourth of all the pre-1851 firms, but account for 40 percent of the pre-1866 failures among the oldest firms.

Table 12.5. The R. G. Dun Sample: Final Year in Business x Year Established x Estimated Worth

	pre-1861	1851–55	1856–60	1861–65	Unknown	Total
Smallest companies (under $15,000)						
1861	1	0	5	0	0	6
1862	0	1	7	1	2	11
1863	0	0	2	1	0	3
1864	1	1	2	2	0	5
1865	4	1	6	4	3	18
1866	0	1	3	4	3	11
1867	0	1	1	1	2	5
1868	1	2	1	4	1	9
1869	0	0	0	2	0	2
1870+	8	22	20	18	28	96
Total	15	29	59	37	39	166
Unknown	9	15	27	7	32	90
% Failed 1861–65	40.0	10.3	46.8	21.6	12.8	25.9
% Survived to 1870	53.3	75.9	42.6	48.6	71.8	57.8
Largest companies (over $49,999)						
1861	1	1	0	0	0	2
1862	1	0	0	0	0	1
1863	0	0	0	0	1	1
1864	0	0	0	1	0	1
1865	1	0	0	0	1	2
1866	1	1	0	0	1	3
1867	1	0	0	2	1	4
1868	0	0	0	0	0	0
1869	0	0	0	0	0	0
1870+	30	7	6	3	13	59
Total	35	9	6	6	17	81
Unknown	2	3	0	1	2	8
% Failed 1861–65	8.6	11.1	0.0	16.7	11.8	8.6
% Survived to 1870	85.7	77.8	100.0	50.0	76.5	72.8

Note: The sample did not include companies formed before 1856 that failed before 1861. Only complete cases were used.

Source: R. G. Dun & Co. Collection, Baker Library, Harvard University Graduate School of Business.

12.4) also display no evident trend. Only five large firms with known dates of origin failed during the war, and three of these date back before 1851. This figure, though, simply reflects the age distribution of the large firms. Thirty-seven of 62 (59.7 percent) of the datable firms with values over $49,999 were at least a decade old in 1861, as opposed to 24 of 198 smaller firms. Table 12.5 suggests the strong relationship between company age and size. But comparisons within specific age cohorts – those firms founded between 1856 and 1860 being the most striking – indicate that size alone provided strong protection against wartime failure.[10]

Table 12.6, which divides t... sampled businesses by type of enterprise, reflects the varied experiences of firms of similar size. Hoteliers, small retailers, and food and grain dealers failed at especially high rates during the war (44, 33, and 37 percent respectively); artisans and light manufacturers seem to have fared slightly better (29 percent); and small clothing producers (24 percent) did better still. These differences are not large, a comparison of small company failures in 1861 is more telling: 1 of 9 (11 percent) hoteliers and 16 of 205 (7.8 percent) retailers and food and grain dealers failed in the war's first year, whereas only 2 of 61 (3.3 percent) clothiers and 2 of 65 (3.1 percent) artisans and light manufacturers failed to survive the crisis. Such data support the conclusion, indicated by the city's building rates (see Table 11.3), that Philadelphia's retailers experienced a "weeding out" period during the secession crisis.

Table 12.6. The R. G. Dun Sample: Final Year in Business x Type of Enterprise

	I[a]	II[b]	III[c]	IV[d]	V[e]	VI[f]	VII[g]	VIII[h]	IX[i]	Total
Unknown	5	0	1	1	1	2	0	0	1	11
1861	10	6	1	2	2	0	0	0	3	24
1862	14	13	0	6	5	0	1	0	5	44
1863	7	0	3	2	4	1	0	2	1	20
1864	6	2	0	1	3	0	0	0	4	16
1865	5	8	0	4	5	2	1	0	5	30
1866	7	5	2	2	1	3	0	0	3	23
1867	6	3	0	3	3	1	0	0	2	18
1868	15	3	0	5	6	3	0	1	6	39
1869	0	4	1	2	1	1	0	0	2	11
1870	19	6	0	7	8	4	6	2	11	63
1870+	37	29	2	27	27	16	6	0	20	164
Total	131	79	10	62	66	33	14	5	63	463

The header also shows "Type of Enterprise" spanning columns III, IV, and V.

[a]I: retail stores (except below).
[b]II: food and grain retailers.
[c]III: hotels, taverns, and inns.
[d]IV: clothing: sales and small manufacturing.
[e]V: artisans and light manufacturing.
[f]VI: brokers, agents, bankers, and shipping.
[g]VII: food, tobacco, and grain importers (major houses).
[h]VIII: major clothing manufacturers.
[i]IX: manufacturing and heavy materials.

Source: R. G. Dun & Co. Collection, Baker Library, Harvard University Graduate School of Business.

Among larger establishment the numbers are small, but certain differences seem apparent. Only 2 of 14 (14.3 percent) large importers and 3 of 31 (10 percent) firms engaged in financial enterprises failed during the war, and no companies in either group failed in 1861. On the other hand, clothing manufacturers and heavy manufacturers and materials wholesalers performed similarly to light manufacturers, with 20 of 67 (29.9 percent) failing during the war years. To summarize, Philadelphia's retailers were hit hardest by the crisis, artisans and manufacturers of all stripes failed at fairly similar rates, and large investors – importers, bankers, shippers – weathered the storm most successfully.

Case histories in the R. G. Dun reports

The R. G. Dun data show that many establishments failed during the first year of the war, and that the panic dealt many more crippling blows that took their toll further down the line. The evidence also illustrates that the smallest and youngest businesses proved to be weakest during the crisis. The reports on specific firms support these conclusions, but individual stories also suggest the diversity of experience within those larger patterns.

In late 1857 twenty-three-year-old Samuel S. Hess opened up a dry goods store with less than $1,000 and no credit to his name. Within a year Hess's business had grown and R. G. Dun's reporter deemed him "safe" for a moderate amount of credit. On the eve of the war, he had "gd cr" and was "dg well." But then the sectional crisis caught up with the dry goods dealer, and in late January 1861 the young business failed without making any settlement. The war broke out soon after W. & R. McKinley had moved their thriving grocery business to a new store. In late 1859 R. G. Dun's ledgers had given the concern an "excellent" credit rating, but a month before Fort Sumter the report read "a little slow recently," and by June the McKinleys had joined Hess in failure.[11]

These were typical stories in 1861. New or overextended small businesses fell rapidly in the face of long months of stagnation. But other concerns managed to weather the crisis. T. E. Lippincott's dry goods store shared much in common with Hess's business. Lippincott went into operation in 1857 at the age of twenty-four with about $2,000 in capital. For two years the business prospered, but in early 1860 Lippincott temporarily went under and had to settle with his

10 Of course these findings are neither surprising nor unique to the war years. Older, larger firms were presumably less likely to fold under any circumstances.
11 Pennsylvania vol. 134:543, 138:133. R. G. Dun & Co. Collection, Baker Library, Harvard University Graduate School of Business (hereafter *RGD*).

creditors. On the eve of the war the young retailer was conducting a largely cash trade, with only moderate short-term credit. But whereas Hess failed almost immediately, Lippincott managed to survive several credit judgments in 1862 without giving up his business.[12]

Even the seemingly least stable small businesses sometimes managed to stay afloat through the troubles of 1861 and 1865. Felix Donnelly, a small grocer and liquor retailer, spent nearly a decade swimming against a current of angry creditors and hostile R. G. Dun agents. In 1854 the R. G. Dun ledger noted that Donnelly was an honest small businessman who was good for small amounts of credit. But in the following year his credit line was "doubtful," and in the next two years he lost a series of credit judgments, leaving the Irish retailer "unworthy of cr" in early 1861. Donnelly pressed on through the war, despite an 1864 report that described him as "a very unpopular man" and called his store "a sm. little hole." Soon after, Donnelly's son, who had long been his partner, took over the concern (and the poor credit rating) and kept it going until at least 1872.[13]

For hatters Franklin Ashby and Adam Rocap the Civil War was just one of a long series of trials. This small business, begun in 1844, enjoyed a "good" credit rating in the early 1850s, but suffered losses in late 1854 that made R. G. Dun's reporter suspect its stability. Ashby and Rocap slowly worked their credit rating up from "limited" to "fair" to "solid"; however, in the crisis of 1857 they suspended payments and then "failed on their extended papers." The pair stumbled through to the end of the decade and into the war years as a cash-only concern. During the early 1860's R. G. Dun's reporters repeatedly noted that they were "poor bus. men" with "very limited [credit] indeed" or entirely "sm. potatoes." But Ashby and Rocap managed to keep their doors open until 1867, when Rocap left the concern.[14]

The experiences of the Donnellys and Ashby and Rocap reflect the greater capacity of established businesses – even unsteady ones – to survive the 1861 crisis. Indeed, both establishments might have been well served by their poor prewar credit ratings. By relying largely on a cash trade, neither suffered the burdens of overextension that destroyed many firms in 1861.[15]

Henry Tryson's credit record tells the same tale at an even smaller scale. Tryson opened up his grocery business in 1850, after his

12 But this success was short-lived. After surviving for several years the young business folded during the postwar decline. See *RGD* 133:54, 296HH.
13 *RGD* 134:563.
14 *RGD* 131:239, 289A.
15 Lippincott's business probably also "profited" from its cash-only status at the start of the war.

brother had failed in the same spot. R. G. Dun's reporter skeptically noted Tryson's "hist of failing" and recommended caution. Twelve months later the grocer temporarily went out of business, but within a few months he was at it again. For the next decade Tryson scratched out a living and earned a reputation for prompt payment of small advances. In 1864 the credit reporter valued the fourteen-year-old concern at a mere $500. Yet Tryson, like Lippincott, managed to make it through the war – only to fail at its conclusion.[16]

One more small business profile suggests both the range of the R. G. Dun reports and the durability of Philadelphia's small entrepreneurs. James Gibbons arrived from California in 1855 with $300 and a "suspect" credit rating. Soon he established himself as an energetic dry goods peddler, good for a small amount of credit. By the Civil War Gibbons had his own store, and in 1863 he moved his prospering business to a new location. The war did not appear to hurt him so much as a major fire in early 1865 and a crippling robbery the following year. These misadventures weakened his credit rating, but soon Gibbons returned to good favor, and he continued to prosper into the 1870s.[17]

The quantitative data suggest that somewhat larger concerns fared better than small businesses. But their individual histories indicate equally diverse experiences. Although smaller grocers struggled, Philip Donahue's moderate-sized grocery and provisions trade apparently survived unscathed, receiving a "good" credit rating at regular intervals from 1860 to 1872. Andrews and Thorn's grocery concern, which began in the early 1850s, enjoyed an unchanged annual rating from 1860 to 1870.[18] John S. Wood's wartime success was far more spectacular. In the mid-1850s, while still in his early twenties, Wood became a commission merchant, trading in leather. By the Civil War he had established himself as a moderate trader, and during the early 1860s he maintained a good credit rating. In the middle of the war Wood was worth an estimated $10,000, but in the last years of the conflict his business boomed. By mid-1866 R. G. Dun listed him as worth between $75,000 and $100,000, and in the following years his prosperity reached even greater heights.[19]

Ludwig Siedenback also prospered during the war, but was unable to sustain his success after the conflict. Siedenback took over his brother's small gentlemen's furnishings business in 1856. In early 1861 R. G. Dun's agent wrote that Siedenback was "gd for his sm

16 *RGD* 133:69.
17 *RGD* 136:347, 665.
18 *RGD* 132:551, 395; 138:253. Andrews died in 1863 and Thorne took over sole control of this business.
19 *RGD* 136:447.

wants" and that "the present troubles as yet do not appear to affect him." In the next few years the German entrepreneur prospered, increasing his estimated worth from $10,000 to 15,000 in 1859, to $20,000 to 30,000 in 1864. In the last year of the war, when many lost their wartime profits, Siedenback's business fared particularly well, raising its worth to $50,000. After the war he maintained an excellent reputation until early 1868, when a major fire and heavy losses in gold and oil stocks ravaged his business.[20]

These four examples describe moderate-sized businesses that survived the secession crisis without difficulty. Although this was the norm, other similarly sized establishments were not so fortunate. Thayer and Cowperthwaite's boot and shoe commission house enjoyed a good reputation during the late 1850s, but suspended payments immediately after the war began.[21] For the next six years the firm carried on business without fully meeting its liabilities or regaining the confidence of the trade. In 1867 the R. G. Dun agent wrote that the company had completely recovered. But according to the reports, this successful struggle owed much to continued financial assistance from the partners' families.[22] Jacob Goldsmith, a middling businessman who lacked such a buffer, failed to keep afloat during the panic. In 1855 Goldsmith joined his brother's clothing store, and three years later he took over the establishment, which R. G. Dun's reporter valued at $10,000. In early 1861 Goldsmith moved his growing business to a new location. This move proved premature, for that May the economic stagnation forced him to secure extensions from his creditors. In the months to come he failed to pay his debts, and in early 1862 the clothier went out of business.[23]

The R. G. Dun records contain evidence of businesses responding to the crisis by turning to war manufacturing or other forms of profiteering, which will be treated next. But the experience of one firm that did not become a war contractor illustrates the war's far-reaching impact. By 1860 Edmund Hindle and Son's machine-making factory had enjoyed ten years of moderate success. Unlike the owners of many other machine works, the Hindles chose not to shift into military manufacturing when the war began. Nevertheless, they benefited from the "war boom" when Alfred Jenks and Son, their chief competitor, abruptly shifted to arms manufacturing. Jenks's move left

---

20 *RGD* 131:284II.
21 The R. G. Dun reports mention no business ties with the South, but perhaps this company, like many of its counterparts, suspended because of lost Southern trade.
22 *RGD* 137:417.
23 *RGD* 135:320B. Goldsmith soon turned his misfortune to his advantage by entering a government contracting partnership with Michael Jacobs. In a short time the two earned $50,000.

a substantial void in the nonwar output of Philadelphia's machinists, and Hindle and Son's Good Intent Factory had a banner year as a result. This fortuitous turn of events helped to carry the factory through several good seasons, but in late 1864 the general business decline took the Hindles' factory as one of its victims.[24]

As we have seen, very few of Philadelphia's largest, most well-established firms folded during the war. Although many joined Jenks and Sons, Merrick and Sons, and Baldwin Locomotives in profiting from military contracts, others merely continued their traditional activities. The glass manufactory of Whitall, Tatum and Company entered 1860 with substantial assets and a solid reputation as the nation's largest glass business. Between 1855 and 1870, R. G. Dun's agents never wavered in giving the firm an "excellent" rating. In 1858 the reporter valued the manufacturing concern at $100,000; by mid-1865 that figure had risen to $750,000.[25] Moore and Campion, cabinetmakers, did not experience so great a wartime boom, but they did enjoy similar stability. In 1858 this firm had been in operation for over twenty years, and the credit reporter listed its worth at over $150,000. Subsequent reports do not note a decline in 1860–1, and in 1865 its estimated value was $250,000.[26]

Some large firms did feel the war's adverse economic pressure. E. W. Bailey and Company's jewelry establishment dated back to the 1840s, and had long been termed an "excellent house." But in April 1861 R. G. Dun's agent wrote that it was "not dg much bus at the present on acct of the political troubles." The difference between Bailey and Company and many small Philadelphia retailers was noted by the credit reporter: "but have an undoubted credit." Bailey and Company rode out the storm without serious difficulty, and in 1863 and 1864 R. G. Dun's records reported that the old establishment had had unusually good years.[27] Even when large firms were affected by the war's economic turmoil, they generally had the strength to survive several difficult years.

Firms with Southern ties

The secession crisis disrupted all forms of Northern business. However, those who traded with the South suffered most as Southern markets closed and rebel debtors refused to meet their obligations. A survey of the R. G. Dun records on Philadelphia's wartime businesses yielded fifty-three firms, engaged in a wide range of

24   *RGD* 135:145.
25   *RGD* 133:69, 130. Before 1857 this firm was called Whitall Brothers and Company.
26   *RGD* 132:511, 630.
27   *RGD* 131:37, 284LL.

Table 12.7. The R. G. Dun Sample: Firms with Southern Ties

| Type of Enterprise | Survived the War Without Suspending? | | |
	Yes	No	Total
Boots/shoes	4	5	9
Clothing	3	4	7
Dry goods	4	0	4
Liquor	1	3	4
Drugs	0	3	3
Saddles	3	0	3
Cloth	1	1	2
Hardware	1	1	2
Hats	0	2	2
Seeds	2	0	2
Books	0	1	1
Chemicals	0	1	1
China	0	1	1
Finance	1	0	1
Guns	1	0	1
Importers	1	0	1
Looms	1	0	1
Mirrors	0	1	1
Notions	0	1	1
Perfume	0	1	1
Shipping	1	0	1
Stoves	1	0	1
Straw goods	0	1	1
Trimmings	0	1	1
Varieties	0	1	1
Total	25	28	53

Note: Two companies survived through the war and failed in late 1865. This explains the slight difference between these figures and those in Table 12.7.

Source: R. G. Dun & Co. Collection, Baker Library, Harvard University Graduate School of Business. See the text and Appendix for a discussion of methods.

enterprises, with prewar Southern ties (see Table 12.7).[28] Nearly all experienced some difficulties as the war commenced, and 30 either suspended or failed before 1866 (Table 12.8). Although a firm's age did not protect it from the loss of Southern revenues, Table 12.8 suggests that well-established businesses were better equipped to survive.[29] Only one of thirteen firms founded before 1851 failed

28 Of course the R. G. Dun reporters might have been more likely to mention businesses with Southern ties that had run into troubles because of those connections.
29 The data are too scanty to permit statistically based conclusions on the role of size in protecting businesses with Southern ties. But it seems that those older firms that fared the best were often quite large. In general, these businesses were larger than those in the R. G. Dun sample.

Table 12.8. The R. G. Dun Sample: Firms with Southern Ties, Year of Origin x Final Year in Business

Final year	Unknown	First Year Pre-1851	1851–62	Total
1861	0	0	4	4
1862	1	1	2	4
1863	3	0	1	4
1864	1	0	0	1
1865	2	0	1	3
1866	2	0	3	5
1867	0	1	1	2
1868	0	0	2	2
1869	0	2	0	2
1870+	7	7	4	18
Over 1865[a]	2	2	2	6
Unknown[b]	2	0	0	2
Total	20	13	20	53
Failed 1861–65	7	1	8	16
% failed	35.0	7.7	40.0	30.2
Survived suspension	4	5	5	14
% survived suspension	20.0	38.5	25.0	26.4
Survived with trouble[c]	2	4	1	7
% survived with trouble	10.0	30.8	5.0	13.2
Survived without trouble	7	3	6	16
% survived without trouble	35.0	23.1	30.0	30.2

[a]Firms with final year over 1865 survived through 1865 but their final year is unknown.
[b]In all calculations I have treated the two cases with unknown final years as survivors of the war.
[c]"Trouble" refers to serious difficulties not resulting in suspension.

Source: R. G. Dun & Co. Collection, Baker Library, Harvard University Graduate School of Business.

between 1861 and 1865, as compared to eight of twenty founded between 1851 and 1862.

As Table 12.7 demonstrates, those who traded with the South dealt in a great variety of goods. Some entered 1861 with sufficient capital to withstand heavy short-term losses, whereas smaller, less stable companies found the burden too great. DeCoursey, Lafoureade & Co., a wealthy cloth firm, was "largely in the southern trade" at the war's outset but R. G. Dun's reporters never wavered in giving this long-established company a strong rating, and in 1864 it enjoyed a net worth estimated at $400,000. Similarly, the dry goods firm of S. B. Bancroft & Co. entered 1861 with $300,000 to $400,000 due it from the South, but by 1865 – after absorbing heavy wartime losses – the firm still enjoyed a reputation as one of the city's best, with a value of a half million dollars.[30]

Other well-established businesses were not so lucky. A. W. Harrison's perfume and ink company had a "good" credit rating in 1857 and a "moderate" rating in 1860 but in December 1860, Harrison, who engaged in a profitable Southern trade, saw dark clouds ahead and asked his creditors if they would grant extensions should he require them. Responding to hostile rumors the following February, Harrison insisted that his credit was still good; however, during the summer of 1861, with many of his assets unreachable in the South, he began to seek extensions. For two years Harrison struggled to keep his business intact, but in mid-1863 he lost a series of credit judgments and by the end of 1863 he had failed and sold out.[31]

For Siter, VanCulen and Glass the end came far more swiftly. This "varieties" firm was founded in 1853 and enjoyed a strong reputation by 1861. In February R. G. Dun's agent wrote that "they do considerable bus. with the South, but very little with the cotton states." He added: "we do not think they will suffer seriously from the present panic." Two months later the firm received an extension on its debts, but its positive reputation enabled it to keep a "fair" credit rating. In August the credit reporter noted that Siter, VanCulen and Glass was "winding up its affairs," and a month later the firm was out of business.[32]

Between the examples of unbending strength and dramatic failure, the R. G. Dun records paint numerous portraits of traders with the South who limped through the war years bloodied but not defeated. Sibley, Molten, and Woodruff, a silk trading company dating back to 1854, entered 1861 with an estimated worth of $150,000; but the onset of war found them with $200,000 in Southern debts, forcing them to suspend their payments and deal only in cash for over a year before fully recovering. The shoe manufacturing partnership of Hendry and Harris entered the war years in "very good standing," but soon failed when it found itself unable to collect $30,000 from Southern debtors. A year later, E. A. Hendry reentered business on his own and slowly paid off the old firm's debts at 40 percent. By the middle of 1864 Hendry's estimated worth was $10,000 (as opposed to $40,000 in 1857), and the company prospered until his death in December 1866.[33]

30 *RGD* 131:284D; 136:573
31 *RGD* 134:638.
32 *RGD* 131:284II.
33 *RGD* 131:284II; 134:445.

Two cases indicate that at least some Philadelphia businessmen were unwilling simply to write off their Southern debts. When the war began, liquor dealer N. Vanbeil left the business in his brother's hands and disappeared into the Confederacy to collect from his debtors personally. For the next four years the business flourished under his brother's watchful eye, but Vanbeil did not return. Finally, at the war's conclusion, a victorious Vanbeil came home amidst rumors that he had earned $80,000 in gold running cotton to Europe. R. G. Dun's reporter could not confirm the stories, but a few months later Vanbeil sold his liquor establishment and moved to New York.[34] The hardware firm of Field, Langstroth and Company took a slightly different route toward recouping its losses. This long-established concern had a "reliable" reputation through the 1850s. When the war began, the firm had a substantial amount of money tied up in the South, but "they managed to follow the Army through Kentucky & Tenn & secured a large amount of cotton in payment for debts out of which they realized a sm fortune."[35]

Firms with government contracts

A survey of the R. G. Dun records yielded 138 firms with government war contracts. This is not a complete list – R. G. Dun's agents did not systematically record all war contractors. But these enterprises substantially reflect the range of military contracting in Philadelphia, and thus serve as an excellent means of observing the impact of war contracting on the city's entrepreneurs.

The R. G. Dun records usually took note of the type of war contract held by each firm. Table 12.9 summarizes this range of local activities. More than a quarter of these firms supplied uniforms to the army; an additional 15 percent furnished boots, shoes, and equipment. Others profited in more unorthodox enterprises. Dr. B. Frank Palmer earned a small fortune supplying the army with artificial limbs. By April 1864 Condit Pruden reportedly had sold the government 100,000 saddletrees, at a profit of between fifty and seventy-five cents each.[36]

Usually war contractors adjusted their established business to meet the army's needs. But in some instances a firm substantially retooled. Before the war, George W. Simons & Brother manufactured gold chains, thimbles, and pencils. In 1861 R. G. Dun's agent reported that this established business had "altered thr machinery for

34 *RGD* 138:213.
35 *RGD* 132:626.
36 *RGD* 133:183; 140:180.

Table 12.9. The R. G. Dun Sample: War Contractors

	Known	Assumed[a]	Total	Percent[b]
Clothing	24	7	31	27.4
Haversacks and canteens	11		11	9.7
Guns / rifles	8		8	7.1
Boots / shoes	6	1	7	6.2
Blankets	6		6	5.3
Saddles	3	2	5	4.4
Tents	4		4	3.5
Swords / bayonets	4		4	3.5
Cannons	3		3	2.7
Ships	3		3	2.7
Bread	2		2	1.8
Wagons	2		2	1.8
Saddle trees	2		2	1.8
Food	2		2	1.8
Coal	1		1	0.9
Brushes	1		1	0.9
Drums	1		1	0.9
Mint acids	1		1	0.9
Lumber	1		1	0.9
Stockings	1		1	0.9
Hospital bedsteads	1		1	0.9
Ship timber	1		1	0.9
Hay and feed	1		1	0.9
Stoves	1		1	0.9
Potatoes	1		1	0.9
Gun locks	1		1	0.9
Propellors	1		1	0.9
Surgical instruments	1		1	0.9
Horses	1		1	0.9
Locomotives	1		1	0.9
Caps	1		1	0.9
Ship engines	1		1	0.9
Drugs	1		1	0.9
Shot and shell	1		1	0.9
Shipping	1		1	0.9
Harness leather	1		1	0.9
Artificial limbs	1		1	0.9
Unknown	35		25	
Total	138		138	100.0

[a]Assumed cases are based on prewar activities rather than on a credit report entry identifying a particular contract.
[b]Percentages are based on a total of 113 cases with known or assumed types of contract.

Source: R. G. Dun & Co. Collection, Baker Library, Harvard University Graduate School of Business.

the mfr of swords & are dg a large & profitable bus." Samuel Sheble and John M. Fisher ran the Fair Mount Fork Works before the war, but in mid-1861 they began manufacturing bayonets and cavalry sabres. This transition required a substantial investment that, the credit reporter noted, had "a tendency to cramp them a little." But

Table 12.10. The R. G. Dun Sample: War Contractors, Final Year in Business

	Complete Cases	Estimated cases	Total
1861	0	0	0
1862	4	0	4
1863	3	0	3
1864	4	1	5
1865	13	0	13
1866	9	4	13
1867	9	3	12
1868	3	8	11
1869	2	3	5
1870+	51	14	65
Total	98	33	131
Out of business 1861–65	24	1	25
% out of business	24.5	3.0	19.1
Data from General Sample (Table 12.1)			
Total	340	112	452
Out of business 1861–65	79	55	134
% out of business	23.2	49.1	29.6

Note: For an explanation of methods and terms see Appendix.

Source: R. G. Dun & Co. Collection, Baker Library, Harvard University Graduate School of Business.

soon the partners began making a healthy profit on their government contracts.[37]

Of course such adjustments often required further shifts at the end of the war. Ex-Colonel William H. Gray "made money" supplying swords to the army, and when the war ended he switched to manufacturing gas fixtures. Others did not readjust so successfully. Sail maker Charles E. Miller went into tent manufacturing when the war began, but by the end of April 1865 his highly successful enterprise had gone out of business. At the outset of the conflict H. G. Clagstone began to manufacture shoulder straps and other military goods. Through 1864 he did fairly well, but by May 1865 he had lost two credit judgments, and soon closed shop and moved to Virginia.[38]

These examples suggest how varied was the experience of Philadelphia's war contractors. Table 12.10 shows that the aggregate failure rate for 131 war contracting firms was quite similar to the general sample of 452 cases described in Table 12.1. Sixty-five of 131 war contractors (49.6 percent) survived until 1870; 50.2 percent of the

37   *RGD* 132:381; 133:296K.
38   *RGD* 141:13; 141:131; 142:6.

larger sample lasted through the war decade. But this apparent similarity masks a clear difference. Only 25 (19.1 percent) war contractors failed between 1861 and 1865, whereas 29.6 percent of the overall sample failed during the war years. It should be noted that many war contracting businesses formed in response to military demand, and thus after the destructive panic of 1861, which helps explain their higher wartime success rate.[39] And as we have seen, many war contractors folded as soon as demand ended, resulting in an 1861 to 1869 failure rate similar to the entire sample.

The R. G. Dun reports of annual fluctuations for war contractors (Table 12.11) provide a further point of comparison with the larger sample. The chronology is by now familiar. A high percentage of these firms ran into trouble in 1857 and in 1861, and roughly a fifth improved in both 1862 and 1863. How do these figures compare with those of other R. G. Dun businesses? Although the timing of peaks and valleys is essentially the same, the war contractors' experiences were far more volatile. A higher percentage of war contractors ran into trouble in 1857 and 1861 than firms in the larger sample. And a much greater share of war contractors experienced substantial gains in the midwar years.

This first fact suggests the possibility that war contractors turned to the government when their normal activities ran into trouble. Such was certainly the case for many companies with Southern ties. The extremely high percentage of war contractors enjoying strong gains in 1862 and 1863 demonstrates that supplying the army was a profitable occupation. But it also could indicate that many of these companies might have been "down" in 1861, making their later successes particularly noteworthy to the credit reporters.

The case studies offer support for the suggestion that war contracting served as a vehicle for recovery. G. Hoff and Company's Cap Manufactory fared well through the 1850s, but suspended in 1861. The firm soon settled its debts and earned new prosperity by winning a government cap contract. The Phoenix Iron Company suspended in 1857 and again in 1861, but boomed during the war by manufacturing cannons. Even musical instrument manufacturer C. M. Zimmerman benefited from the recuperative powers of the war. Through the 1850s he struggled along with little or no credit rating. But late in the war Zimmerman won a contract to furnish drums to the government, and R. G. Dun's agent listed him as worth $15,000 and "good for mod amts." Beggs and Rowland, Philadelphia wheelwrights, are a dramatic illustration of this phenomenon. In May 1861, R. G. Dun's ledger read that the panic had left the partnership "a little tight," but the

39 Of course the war-induced profits also helped explain these successes.

Table 12.11. The R. G. Dun Sample: War Contractors, Annual Fluctuations, 1855–69

	1855	1856	1857	1858	1859	1860	1861	1862	1863	1864	1865	1866	1867	1868	1869
Total	57	62	72	81	88	97	112	120	122	125	110	88	73	62	59
Rose	0	0	0	1	2	0	6	26	23	10	2	1	0	0	0
Declined	0	0	0	1	1	4	5	9	0	2	4	5	1	0	1
Trouble	0	0	8	3	1	4	10	2	7	0	4	1	4	1	0
Unknown	37	35	27	22	22	15	13	8	4	2	4	14	22	29	27
Out of business							0	4	3	5	13	13	12	11	5
% Rose	0	0	0	1	2	0	5	22	19	8	2	1	0	0	0
% Declined	0	0	0	1	1	4	4	8	0	2	4	6	1	0	2
% Trouble	0	0	11	4	1	4	9	2	6	0	4	1	5	2	0
% Out of business							0	3	2	4	12	15	16	18	8.5
Data from General Sample (Table 12.2)															
% Rose	0	0	0	0	1	0	1	3	3	2	1	0	1	0	0
% Declined	1	1	1	1	1	1	3	4	1	3	1	1	3	1	1
% Trouble	1	1	3	3	1	2	6	4	1	3	1	0	2	2	1
% Out of business							7	12	6	5	10	8	7	17	5

Note: The data from 1855–60 are given to show the prewar fluctuation. These figures are not comparable to the later data because they do not include companies formed before 1856 which failed before 1861. See Table 12.2 for definitions of categories.

Source: R. G. Dun & Co. Collection, Baker Library, Harvard University Graduate School of Business.

Table 12.12. The R. G. Dun Sample: War Contractors, Year of Origin x Final Year in Business

	Pre-1851	1851–55	1856–60	1861–65	Unknown	Total
1860	0	0	0	0	0	0
1861	0	0	0	0	0	0
1862	0	0	1	2	1	4
1863	0	0	0	1	2	3
1864	1	0	0	3	1	5
1865	0	1	4	4	4	13
1866	1	2	1	6	3	13
1867	1	2	4	2	3	12
1868	3	2	0	2	4	11
1869	1	2	1	1	0	5
1870+	21	13	9	8	14	65
Unknown	3	1	0	1	2	7
Total	31	23	20	30	34	138
Failed 1861–65	1	1	5	10	8	25
% Failed 1861–65	3.3	4.5	33.3	50.0	30.8	22.1
% Survived to 1870	75.0	59.1	45.0	27.6	43.8	49.6

Note: This table includes both complete and estimated cases. Percentages do not include cases with unknown final years.

Source: R. G. Dun & Co. Collection, Baker Library, Harvard University Graduate School of Business.

reporter was confident that they would "come out all right" with the aid of a government contract. Shortly thereafter, though, the firm suffered heavy losses in a fire. This second blow could easily have crippled them, but according to the R. G. Dun agent the company "pushed forward thr Government contracts as fast as possible," and soon triumphed over adversity.[40]

Tables 12.12 and 12.13 consider the importance of age and size in dictating the success of Philadelphia's government contractors. Table 12.12 demonstrates that, as in the general sample, longer-established war contractors fared best during the war. Seventy-five percent of the war contracting firms founded before 1851 survived until 1870, whereas only 45 percent of the firms begun between 1856 and 1860 did so. Both of these figures are slightly higher than the record of the general sample.[41] Only eight of thirty (27.6 percent) war contracting firms founded during the war survived until 1870, as opposed to 40.8 percent among the general sample. This is further evidence that firms

40   RGD 132:484; 134:543; 134:557; 134:645.
41   This presumably reflects the larger average size of war contracting companies.

Table 12.13. The R. G. Dun Sample:
War Contractors, Final Year in Business x Estimated Worth

	I	II	III	IV	V	Unknown	Total
1861	0	0	0	0	0	0	0
1862	0	0	1	0	2	1	4
1863	2	0	1	0	0	0	3
1864	0	1	2	0	0	1	4
1865	5	1	2	0	4	1	13
1866	1	4	2	1	1	0	9
1867	3	2	1	1	1	1	9
1868	3	0	0	0	0	0	3
1869	0	0	2	0	0	0	2
1870+	24	9	8	5	4	1	51
Unknown	12	7	9	1	6	5	40
Total	50	24	28	8	18	10	138
% Failed 1861–65	18	12	32	0	50	60	24
% Survived to 1870	63	53	42	71	33	20	52

Note: See Table 12.4 for definitions of categories. Only complete cases were used. The percentages do not include cases with unknown final years. See the text and Appendix for sources and methods.

Source: R. G. Dun & Co. Collection, Baker Library, Harvard University Graduate School of Business.

founded to fill war contracts often went out of business when the war ended.[42]

Table 12.12 also allows us to compare the age of war contracting businesses with Philadelphia firms as a whole. Thirty percent of the war contracting businesses formed before 1851, as compared to 25 percent of the general sample. Conversely, 40 percent of the general companies were formed in the five prewar years, as opposed to 19 percent of the war contractors. Among established companies, older firms were apparently somewhat better prepared to win war contracts. At the same time, Table 12.12 indicates that a disproportionate number of companies founded between 1861 and 1865 went into military contracting (29 percent as opposed to 20 percent in the general sample), suggesting that the war presented attractive options for hopeful entrepreneurs.

Table 12.13 considers the role of wealth in creating successful war contractors. Once again, the pattern mirrors the general sample:

42 Of course this does not necessarily indicate "failure" in any damaging sense. Some war contractors retired rich; others shut down their operations and went on to other profitable endeavors. But many struggled through the post-war years.

larger companies did better than smaller ones. The largest war contractors, however, were not quite as impregnable as in the general
sample. Only 4 of 43 (9.3 percent) sampled firms worth over $100,000
(with known or estimated final years) went out of business during the
war, and one of these folded during the 1861 panic. In contrast, 7 of
38 (18.4 percent) large war contractors closed between 1861 and 1865.
This table also shows that Philadelphia's war contracting firms were,
on average, larger than the norm. Of 128 war contractors with estimated sizes, 39 percent percent were worth $100,000 or more. Only
12 percent of the general sample firms were this large. Conversely, 57
percent of the sampled firms, and only 14 percent of the war contractors had estimated worths under $15,000.[43] But primarily the data
reflect the fact that war contracting companies were usually manufacturers, whereas a large share of the sampled establishments were
small retailers.[44]

The R. G. Dun records demonstrate that Philadelphia's war contractors were a mixed lot. Some became quite wealthy along the way.
Before the war, Emanuel Hey and his brother ran a small wool and
worsted establishment, valued at about $10,000 in late 1859. The Heys
engaged in government work throughout the conflict, and by February 1865 their firm's estimated value had risen to $100,000.[45] But
others could not stay afloat, even with the aid of government contracts. Henry W. Scott dealt in fancy goods before the war. In 1857 his
company failed, and he struggled on with little credit until he won an
army clothing contract in 1862. In late 1862 R. G. Dun's agent reported that Scott had made money on government work, but in early
1863 the Philadelphian failed once again.[46] In at least four cases local
war contractors struggled because the government was slow in paying its bills.[47]

In his study of Philadelphia textiles, Philip Scranton sought to
trace the histories of several local contractors. He was able to find
1860 and 1870 census data on twenty-five known contractors or sub-
contractors. Scranton concluded that "the paired characteristics of
flexibility and specialization" marked the wartime activities of these
mills. All six blanket contractors, for instance, had been occupied in

---

43 These figures are partly a product of the estimation procedure, which typically
    evaluated firms based on their 1864 worth and therefore inflated the value of
    prosperous war contractors. See Appendix.
44 Combining the age and wealth variables yields predictable results. At one end of
    the spectrum, 81 percent of the war contractors worth $50,000 or more and
    founded before 1856 survived until 1870. At the other end, only 36 percent of the
    smaller firms founded between 1856 and 1865 survived through the war decade.
45 *RGD* 134:603.
46 *RGD* 136:380.
47 *RGD* 135:320; 136:443; 137:456; 140:156.

other textile a͞ti͞.͞.͞ties in 1860. Scranton also found that nearly all
twenty-five firms expanded over the war decade, indicating the economic viability of war contracting.[48]

The evidence from both the fraud hearings (discussed in Chapter
11) and the R. G. Dun records reinforce the conclusion that Philadelphia's war contractors were particularly flexible. In some cases
businessmen, such as William Cozens, profited through the sale of
products they knew very little about. In other instances, as we have
seen, manufacturers devoted considerable capital to switching their
machinery to accommodate war demands. Clearly, the fortunes of
war often went to the most adventuresome entrepreneurs.[49]

John Rice's experiences reflect this pattern. Until the early 1850s
Rice made his living as a building contractor. Then he gave up
building entirely and bought part of a marble quarry. In mid-1856
R. G. Dun's agent wrote that the forty-five-year-old Rice was "bold in
his undertakings" and had "good judgment." Within a year this
boldness had led him into a lost credit judgment, but by 1859 R. G.
Dun's records once again labeled him "safe & reliable," and when the
war came he was a rich man. In December 1861 a R. G. Dun reporter
called Rice "A very energetic bus. man" and "a large & bold oper-
ator." The report added that the ex-builder and one-time quarry
owner had "taken a large contract for manufg muskets." This contract
apparently served him well, for by 1867 Rice, who was then listed as
an architect, was worth more than $100,000. Rice's record of flexibility
is certainly impressive, but not unique. Indeed, it was this ability to
adapt to new circumstances that gave Philadelphians a dominant role
in supplying the Union army.

A shoddy aristocracy?

In July 1864 a *Harper's Magazine* article called "The Fortunes of War"
attacked the "enterprising money-getters" who had profited from the
nation's misfortunes. These men, the article charged, initially built
fortunes on the sale of cheap "shoddy" and then later prospered by
stock speculation.[50] Such claims appeared frequently in the North's
magazines and newspapers. We have seen that there were many in

---

48 Philip Scranton, *Proprietary Capitalism: The Textile Manufacture at Philadelphia, 1800–
    1885* (Philadelphia, 1983) 294–300. Of course this last point is biased in including
    only those firms that survived until 1870.
49 For instance, Cozens attributed his war success to gambling on the profitability of
    cotton duck when the war began.
50 Robert Tomes, "The Fortunes of War," *Harper's New Monthly Magazine* 29 (July
    1864): 227–31.

Table 12.14. The R. G. Dun Sample:
Men with Incomes over $100,000 in 1864

Major Occupation	Number	Wealthy Before War	Rich / richer During War
Iron works	6	5	3
Coal	4	2	4
Commission merchant	3	3	
Locomotive manufacturer	3	3	3
Banker	2	2	2
Wool manufacturer	2	1	2
Distiller	1	1	
Drugs	1	1	
Gas coal company / gas meters	1	1	
Spice dealer	1	1	1
Steam engine manufacturer	1	1	1
Steam propeller manufacturer	1	1	
Total	26	22	16

Note: This table only summarizes information in the R. G. Dun Credit reports. Ten of the 36 men with incomes over $100,000 do not appear in these volumes. These include a banker, a manufacturer, and an engineer all of whom were wealthy before the war. The R. G. Dun reports noted that seven of these men had wartime government contracts, but only one—William L. Hunter, Jr.—appears to have become rich through these contracts.

Sources: "The Rich Men of Philadelphia" — Income Tax of the Residents of Philadelphia and Bucks County for the Year Ending April 30, 1865 (Philadelphia, 1865); R. G. Dun & Co. Collection, Baker Library, Harvard University Graduate School of Business.

Philadelphia who profited handsomely from the war. But one question remains: Were the city's wealthiest men war profiteers?

At the close of the war, Philadelphia's book dealers sold a printed summary of the "Rich Men of Philadelphia" based on income tax returns for the year ending on April 20, 1865. The list included thirty-six men who had annual incomes of over $100,000. A search of the R. G. Dun index yielded reports on twenty-six of these prosperous Philadelphians. Their wartime experiences are summarized in Table 12.14. The occupations (or sources of income) of these men reflect the nature of mid-nineteenth century Philadelphia's economy. The great majority were involved in either manufacturing or mining. Only five were engaged in some form of importing, and two – F. A. Drexel and A. J. Drexel – were in banking. The R. G. Dun records suggest that ten of these men did not became appreciably more wealthy during the war; only four clearly become rich because of the conflict. Of seven with wartime government contracts, only one, William L. Hunter, Jr., gained great wealth thereby.

In 1858 Hunter, a twenty-nine-year-old with "little or no means," became a member of the new clothing firm, Lippincott, Hunter and Scott. This partnership ran into trouble in 1859, but managed to win an army clothing contract in 1861. At first this seemed a successful arrangement, but at the end of 1861 the partnership dissolved. Hunter and Scott took their profits, founded a coal company, and began trading in Treasury notes and government securities. In November Hunter and Scott also dissolved, and Hunter went into the coal business in his own name. On June 30, 1864, R. G. Dun's agent cataloged Hunter's wartime activities:

> H. is 35. formerly in clothing bus. at the commencement of the war went to Washington, D.C. & made an immense sum of money rebuilding RRs came back here & started in the coal bus is a bold & daring operator, worth 300m$ [$300,000] (has various partners in his various enterprises such as Jay Cooke, Wm G. Moorhead & others) is dg a large bus has contracts for supplying Govt vessels making money rapidly and deemed perfectly good.[51]

Hunter's successes continued for at least the next few years. The tax list shows him with an income of $163,000 in the last year of the war, and by October 1865 his estimated worth had risen to $500,000. In January 1867 he went out of business, but the report gives no evidence of any troubles that might have precipitated that move.

Hunter's story is an extreme example of the business possibilities existing during wartime. At one point or another he profited from clothing contracts, government railroad building, military shipping, Treasury bills, and government securities. Despite this exception, it appears that Philadelphia's wealthiest businessmen earned their money primarily through established channels, perhaps supplementing their incomes through government contracting or speculation.

Conclusion

In 1860 Philadelphia was one of America's leading manufacturing and commercial centers. Five years of war did much to change its economic life, but did not fundamentally alter its character. Rather, it underscored the strength and flexibility of the Philadelphia economy.

Citizens on the home front faced rising prices, declining real wages, lost Southern markets, and periodic shortages. In Philadelphia, as in the rest of the Union, wartime economic change occurred in three overlapping stages. The first, beginning with the initial rumors of secession and continuing through the middle of 1862, saw the economy struggling through a panic that rivaled the

51   *RGD* 137:293.

one in 1857. The second stage, in which businesses recovered and then boomed, began for some military contractors as early as the end of 1861 and carried most of the city through three years of prosperity. As the war drew to a close, the economy went through a third stage in which government contracts dried up, prices fell, and many Philadelphians suffered through a decline lasting into the postwar years.

These peaks and valleys affected every sector of Philadelphia's business community, but with widely-differing results. The city's largest and best-established firms generally weathered the storm with the least difficulty, whereas its smaller businesses and those most reliant on credit frequently failed. Many recovered from lost Southern ties or 1861 suspensions by winning government contracts. Others found different ways to turn war enthusiasm to their advantage.

By concentrating on a single city, it has been possible to go beyond the large patterns to explore the rich variations they often obscured. This investigation suggests that although the war touched every level of Philadelphia's economy, it left ample room for individual flexibility. The nature of the conflict fostered this diversity. At the war's outset the War Department had to outfit a massive army with almost no preparation. It depended heavily on the private sector for all supplies necessary to keep its soldiers housed, clothed, fed, and armed. And although organized, centralized efficiency replaced confused individualism, the federal contracting system continued to rely on broad based participation by Philadelphia entrepreneurs, rather than centralizing government contracting in a few hands.[52]

But the flexibility that allowed Philadelphians to prosper during the war also left them relatively unchanged at its conclusion. Frequently, I have tried to draw a distinction between structural and institutional "change" on the one hand, and "adjustment" on the other. The war certainly led some Philadelphians to "change" in the sense of altering established economic practices to meet the conflict's new tests. But many merely "adjusted" their activities in response to short-term economic shifts. Tailors made military clothing. Sailmakers sold tents. Pitchfork manufacturers produced bayonets.

In the years immediately following the war, business failures rose as the city adjusted to peacetime, but the steady growth in building rates suggests an economy that continued to prosper. Nevertheless, real prices – although they declined – remained above antebellum levels throughout the decade, and the almshouse lists

52 This "decentralized" experience with contracting was in direct contrast with contracting procedures during World War II. In that conflict 100 defense contractors were responsible for two-thirds of the nation's $240 billion war contracting, and thousands of small businesses, unable to profit from the war boom, failed. See James L. Abrahamson, *The American Home Front* (Washington, D.C., 1983), 149.

reached record highs in 1866 and 1867.[53] When the dust settled in the late 1860s, Philadelphia's economy looked much as it had a decade before. Among manufacturers, only the textile firms – which had turned from cotton to wool – found that their wartime adjustments produced permanent change. Others parlayed wartime profits into increased capital investments and subsequent postwar growth.[54] But the shape of that development seemed to be largely undisturbed by the war.[55] Elsewhere in Philadelphia's economic world, Jay Cooke's energetic sales of Treasury bonds helped return the city's financial sector to national prominence,[56] while, as we have seen, the National Banking Act brought the city's banks into the federal system.

The key to the economic "impact" of the war on Philadelphia lies in the meaning of the word. The city's experience provides little reason to disagree with those scholars who have minimized the war's role in accelerating industrialization. But for the men and women on the Philadelphia home front, the Civil War was an important economic event that substantially, if temporarily, affected their material lives.

53 See Tables 11.1, 11.2, 11.3.
54 Philadelphia's railroad companies were one sector that fared particularly well.
55 Perhaps the postwar expansion of ironclad building at Cramp's Shipyard is an exception.
56 See Ellis P. Oberholtzer, *Jay Cooke, Financier of the Civil War*, 2 vols. (Philadelphia, 1907); Henrietta M. Larson, *Jay Cooke, Private Banker* (Cambridge, Mass., 1936).

13 Conclusion: Toward the Centennial City

The Civil War in Philadelphia

The Civil War left its mark on all who lived through it. The human price of fighting a major war was great: 360,000 Union and 260,000 Confederate soldiers lost their lives. The burden of raising, arming, equipping, transporting, and caring for enormous armies raised unprecedented challenges for both sides. In the North a set of centralized systems emerged. Individual citizens experienced these new national structures in a variety of ways, giving Philadelphians numerous experiences in common with people in all corners of the Union.

Enlistees, conscripts, and deserters came into contact with different aspects of the expanding national military system. Men on battlefields from Mississippi to Gettysburg were ministered to by representatives from the two national relief commissions. The war's economic shifts and the accompanying banking, tariff, currency, and tax legislation were felt by businessmen and laborers across the North. Government contractors and their employees fit into Quartermaster General Montgomery Meigs's national supply structure. And throughout the loyal states, citizens read newspaper accounts of the same battles and celebrated shared patriotic holidays.

These common experiences underline the war's role as a nationalizing, centralizing force.[1] But our investigation of Philadelphia during the Civil War has revealed strong continuities with the past persisting alongside these shifts. Nearly every facet of the war effort depended on the successful integration of diverse voluntary efforts. This was accomplished by appealing to patriotism and self-interest through a web of established associational ties.

In the spring of 1861 many of Philadelphia's recruits volunteered in ethnic, occupational, and fraternal groups. Calls for emergency troops during the 1862 and 1863 Confederate invasions attracted companies from factories, clubs, and churches. Although a national military structure did emerge, emergency recruits relied on Philadelphia's existing associational groups. When patriotism alone

---

1 For an account of the war's centralizing aspects see Morton Keller, *Affairs of State: Public Life in Late Nineteenth Century America* (Cambridge, Mass., 1977), 13–30.

could not fill the ranks, the Union turned to conscription. Philadelphians, fearing disruptive drafting, formed local and citywide groups to raise large bounty funds. These efforts, too, revealed the persistence of private, localized initiatives. Although the City Council appropriated public money to the bounty funds, Philadelphia owed much of its spectacular recruiting success to ward-level fund-raising.

The war's casualties – wounded soldiers, families of volunteers, refugees, and contrabands – attracted benevolent responses from many Philadelphians. Dozens of local societies evolved out of spontaneous gatherings of concerned citizens. Often these organizations attracted volunteers from a specific neighborhood, church, or ethnic group. And repeatedly they organized along traditional lines. In the 1864 Sanitary Fair Philadelphia aided the nationwide relief commission. But even this large event depended on the efforts of small groups working through familiar associational ties.

Whereas many Philadelphians made sacrifices to help recruit and care for the Union's soldiers, the war presented other citizens with attractive economic opportunities. Some patriotic local women responded to the national crisis by sewing uniforms for volunteers, but soon the task of outfitting the troops fell to quartermasters, military contractors, and thousands of wage earners. Here again, Philadelphia's diversity and flexibility served it well. Hundreds of local establishments quickly shifted to war production, often finding that the military's demands pulled them out of war-induced economic troubles.

The wartime need for men, medical care, and materials drew enthusiastic voluntary responses from thousands of Philadelphians. The conflict also disrupted other facets of life in the city, requiring adjustments of all citizens. News from the battlefield and controversial decisions from Washington affected the public mood at the home front, sometimes shaping traditional civic rituals or creating moments of particular tension. Soldiers from all over the North passed through Philadelphia, producing frequent martial displays and adding a new disorderly element to the city's streets. The secession crisis and subsequent economic boom touched all local businessmen. And wartime inflation and declining real wages drove Philadelphia's workers to collective action. Each of these disruptions changed Philadelphia's wartime experience. But we have found that the city answered the various threats to its social and economic order without abandoning traditional practices.

Let us return, then, to Arthur Marwick's four "tiers," with which we began this study. Many Philadelphians felt the war's "destructive aspects" – the first tier – in the form of lost friends and loved ones, but the economy prospered despite a persistent inflation. Whereas Sherman's March brought total warfare to the Southern home front and Grant's 1864 campaigns in the East displayed the devastating capabilities of unrelenting offensives, the Civil War's destructive aspects never threatened to topple life in the City of Brotherly Love.

Thus our attention has been focused more on the war's "test aspects." We have seen that most of Philadelphia's adjustments to the Civil War emerged out of familiar associational ties and traditional practices. Its citizens responded to the war's diverse challenges – threatened drafts, calls for benevolence, visiting heroes, rebel invasions, economic dislocation – by turning to peacetime experiences for guidance. The city government was rarely called on to surpass its prewar role. Public monies went to the bounty funds and aid to families of volunteers. But in each case voluntary contributions supplemented the appropriations. Civic rituals often occurred without government sponsorship. Recruiting and government contracting tied citizens' efforts to a federal structure, only involving city officials in emergencies.

In the course of these adjustments new local organizations such as the Union League, the refreshment saloons, and ward bounty associations emerged, but I have argued that the strong continuities with the past (in the origins, organization, and membership of such new bodies, for instance) suggest a city successfully withstanding the "tests" posed by the Civil War. Such an argument implies that other roads *could* have been taken, and periodically other possibilities have been noted or implied. Certainly the most frequent observation has been that the forces of "localism" weighed in against centralizing impulses at both the city and federal levels. This persistent localism demonstrates that Philadelphians and their institutions were quite capable of meeting challenges without dramatic reshaping.[2] But it also says something about the nature of the Civil War. Although the centralizing forces of conscription, war contracting, suppression of dissent, and national benevolence were consistently present, rarely was centralized control a specific goal.[3] Frequently, in fact, the Union's war interests were best served by appealing to local voluntarism. Thus recruiting, contracting, and voluntarism all profited from

2 This relatively peaceful survival of an established world was certainly not the norm. The various episodes of urban rioting suggest the dislocating forces unleashed by wartime tensions (see Chapter 6). Michael Frisch's study of Springfield, Massachusetts demonstrated the economic impact of war contracting on a much smaller city. See M. Frisch, *Town into City: Springfield, Massachusetts and the Meaning of Community, 1840–1880* (Cambridge, Mass., 1972).
3 The United States Sanitary Commission is an exception.

their distinctly decentralized components.[4] In later wars the rejection of competitive bounties and local enlistment quotas removed a critical impulse to local recruiting; the military's need for contributions from heavy industry made centralized contracting more efficient; and as the federal government took on the tasks of soldiers' relief and propaganda, patriotic volunteers became increasingly under government direction.[5]

What of Marwick's third tier: "participation aspects"? Once again, Philadelphia's Civil War experience suggests more continuity than change for most social groups. Although this conflict, like those in the next century, brought thousands of women into the workplace, there is little evidence of expanding female occupations and, more important, Philadelphia's sewing women bore the brunt of an unfair subcontracting system and a crippling inflation without evolving beyond traditional, paternalistic forms of labor activism. For Philadelphia's legions of female volunteers, the war brought dozens of avenues for activism and quite a bit of recognition both during and immediately after the war. But it appears that the roles of women in the city's complex benevolent mosaic changed less between 1860 and 1870 than it did between 1875 and 1885.[6]

Philadelphia's workers "participated" in all aspects of the wartime experience, but they do not seem to have parlayed their patriotic contributions into substantive gains. A favorable labor market allowed for active midwar unionization and frequent concessions for the better-skilled craftsmen; however, the inevitable postwar decline took a familiar toll. Thus the war's lasting impact on organized labor is unclear.[7]

4   And critical but "nonessential" aspects of the war effort, such as civic ritual, were most conveniently left in private hands rather than taxing the resources of the city government.
5   America's experience in both world wars, like Philadelphia's during the Civil War, combined localized voluntarism with centralized direction. But clearly the balance had shifted toward centralized, federal control during the later wars. On World War I see David M. Kennedy, *Over Here: The First World War and American Society* (New York, 1980), 59–63 (Committeee on Public Information); 113–16 (Council of National Defense and Civilian Advisory Commission); 144–50 (Selective Service System); and *passim*. Despite the range of federal commissions, Kennedy argues that Wilson's consistent goal was to tap into American voluntarism. See Kennedy, *Over Here*, 142–3, 150–2. On World War II see Richard Polenberg, *War and Society: The United States, 1941–1945* (Philadelphia, 1972), 5–19 (War Production Board); 20–2 (War Manpower Commission); 51–4 (Offices of Censorship and War Information). Polenberg notes that even during World War II economic controls relied on "a heavy emphasis on willing consent" and numerous other aspects of the war effort profited from enthusiastic voluntarism on the home front. See Polenberg, *War and Society*, 36, 29, 132–3. On both wars see James L. Abrahamson, *The American Home Front* (Washington, D.C., 1983).
6   We will say more about this apparent shift in the discussion of the Centennial Exhibition.
7   See the next section for a discussion of the 1877 strike.

The wartime gains for black Americans are perhaps best measured at the national level. Many black Philadelphians jumped at the
opportunity to fight the Confederacy, and that military participation
certainly figured in the postwar decision to desegregate the city's
streetcars. But that link should not be overstated. In fact, the desegregation legislation came at the statewide level, and local resistance to black rights persisted into the postwar years.[8]

I have, as promised, had less to say about Marwick's fourth tier:
war's "psychological aspects." We have seen that Philadelphians
facing wartime losses adapted traditional "coping mechanisms" to
new circumstances by turning to letters to replace more personal
contacts. But this hardly speaks to the larger psychological implications of four years of carnage. If such things can be measured,
the task would require quite different modes of analysis. Moreover,
the true "impact" of the war might not fully emerge for decades to
come. Although I prefer to steer clear of that psychological terrain,
there is certainly value in glancing ahead to the postwar decades to
see how an older Philadelphia addressed a comparable set of challenges.

The centennial city

During four years of war Philadelphia functioned much as it had for
the previous decades. The city government continued in the role
established by the 1854 consolidation. A decade after the war Philadelphia experienced two new challenges: It hosted the national
centennial in 1876 and it faced threats of labor riots in 1877. Philadelphia's responses to these two tests reveal strong continuities with
the past as well as signs that another decade of growth had placed
more control in the hands of public officials.

In 1870 Philadelphia's population was 674,000, an increase of
nearly 110,000 over 1860. By 1876 the city's estimated population had
jumped to 817,000.[9] Roughly 27 percent of its people were foreign
born in 1870, a figure slightly less than that of a decade before and the
lowest among major Northern cities. As in 1860, most of Philadelphia's immigrants were from Ireland and Germany.[10] One result
of the war was to place political control of the city in the hands of the

8   See Philip S. Foner, "The Battle to End Discrimination Against Negroes on Philadel-
    phia's Streetcars," 2 parts *Pennsylvania History* 40 (July 1973): 261–90; (October 1973):
    355–79.
9   Dorothy Gondos Beers, "The Centennial City, 1865–1876" in *Philadelphia: A 300-Year
    History*, ed. Russell F. Weigley (New York, 1982), 419–20.
10 Allen F. David, "Introduction," in *The Peoples of Philadelphia: A History of Ethnic
    Groups and Lower-Class Life, 1790–1940*, eds. Allen F. Davis and Mark H. Haller
    (Philadelphia, 1973), 9; Scott Campbell Brown, "Migrants and Workers in Philadel-
    phia: 1850 to 1870" (Ph.D diss., University of Pennsylvania, 1981), 27.

334   **Conclusion**

Republican Party. Local government became dominated by corrupt political machines, with a new breed of bosses replacing the traditional social elites of the antebellum years. William S. ("Sweet William") Stokley, who won the mayorality in 1871, lacked the respectability of earlier civic leaders, though he shared a passion for law and order with wartime Mayor Alexander Henry.[11]

Philadelphia's political leadership shifted in the postwar years, but its economy continued to expand along familiar lines. Its relationship to the hinterlands and easy access to iron and coal continued to provide the stimulus for industrial growth. And as in the antebellum years, the local economy was susceptible to sudden panics. In September 1873 Jay Cooke and Company failed, and several other Philadelphia financial institutions soon followed. In the subsequent months numerous local factories closed, forcing laborers out of work. The ensuing depression destroyed many of the recent gains of the city's labor unions. Thus in 1873 Philadelphia's economy and labor movement had to cope with hard times akin to those of 1837, 1857, and 1861.[12] Prewar patterns of disorder and racial tension also continued in the 1870s. During the 1871 election whites battled blacks seeking to exercise their newly won franchise. Three blacks were killed in the rioting, and several blacks and whites were wounded. This was worse than wartime riots, largely because the city's police force refused to protect blacks seeking to vote and instead joined in the attacks.[13]

Philadelphia responded to economic and social disruptions in the mid-1870s much as it had during the Civil War. But the most important event of the decade came in 1876 when the entire world watched as the City of Brotherly Love staged the nation's Centennial Exhibition.

Philadelphia's centennial year began with a grander version of its traditional New Year's Day celebrations. An English visitor who witnessed the midnight celebration on New Year's Eve described "the most extraordinary noise ever heard," when "every bell, whistle, or other instrument that would make a noise [was] put into requisition." That evening many buildings displayed illuminations, and citizens paraded in the streets. When the New Year's Day came to a close, a large crowd watched as Mayor Stokley raised a flag above Independence Hall. As they had during the war, Philadelphians com-

11 Beers, "The Centennial City," 436–7, 440.
12 Beers, "The Centennial City," 428, 432–4; Alexander K. McClure, *Old Time Notes of Pennsylvania*, 2 vols. (Philadelphia, 1905), 2:453.
13 Henry C. Silcox, "Nineteenth Century Philadelphia Black Militant: Octavius V. Catto (1839–1871)," *Pennsylvania History* 44 (January 1973): 73–4.

memorated the day with a combination of private and public celebrations.[14]

When Independence Day 1876 arrived, Philadelphians staged several days of celebrations. On July 3 the Grand Army of the Republic paraded. That evening an estimated 300,000 people packed downtown streets to watch a grand torchlight parade of "representatives of trades and industries, social and political clubs, and foreign visitors." At midnight the statehouse bell chimed, and the city erupted in cheers. On the Fourth the celebrations centered on Independence Square where national politicians and veterans joined in a day of oratory and military parading, followed by a fireworks display at Fairmount Park.[15] Henry Crew, who was visiting Philadelphia, wrote: "I suppose [that Independence Day] was celebrated today very much as it was this day one hundred years ago, except on a larger scale. . . . there has been a terrible racket of fire-crackers, cannon and pistols."[16]

Crew was correct in his view that the 1876 Fourth of July celebrations were grander versions of traditional rituals. Patriotic oratory, public fireworks, noisy street celebrations, and parades by military groups, labor organizations, and private societies had long been part of Philadelphia's Independence Day festivities. But during the Civil War the City Council usually left such activities in private hands, preferring to spend public monies on war-related concerns. In 1876 the city government spent $10,000 on the Fourth of July fireworks display and an additional $9,966 on the Independence Square festivities. These expenditures added a centralized, government-sponsored event to a traditionally decentralized holiday.[17]

Although Philadelphia celebrated New Year's Day and July 4 with particular enthusiasm in 1876, the city focused most of its attention on the grand Centennial Exhibition. The exhibition's planning and organization followed some of the patterns set by the 1864 Great Sanitary Fair. But the two events were different, suggesting how Philadelphia had evolved in the postwar decade.

The idea that Philadelphia should host the nation's centennial celebration was first raised in 1866. In 1870 the Select Council official-

14 William Randel, ed., "John Lewis Reports the Centennial," *Pennsylvania Magazine of History and Biography* 79 (July 1955): 367; Beers, "The Centennial City," 459. For the history of New Year's celebrations see Susan G. Davis, " 'Making Night Hideous' ": Christmas Revelry and Public Order in Nineteenth-Century Philadelphia," *American Quarterly* 34 (Summer 1982): 185–99.

15 J. Thomas Scharf and Thompson Westcott, *History of Philadelphia, 1609–1884*, 3 vols. (Philadelphia, 1884), 1:848, McClure, *Old Time Notes*, 1:846–7.

16 William H. Crew, ed., "Centennial Notes," *Pennsylvania Magazine of History and Biography* 100 (July 1976): 408–9.

17 City Controller, *23rd Annual Report of the City Controller 1876* (Philadelphia, 1877), 60–1.

ly resolved to hold an international exhibition, and soon after the state legislature voted its support of the proposal. The following year Congress passed a bill naming Philadelphia the official site of the Centennial Exhibition and providing for the selection of exhibition commissioners from each state. With this move the national government gave its approval to the plan (while refusing to provide financial backing). In 1872 Congress authorized the creation of a Centennial Board of Finance to sell shares of stock in the exhibition. The Board of Finance was dominated by the same core of Philadelphia elites who had orchestrated the Sanitary Fair and other wartime activities.[18]

The Board of Finance had to raise $10 million to ensure the exhibition's success. In early 1873 the City Council appropriated $500,000 to the fund, eventually donating a total of $1.5 million. The State Legislature added $1 million to finance the construction of a permanent Memorial Hall on the exhibition site. Philadelphians held numerous fund-raising mass meetings, and in March 1874 a Citizens' Centennial Trade Committee formed to promote the sale of stock. The city's coal, railroad, and lumber companies made large donations, as did local publishers, printers, fraternal societies, and other financial and social organizations. But by mid-1874 only $1.5 million in stock had been sold, mostly in Philadelphia. The U.S. government persistently refused to provide financial support for the project, but in March 1875 Congress voted $500,000 to fund a United States Government building at the exhibition. Finally, as the exhibition's opening day approached, Congress lent the Board of Finance $1.5 million to guarantee that the exhibition would open.[19]

The Centennial Exhibition, modeled on the world's fairs in London (1851), Paris (1855 and 1867), New York (1853), and Vienna (1873), featured displays of industrial progress from across the globe, filling more than 200 buildings and covering 450 acres of Fairmount Park. After various construction delays, the exhibition opened on May 10. During the next six months more than 10 million visitors came to Philadelphia to share in the celebration.[20] How did the 1876

18 John Welsh – who had headed the Executive Committee of the Great Sanitary Fair – served as president of the Board of Finance, which had fifteen Philadelphians among its twenty-five members. Welsh and seven other board members had been founding members of the Union League. See Faith K. Pizor, "Preparations for the Centennial Exhibition of 1876," *Pennsylvania Magazine of History and Biography* 94 (April 1970): 213–19; Maxwell Whiteman, *Gentlemen in Crisis: The First Century of The Union League of Philadelphia* (Phildelphia, 1975), 132. For an excellent description of the exhibition see James D. McCabe, *The Illustrated History of the Centennial Exhibition* (1876; Philadelphia, 1975).
19 Pizor, "Preparations for the Centennial," 223, 228, 231; Beers, "The Centennial City," 460–1.
20 Beers, "The Centennial City," 462–70; Pizor, "Preparations for the Centennial," 213–14. For visitors' descriptions see Randel, ed., "John Lewis Reports the Centennial," 365–74; Crew, "Centennial Notes," 410–13.

exhibition compare with the Great Sanitary Fair of 1864? The Centennial Exhibition's physical layout was much like its wartime predecessor, but on a grander scale. Both fairs featured special horticultural, art, and manufacturing displays. Each had a section reserved for guns and military regalia. Both boasted elaborate restaurants as well as oddities from around the world. For the visitor, the biggest difference was that the 1876 exhibition was much more ambitious than the earlier fair, and included many more international displays. And whereas the Sanitary Fair was completely dismantled after a few weeks, the Centennial Exhibition lasted for half a year, and some of its buildings remained as permanent structures. The events also differed in that each part of the Sanitary Fair was designed to raise money, whereas the exhibition's organizers sought to celebrate the national anniversary by displaying America's technological progress to the world.[21]

Apart from its scale and international aspect, one display in particular set the Centennial Exhibition apart from the Sanitary Fair. In 1864 Philadelphia's women were quite active in most facets of the fair's organization, but their activities did not involve new gender roles. In 1876 the Citizens' Centennial Finance Committee formed a women's committee headed by thirteen prominent Philadelphia women. This body carried out a grass roots fund-raising campaign that quickly collected $40,000. When it became evident that the Centennial Exhibition's male organizers had made no plans to display women's work, the women's committee collected an additional $30,000 to finance the construction of a women's building. The Women's Pavilion housed an eclectic assortment of displays, ranging from a six horsepower engine to a head carved out of butter, all produced by women. In a fair that heralded the nation's progress, this exhibit explicitly acknowledged women's role in that development.[22]

The most illuminating differences between the two fairs were not in what they displayed but in how they were organized. As we have seen, the Executive Committee of Philadelphia's Sanitary Fair acted independently of the national Sanitary Commission and without any government aid. The fair owed its success to the energetic efforts of local volunteers. The 1876 Centennial Exhibition, however, received large donations from the city, state, and federal governments as well as financial support from foreign nations. The exhibition enjoyed such broad support because it was not a local event, but a national

21 Whereas the Sanitary Fair had been stocked with tables of items for visitors to purchase, the Centennial Exhibition's were not for sale.
22 Beers, "The Centennial City," 461; McCabe, *Illustrated History*, 218–20; Randel, ed., "John Lewis Reports the Centennial," 369.

celebration hosted by Philadelphia. But despite these differences, the Centennial Exhibition's organization and financing was quite similar to the Sanitary Fair. Both fairs relied on the direction of a handful of Philadelphia elites, the voluntary efforts of hundreds of local men and women, and the financial support of the city's businesses, fraternal societies, and private citizens.

In July 1877 violence disrupted many Northern cities, as railroad workers battled in response to layoffs forced by the depression.[23] Pennsylvania suffered some of the worst disturbances, leading Philadelphians to fear for the safety of their own city. When he learned of rioting in Pittsburgh, Pennsylvania Railroad President Thomas A. Scott telegraphed Mayor Stokley, who was vacationing in New Jersey. Stokley immediately returned home and called out a large police detail to gather near the West Philadelphia depot, where a large crowd had assembled. On Sunday July 22, as word of the Pittsburgh violence filtered into Philadelphia, Stokley issued a proclamation reminiscent of Mayor Henry's April 1861 official notice: He appealed to the crowd's sense of patriotism and civic pride and warned that any disturbance would be answered with force. That afternoon Stokley went to the depot to personally direct the police in dispersing the crowd.

On the evening of the twenty-second Philadelphia's railroad workers finally voted to strike. Stokley once again sent 600 police officers to clear the depot. This measure resulted in a brief scuffle, a few shots were fired, and the mob scattered. On Monday morning police battled the mob; someone set an oil train on fire. The mayor responded by ordering the city's entire 1,280-man police force to West Philadelphia. Meanwhile, the Pennsylvania Railroad's President Scott had telegraphed Harrisburg for federal troops, and shortly after noon about 200 armed men arrived. That afternoon Mayor Stokley held a meeting of 200 leading citizens to discuss the situation. This body named a six-member Committee of Safety to aid in preserving the peace. Stokley and the committee agreed to recruit an additional 1,200 police officers. Because the mayor had no authorization to pay such a force, thirty-five local businesses lent the city $18,144 to meet the emergency. On Tuesday more federal troops reached Philadelphia, bringing the number of armed men in the city to over 5,000. With such a force on hand, Philadelphia experienced no more serious disturbances, despite continued reports of violence from other parts of the state. However, the newly expanded police force continued to follow orders and disperse public gatherings. On several occasions

23 Robert V. Bruce, 1877: *Year of Violence* (Indianapolis, 1959); Philip S. Foner, *History of the Labor Movement in the United States* (1947; New York, 1972), 464–74.

officers provoked violence by charging and breaking up labor meetings. One such incident resulted in the shooting of an eighteen-year-old worker, the only fatality of the Philadelphia riots. Stokley's enthusiasm for controlling his city also led him to order the confiscation of the *Labor Standard*, a New York labor newspaper.[24]

How did Philadelphia's handling of the July 1877 turmoil compare with its wartime experience? To some degree Philadelphians responded to the 1877 dangers as they had to the diverse challenges of the Civil War. As in July 1863 when draft riots broke out in New York City, Philadelphia profited from advance warning of possible disorder. On each occasion local police were positioned in potentially dangerous areas, and city officials and private citizens telegraphed for additional federal troops. Stokley used official proclamations, personal appearances, and aggressive manipulation of his police force to ensure order, much as Alexander Henry had done during the war. And the postwar mayor repeatedly employed the same strong preemptive measures that Henry had found so successful.

Stokley's decision to call on leading private citizens to recruit and fund the enlarged police force hearkened back to traditional practices. In 1844 a mass meeting of citizens discussed the need for public order. During the war, too, private efforts complemented government measures to aid families of volunteers, raise bounty funds, and care for wounded soldiers. And as wartime military policies sometimes generated controversy and violence in Philadelphia's streets, Stokely's men also created disturbances while trying to maintain control. Finally, in 1877, as during the war, government officials sacrificed constitutional rights in the pursuit of order by confiscating hostile newspapers and silencing potentially disruptive speakers.

But some of Stokley's methods were new. Mayor Henry's police force never charged an assembled mob. This response to the railroad riots was more reminiscent of Colonel Cadwalader's handling of the ethnic riots of 1844. Stokley's orders to break up public meetings also differed from Henry's policy of sending his police force to protect potentially disruptive Democratic meetings from hostile attacks. Thus Stokely's heavy-handed mayoralty did differ significantly from his wartime predecessor. But perhaps the differences say more about the city's two leaders than it does about war-induced change.

The North entered the Civil War to preserve a union fractured by secession. Before the conflict's conclusion the nation had undergone

---

24 Philip English Mackey, "Law and Order, 1877: Philadelphia's Response to the Railroad Riots," *Pennsylvania Magazine* 96 (April 1972): 183–202; Scharf and Westcott, *History of Philadelphia,* 1:848.

unanticipated changes. Slavery had been abolished, the powers of the presidency had expanded, an enormous military and contracting structure had emerged, and the army's ranks had been filled with conscripts, hired substitutes, and black volunteers. This study has asked how the Civil War changed life at the local level. One conclusion has been that the war's impact was broadly felt. Although Philadelphia never had to fight off a Confederate attack, its citizens repeatedly felt the war's presence. But still, the war did not change how Philadelphians responded to pressing needs. Despite new circumstances, they persistently answered the conflict's challenges by relying on familiar responses. The federal government had to expand in order to fight a modern war. But men and women on the home front had the personal and institutional tools at hand to bear the burden of four years of warfare.

How far can we generalize such conclusions? Certainly most Northern communities shared the same set of wartime challenges. But several traits made Philadelphia's experience distinct. First, its location made occasional fears of invasion especially palpable, while also producing a far greater military presence than that in more distant cities. Second, the size of Philadelphia's population and economy made it better able to absorb new challenges without major changes. Finally, Philadelphia was at a particularly flexible stage in its development when the war broke out.

Between consolidation in 1854 and the Centennial Exhibition of 1876, Philadelphia grew dramatically. The Civil War, falling between these two dates, found Philadelphia with a new political structure, an active police force, a complex, changing economy, and long-established neighborhoods, associations, and traditions. The conflict posed varied short-term challenges, forcing numerous adjustments but few concrete changes. By 1876 Philadelphia had experienced another decade of growth and development. Its responses to the Centennial Exhibition, Independence Day 1876, and the 1877 riots combined traditional practices dominated by private citizens and groups with expanding initiatives by public officials. If we consider the Sanitary Fair of 1864 as a benchmark, it would appear that the city "changed" at least at much in these dozen postwar years as it had in the previous decade.

Appendix: The R. G. Dun data

The R. G. Dun credit reports are housed in the manuscript room at Baker Library, Harvard University Graduate School of Business. They include twelve large ledgers for Philadelphia County, with entries for the years 1855 to 1865. The sample I used is made up of every firm described on every twentieth page that fits either of the following criteria: (1) It existed at some point between 1861 and 1865; or (2) it was founded between 1856 and 1860. The first criterion includes all businesses existing during the war years. The second adds young firms that failed before the war began, thus providing a basis of comparison with young companies that were founded during the war and failed before 1866. For each sampled business full information for the years 1850 to 1870 were recorded. Often the R. G. Dun records for a single company were continued on several pages, with notations telling the reader where to find the previous or subsequent entries. Whenever necessary, the sampled businesses were traced both forward and backward to achieve as complete information as possible. This procedure yielded 491 cases, including 21 founded between 1856 and 1860 that did not survive to 1861.

By including cases from every twentieth page, the sample covered roughly 5 percent of the applicable cases. The actual percentage was in fact slightly higher because in 48 cases the additional data from earlier or later pages fit one of the criteria just described. Thus the sampling procedure would have picked up such a firm on either page; and the sample included slightly more than 5 percent of all cases. Assuming that the other 443 (491 minus 48) cases each represent 19 nonsampled cases, and the 48 cases that could have been sampled on either of two pages represent 9 nonsampled cases, the total eligible cases in the records is: $(443 \times 20) + (48 \times 10) = 9340$. Thus the sample of 491 firms includes about 5.3 percent of the total, or one-nineteenth of all eligible cases in the R. G. Dun records.

Much of the discussion of the R. G. Dun evidence in this text relies on quantitative manipulation of the data. Although I am confident that my conclusions do not overextend the evidence, it is important to take note of the problems inherent in working with this material. One problem stemmed from the fact that much of the evidence was highly subjective. The reporters took their information from interviews, observations, and printed records. This made their estimates of a business's worth or age somewhat inexact.[1] On the other hand, R. G. Dun's success rested on a reputation for reliability and the reporters were in good positions to make accurate judgments. The frequent incompleteness of the entries was a larger obstacle. Often R. G. Dun's agents omitted the exact date of founding or failure. In one entry a company might appear perfectly strong and in the next entry, several years later, the reporter would simply record that it had gone "out of business." Moreover, in many cases the agents failed to give a dollar estimate of net worth. To overcome these problems I adopted various estimation procedures.

Businesses in the R. G. Dun records folded for a variety of reasons. Usually the reporters noted why a business closed, but often the entry merely stated that the business ceased operation. In the tables accompanying the text an establishment was listed as "out of business" if one of the following occurred: the business failed; the owner sold out; the owner died (if there were no partners); the establishment moved out of the city; or, in a few cases, a struggling firm only survived after a new partner stepped in with a large amount of capital. (Thus "out of business" does not necessarily mean that the firm had faced financial difficulties.) Conversely, these tables do not include cases where the business merely suspended payments temporarily; moved within the city; or changed its partnership structure without substantially changing the capitalization.

Most of the tables from the R. G. Dun data include two sets of figures. The first includes only those cases of which I am most confident. The second adds estimates based on less complete information. The first figures, called "complete cases," include the following information:

First year of operation:
1. Exact date given *or*
2. First entry states that company is a new firm *or*
3. Explicit statement of the age of the company given *or*
4. Entries predate 1851.

Final year of operation:
1. Exact date given *or*
2. Entry announcing end of business within a year after previous entry (recorded as year of last entry) *or*
3. Entries after 1869.

---

1 The wealth estimates cluster around 1864, suggesting that the reporters made heavy use of the tax list of that year. Occasionally several entries for the same establishment gave inconsistent age estimates.

The second, called "estimates," add the following:

First year of operation:

1. First entry between 1851 and 1853 and the business is clearly well established (pre-1851) *or*
2. Entry narrows year of origin down to one of the five-year intervals used in tables.

Final year of operation:

1. Where there is more than one year between a company's demise and the previous entry the estimated final year is the exact midpoint between the last two entries *except when:*
2. The next-to-last entry shows that the company was in serious difficulties. In these cases the estimated final year is the year after the next-to-last entry.

Several factors inhibit an exact analysis of the role of size in guaranteeing success. First, estimates of worth were not given every year. Second, companies obviously changed size throughout the war. By using only five wealth categories, I believe that I was able to blur the finer distinctions and thus circumvent the worst of these difficulties. Usually the agents gave enough evidence to place each firm in one of the defined categories.[2] Because the estimates of worth were most complete for 1864, I used that year as my base year whenever possible. Of course an 1861 figure is not perfectly comparable to an 1864 estimate reflecting three years of growth and inflation. Few establishments, however, grew so fast that they moved more than one "size category" in the course of the war. Moreover, the agents often used descriptive terms (such as "small" or "moderate") that they presumably would adjust as the dollar fell. Thus a "moderate" business in 1861 might have had a smaller actual dollar value than a similarly "moderate" establishment three years later.

---

2   By matching descriptions with recorded worth estimates, it was usually possible to translate the standard descriptive terms into the appropriate dollar figures when the agents failed to give an explicit valuation.

Bibliographic Essay

This bibliographic essay will concentrate on those documents and scholarly works I have found most useful. The footnotes in each chapter provide a much fuller discussion of the primary and secondary literature on each topic. Readers seeking a general list of sources on the Northern home front may wish to consult the bibliographic sources noted in the Secondary Literature section.

Manuscripts: Personal papers

In the course of my research I examined over a hundred collections of personal papers; more than fifty are cited in this book. The majority of these are housed in the fine manuscript collection of Philadelphia's Historical Society of Pennsylvania (HSP in the footnotes). Of these, the most useful are: the diaries of Lewis and Mary Ashhurst, an unusual case of separate diaries by a husband and wife; the diary of glass manufacturer Henry Benners; the William B. N. Cozens Papers, a collection of roughly a hundred items pertaining to his arrest for defrauding the government; the diary of George W. Fahnestock, a detailed and indexed diary of a wealthy drug merchant; the Horace H. Furness Papers, containing extensive printed and manuscript material pertaining to the Sanitary Fair; the letterbook of prominent businessman and inventor Joseph Harrison, who was responsible for the fair's Art Gallery; the letters of George F. Lee, a local businessman; the correspondence between John W. Lynch and his fiancée, Bessie Mustin; the diary of Susan Trautwine MacManus, a marvelously detailed journal spanning the entire war; the diary of patternmaker Washington Penrose; the diary of Sallie M. Stokes, a tiny volume full of comments about her soldier brother; the diary of Katherine Brinley Wharton, one of the richest journals in the collection; and the diary of Septunius Winner, composer of "Little Brown Jug."

The manuscript collection at the Haverford College Library (Haverford, Pa.) includes the diaries of local Quakers Jacob R. Elfreth, Sr., Jacob R. Elfreth, Jr., and Anna Yarnall as well as the fascinating diary of Quaker draftee Edward G. Smedley, which he kept while in the conscript barracks in Philadelphia in 1863. Swarthmore College Library has two particularly useful Quaker diaries: Anna Ferris, a Wilmington resident and frequent visitor to Philadelphia, and William Eyre, a local building contractor. The most useful Philadelphia diary in the Manuscript Room of the Library of Congress (Washington, D.C.) is the diary of Mary Dreer, in the Papers of Edwin Greble. The girlhood diary of Anna Mercer LaRoche Francis, the daughter of a prominent local Democrat, is in the manuscript room of the Columbia University Library. The diary of James Tyndale Mitchell is in a private collection.

Manuscripts: Institutional records

My analysis of the war's impact on businesses makes extensive use of the R. G. Dun Credit Reports, housed in the Manuscript Room of Baker Library, Harvard University Graduate School of Business (Cambridge, Mass.). See Chapter 12 and the Appendix for a full discussion of this rich source.

The Papers of the National Typographical Union #2 are on microfilm in Lamont Library, Harvard University.

The "Minutes of the Meeting for Sufferings of Philadelphia, 1860–1867" are in the William H. S. Wood Collection, Haverford College Library. This source reports the Meetings of Philadelphia Quakers held in response to the war and eventually to the conscription legislation.

In addition to its collection of printed materials, the Historical Society of Pennsylvania also has extensive manuscript materials on various aspects of recruiting and benevolence. These include the account book of the "Fund for the Relief of the Families of the Philadelphia Volunteers," Peter Williamson Papers; Papers of the Antediluvian Society Infants' Clothing Association; Papers of the Magdalen Society of Philadelphia; and Minutes of the Union Benevolent Association. Material on the Sanitary Fair is scattered throughout the collection. See the Furness Papers; "Great Sanitary Fair–Miscellaneous Material"; and "U.S. Sanitary Commission and Fair Papers." The minute books of several fair committees are catalogued separately.

Manuscripts: Government documents

The final reports of the local provost marshals provide a valuable account of the responses to conscription. For Philadelphia see Provost Marshals, Pennsylvania Districts 1 through 5, "Historical Reports," microfilm M1163 (reel #4), National Archives, Washington, D.C. The records of the local Boards of Enrollment are in Record Group 110 (RG 110), National Archives. For this study I used the following documents: "Enrollment of Citizens Within the Eighth Precinct of the First Ward, Philadelphia, liable to Military service, . . . August 9th, 1862," #2794, RG 110; "Board of Enrollment, First District, Pennsylvania– Letters Sent," #2813, RG 110; "Provost Marshal General's Bureau, Pennsylvania–Eastern Division–1st District, Letters Received" (1863– 1865), #2816, RG 110; "Proceedings of the Board of Enrollment, First District, Pennsylvania," #2823, RG 110; and "Descriptive List of Deserters and Persons Arrested in the First District, Pennsylvania," #2834, RG 110.

Material on local government contracting is in the National Archives, Philadelphia Branch, Record Group 92 (RG 92). I used the "Abstracts of Contracts, 1862–1864," #2226, RG 92 (a thirty-two-page volume listing nearly 300 contracts for various items, excluding food, uniforms, and tents); "Register of Contracts Relating to the Supplying of Clothing and Equipage," #2227, RG 92 (a forty-five-page volume listing roughly 1,500 contracts); and the "List of Employees Classifies for Employment" at Schuylkill Arsenal, #2328, RG 92 (classified potential workers by military experience).

Newspapers and journals

I generally relied on two daily newspapers, the *Philadelphia Public Ledger* and the *Evening Bulletin,* for accounts of events. The *Christian Recorder* offers the perspective of the black community; *Fincher's Trades' Review* was a major Philadelphia-based labor newspaper; the *Friends' Intelligencer* provides a Quaker viewpoint; and the *Germantown Telegraph* is an excellent local weekly. *Godey's Lady's Book,* a Philadelphia-based magazine, provided some useful material. I also consulted the following citywide papers for material on specific events: the *North American and United States Gazette,* the *Philadelphia Inquirer,* the *Philadelphia Press,* and *Poulson's American Daily Advertiser* (1814–1815). Among the national periodic literature, the most useful were the *Merchants' Magazine and Commercial Review* (New York), the *New York Times,* and *Scientific American* (New York).

Published primary sources

Most of the best collections of personal papers are only available in manuscript form. Among the published papers of Civil War Philadelphians, *A Philadelphia Perspective: The Diary of Sidney George Fisher,* edited by Nicolas B. Wainwright (Phiiladelphia, 1967) is an invaluable daily commentary by a member of Philadelphia's elite. "Sarah Butler Wister's Civil War Diary," edited by Fanny Kemble Wister, *Pennsylvania Magazine of History and Biography* 102 (July 1978): 271–327, is a good account of the war's first months by the daughter of Southern sympathizer, Pierce Butler. Excerpts of artist Joseph Boggs Beale's wartime diary are published in "Education of an Artist: The Diary of Joseph Boggs Beale, 1856–1867," edited by Nicholas B. Wainwright, *Pennsylvania Magazine of History and Biography* 103 (April 1979): 222–51. And for a fascinating collection of undelivered letters to men in the field see " 'Come home soon and dont delay': Letters from the Home Front: July, 1861," edited by Edward G. Longacre, *Pennsylvania Magazine of History and Biography* 100 (July 1976): 395–406. For this study I have used the manuscript versions of the Beale diary and the "Letters from the Home Front" rather than the edited published versions. Both are housed in the Historical Society of Pennsylvania.

Among printed city documents the most useful were the *Annual Messages* of the mayors of Philadelphia; *The Journal of the Select Council of the City of Philadelphia; The Journal of the Common Council of the City of Philadelphia;* the *Annual Reports* of the city controller; and the *Report of the City Bounty Fund Commission* (1865).

Many of the most important documents pertaining to political arrests, government contracting, and the preparations for the draft are published in United States War Department, *The War of the Rebellion: A Compilation of the Official Records of the Union and Confederate Armies,* 128 vols. (Washington, D.C., 1880–1901). For the final results of the draft see James B. Fry's "Final Report to the Secretary of War by the Provost Marshal General," *Journal of the House of Representatives,* 39th Cong., 1st sess., House Executive Document 1, vol. 4 (Washington, D.C., 1866).

My discussion of benevolent organizations makes extensive use of the printed annual reports of numerous private institutions. Most of these are in the collections of the Historical Society of Pennsylvania or the Library Company of Philadelphia. The Historical Society also has the published reports of several ward-level bounty fund committees. Both the Historical Society and the Library Company have large collections of printed materials relating to the Great Sanitary Fair. The only copy of the official *List of Committee Members of the Great Central Fair for the U.S. Sanitary Commission held in Philadelphia* (Philadelphia, 1864) that I found is in Box 5, F-1, Furness Papers, HSP. I obtained my copy of *Our Daily Fare,* the official newspaper of the Sanitary Fair, in the manuscript room of the Columbia University Library, New York.

My analysis of manufacturing changes in based on Lorin Blodget's *Manufactures of Philadelphia. Census of 1860* (Philadelphia, 1861) and his *The Industries of Philadelphia, as shown by the Manufacturing Census of 1870* (Philadelphia, 1877). Blodget's tables are based on the Bureau of the Census data. I have also used Edwin T. Freedley's 1866 manufacturing estimates in *Philadelphia and its Manufactures* (Philadelphia, 1867). These are useful middecade estimates, although they are certainly not as accurate as the census returns. The *Annual Reports of the Philadelphia Board of Trade* and the *Annual Reports of the Corn Exchange Association of Philadelphia* include valuable material on the local economy. I have used *McElroy's City Directory* for addresses and occupations.

Secondary literature

The best place to begin any study of the Civil War is still Allan Nevins's *The War for the Union*, 4 vols. (New York, 1959 to 1971). For general factual material on the war years I have relied on James M. McPherson's excellent single-volume history, *Ordeal By Fire: The Civil War and Reconstruction* (New York, 1982). Anyone embarking on a Civil War study today should consult three sources that appeared as this volume was nearing completion. James M. McPherson's *Battle Cry of Freedom: The Civil War Era* (New York, 1988) is now the leading study of the war years. Until very recently, Emerson David Fite's *Social and Economic Conditions in the North* (New York, 1910) stood as the only history of the North during the Civil War. Philip Shaw Paludan's *"A People's Contest": The Union and Civil War, 1861–1865* (New York, 1988) now joins Fite's study. Both McPherson's and Paludan's books have excellent bibliographic essays. The student seeking a broader discussion of sources should consult Eugene C. Murdock's *The Civil War in the North: A Selective Annotated Bibliography* (New York, 1987) that includes 5,608 entries.

Russell F. Weigley's edited *Philadelphia: A 300-Year History* (New York, 1982) is an invaluable collaborative history of the city, but researchers should not neglect John Thomas Scharf and Thompson Westcott's densely packed three-volume *History of Philadelphia, 1609–1884* (Philadelphia, 1884). For general treatments of Philadelphia during the war see Russell Weigley's "The Border City in the Civil War, 1854–1865" in his *Philadelphia*, 363–416 and Winnifred K. MacKay, "Philadelphia During the Civil War, 1861–1865," *Pennsylvania Magazine of History and Biography* 98 (April 1972): 3–49. William Dusinberre's *Civil War Issues in Philadelphia, 1856–1865* (Philadelphia, 1965) concentrates on political issues. Frank H. Taylor's *Philadelphia in the Civil War, 1861–1865* (Philadelphia, 1913) is particularly useful on local hospitals and the activities of Philadelphia's regiments.

Several monographs have contributed to my understanding of antebellum Philadelphia. The second part of Sam Bass Warner, Jr.'s *The Private City: Philadelphia in Three Periods of its Growth* (Philadelphia, 1968) discusses the development of the "Big City" from 1830 to 1860. On antebellum civic ritual see Susan G. Davis, *Parades and Power: Street Theater in Nineteenth-Century Philadelphia* (Philadelphia, 1986); on rioting, Michael Jay Feldberg, "The Philadelphia Riots of 1844: A Social History" (Ph.D. diss., University of Rochester, 1970) and *The Turbulent Era: Riot and Disorder in Jacksonian America* (New York, 1980); on organized benevolence, Eudice Glassberg, "Philadelphians in Need: Client Experiences With Two Benevolent Societies, 1830–1880," (Ph.D. diss., University of Pennsylvania, 1979); on labor, Bruce Laurie, *Working People of Philadelphia, 1800–1860* (Philadelphia, 1980); on the economy, Diane Lindstrom, *Economic Development in the Philadelphia Region, 1810–1850* (New York, 1978); and for an excellent study that spans the war years see Philip Scranton, *Proprietary Capitalism: The Textile Manufacture at Philadelphia, 1800–1885* (Philadelphia, 1983).

Index

Abbott, Edith, 194
abolitionism, 2
Age, 6, 183, 190, 233
almshouse population, 271
Anderson, Robert, 105
Antediluvian Society's Infants' Clothing
    Association, 118
Antietam, Battle of, 6, 20
arrests
    in other wartime cities, 194–5
    political, 179–80, 182
    postwar patterns, 213–4
    wartime statistics for Philadelphia,
    195–203
Ashhurst, Lewis, 6–7, 8, 59
Ashhurst, Mary, 7, 56, 61, 62, 80, 143
Ashhurst, Richard Lewis, 66

Baker, E. D., 107
Baldwin Locomotive Works, 220, 239,
    254, 264, 275, 280, 283
banking, 276–9
Beale, Joseph Boggs, 85–6, 105, 144,
    156, 159
Beard, Charles and Mary, 251
benevolence, 117–46, 164–9, 330
    antebellum, 118–9
    continuity and change, 133–8
    established charities in wartime, 119–
    23
    fund-raising, 136–8
    Philadelphia's reputation, 117–8
    postwar, 165–9
    volunteers, 138–44
    wartime donations, 132–3
    and wartime needy, 123–6
    wartime organizations, 126–32
    and women, 133–4
    and workers, 222
    see also particular organizations, Great
    Sanitary Fair
Benners, Henry, 8, 93, 158, 204, 220
blacks, 333
    aid to freedmen, 124
    arrest rates, 201
    benevolence of, 136
    bounties, 49
    population, 1
    in postwar Philadelphia, 334
    recruiting and enlistment, 45–9, 184–5
    streetcar desegregation, 48n
    volunteers, 7, 104
    see also Camp William Penn
Blanchard, Anna, 93, 104, 155, 158, 159
Blodget, Lorin, 257, 270–1
Boileau, Albert, 182–3

Bond, L. Montgomery, 147, 154, 160
Boston, 1863 draft riot, 177n
bounties, 17–8, 29–34, 330, 331
    to blacks, 49
    Citizens' Bounty Fund, 18–9, 28, 33
    City Bounty Fund, 17, 30, 31
    federal, 29–30
    private donations, 18, 278
    ward associations, 28, 31–3, 330, 331
    see also City Bounty Fund
Bowlby, John, 58n
Bremner, Robert, 132, 136
Brockett, Linus P., 132
Brown, Andrew, 73
building industry, 274–6
Butler, Pierce, 179

Cameron, Simon, 14, 16
Camp William Penn, 47–8, 104, 203,
    206, 207
casualties, wartime, 329
centennial celebration, 334–8
Centennial Exhibition, 335–8
Central Employment Association, 120
Central Soup Society, 120
centralization, and the Civil War, 52,
    329, 331–2
    and benevolence, 164–5
    and public order, 215–6
    see also specific topics
Chase, Salmon P., 14
Christian Observer, 179
Christian Recorder, 45, 46, 47, 49, 125,
    184, 185
Christian Commission, *see* United States
    Christian Commission
Cincinnati, 175, 177
Citizens' Bounty Fund, 18–9, 28, 33
    Citizens' Bounty Fund Committee, 47
Citizens' Volunteer Hospital Associa-
    tion, 130, 134, 137
City Bounty Fund, 17, 30–1
    City Bounty Fund Commission, 135
City Council, *see* Philadelphia City
    Council
civic rituals, 85–116
    antebellum traditions, 87–90
    postwar, 108–13
    rituals of wartime, 101–8
    traditional rituals in wartime, 90–101
    see also Independence Day, George
    Washington's Birthday, City
    Council
Clinton, Catherine, 136
Cochran, Thomas C., 251
Colton, Ball, 73–4

Colton, Will, 63, 73–4
Commission for the Relief of Families of Volunteers, 123–4, 135
conscription, 25–9
    1862 militia draft, 18
    1863, 7
    and concern for disorder, 185–7, 189
    evasion, 180
    exemptions, 37
    individual responses, 37–9
    protests, 18
    results, 26, 40–5
    violent resistance, 27, 175–6
    see also Enrollment Act, recruiting and enlistment
Constitution, anniversary celebration, 91–2
construction, see building industry
contrabands, see blacks
Cooke, Jay, 267, 277–8, 290, 328, 334
Cooper Shop Soldiers' Home, 137
Cooper Shop Volunteer Refreshment Saloon, 127, 129, 135
cooperative stores, 247–8
Copperheads, 6, 183–4, 187 see also Democrats
Cozens, William B., 289–90, 291, 298, 324
Crew, Henry, 335
crime, see arrests
Crossman, G. H., 288
Curtin, Andrew G., 7, 14, 16, 19–20, 22, 93, 148–9, 287

death and mourning, 54–60
    in nineteenth century America, 54
    Philadelphia's wartime casualties, 54
death bed scenes, 48–9
Democrats, 6, 180, 181–3, 187, 188–9 see also elections
deserters, 211–3
Detroit, 175–6, 177
Dicey, Edward, 63
disorder
    after Fort Sumter, 170–3
    in antebellum Philadelphia, 173–5
    1877 riots, 338–9
    in other Civil War cities, 175–8
    in postwar Philadelphia, 216
    and soldiers in Philadelphia, 203–13
    wartime episodes, 178–90
    see also police, arrests
Dougherty, Daniel, 94
Douglass, Frederick, 46, 48
Doyle, Don Harrison, 90
draft, see conscription
Dreer, Mary, 159
Dun, R. G., and Company credit reports, 266, 341–3
    business failures in, 300–7

case histories, 307–12
companies with government contracts, 316–23
companies with Southern ties, 312–6
origin, 299–300
war profiteers, 324–6
see also economy

Earnhart, Hugh G., 41
economic impact of the Civil War, 264–5
    historiography, 251–3
    see also economy
economy, 326–8, 330
    in antebellum Philadelphia, 253–4
    case histories, 292–8
    and government contracting, 283–91
    impact of the Civil War, 264–5
    manufacturing change over the war decade, 254–6
    in the secession crisis, 266–71
    sectoral shifts, 257–64
    in various sectors, 271–83
    see also workers, wages, R. G. Dun and Company
eight hour movement, 247–8
elections, presidential
    1856, 2
    1860, 2
    1864, 2, 8, 188–9
Elfreth, Jacob, Jr., 5, 8, 37–8, 159
Elfreth, Jacob, Sr., 7, 37–8, 50, 61, 62, 91, 97, 112, 204
Ellsworth, Elmer, 106
Emancipation Proclamation, 46, 48, 175, 182
Engerman, Stanley, 252, 257
enlistment, see recruiting and enlistment, conscription
Enrollment Act, 25–6, 36–7, 39–40
Evening Journal, 182
Eyre, William, 3, 55, 269, 274

Fahnestock, George W., 6, 38, 48, 60, 103, 158, 159, 182, 183, 274
Feldberg, Michael, 175
Female Hebrew Benevolent Society, 136
Ferris, Anna, 7, 55, 124, 155, 159, 204
Fincher, Jonathan, 36–7, 221, 223, 230, 234–6, 239–40, 241, 247–8, 250
Fincher's Trades' Review, 36, 221, 222, 231, 234, 236, 243–5, 247, 248
Fisher, Sidney George, 5, 6, 12, 60, 89, 92, 98–9, 159, 172, 179, 182, 183, 184, 207, 269, 271
Fisk, Wilbur, 127–9
Fite, Emerson, 274
Foner, Philip S., 220
Fort Sumter, responses in Philadelphia, 4–5, 101–102, 170–173

Fredrickson, George M., 164
Freedley, Edwin T., 255–263
Frickey, Edwin, 256
Friends' Association for the Aid and Elevation of the Freedmen, 125
Friends' Asylum for the Insane, 120, 121
Fry, James B., 25, 51, 186
funeral processions, 106–7, 109–12

George Washington's birthday celebrations, 86, 92–3, 95–6, 97–8, 99–100
Germans
 aid to families of volunteers, 124
 enlistment, 29
 population, 1
 rituals, 100–1, 104
Gettysburg, Battle of, 6–7, 96, 104
 emergency troops, 22–4
Goldin, Claudia, 252
government contracting
 and R. G. Dun credit reports, 316–23
 and the economy, 283–91
Gratz, Rebecca, 56, 57–8, 59
Great Central Fair, see Great Sanitary Fair
Great Sanitary Fair, 7, 132, 136, 146–65, 330
 committees and volunteers, 153
 contributions and contributors, 157–62
 and the 1876 Centennial Exhibition, 335
 and gender roles, 151–7
 Lincoln's visit, 150–1
 and Philadelphia's benevolent traditions, 162–4
 physical description, 149–50
 and wartime centralization, 164–5
Greble, John T., 106

Hacker, Isaiah, 189
Hacker, Louis, 251
Hale, John M., 61
Hale, R. C., 287, 288
Harrison, Benjamin, 110–1
Harrison, Joseph, 155, 274
Hebrew Relief Association, 136
Henry, Alexander, 2, 7, 16, 18, 19, 22, 92, 94, 99, 148, 174–5, 334, 338, 339
 and disorder, 183, 170–2, 185, 190, 191–2
 and police force, 195
Home Guard, 5, 16, 21, 23
Hoover, Ethel, 255, 256, 274
hospitals, 130
How a Free People Conduct a Long War, 114

immigrants, see Irish, German
Independence Day celebrations, 90–1, 93–4, 96–7, 98–9
 1876, 335
Indigent Widows' and Single Women's Society, 118, 121, 122
Infant School, 119
Ingersoll, Charles, 95, 180, 190
Ingersoll, Edward, 190
Irish
 antebellum rioting against, 173–4
 enlistment, 29
 parades for troops, 106
 population, 1
 St. Patrick's Day, 100

Jackson, Andrew, 88
Jewish, benevolence, 136
Jones, William Thomas, 72–3

Kett, Joseph, 72n, 79

labor, see workers
Ladies' Aid Society, 127, 132, 133
Ladies Association for Soldiers' Relief, 127, 133
Ladies' Hebrew Association for the Relief of Sick and Wounded Soldiers, 136
Lafayette, Marquis de, 87–8
Lane, Roger, 177n
LaRoche, Anna, 183, 189
Lee, George F., 294–8
Levine, Peter, 40–1
Lewis, Frank, 252
Lincoln, Abraham, 2, 3, 19
 assassination, 8, 189
 1861 visit to Philadelphia, 85–7, 218
 funeral procession, 109–12
 visit to the Great Sanitary Fair, 105, 150–1
 and labor, 218, 245
 see also elections, presidential
Lincoln, Mary Todd, 105
Lindstrom, Diane, 265
Lynch, John W., 67, 69–71, 81

Machinists' and Blacksmiths' Union, 239–40
Magdalen Society, 122
mail, 80–1
manufacturing
 expansion over the war decade, 254–6
 sectoral shifts, 257–64
 see also economy
Marklee, Amanda, 141–2
Marwick, Arthur, x–xii, 250, 330–3
Massachusetts
 manufacturing, 256

McClellan, George B., 105
McManus, Susan Trautwine, *see* Susan Trautwine
McMichael, Morton, 197, 214
McPherson, James, 36
Meade, George, 105
Meigs, Montgomery, 286, 288–9, 291, 329
Merchants' Fund, 118, 121, 122
Mickle, Isaac, 110
Miller, Tamara, 82
Mitchell, James Tyndale, 5, 7, 12, 20–1, 24, 35, 56, 77–8, 91, 97, 156, 159
Molders' Union, 237–9
Monkkonen, Eric, 195, 214
Montgomery, David, 222, 236
mourning, *see* death and mourning
Murdock, Eugene C., 41
Mustin, Bessie, 67, 69–71, 81

National Typographical Union #2, 220
  antebellum, 231
  voluntarism, 222
  wartime experience, 231–3
National Workingmen's convention, 86
Nevins, Allan, 14, 115, 286–91
New York City
  1863 draft riots, 34, 175, 177, 184, 222–3
  election day 1864, 178n
  Metropolitan Fair, 146
  recruiting, 34
New York (state)
  conscription results, 40–1
  manufacturing, 256
Norton, Mary Beth, 82

Oberholtzer, Ellis Paxson, 107
Ohio, conscription in, 41

Palmetto Flag, 170–2
pamphlets, political, 114–6
parades, *see* civic rituals
Patterson, Robert, 86–7
Patterson Regiment, letters from, 56, 62, 66, 67–8
Peace Democrats, *see* Democrats, Copperheads
Penn Relief Association, 130, 133, 135, 137
Penrose, Washington, 91, 144, 292–4, 297–8
People's Party, 2
Philadelphia
  antebellum economy, 253–4
  antebellum militia, 11
  benevolent reputation, 117–8
  1854 Consolidation Act, 1
  military participation, 11, 35
  population, 1, 333
  in the postwar decades, 333–9

wartime casualties, 54
  see also specific topics
Philadelphia City Council (Select and Common), 330
  aid to families of volunteers, 17, 95, 123
  appropriations for city defense, 16, 20, 22, 95
  and the Centennial Exhibition, 335–6
  City Bounty Fund, 17, 30–1, 95
  support of civic rituals, 89–90, 92–3, 97, 108, 110, 112
Philadelphia Society for the Employment and Instruction of the Poor, 119, 122–3, 134, 166–7
Philadelphia Society for Organizing Charitable Relief and Repressing Mendicancy, 168
Pleasonton, A. J., 16, 22, 23
Plitt, Mrs. George, 154
police, 174, 191, 192, 195–7, 215–6
police, *see also* disorder
Polish celebrations, 101
Port Washington, Wisconsin, 175, 177
prices, 273–4 *see also* economy
Provident Society, 118
provost marshals, 215–6
  as disorderly force, 212–3
  and military arrests, 209, 211
  see also conscription
Public Ledger, violent incidents reported in, 204–5

Quakers
  and enlistment, 49
  responses to conscription, 49–52

railroads, 279–80
recruiting and enlistment, 329–30
  blacks, 7, 45–9
  characteristics of soldiers, 35–6
  1861 ninety day troops, 5, 11–4
  1862 emergency troops, 19–21
  1863 emergency troops, 7, 21–4
  English, 12
  Germans, 12, 29
  Irish, 12, 29
  in New York, 34
  Quakers, 49–52
  three year regiments, 5–6, 14–7
  workers, 219–21
  see also bounties, conscription
Reed, William B., 114
Richardson, Sarah, 55, 143
Richmond, 1863 bread riots, 176, 177
rituals, *see* civic rituals
Rosenblatt, Paul C., 55, 57, 64, 81
Russell, William Howard, 175
Ryan, Mary, 72n, 79n

St. Patrick's Day, 100
Salsbury, Stephen, 251
Sanitary Commission, *see* United States
    Sanitary Commission
Saum, Lewis O., 55
Schneider, John, 174
Scott, Anne Firor, 133
Scott, Thomas A., 338
Scranton, Philip, 264, 282, 285, 323
secession crisis, and the economy, 266–
    71
separation
    antebellum, 79–82
    and mail, 80–1
    responses to wartime, 60–78
    and western migrants, 80
Shaw, Peter, 87
shipping, 280–1
Slemmer, Lieutenant, 105
Smedley, Edward, 50
Smith, J. L., 56, 71–2, 80
Smith, Thomas W., 73, 80–1
soldiers in Philadelphia
    disruptive aspects, 203–13
    postwar return, 213–4
Soldiers' Aid Society, 138
Somkin, Fred, 55, 87
Spencer, Anna, 144
Spring Garden Soup Society, 120
Stansell, Christine, 67n
Stanton, Edwin M., 18, 50, 185, 288–9
    and labor, 245
Stearns, George L., 47
Stillé, Charles Janeway, 114
Stokes, Sallie, 74–7, 81
Stokley, William S., 216, 334, 338–9
Supervising Committee for Recruiting
    Colored Troops, 47–8
Sylvis, William H., 217, 219, 221, 230,
    237–9, 250

Taylor, Frank H., 35
textile industry, 254, 263, 282–3, 285–6
Thompson, John J., 165
trade, Philadelphia's wartime, 276
Trautwine, Susan R., 56, 59–60, 62, 63–
    6, 140–1, 159
Trexler, Richard, 87
Tyler, John, 88

Union Benevolent Association, 119, 120,
    121, 123, 134, 166
Union Freedman's Relief Association of
    West Philadelphia, 125
Union League, 6, 95–6, 115–6, 147, 331
Union Volunteer Refreshment Saloon,
    129
unions, labor
    antebellum, 227–30
    wartime, 231–40

see also National Typographical
    Union, Molders' Union,
    Machinists' and Blacksmiths' Union
United States Congress, 336
United States Christian Commission,
    126
United States Sanitary Commission, 7,
    126, 132, 135, 146–7, 164–5

Vallandigham, Clement, 183
Van Wyck Committee, 288
Vartanian, Pershing, 251
Vicksburg, Battle of, 107–8
voluntarism, *see* benevolence

wages, 224–6
Walker, Lewis, 38
Waln, Edward, 112
Warner, Sam Bass, 1
Washington Grays, 12
Welsh, John, 147
Wharton, Henry, 39
Wharton, Katherine Brinley, 4, 5, 7, 8,
    56–7, 58–9, 60–1, 62, 104, 111, 142–3
White, Jacob A., 49
Wiley, Bell, 35
Williamson, Jeffrey, 252, 298
Wilson, John A., 39
Winder, William H., 179–80
Wistar, Mrs. Caleb, 144
Wister, Sarah Butler, 4, 63, 102, 104,
    138–9, 172, 179
women, 332
    and benevolence, 133–4
    and the Centennial Exhibition, 337
    government contract workers, 287
    and the Great Sanitary Fair, 153
    and postwar benevolence, 168–9
    workers, 242–7
Women's Association of Philadelphia
    for the Relief of the Freedmen, 124
Women's Employment Society, Ger-
    mantown, 120
workers, 332
    and class antagonisms, 221, 249
    employment structure, 226–7
    government contract work, 240–5
    military service, 219–21
    organized labor, 227–40
    postwar, 250
    response to conscription, 221
    and the secession crisis, 217–9, 223–5
    voluntarism, 222
    wages, 224–6
    and war contracting, 269–70
    women, 242–5, 246–7
    see also wages, unions
World War I, xi, 165n, 332n
World War II, xi, 327n, 332n

Yarnall, Anna, 3, 6